Yamada-kun and the Seven Witches

9

MIKI YOSHIKAWA

GRR!
SHAKE
SHAKE

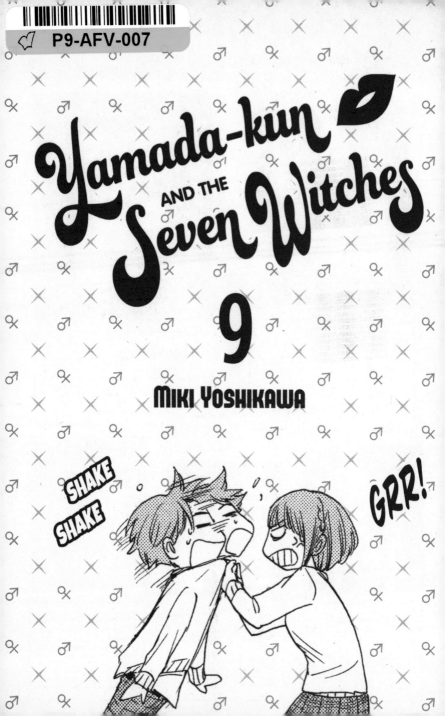

Ryu Yamada

A second-year at Suzaku High School and part of the Supernatural Studies Club. He's loathed by his schoolmates for some reason. He's known as the "Copy Guy" and possesses the ability to copy the power of whichever witch he kisses.

Urara Shiraishi

A second-year at Suzaku High School and president of the Supernatural Studies Club. A coolheaded girl who's always studying. She's known as the "Switch Witch" and switches bodies with the person whom she kisses. Her smile, which she shows from time to time, is so cute that it should be illegal.

Toranosuke Miyamura

A second-year at Suzaku High School. He's the vice-president of the Supernatural Studies Club and Student Council. The polar opposite of Yamada, he's the most popular kid in school. He's very curious and sharp, but his perverted streak is a problem.

Miyabi Itou

A second-year at Suzaku High School and part of the Supernatural Studies Club. She's the only member of the club who's into the occult. She's surprisingly popular with boys.

Kentaro Tsubaki

A second-year at Suzaku High School and part of the Supernatural Studies Club. He is both scholarly and a good fighter, and he used to live abroad. However, he's also an odd fellow who fries up some tempura when he starts to feel lonely.

Meiko Otsuka

A second-year at Suzaku High School and member of the Manga Studies Club. She is known as the "Thought Witch" and can perform telepathic communication with the person whom she kisses.

Haruma Yamazaki

A third-year at Suzaku High School and president of the Student Council. He's a crafty guy who holds many secrets. And he has a dirty mind.

Rika Saionji

A third-year at Suzaku High School and the seventh witch. She appears before anyone who knows the identities of all seven witches. She doesn't wear panties and appears and disappears when you least expect it. She's what you might call…"abnormal."

Nene Odagiri

A second-year at Suzaku High School. She shares the position of Student Council vice-president with Miyamura. She is known as the "Charm Witch" and makes the person whom she kisses fall in love with her.

Noa Takigawa

A first-year at Suzaku High School. A little rascal who is infatuated with Yamada. She is known as the "Retrocognition Witch" and by way of dreams can see the past trauma of whomever she kisses.

Mikoto Asuka

A third-year at Suzaku High School and vice president of the Student Council. She loves the Student Council president and is super sadistic! She used to be the "Invisible Witch" but had her power erased by Tamaki.

Ushio Igarashi

A second-year at Suzaku High School. He is the loyal minion of the cunning Odagiri. He was Yamada's friend in junior high.

Maria Sarushima

A second-year at Suzaku High School. She's a kissing-fiend who used to live abroad. She is known as the "Prediction Witch" and can see the future from the perspective of the person whom she kisses.

Shinichi Tamaki

A second-year at Suzaku High School. A guy with an attitude who's aiming to be the next Student Council president. He's known as the "Capture Guy" and steals the power of the witch whom he kisses. He currently possesses the ability to turn invisible.

CONTENTS

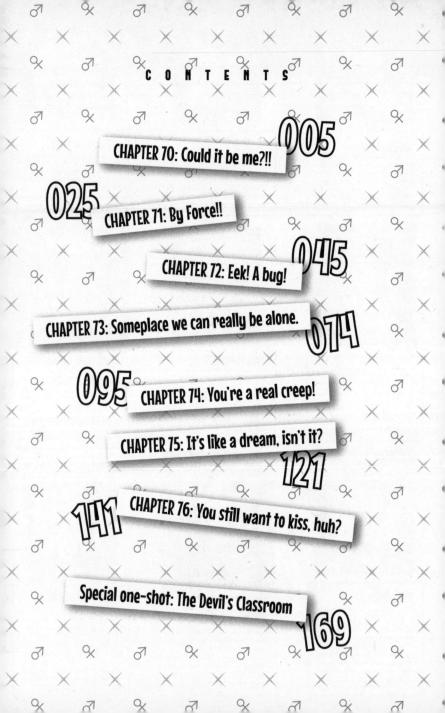

CHAPTER 70: Could it be me?!!

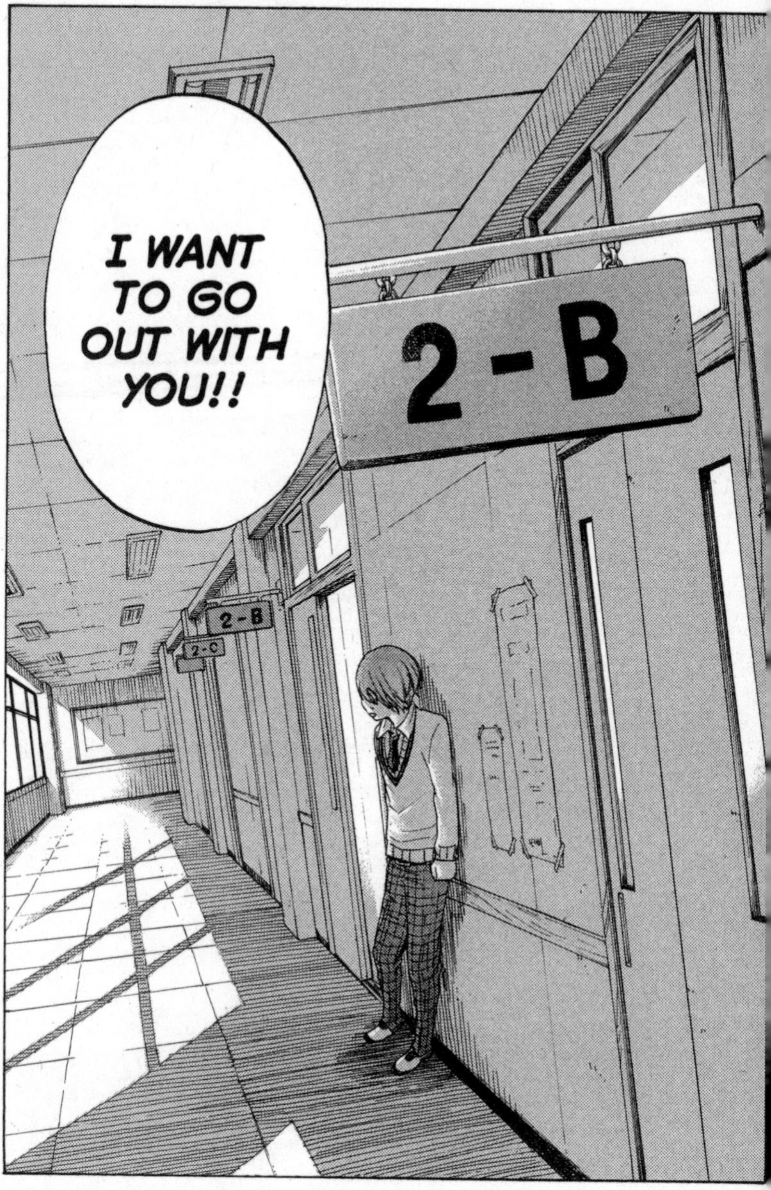
I WANT TO GO OUT WITH YOU!!
2-B
2-B
2-C

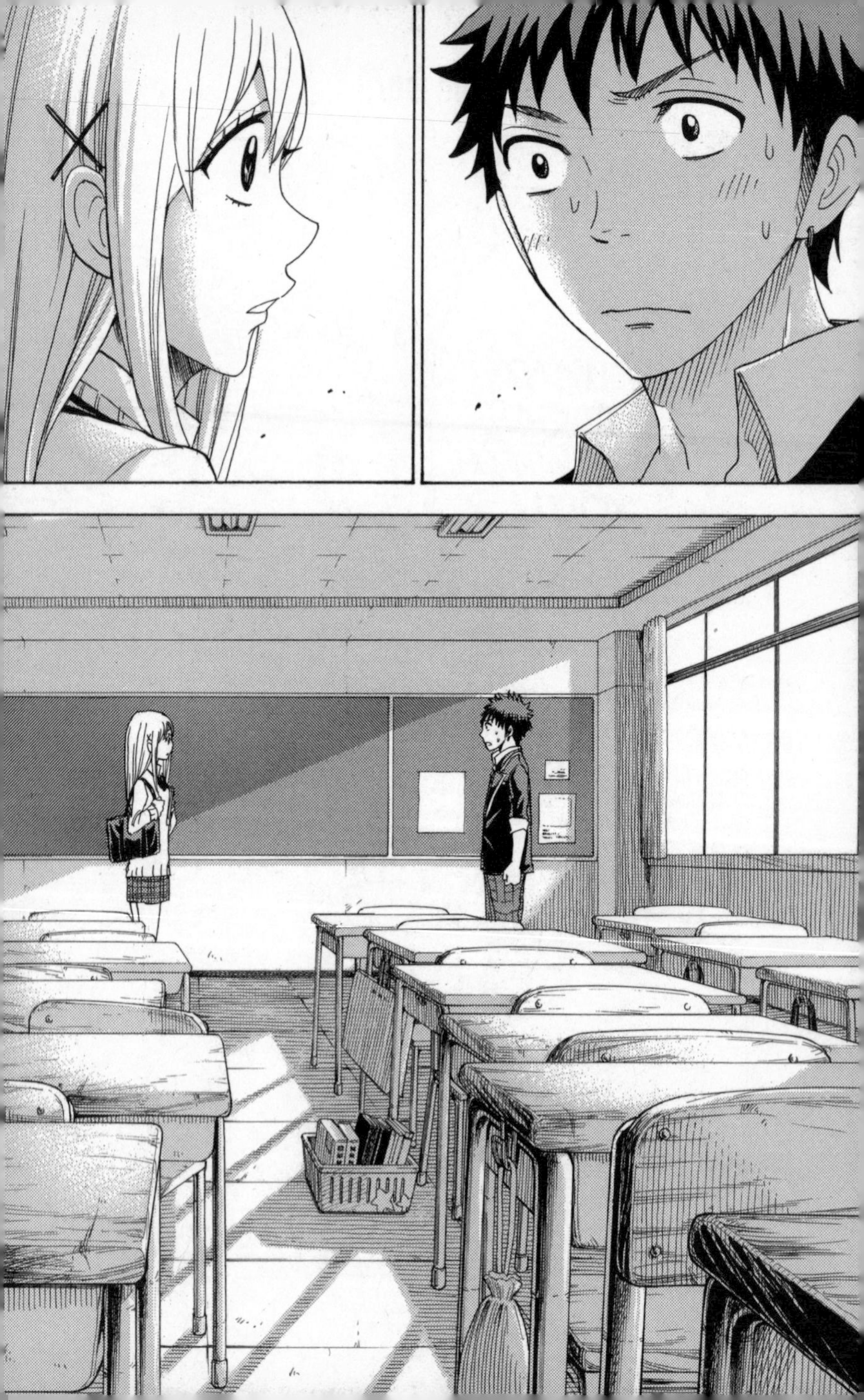

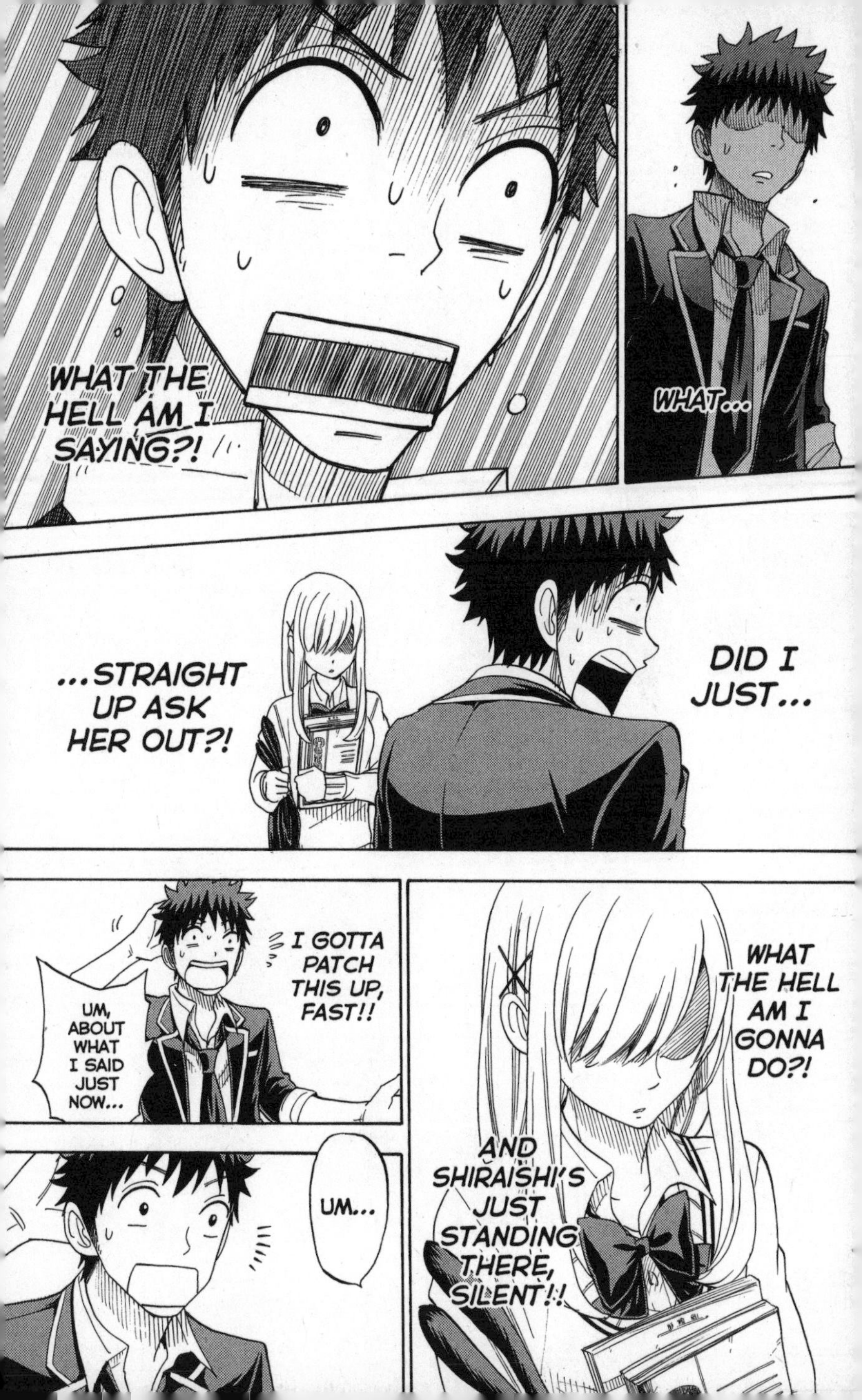
WHAT...
WHAT THE HELL AM I SAYING?!
DID I JUST...
...STRAIGHT UP ASK HER OUT?!
WHAT THE HELL AM I GONNA DO?!
AND SHIRAISHI'S JUST STANDING THERE, SILENT!!
I GOTTA PATCH THIS UP, FAST!!
UM, ABOUT WHAT I SAID JUST NOW...
UM...

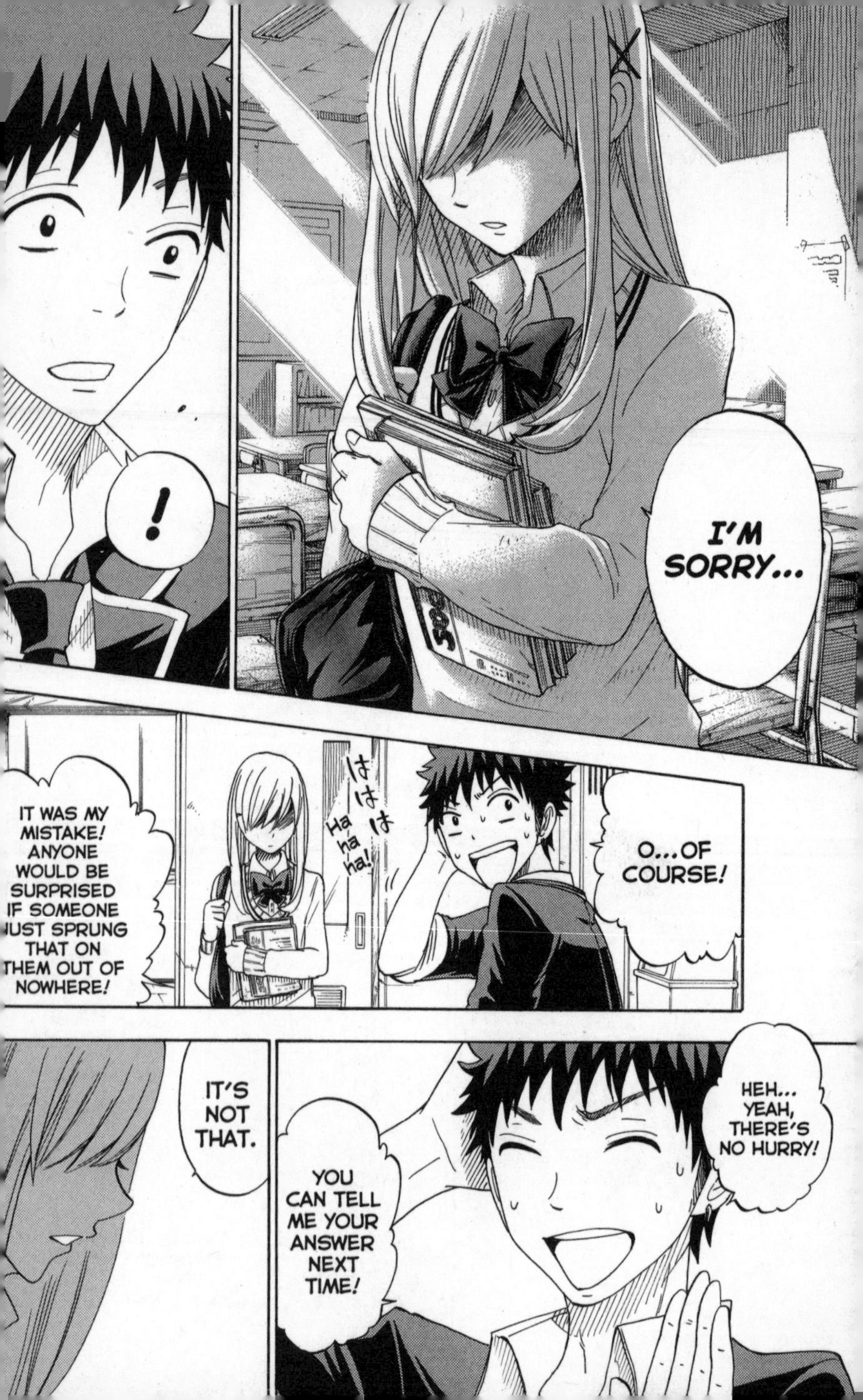
I'M SORRY...
!
O...OF COURSE!
ははは
Ha ha ha!
IT WAS MY MISTAKE! ANYONE WOULD BE SURPRISED IF SOMEONE JUST SPRUNG THAT ON THEM OUT OF NOWHERE!
HEH... YEAH, THERE'S NO HURRY!
YOU CAN TELL ME YOUR ANSWER NEXT TIME!
IT'S NOT THAT.

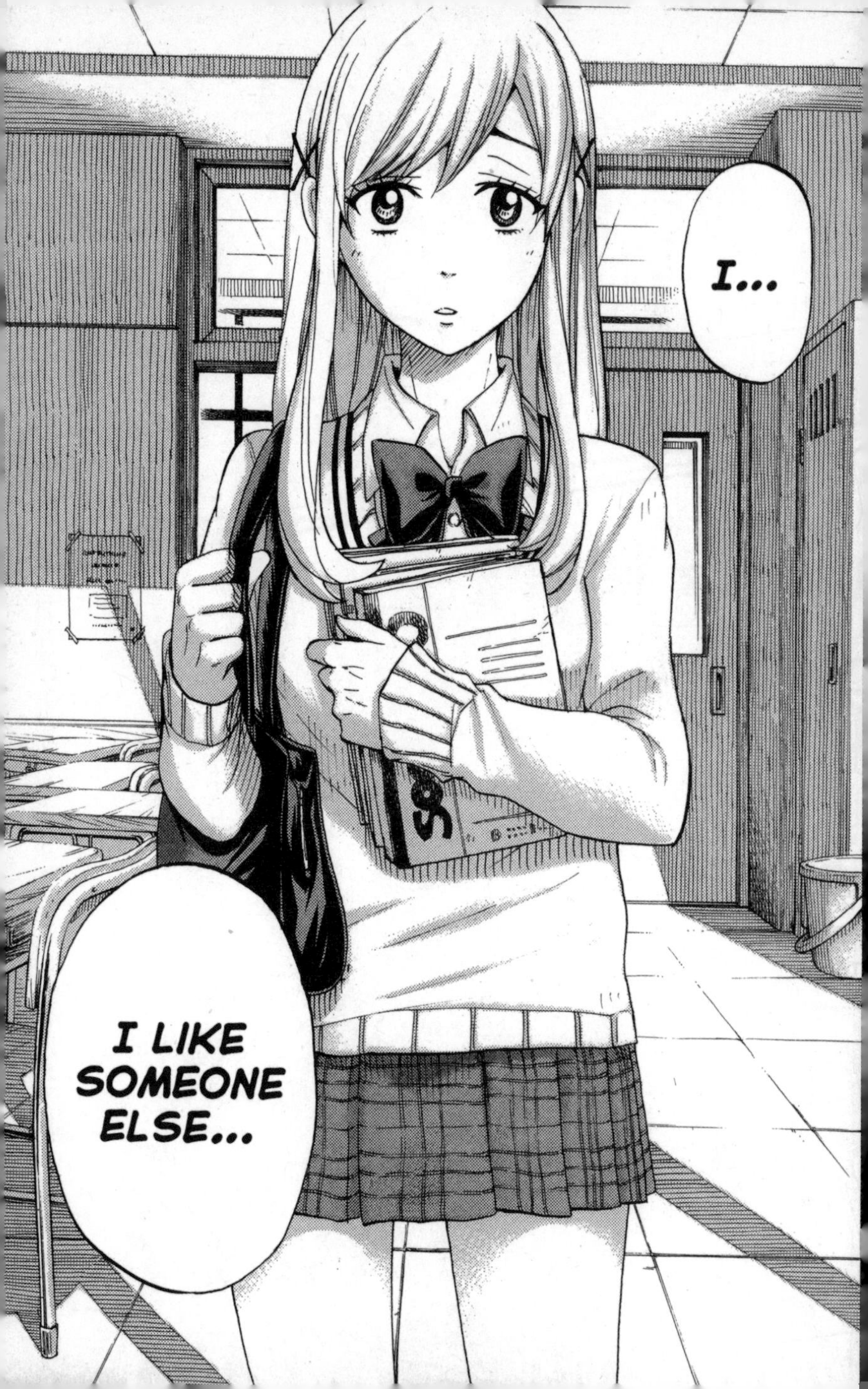
I...
I LIKE SOMEONE ELSE...

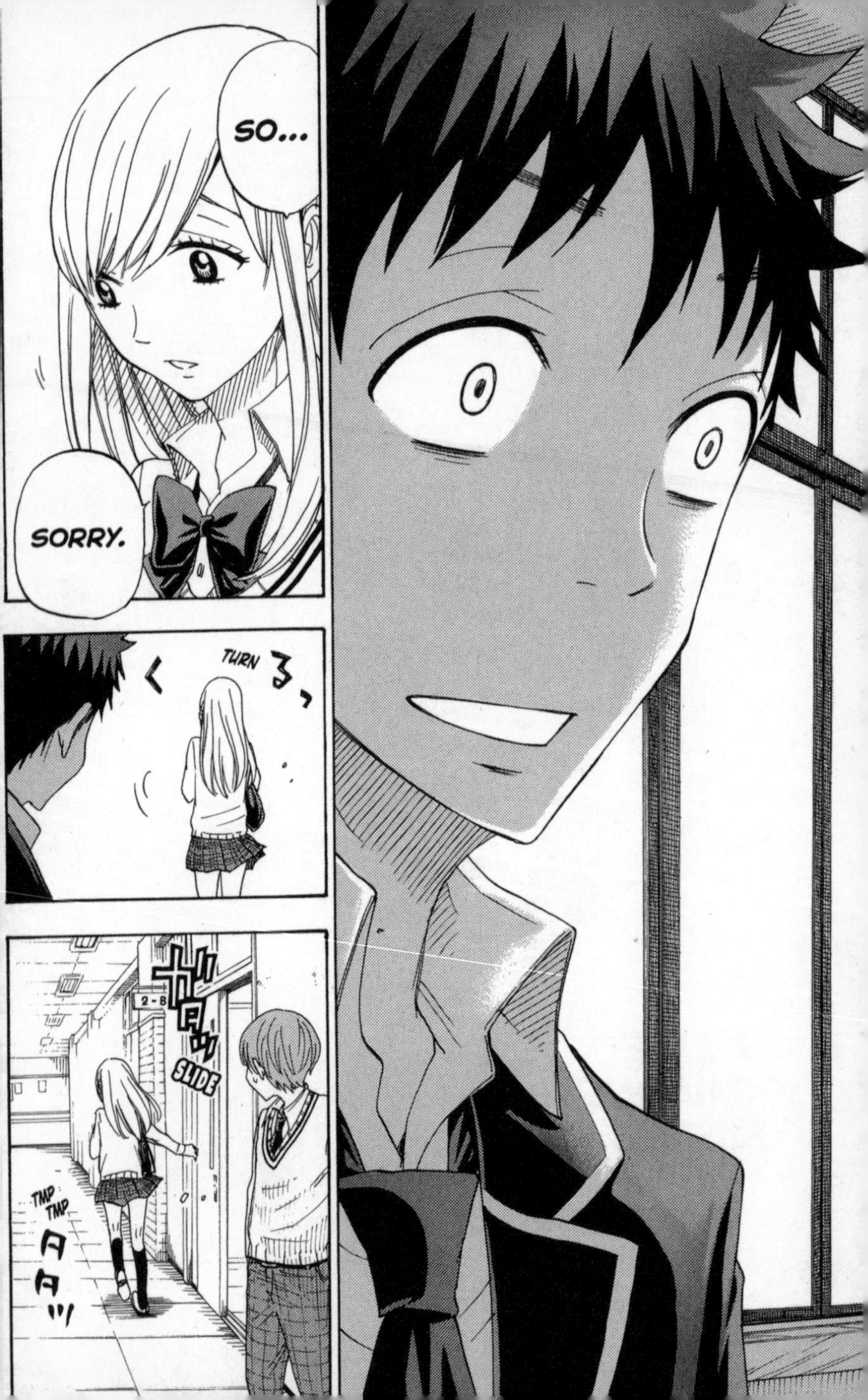
SO...
SORRY.
TURN
2-8
SLIDE
TMP TMP

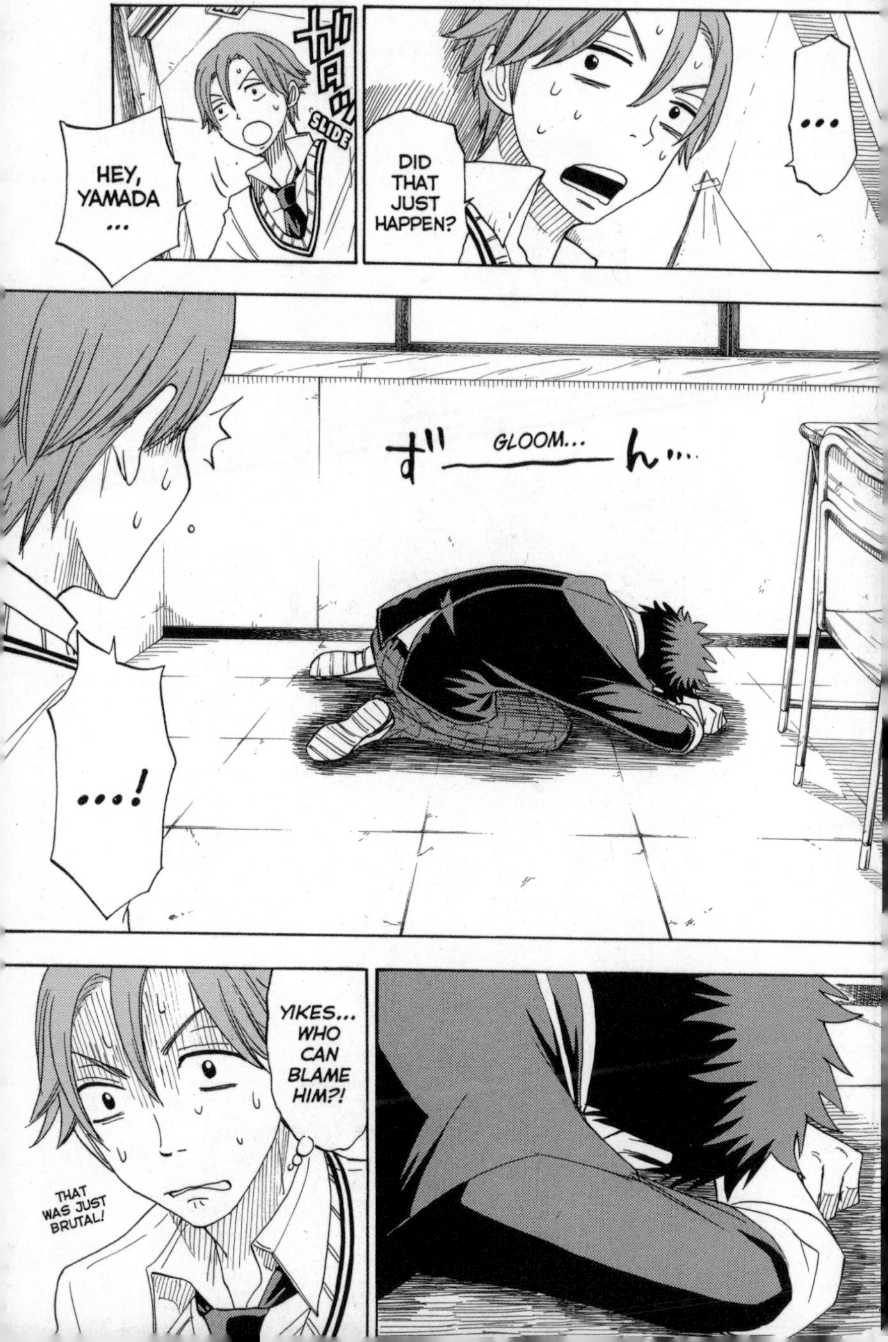
...
DID THAT JUST HAPPEN?
ガラッ
SLIDE
HEY, YAMADA ...
ずーーん…
GLOOM...
...!
YIKES... WHO CAN BLAME HIM?!
THAT WAS JUST BRUTAL!

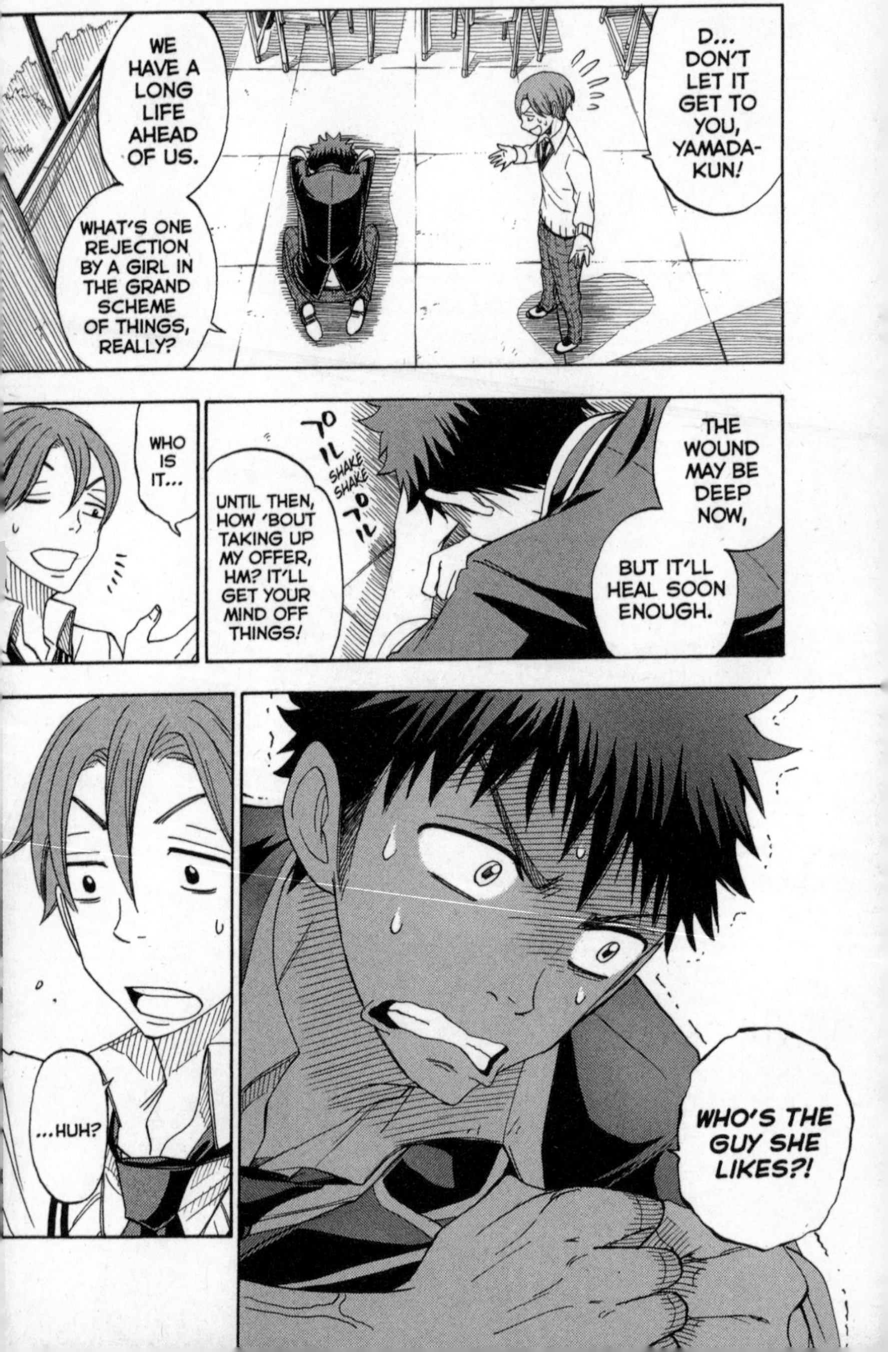
D... DON'T LET IT GET TO YOU, YAMADA-KUN!
WE HAVE A LONG LIFE AHEAD OF US.
WHAT'S ONE REJECTION BY A GIRL IN THE GRAND SCHEME OF THINGS, REALLY?
THE WOUND MAY BE DEEP NOW,
BUT IT'LL HEAL SOON ENOUGH.
SHAKE SHAKE
UNTIL THEN, HOW 'BOUT TAKING UP MY OFFER, HM? IT'LL GET YOUR MIND OFF THINGS!
WHO IS IT...
WHO'S THE GUY SHE LIKES?!
...HUH?

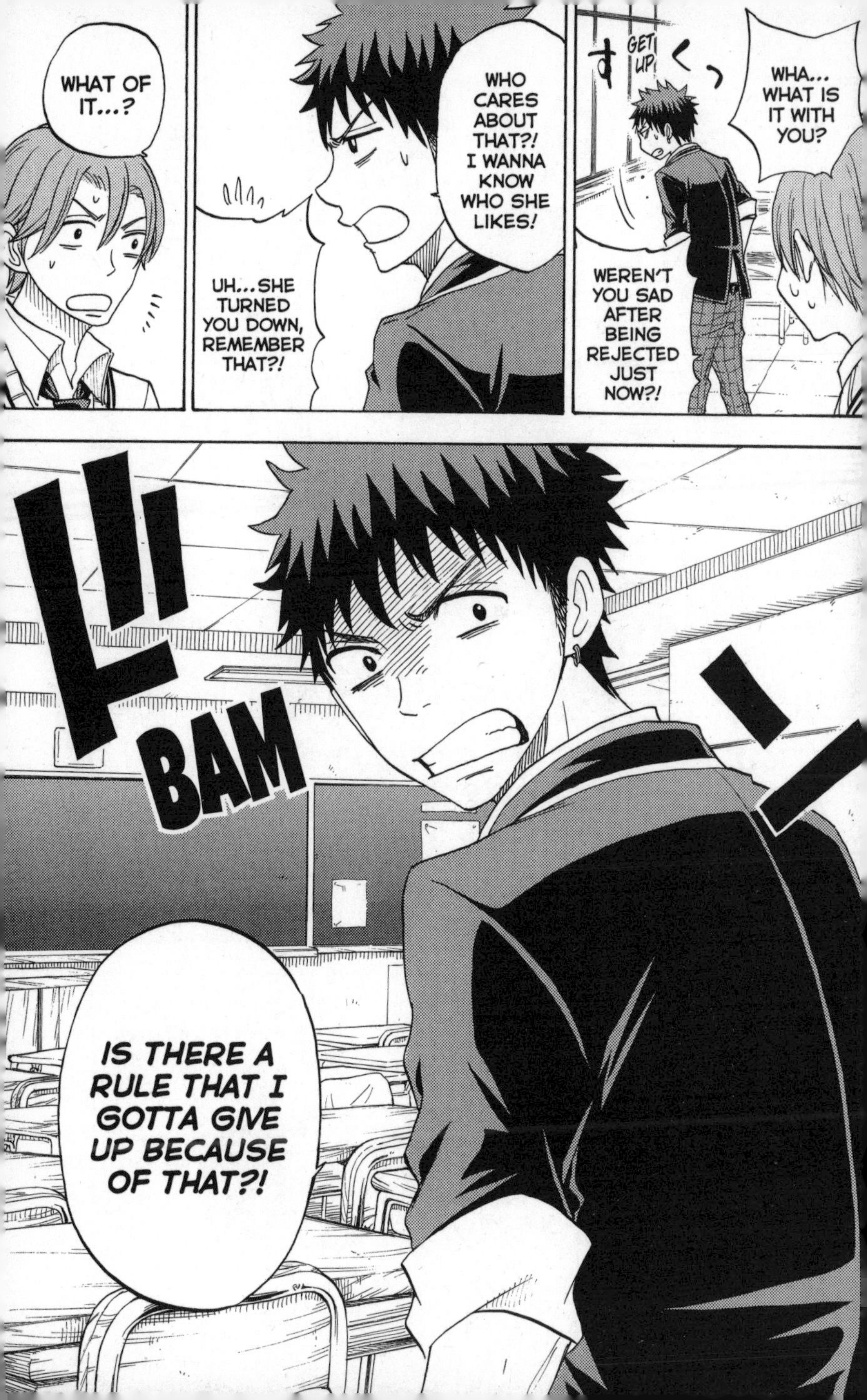
WHA... WHAT IS IT WITH YOU?
GET UP
WEREN'T YOU SAD AFTER BEING REJECTED JUST NOW?!
WHO CARES ABOUT THAT?! I WANNA KNOW WHO SHE LIKES!
UH...SHE TURNED YOU DOWN, REMEMBER THAT?!
WHAT OF IT...?
BAM
IS THERE A RULE THAT I GOTTA GIVE UP BECAUSE OF THAT?!

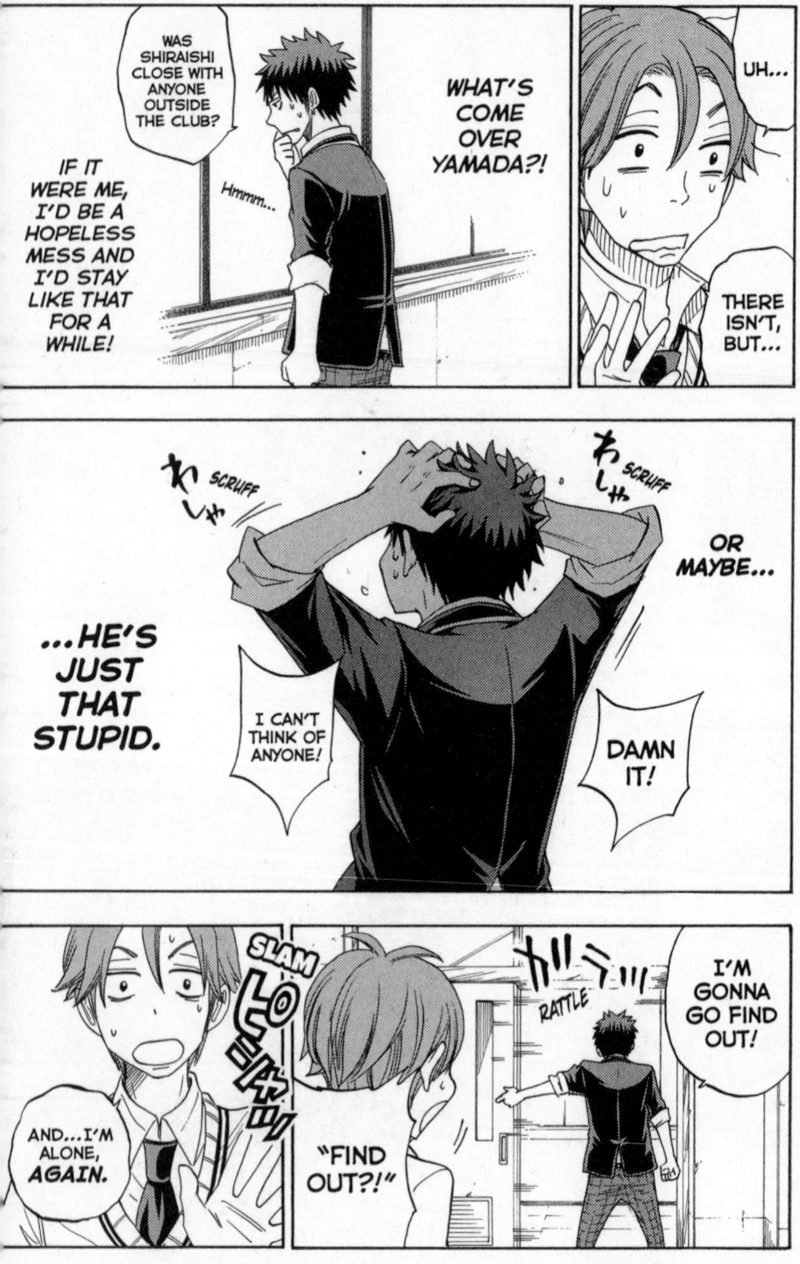
UH...
THERE ISN'T, BUT...
WHAT'S COME OVER YAMADA?!
WAS SHIRAISHI CLOSE WITH ANYONE OUTSIDE THE CLUB?
Hmmm...
IF IT WERE ME, I'D BE A HOPELESS MESS AND I'D STAY LIKE THAT FOR A WHILE!
わしゃ SCRUFF
OR MAYBE...
DAMN IT!
I CAN'T THINK OF ANYONE!
わしゃ SCRUFF
...HE'S JUST THAT STUPID.
I'M GONNA GO FIND OUT!
RATTLE
"FIND OUT?!"
SLAM
AND...I'M ALONE, AGAIN.

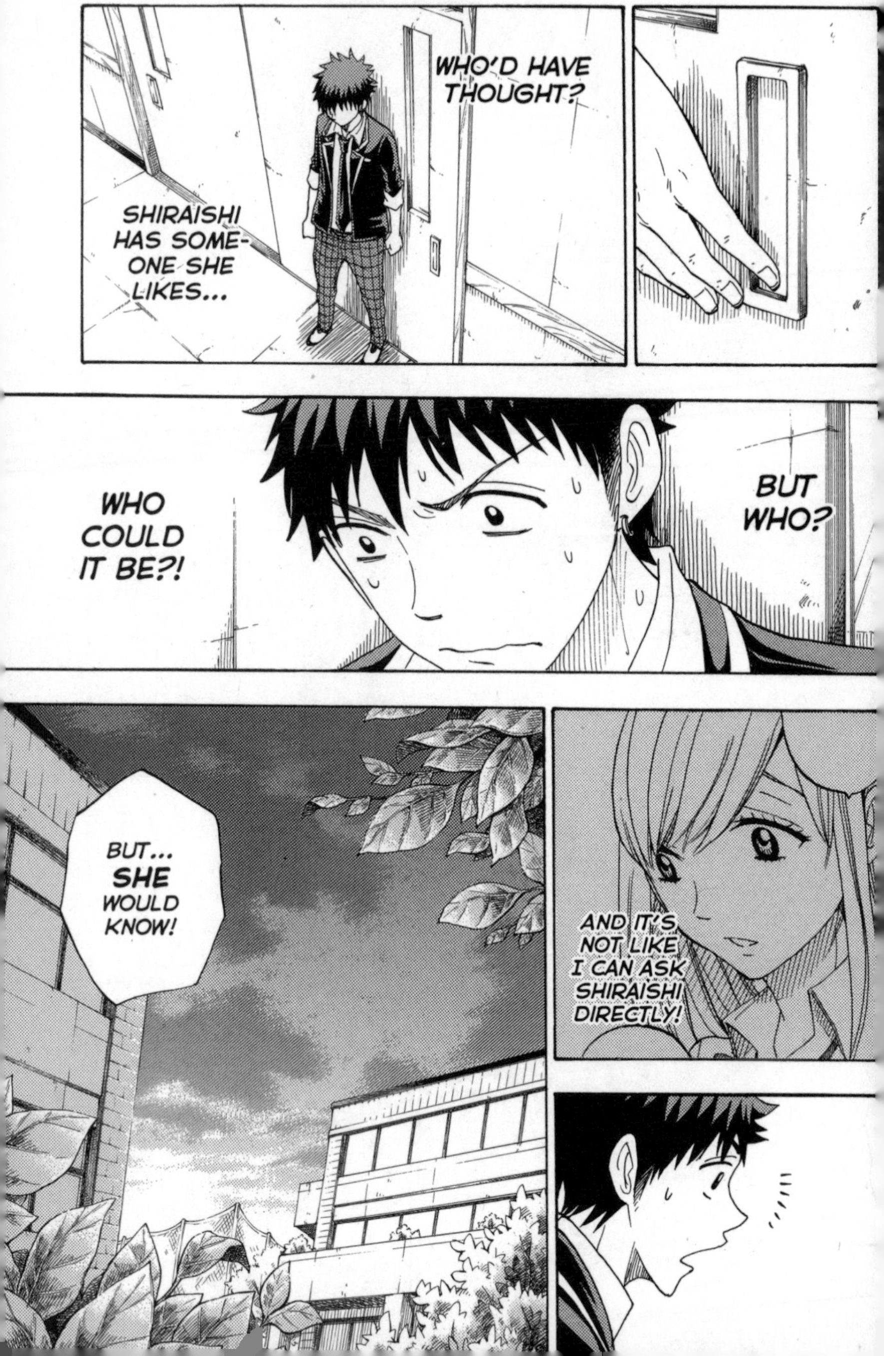
WHO'D HAVE THOUGHT?
SHIRAISHI HAS SOME-ONE SHE LIKES...
BUT WHO?
WHO COULD IT BE?!
AND IT'S NOT LIKE I CAN ASK SHIRAISHI DIRECTLY!
BUT... SHE WOULD KNOW!

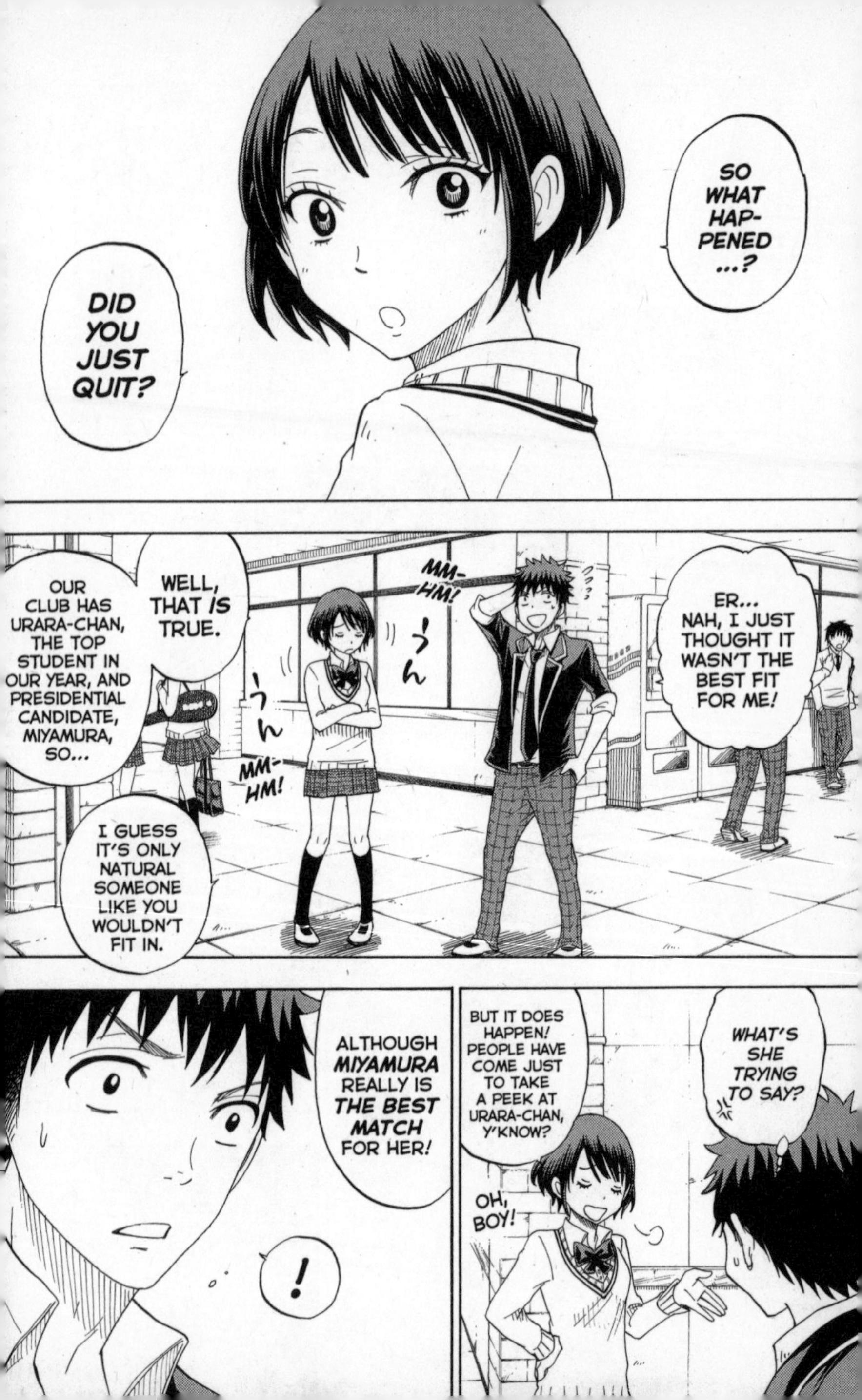
SO WHAT HAP-PENED ...?
DID YOU JUST QUIT?
ER... NAH, I JUST THOUGHT IT WASN'T THE BEST FIT FOR ME!
MM-HM!
うん
WELL, THAT IS TRUE.
OUR CLUB HAS URARA-CHAN, THE TOP STUDENT IN OUR YEAR, AND PRESIDENTIAL CANDIDATE, MIYAMURA, SO...
うん
MM-HM!
I GUESS IT'S ONLY NATURAL SOMEONE LIKE YOU WOULDN'T FIT IN.
WHAT'S SHE TRYING TO SAY?
BUT IT DOES HAPPEN! PEOPLE HAVE COME JUST TO TAKE A PEEK AT URARA-CHAN, Y'KNOW?
OH, BOY!
ALTHOUGH MIYAMURA REALLY IS THE BEST MATCH FOR HER!
!

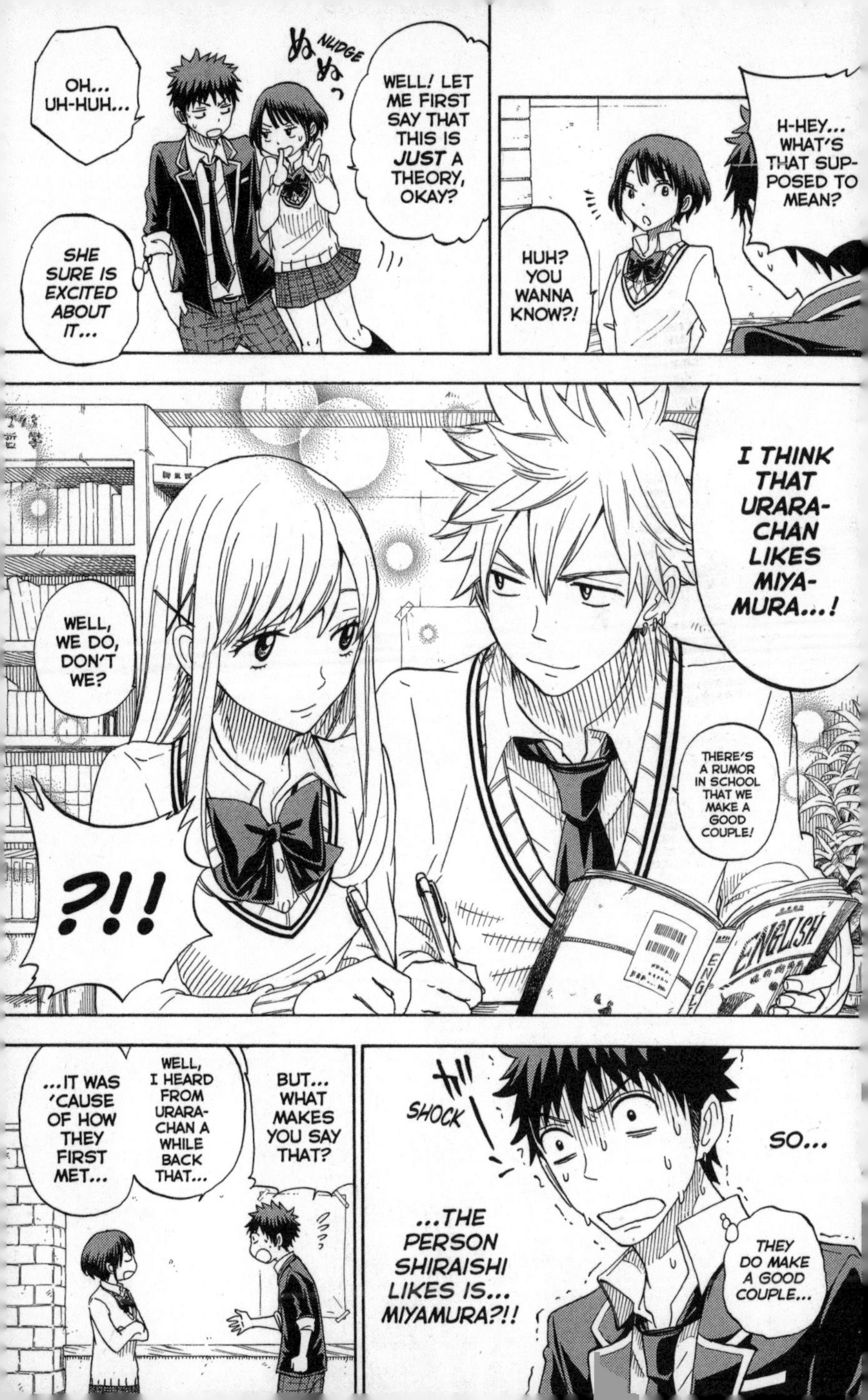

H-HEY... WHAT'S THAT SUPPOSED TO MEAN?
HUH? YOU WANNA KNOW?!
WELL! LET ME FIRST SAY THAT THIS IS JUST A THEORY, OKAY?
NUDGE
OH... UH-HUH...
SHE SURE IS EXCITED ABOUT IT...
I THINK THAT URARA-CHAN LIKES MIYAMURA...!
THERE'S A RUMOR IN SCHOOL THAT WE MAKE A GOOD COUPLE!
WELL, WE DO, DON'T WE?
?!!
SO...
SHOCK
...THE PERSON SHIRAISHI LIKES IS... MIYAMURA?!!
THEY DO MAKE A GOOD COUPLE...
BUT... WHAT MAKES YOU SAY THAT?
WELL, I HEARD FROM URARA-CHAN A WHILE BACK THAT...
...IT WAS 'CAUSE OF HOW THEY FIRST MET...

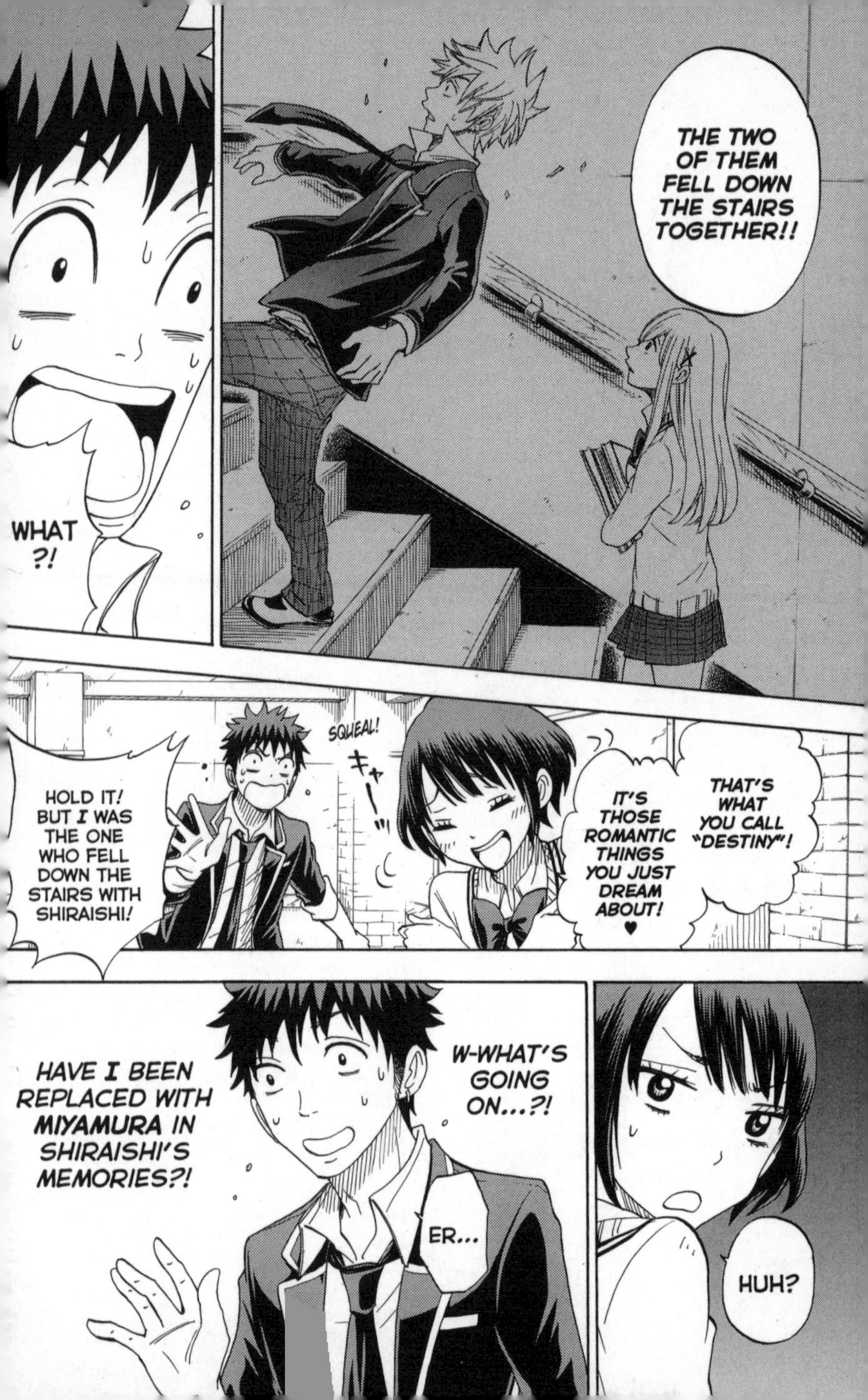
THE TWO OF THEM FELL DOWN THE STAIRS TOGETHER!!
WHAT ?!
THAT'S WHAT YOU CALL "DESTINY"!
IT'S THOSE ROMANTIC THINGS YOU JUST DREAM ABOUT! ♥
SQUEAL!
キャーッ
HOLD IT! BUT I WAS THE ONE WHO FELL DOWN THE STAIRS WITH SHIRAISHI!
HUH?
W-WHAT'S GOING ON...?!
HAVE I BEEN REPLACED WITH MIYAMURA IN SHIRAISHI'S MEMORIES?!
ER...

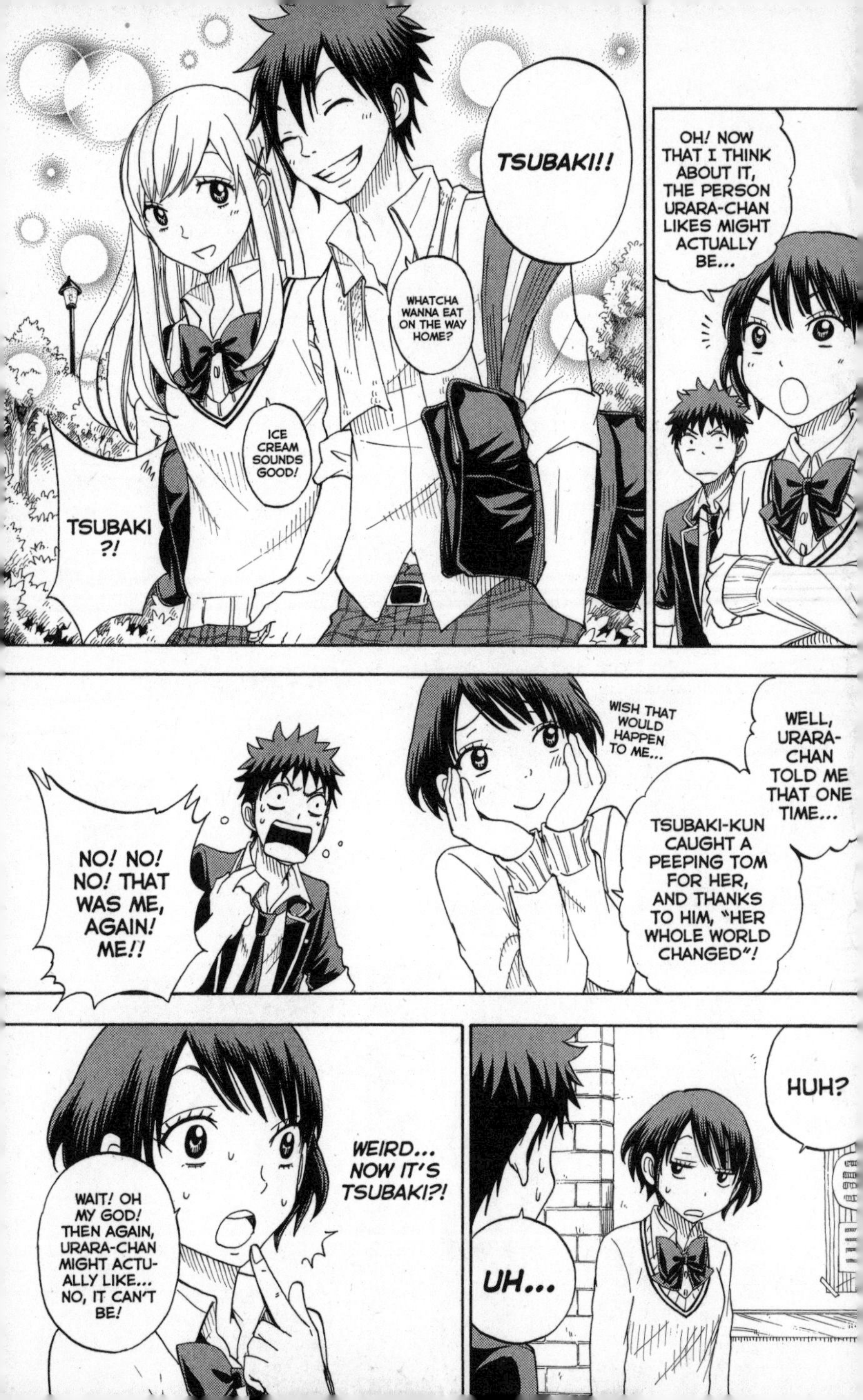
OH! NOW THAT I THINK ABOUT IT, THE PERSON URARA-CHAN LIKES MIGHT ACTUALLY BE...
TSUBAKI!!
WHATCHA WANNA EAT ON THE WAY HOME?
ICE CREAM SOUNDS GOOD!
TSUBAKI ?!
WELL, URARA-CHAN TOLD ME THAT ONE TIME...
TSUBAKI-KUN CAUGHT A PEEPING TOM FOR HER, AND THANKS TO HIM, "HER WHOLE WORLD CHANGED"!
WISH THAT WOULD HAPPEN TO ME...
NO! NO! NO! THAT WAS ME, AGAIN! ME!!
HUH?
UH...
WEIRD... NOW IT'S TSUBAKI?!
WAIT! OH MY GOD! THEN AGAIN, URARA-CHAN MIGHT ACTU-ALLY LIKE... NO, IT CAN'T BE!

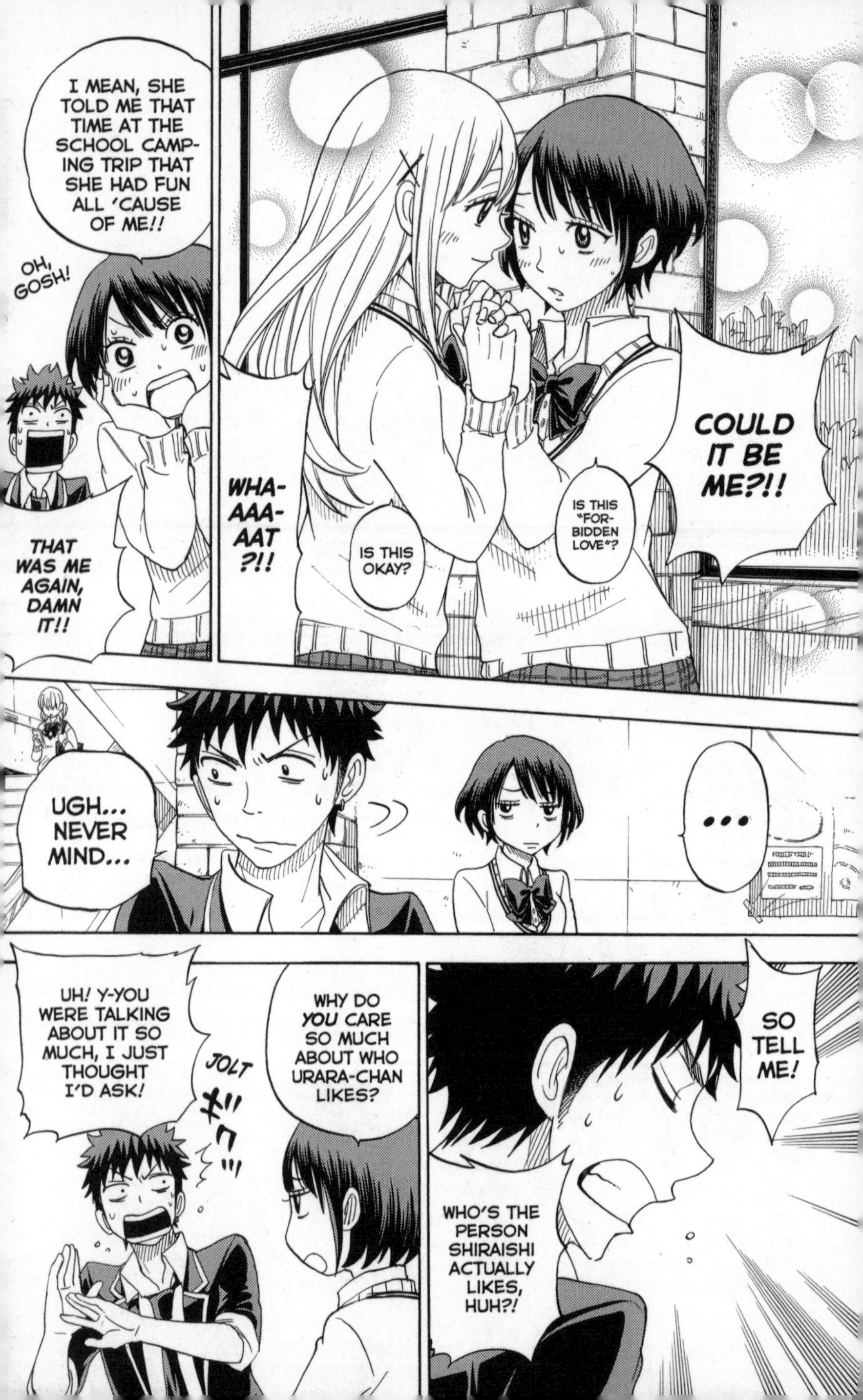
COULD IT BE ME?!!
IS THIS "FORBIDDEN LOVE"?
IS THIS OKAY?
WHAAAAAAT?!!
I MEAN, SHE TOLD ME THAT TIME AT THE SCHOOL CAMPING TRIP THAT SHE HAD FUN ALL 'CAUSE OF ME!!
OH, GOSH!
THAT WAS ME AGAIN, DAMN IT!!
...
UGH... NEVER MIND...
SO TELL ME!
WHO'S THE PERSON SHIRAISHI ACTUALLY LIKES, HUH?!
WHY DO YOU CARE SO MUCH ABOUT WHO URARA-CHAN LIKES?
JOLT
UH! Y-YOU WERE TALKING ABOUT IT SO MUCH, I JUST THOUGHT I'D ASK!

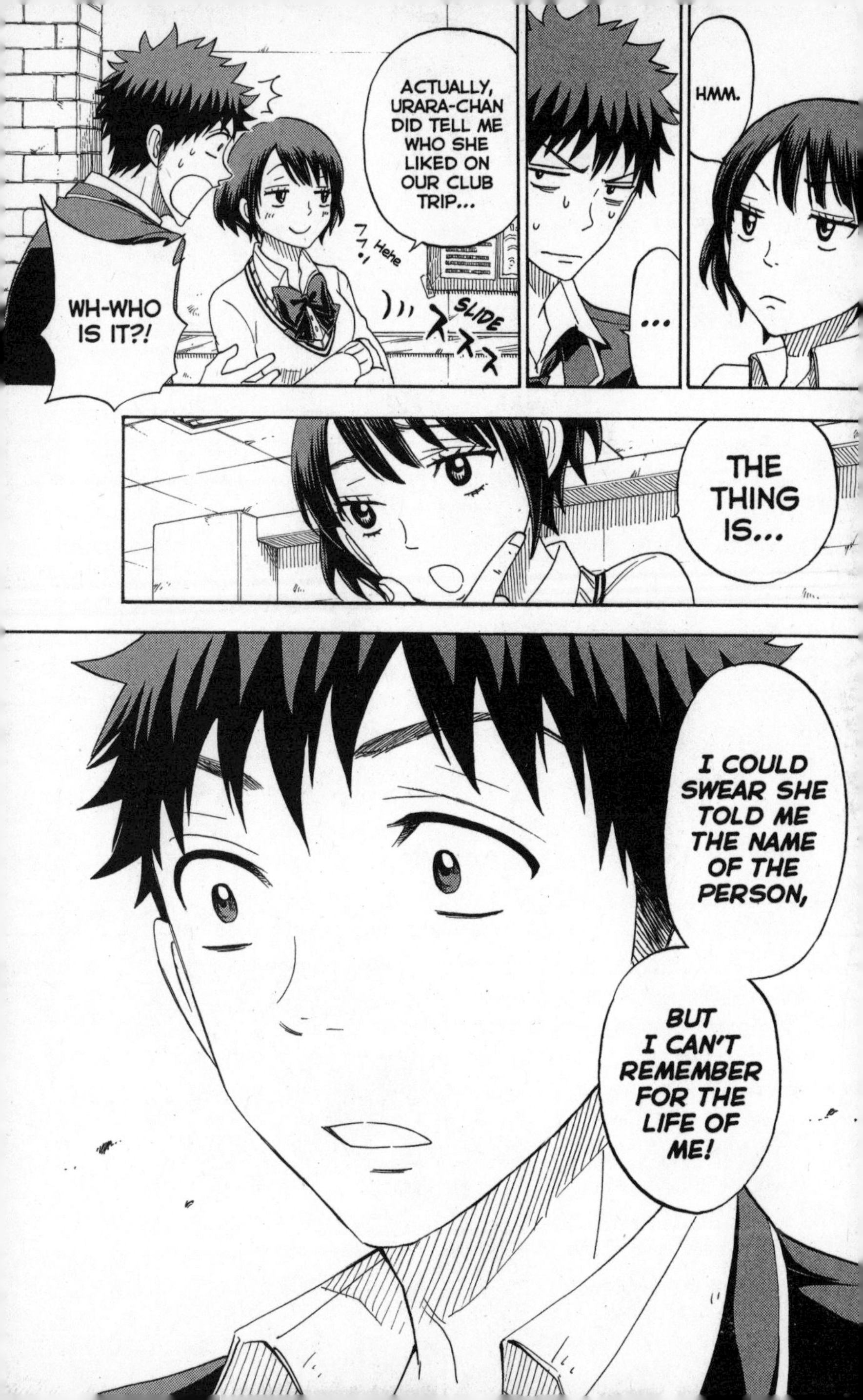
HMM.
...
ACTUALLY, URARA-CHAN DID TELL ME WHO SHE LIKED ON OUR CLUB TRIP...
Hehe
SLIDE
WH-WHO IS IT?!
THE THING IS...
I COULD SWEAR SHE TOLD ME THE NAME OF THE PERSON,
BUT I CAN'T REMEMBER FOR THE LIFE OF ME!

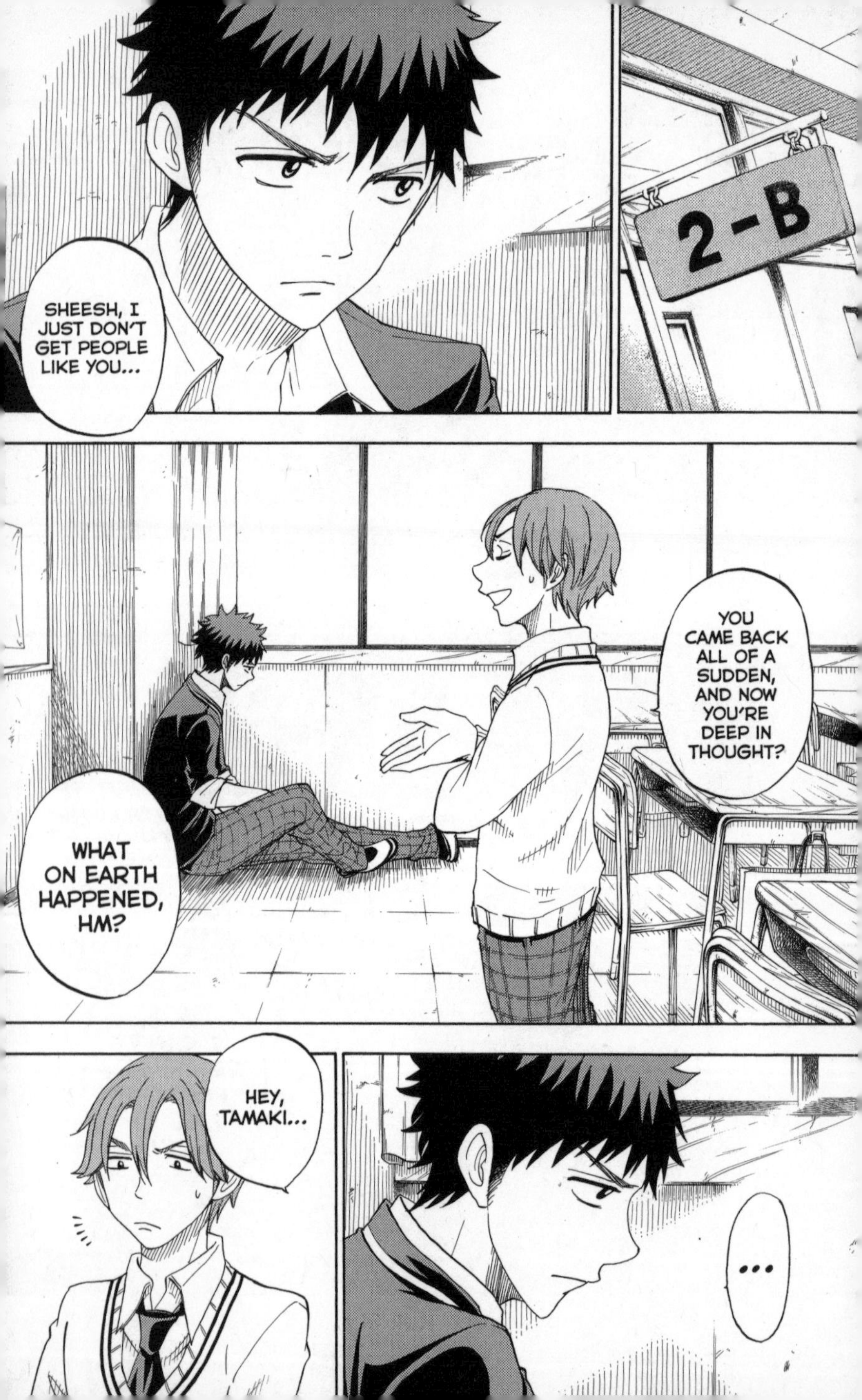
2-B
SHEESH, I JUST DON'T GET PEOPLE LIKE YOU...
YOU CAME BACK ALL OF A SUDDEN, AND NOW YOU'RE DEEP IN THOUGHT?
WHAT ON EARTH HAPPENED, HM?
...
HEY, TAMAKI...

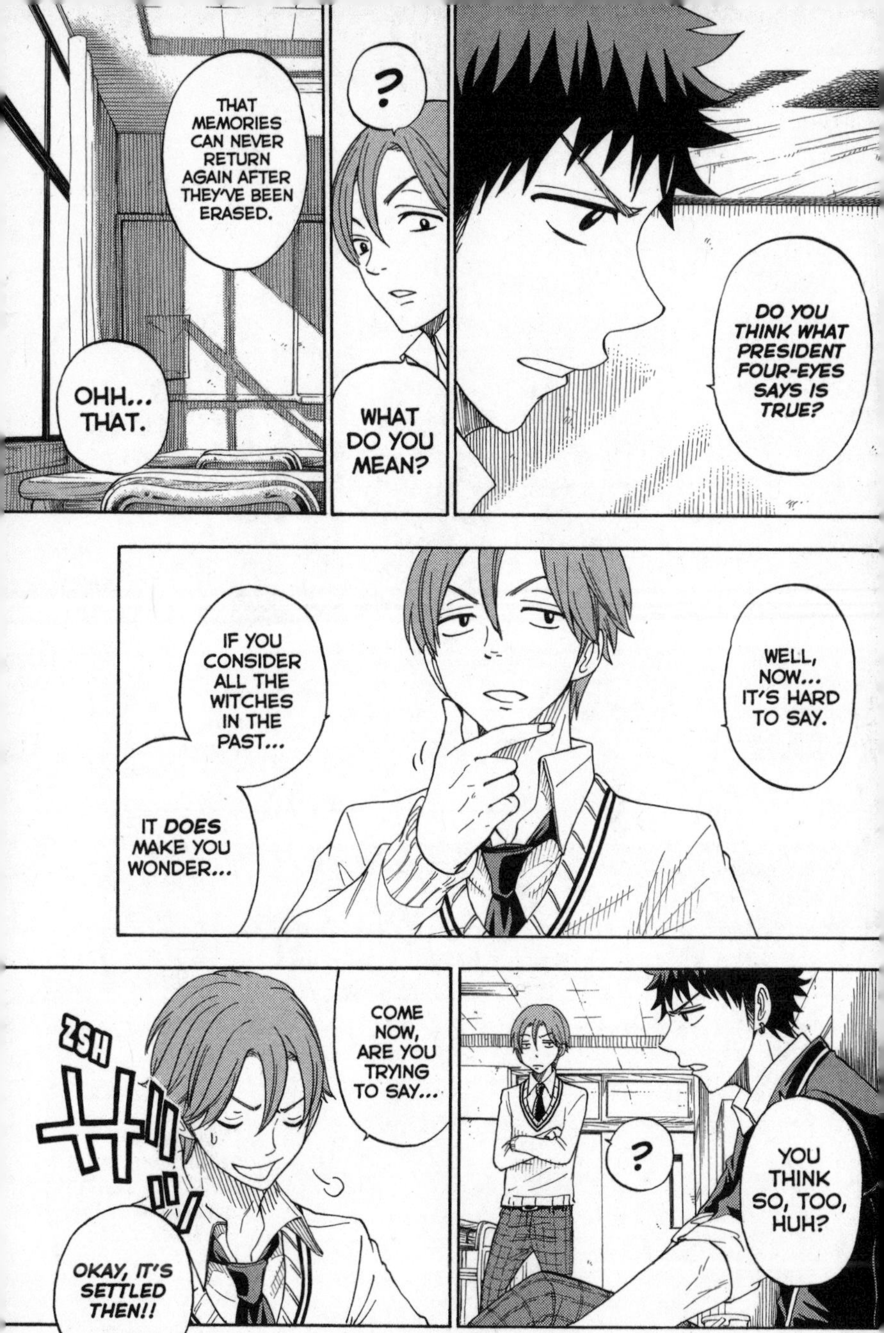
DO YOU THINK WHAT PRESIDENT FOUR-EYES SAYS IS TRUE?
?
WHAT DO YOU MEAN?
THAT MEMORIES CAN NEVER RETURN AGAIN AFTER THEY'VE BEEN ERASED.
OHH... THAT.
WELL, NOW... IT'S HARD TO SAY.
IF YOU CONSIDER ALL THE WITCHES IN THE PAST...
IT *DOES* MAKE YOU WONDER...
YOU THINK SO, TOO, HUH?
?
COME NOW, ARE YOU TRYING TO SAY...
ZSH
OKAY, IT'S SETTLED THEN!!

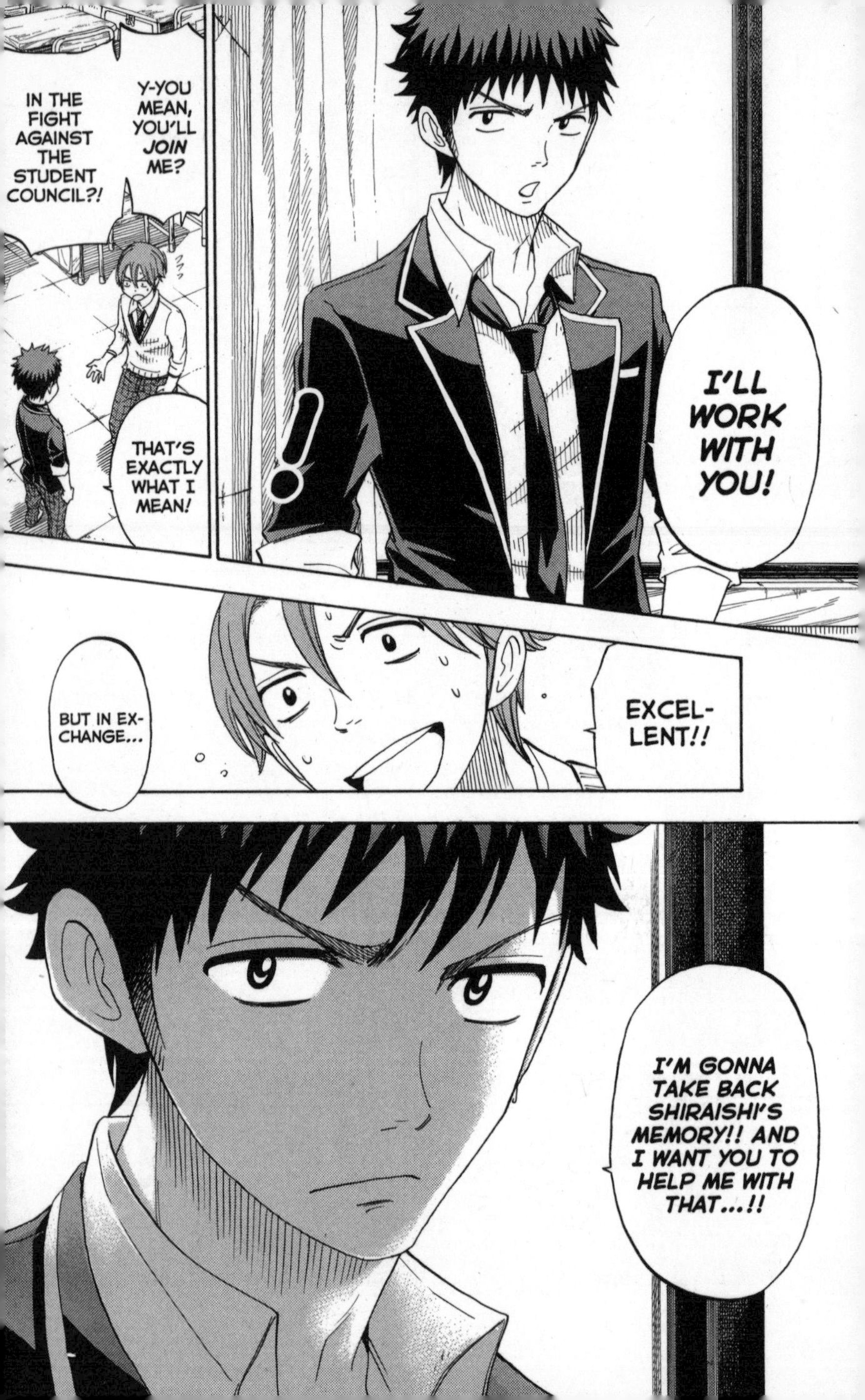
I'LL WORK WITH YOU!
Y-YOU MEAN, YOU'LL *JOIN* ME?
IN THE FIGHT AGAINST THE STUDENT COUNCIL?!
THAT'S EXACTLY WHAT I MEAN!
EXCEL-LENT!!
BUT IN EX-CHANGE...
I'M GONNA TAKE BACK SHIRAISHI'S MEMORY!! AND I WANT YOU TO HELP ME WITH THAT...!!

CHAPTER 71: Charge!!

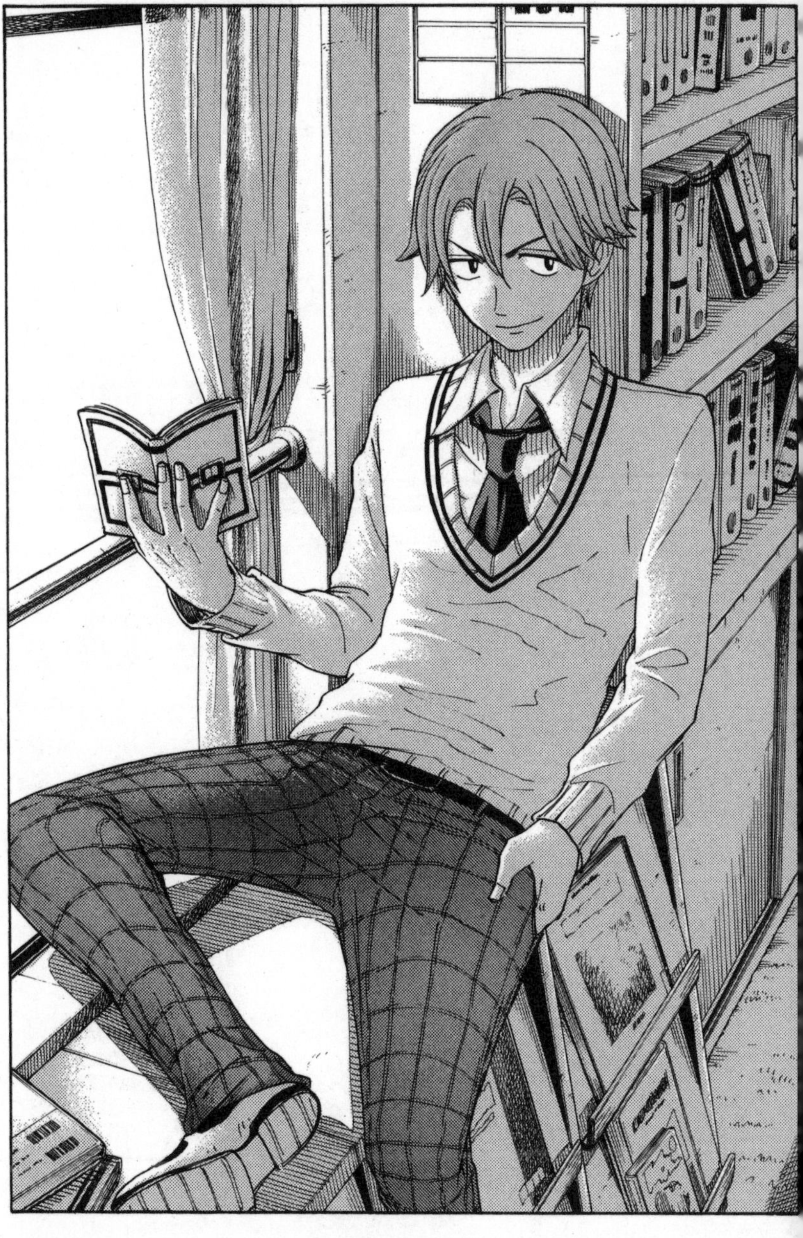

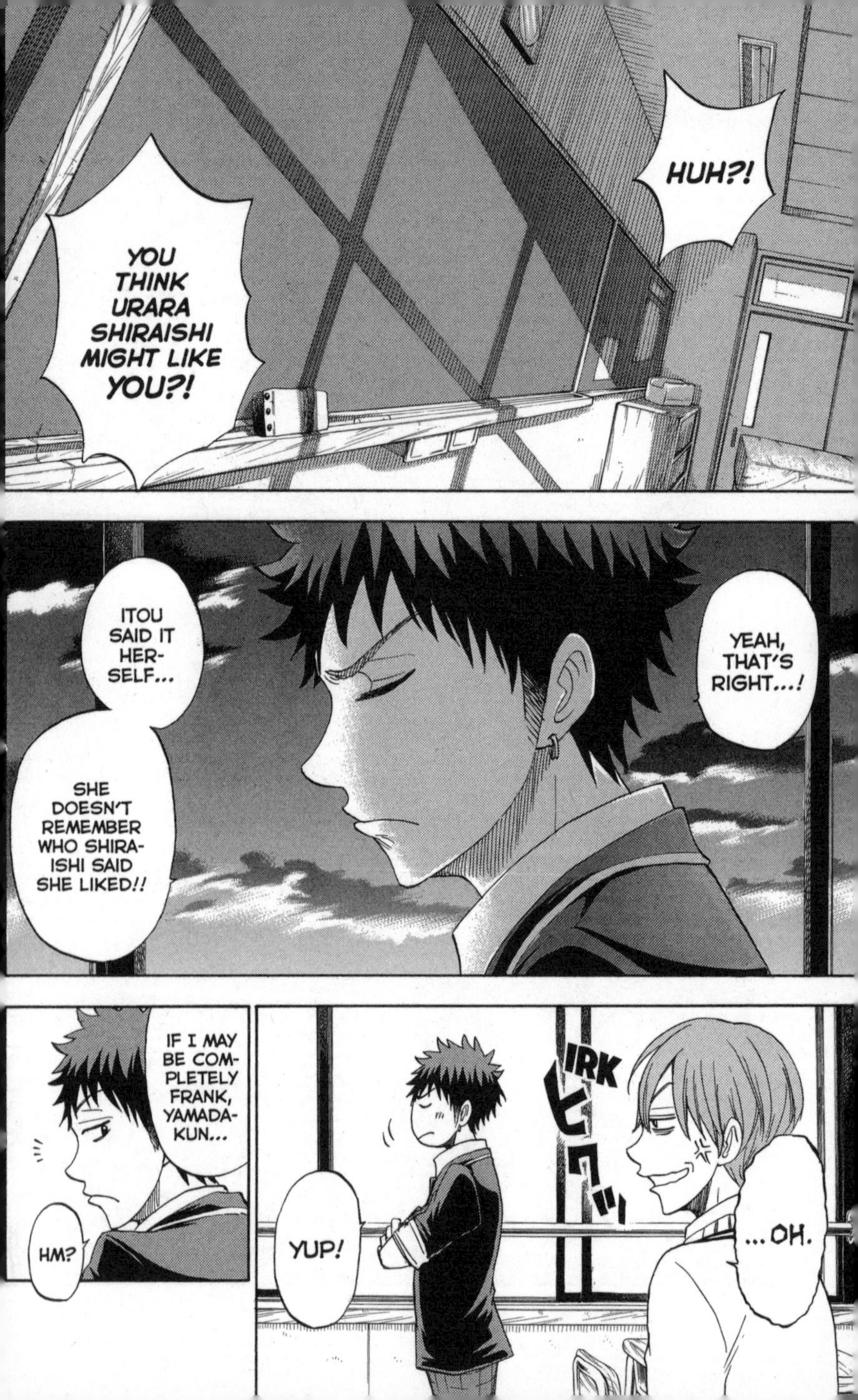
HUH?!
YOU THINK URARA SHIRAISHI MIGHT LIKE YOU?!
YEAH, THAT'S RIGHT...!
ITOU SAID IT HER-SELF...
SHE DOESN'T REMEMBER WHO SHIRA-ISHI SAID SHE LIKED!!
IRK
...OH.
YUP!
IF I MAY BE COM-PLETELY FRANK, YAMADA-KUN...
HM?

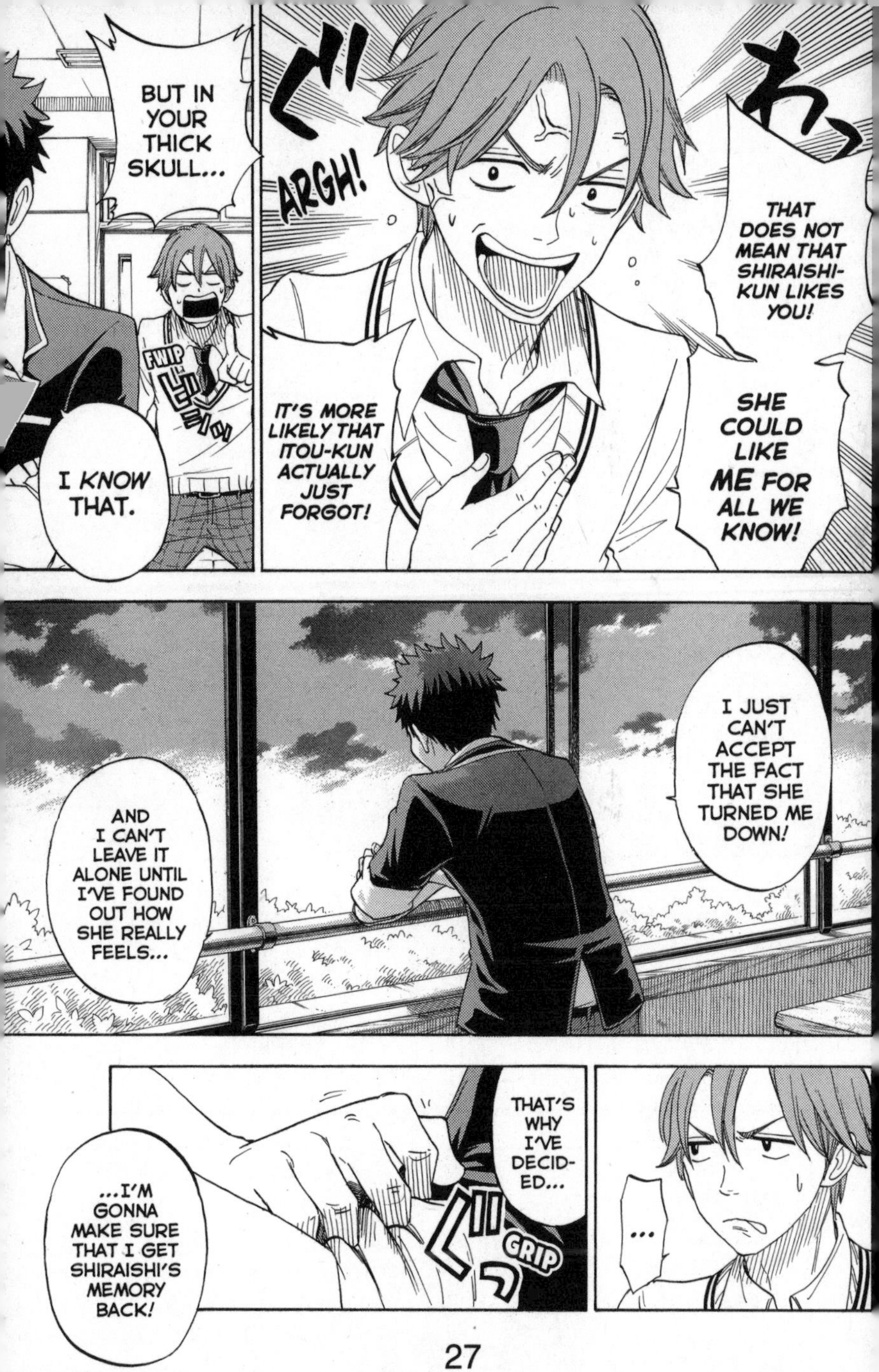

THAT DOES NOT MEAN THAT SHIRAISHI-KUN LIKES YOU!
SHE COULD LIKE ME FOR ALL WE KNOW!
ARGH!
IT'S MORE LIKELY THAT ITOU-KUN ACTUALLY JUST FORGOT!
BUT IN YOUR THICK SKULL...
FWIP
I KNOW THAT.
I JUST CAN'T ACCEPT THE FACT THAT SHE TURNED ME DOWN!
AND I CAN'T LEAVE IT ALONE UNTIL I'VE FOUND OUT HOW SHE REALLY FEELS...
...
THAT'S WHY I'VE DECID-ED...
GRIP
...I'M GONNA MAKE SURE THAT I GET SHIRAISHI'S MEMORY BACK!

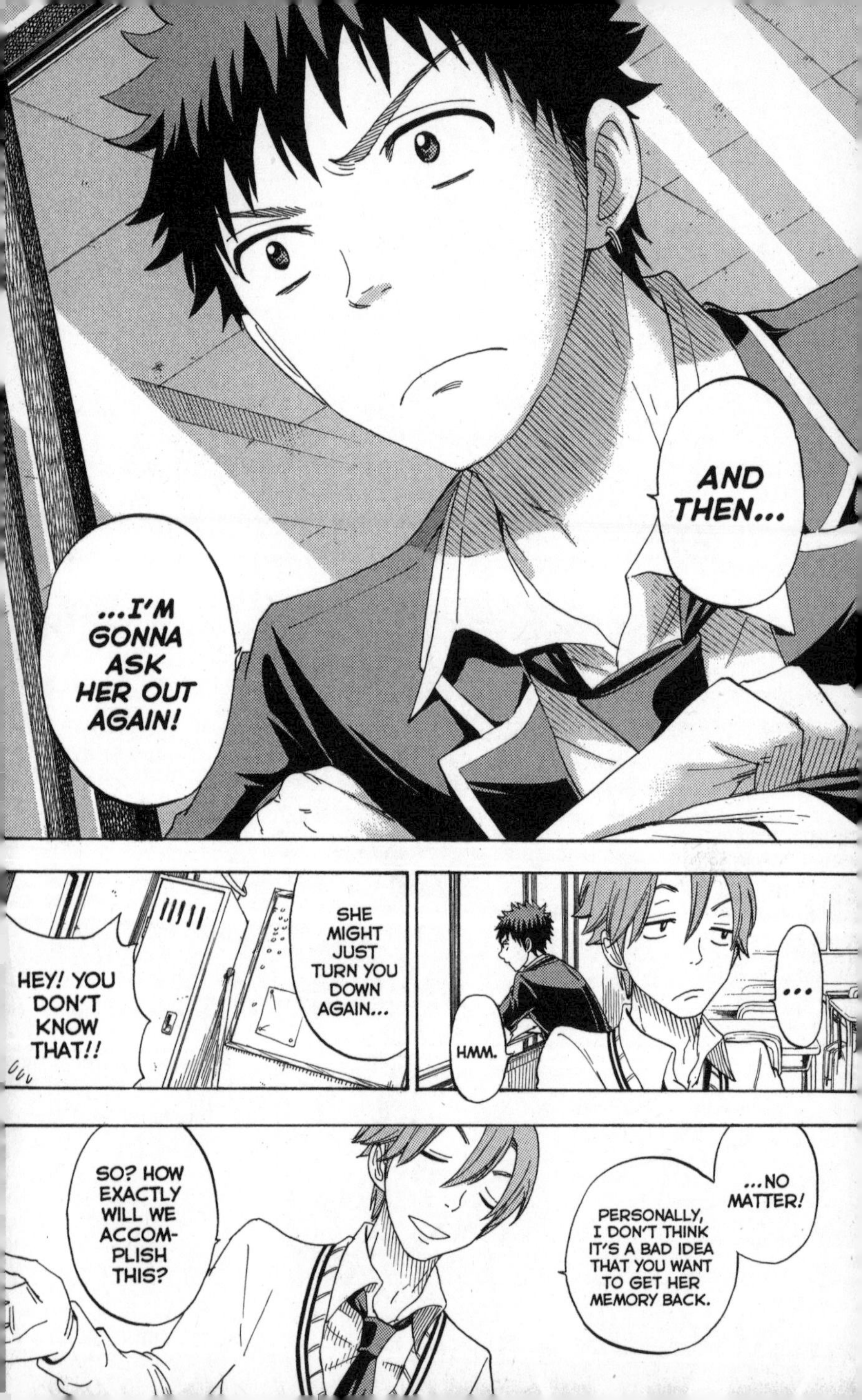
AND THEN...
...I'M GONNA ASK HER OUT AGAIN!
...
HMM.
SHE MIGHT JUST TURN YOU DOWN AGAIN...
HEY! YOU DON'T KNOW THAT!!
...NO MATTER!
PERSONALLY, I DON'T THINK IT'S A BAD IDEA THAT YOU WANT TO GET HER MEMORY BACK.
SO? HOW EXACTLY WILL WE ACCOMPLISH THIS?

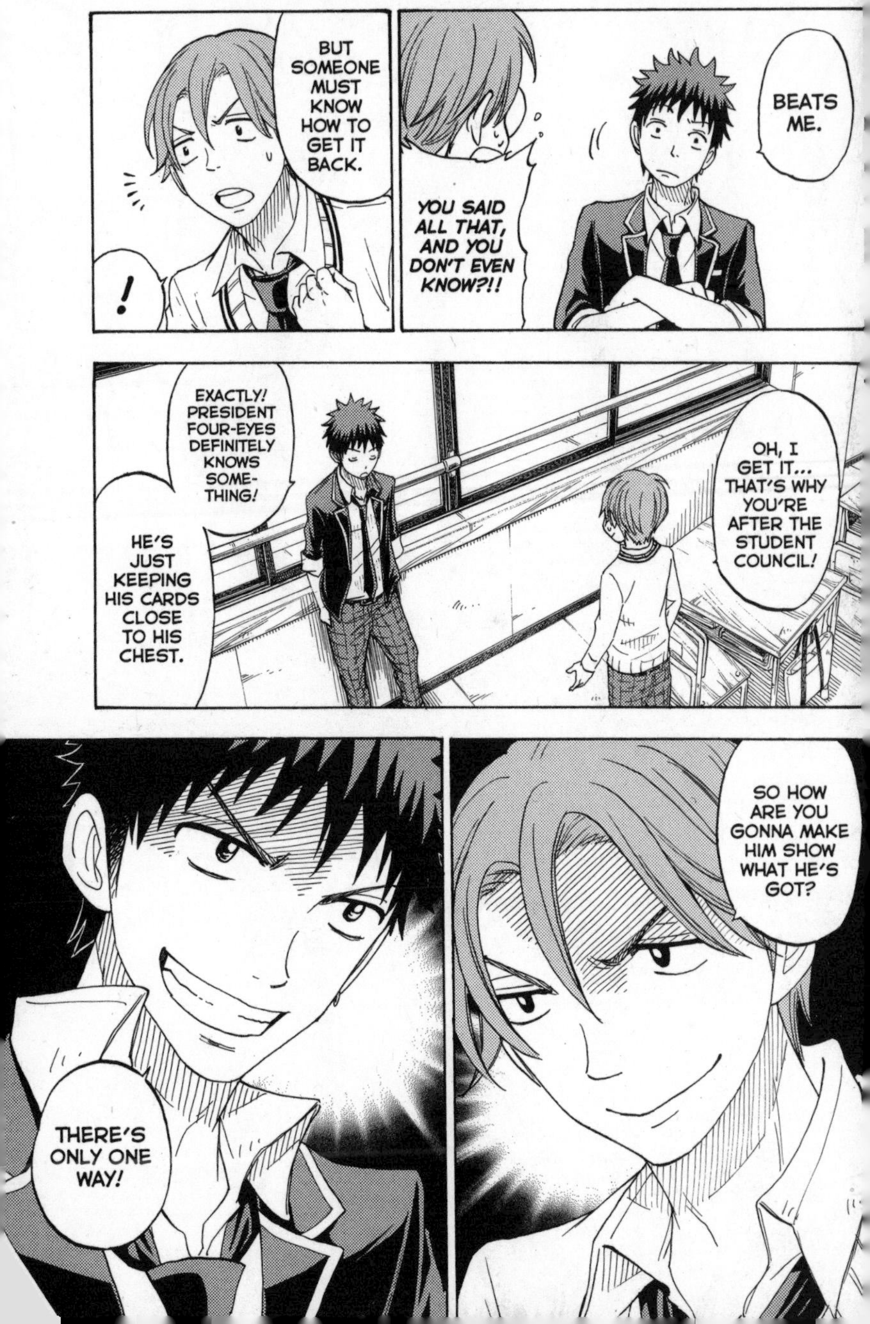
BEATS ME.
YOU SAID ALL THAT, AND YOU DON'T EVEN KNOW?!!
BUT SOMEONE MUST KNOW HOW TO GET IT BACK.
!
OH, I GET IT... THAT'S WHY YOU'RE AFTER THE STUDENT COUNCIL!
EXACTLY! PRESIDENT FOUR-EYES DEFINITELY KNOWS SOME-THING!
HE'S JUST KEEPING HIS CARDS CLOSE TO HIS CHEST.
SO HOW ARE YOU GONNA MAKE HIM SHOW WHAT HE'S GOT?
THERE'S ONLY ONE WAY!

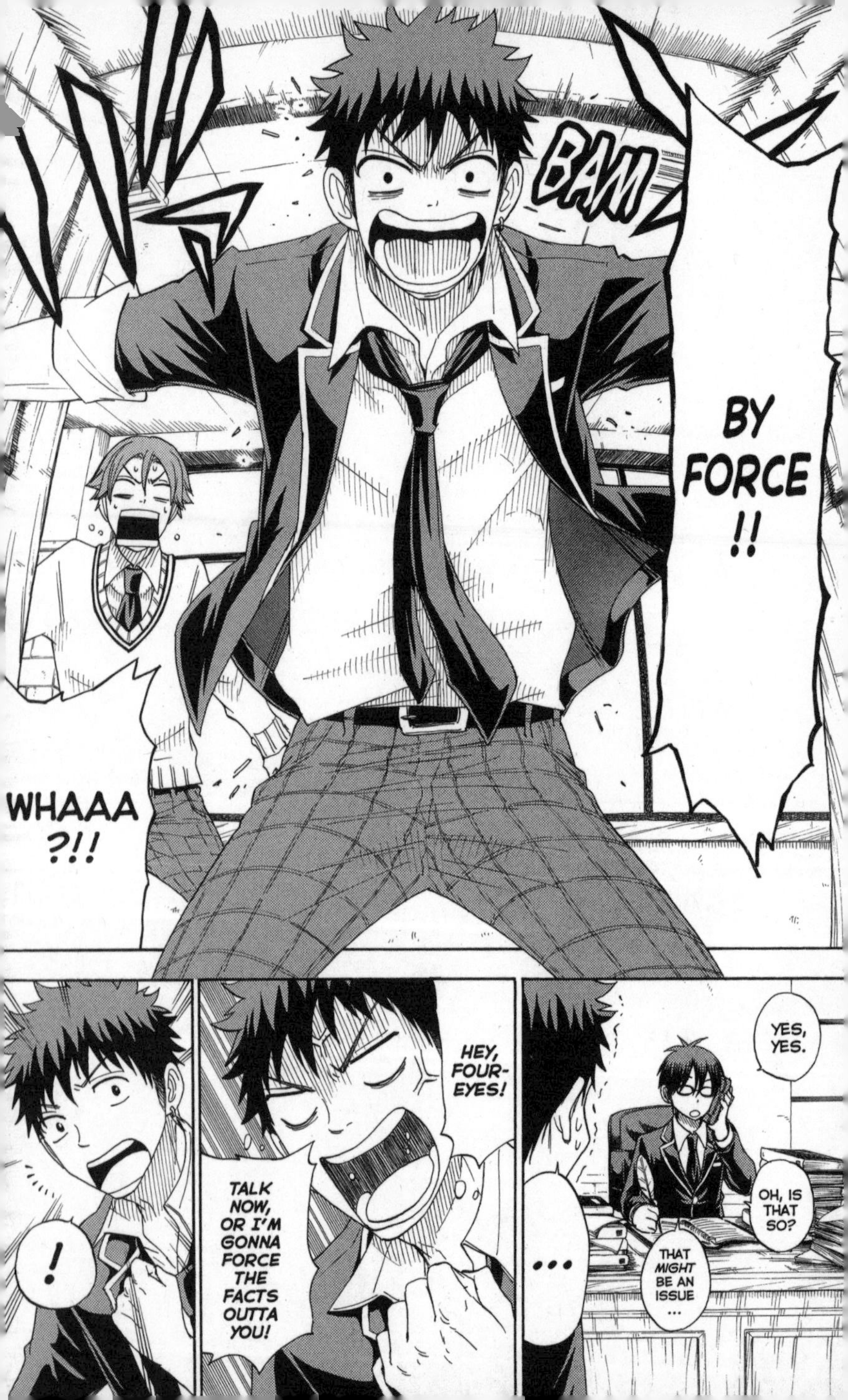
BAM
BY FORCE!!
WHAAA?!!
YES, YES.
OH, IS THAT SO?
THAT MIGHT BE AN ISSUE ...
...
HEY, FOUR-EYES!
TALK NOW, OR I'M GONNA FORCE THE FACTS OUTTA YOU!
!

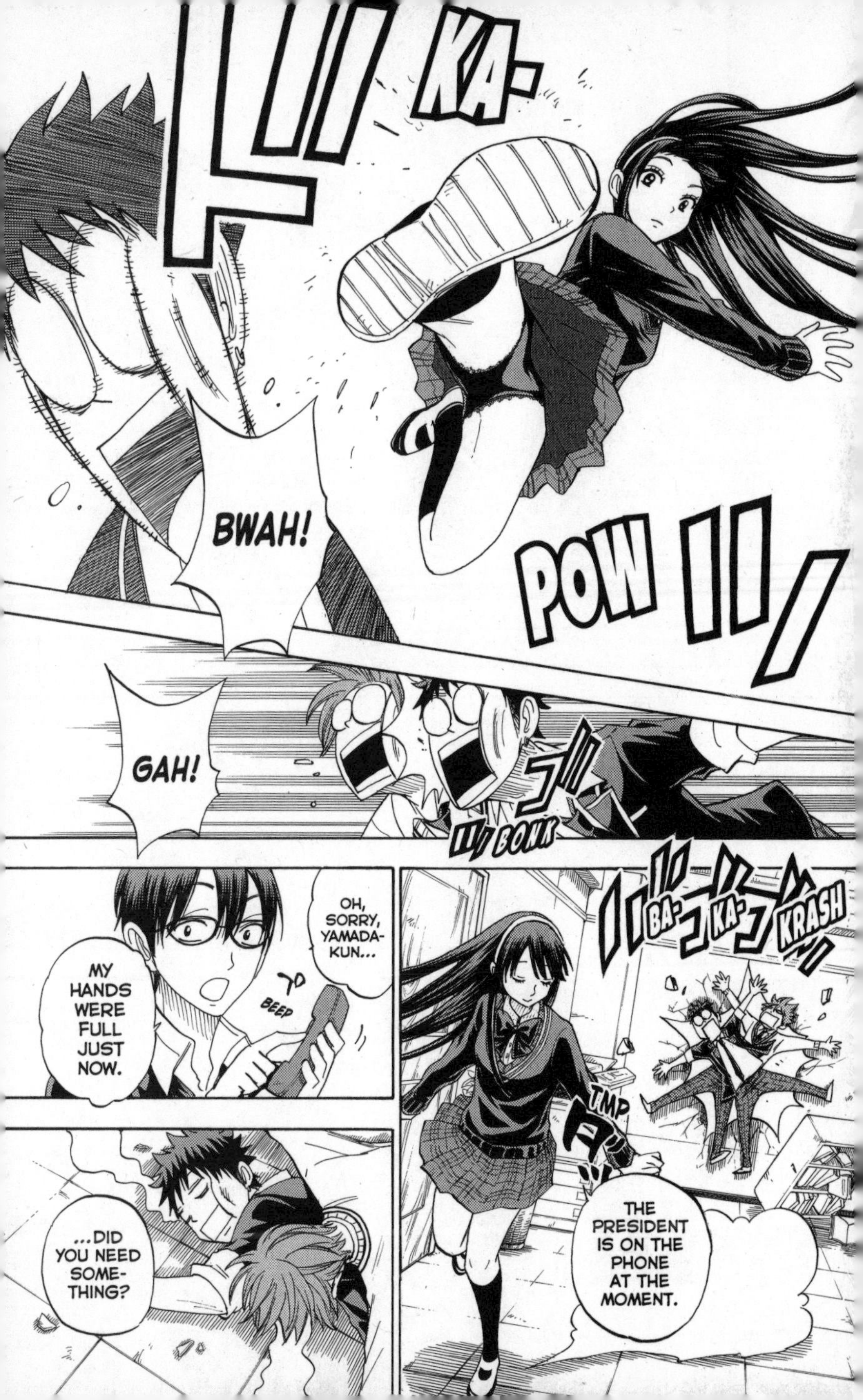
KA-
BWAH!
POW
GAH!
BONK
BA- KA- KRASH
TMP
THE PRESIDENT IS ON THE PHONE AT THE MOMENT.
OH, SORRY, YAMADA-KUN...
MY HANDS WERE FULL JUST NOW.
BEEP
...DID YOU NEED SOME-THING?

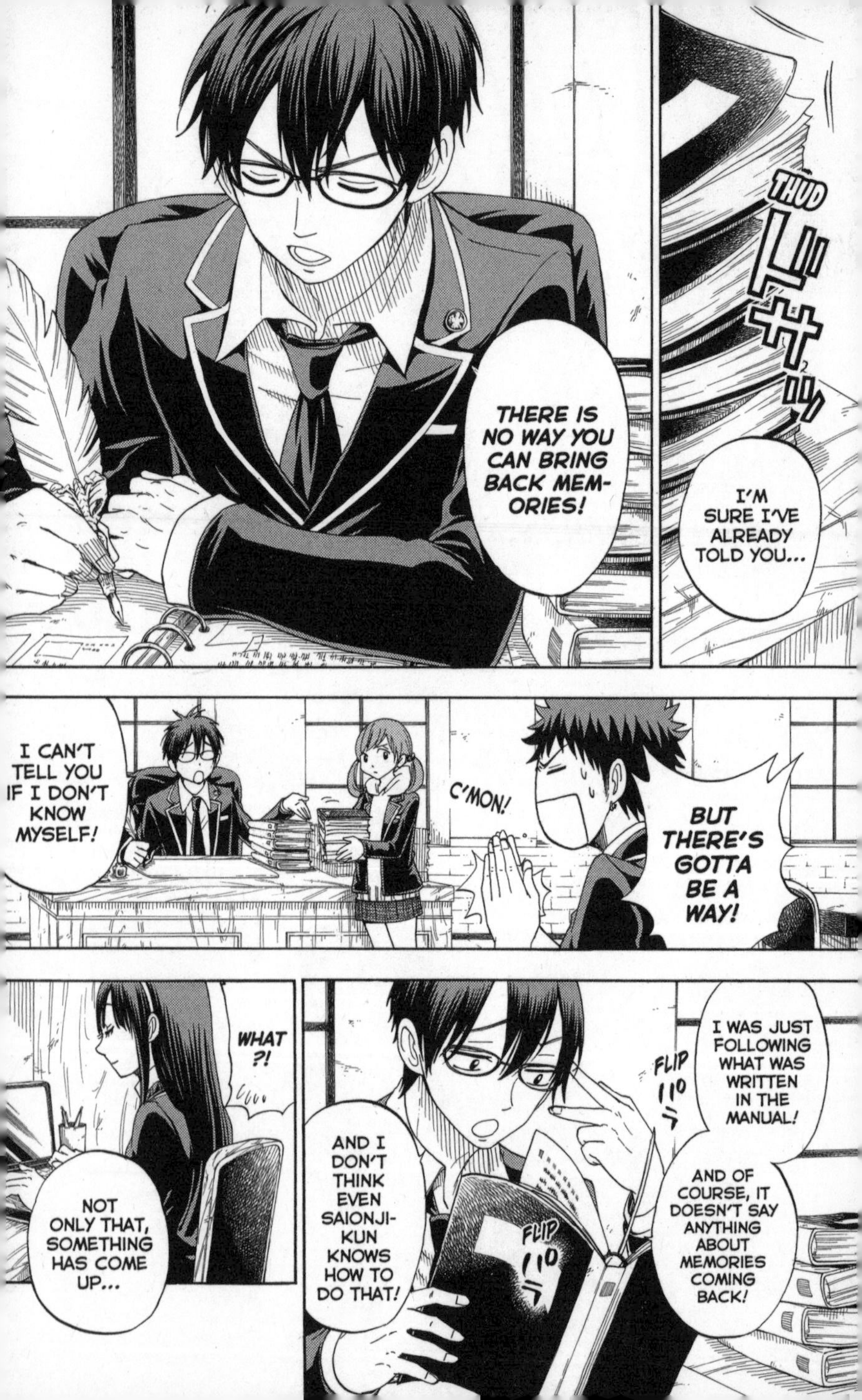
THUD
I'M SURE I'VE ALREADY TOLD YOU...
THERE IS NO WAY YOU CAN BRING BACK MEM-ORIES!
BUT THERE'S GOTTA BE A WAY!
C'MON!
I CAN'T TELL YOU IF I DON'T KNOW MYSELF!
I WAS JUST FOLLOWING WHAT WAS WRITTEN IN THE MANUAL!
FLIP
AND OF COURSE, IT DOESN'T SAY ANYTHING ABOUT MEMORIES COMING BACK!
FLIP
AND I DON'T THINK EVEN SAIONJI-KUN KNOWS HOW TO DO THAT!
WHAT?!
NOT ONLY THAT, SOMETHING HAS COME UP...

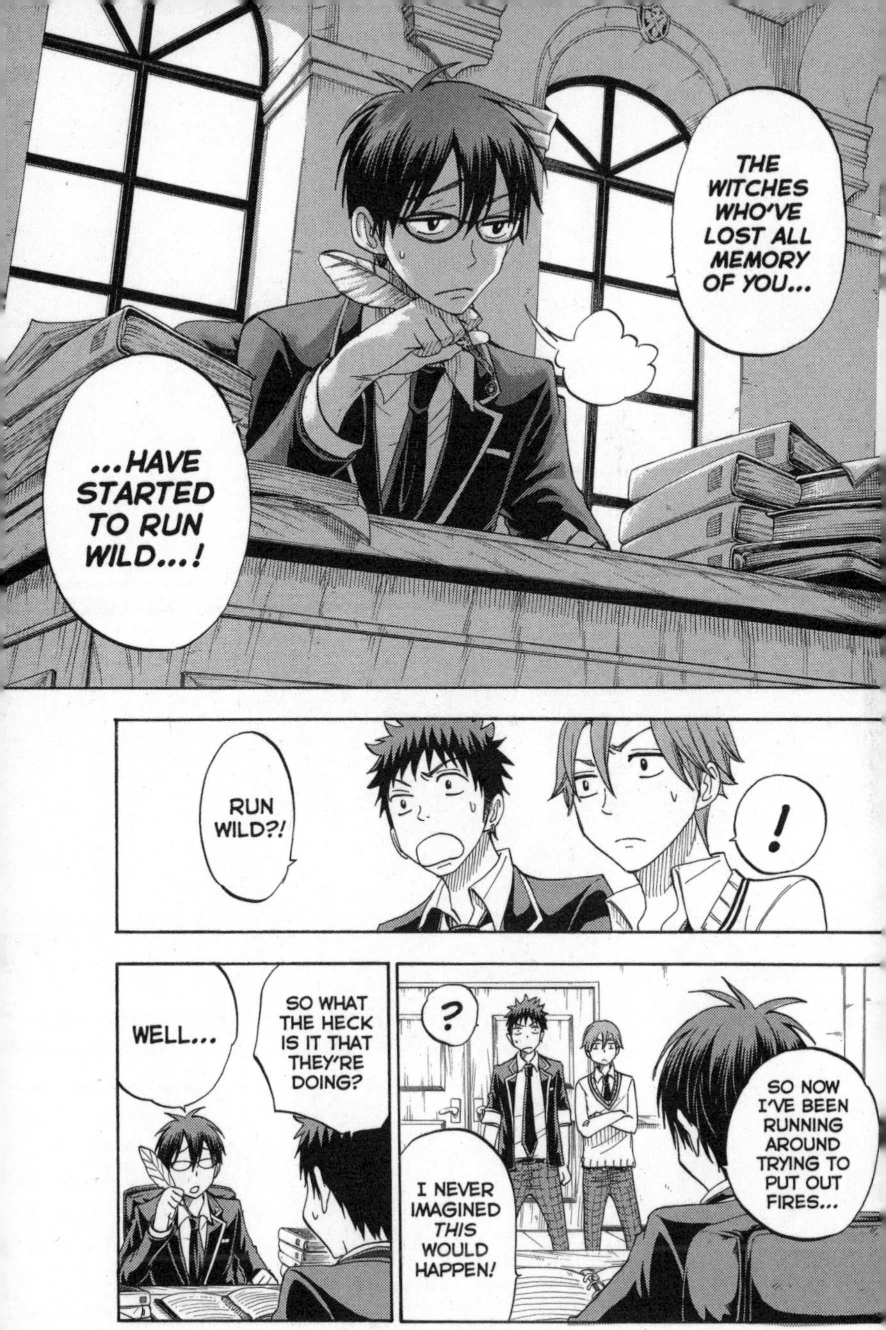
THE WITCHES WHO'VE LOST ALL MEMORY OF YOU...
...HAVE STARTED TO RUN WILD...!
!
RUN WILD?!
?
SO NOW I'VE BEEN RUNNING AROUND TRYING TO PUT OUT FIRES...
I NEVER IMAGINED *THIS* WOULD HAPPEN!
SO WHAT THE HECK IS IT THAT THEY'RE DOING?
WELL...

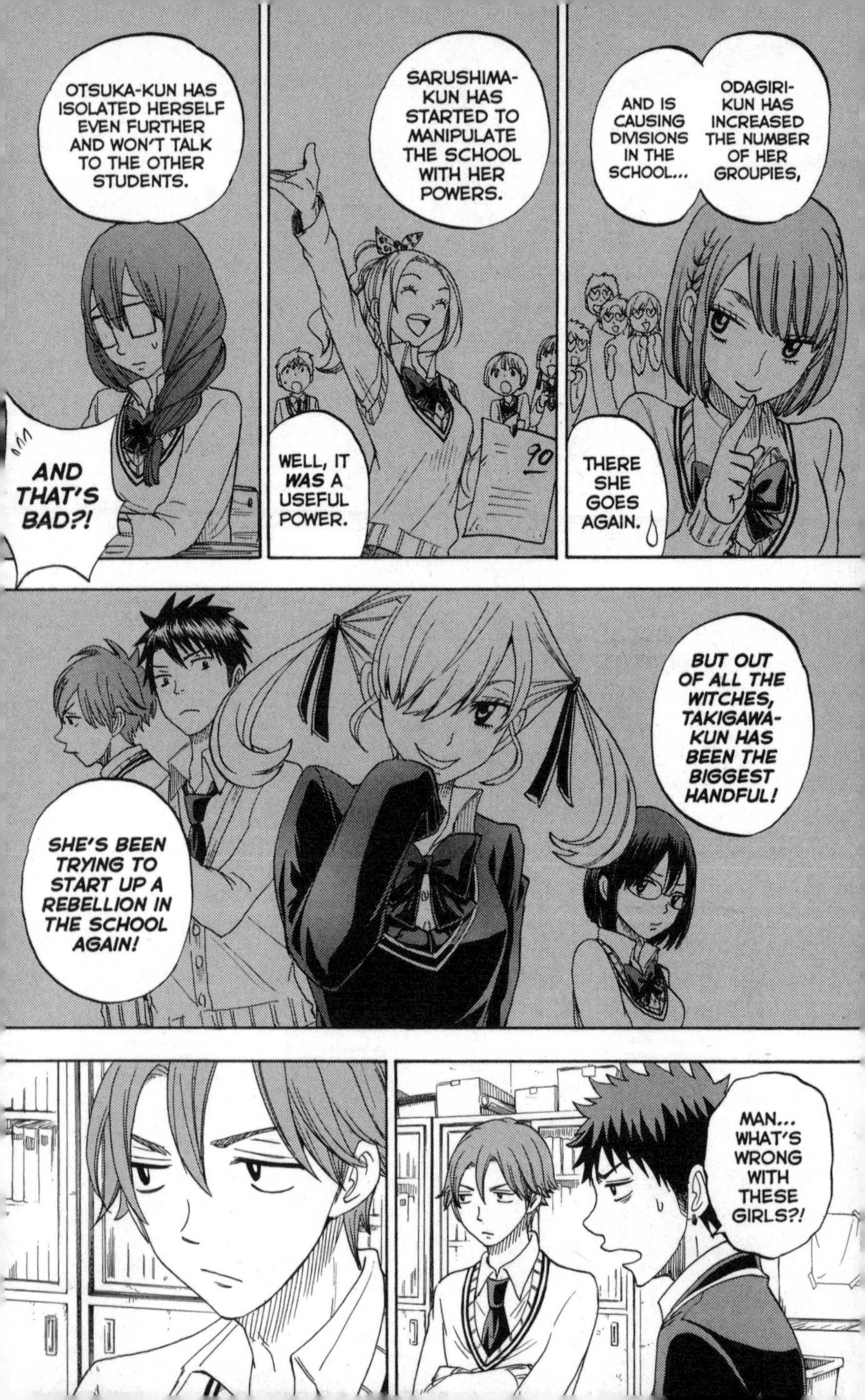
ODAGIRI-KUN HAS INCREASED THE NUMBER OF HER GROUPIES,
AND IS CAUSING DIVISIONS IN THE SCHOOL...
THERE SHE GOES AGAIN.
SARUSHIMA-KUN HAS STARTED TO MANIPULATE THE SCHOOL WITH HER POWERS.
90
WELL, IT *WAS* A USEFUL POWER.
OTSUKA-KUN HAS ISOLATED HERSELF EVEN FURTHER AND WON'T TALK TO THE OTHER STUDENTS.
AND THAT'S BAD?!
BUT OUT OF ALL THE WITCHES, TAKIGAWA-KUN HAS BEEN THE BIGGEST HANDFUL!
SHE'S BEEN TRYING TO START UP A REBELLION IN THE SCHOOL AGAIN!
MAN... WHAT'S WRONG WITH THESE GIRLS?!

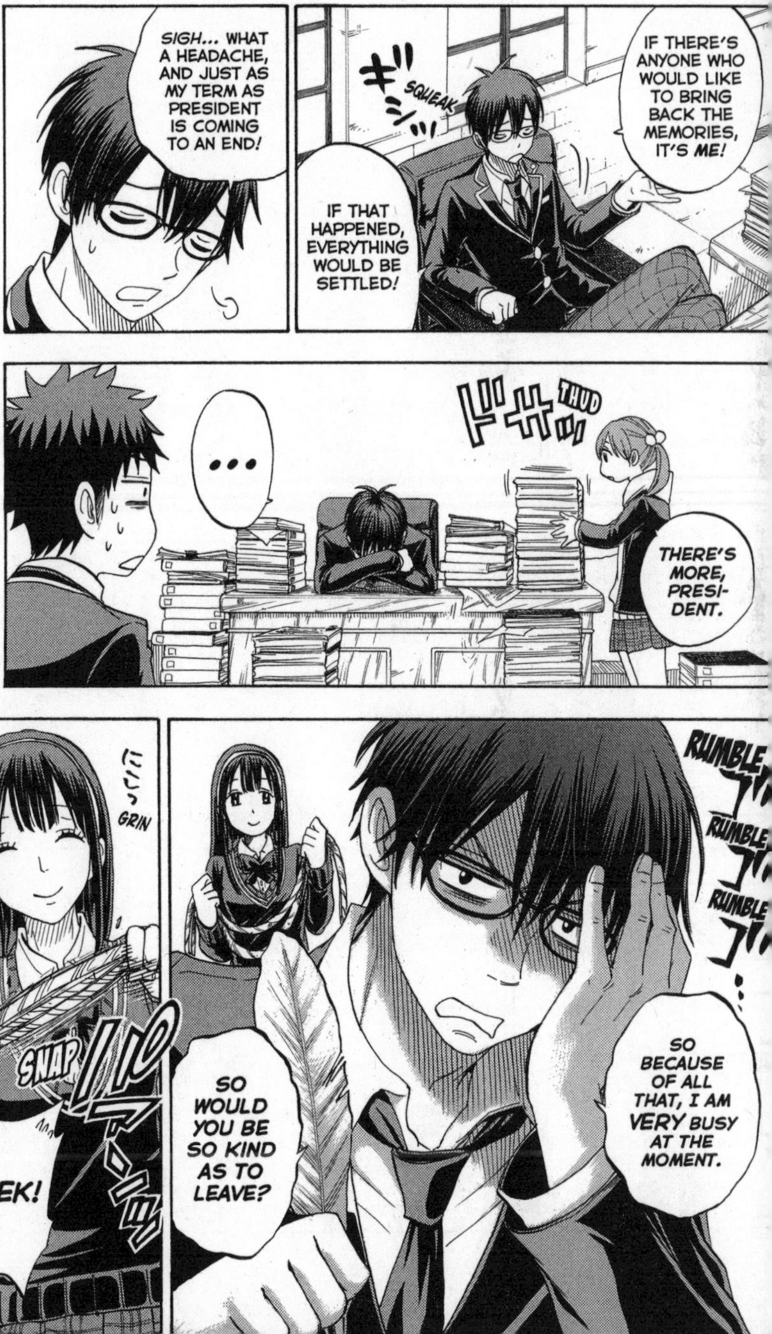
IF THERE'S ANYONE WHO WOULD LIKE TO BRING BACK THE MEMORIES, IT'S ME!
ギシッ
SQUEAK
IF THAT HAPPENED, EVERYTHING WOULD BE SETTLED!
SIGH... WHAT A HEADACHE, AND JUST AS MY TERM AS PRESIDENT IS COMING TO AN END!
ドカッ
THUD
THERE'S MORE, PRESIDENT.
...
RUMBLE
RUMBLE
RUMBLE
SO BECAUSE OF ALL THAT, I AM VERY BUSY AT THE MOMENT.
SO WOULD YOU BE SO KIND AS TO LEAVE?
にこっ
GRIN
SNAP
EEEK!

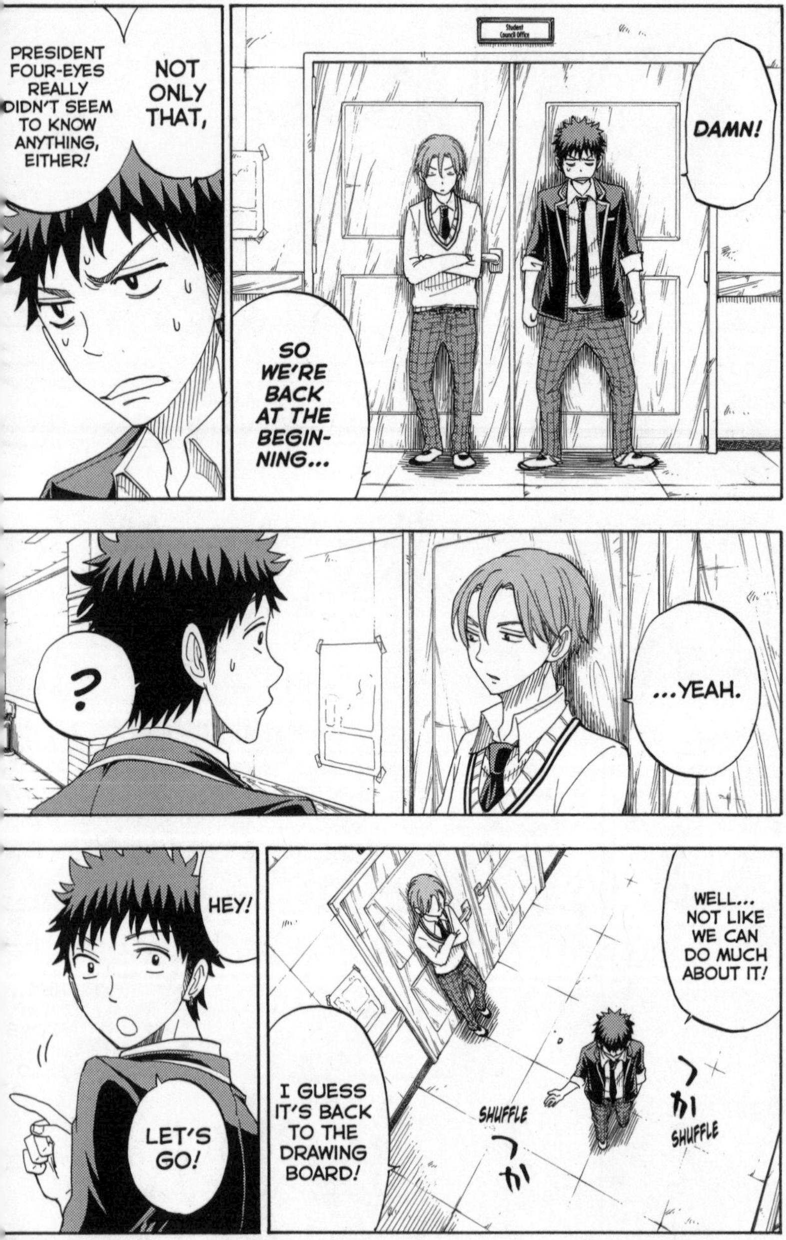
Student Council Office
DAMN!
SO WE'RE BACK AT THE BEGIN-NING...
NOT ONLY THAT,
PRESIDENT FOUR-EYES REALLY DIDN'T SEEM TO KNOW ANYTHING, EITHER!
...YEAH.
?
WELL... NOT LIKE WE CAN DO MUCH ABOUT IT!
SHUFFLE
SHUFFLE
I GUESS IT'S BACK TO THE DRAWING BOARD!
HEY!
LET'S GO!

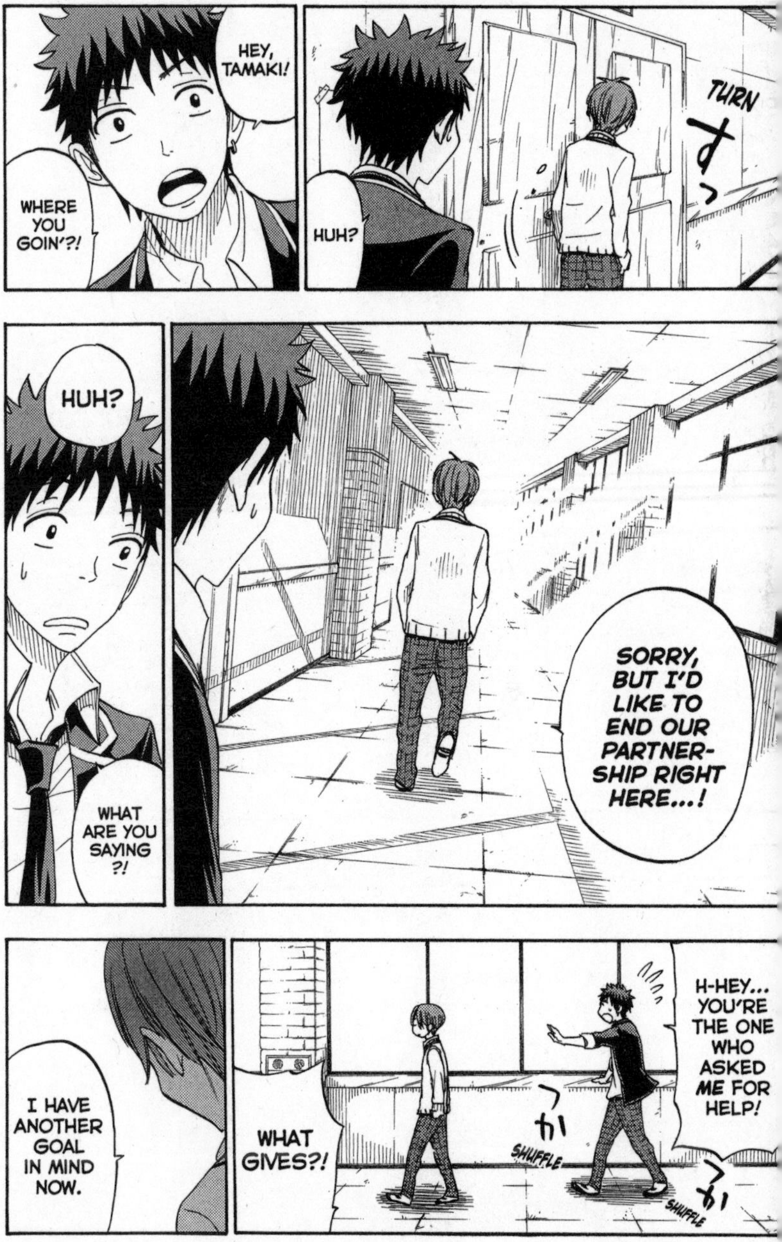
TURN
すっ
HUH?
HEY, TAMAKI!
WHERE YOU GOIN'?!
SORRY, BUT I'D LIKE TO END OUR PARTNER-SHIP RIGHT HERE...!
HUH?
WHAT ARE YOU SAYING ?!
H-HEY... YOU'RE THE ONE WHO ASKED ME FOR HELP!
つか
SHUFFLE
つか
SHUFFLE
WHAT GIVES?!
I HAVE ANOTHER GOAL IN MIND NOW.

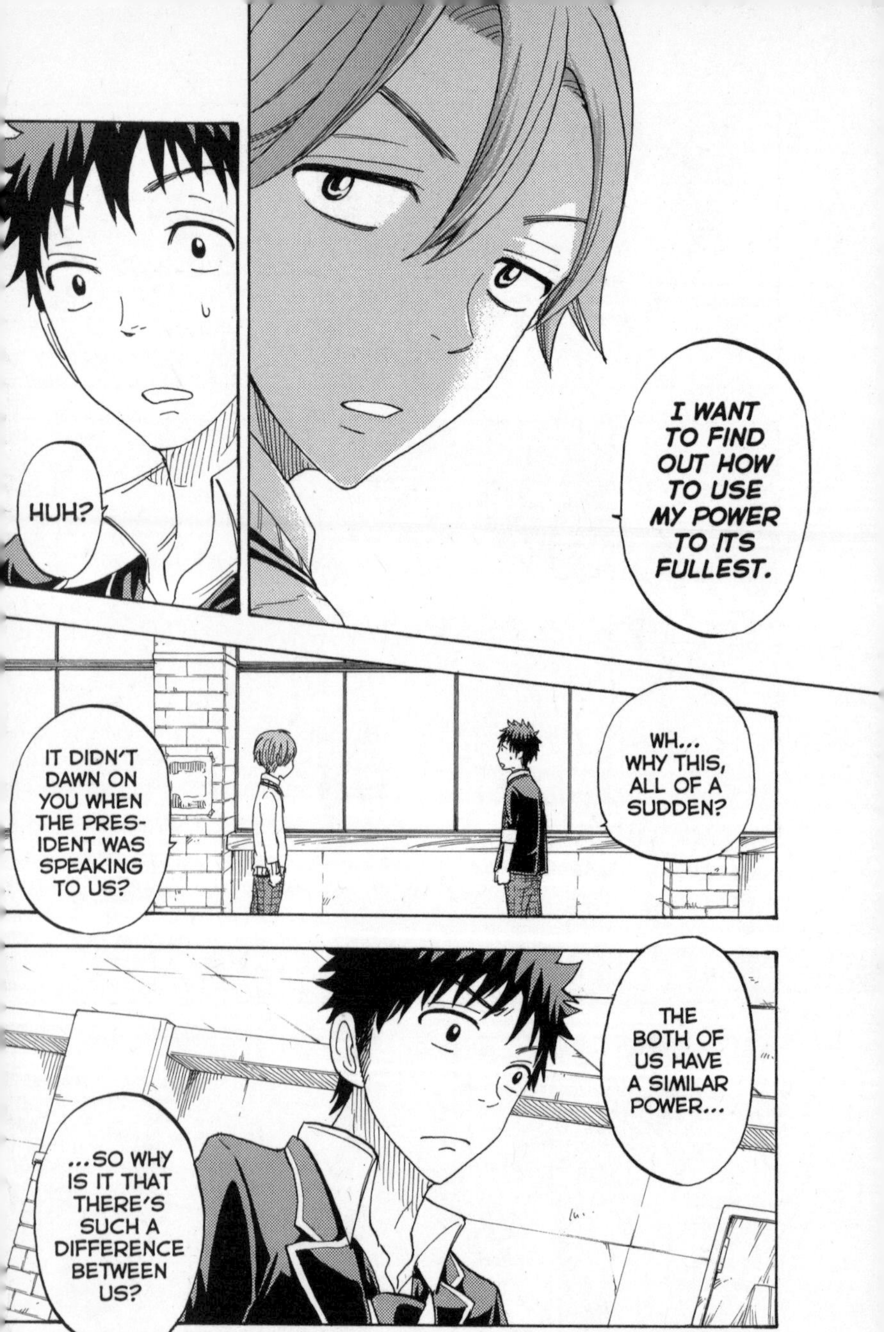
I WANT TO FIND OUT HOW TO USE MY POWER TO ITS FULLEST.
HUH?
WH... WHY THIS, ALL OF A SUDDEN?
IT DIDN'T DAWN ON YOU WHEN THE PRES-IDENT WAS SPEAKING TO US?
THE BOTH OF US HAVE A SIMILAR POWER...
...SO WHY IS IT THAT THERE'S SUCH A DIFFERENCE BETWEEN US?

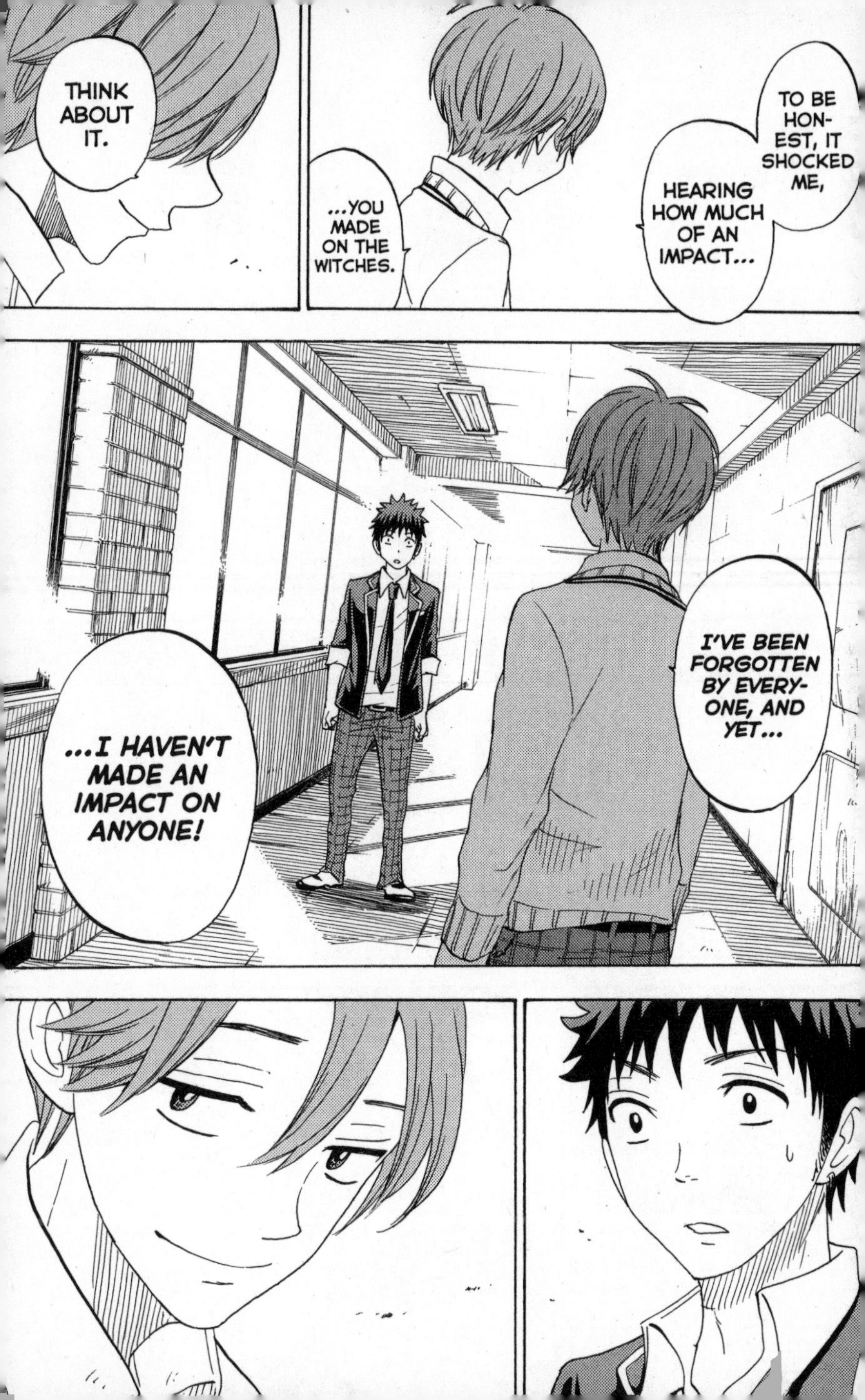
TO BE HONEST, IT SHOCKED ME,
HEARING HOW MUCH OF AN IMPACT...
...YOU MADE ON THE WITCHES.
THINK ABOUT IT.
I'VE BEEN FORGOTTEN BY EVERYONE, AND YET...
...I HAVEN'T MADE AN IMPACT ON ANYONE!

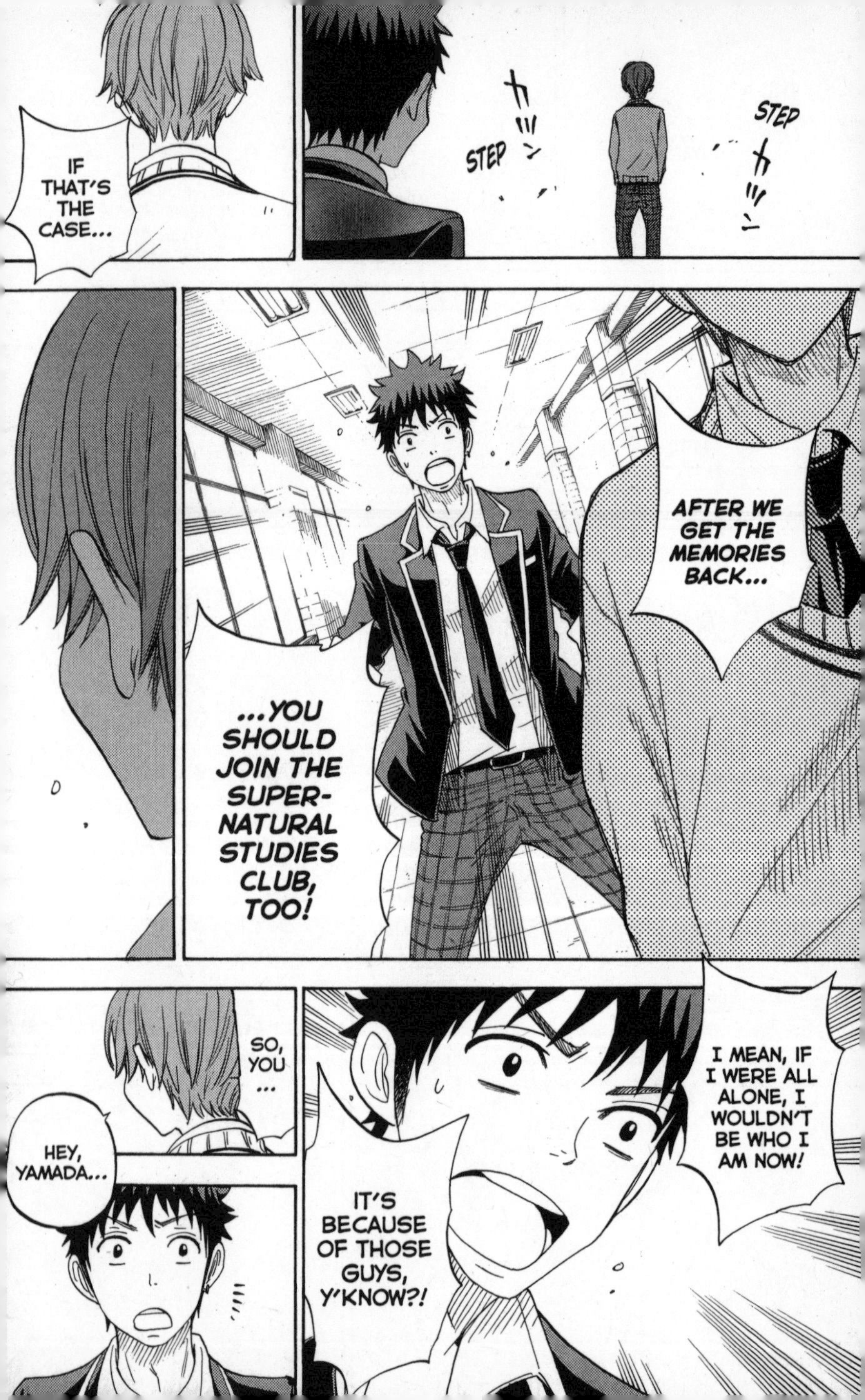
STEP
STEP
IF THAT'S THE CASE...
AFTER WE GET THE MEMORIES BACK...
...YOU SHOULD JOIN THE SUPER-NATURAL STUDIES CLUB, TOO!
I MEAN, IF I WERE ALL ALONE, I WOULDN'T BE WHO I AM NOW!
IT'S BECAUSE OF THOSE GUYS, Y'KNOW?!
SO, YOU ...
HEY, YAMADA...
!!!!

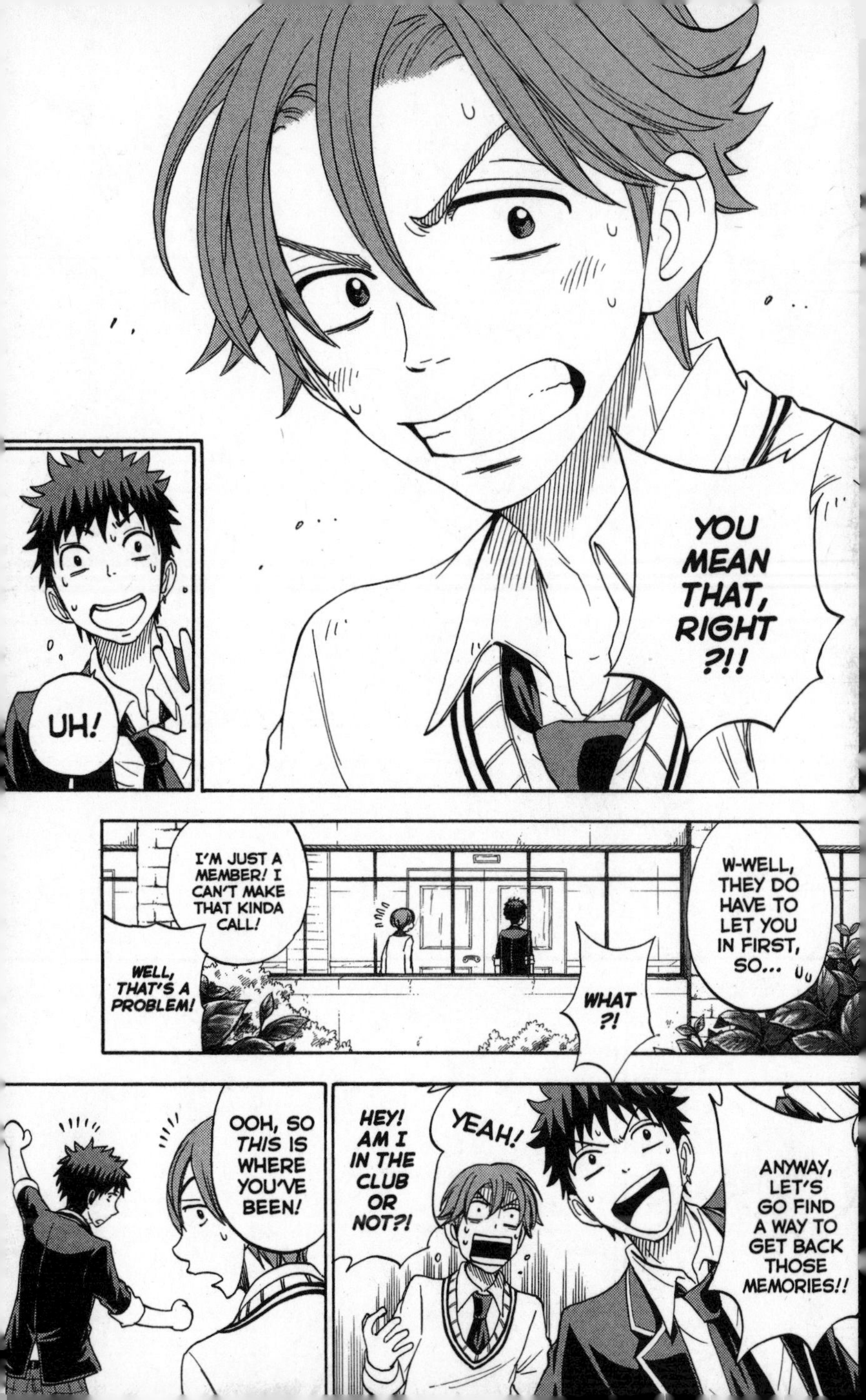
YOU MEAN THAT, RIGHT?!!
UH!
W-WELL, THEY DO HAVE TO LET YOU IN FIRST, SO...
WHAT?!
I'M JUST A MEMBER! I CAN'T MAKE THAT KINDA CALL!
WELL, THAT'S A PROBLEM!
ANYWAY, LET'S GO FIND A WAY TO GET BACK THOSE MEMORIES!!
YEAH!
HEY! AM I IN THE CLUB OR NOT?!
OOH, SO *THIS* IS WHERE YOU'VE BEEN!

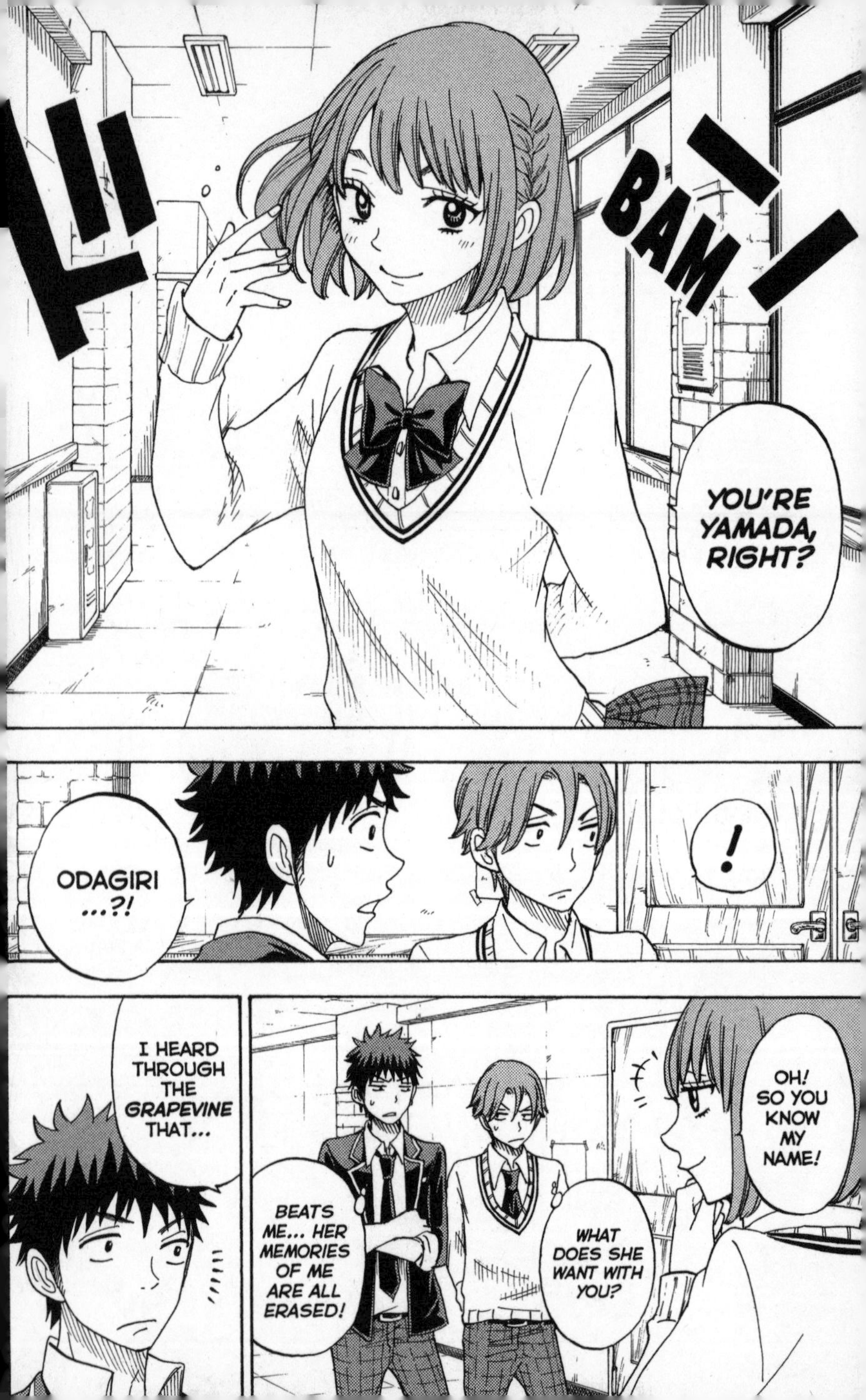
BAM
YOU'RE YAMADA, RIGHT?
!
ODAGIRI ...?!
OH! SO YOU KNOW MY NAME!
WHAT DOES SHE WANT WITH YOU?
BEATS ME... HER MEMORIES OF ME ARE ALL ERASED!
I HEARD THROUGH THE GRAPEVINE THAT...

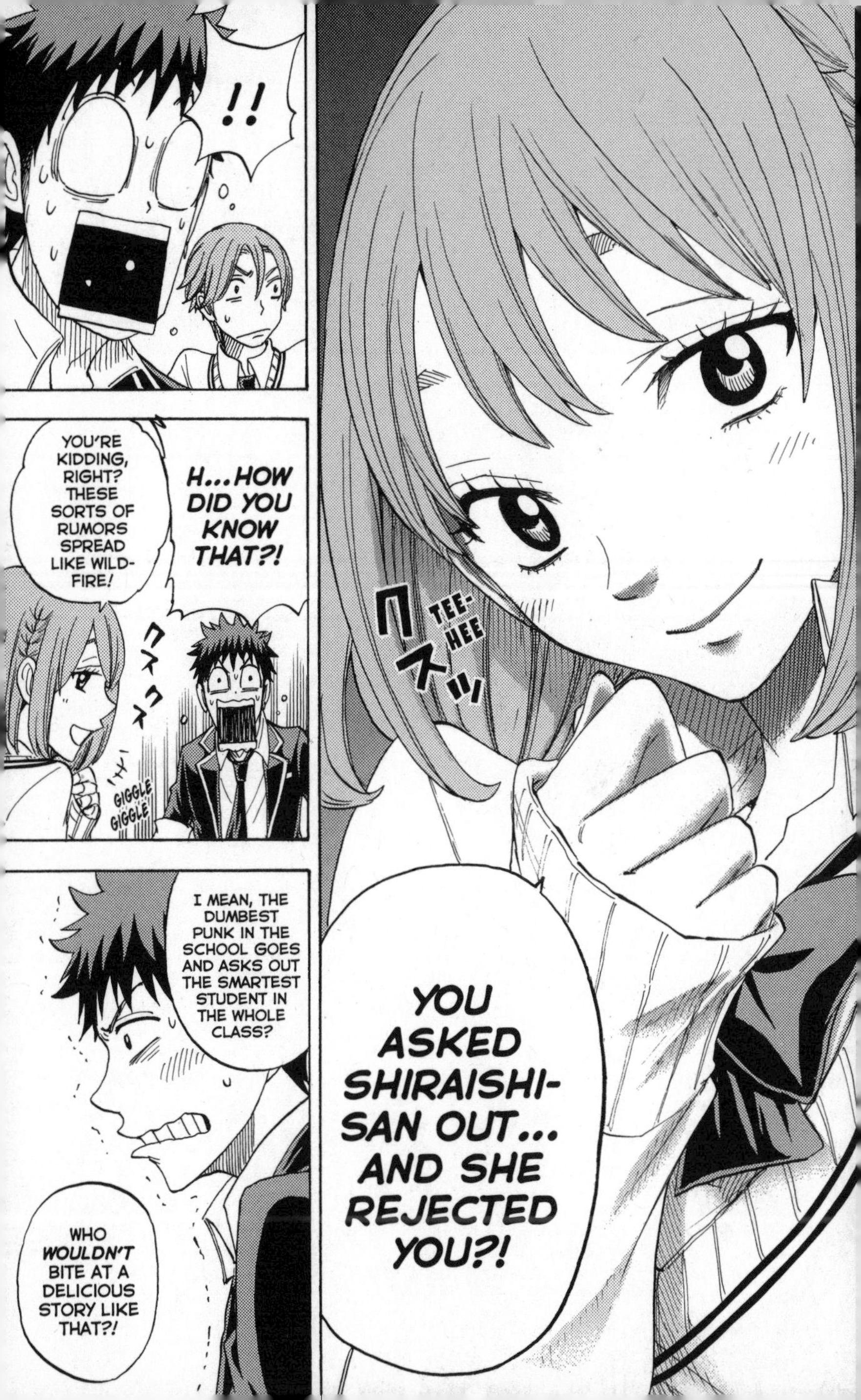
ニコッ
TEE-HEE
YOU ASKED SHIRAISHI-SAN OUT... AND SHE REJECTED YOU?!
!!
H...HOW DID YOU KNOW THAT?!
YOU'RE KIDDING, RIGHT? THESE SORTS OF RUMORS SPREAD LIKE WILD-FIRE!
クスクス
GIGGLE GIGGLE
I MEAN, THE DUMBEST PUNK IN THE SCHOOL GOES AND ASKS OUT THE SMARTEST STUDENT IN THE WHOLE CLASS?
WHO WOULDN'T BITE AT A DELICIOUS STORY LIKE THAT?!

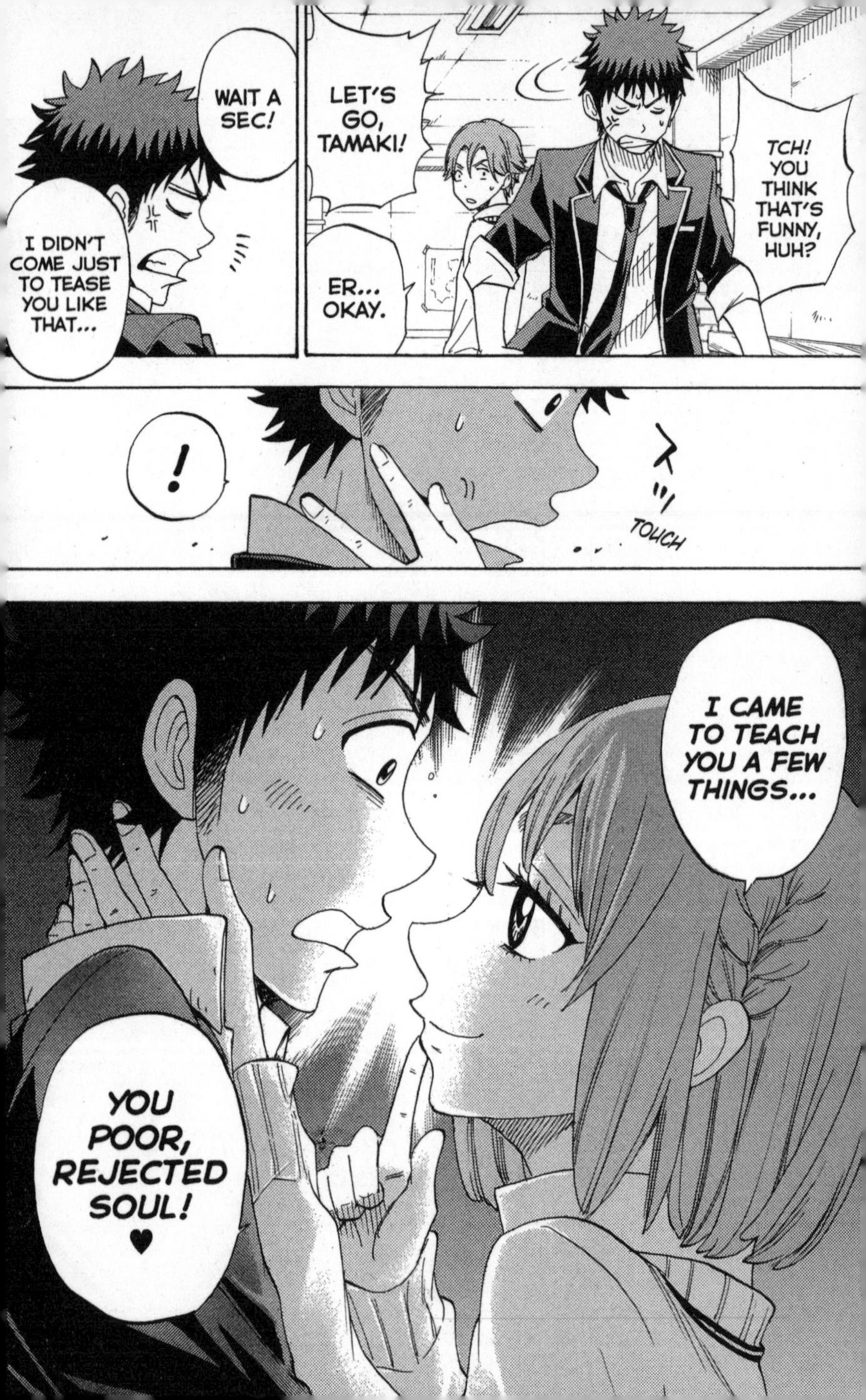
TCH! YOU THINK THAT'S FUNNY, HUH?
LET'S GO, TAMAKI!
ER... OKAY.
WAIT A SEC!
I DIDN'T COME JUST TO TEASE YOU LIKE THAT...
TOUCH
!
I CAME TO TEACH YOU A FEW THINGS...
YOU POOR, REJECTED SOUL! ♥

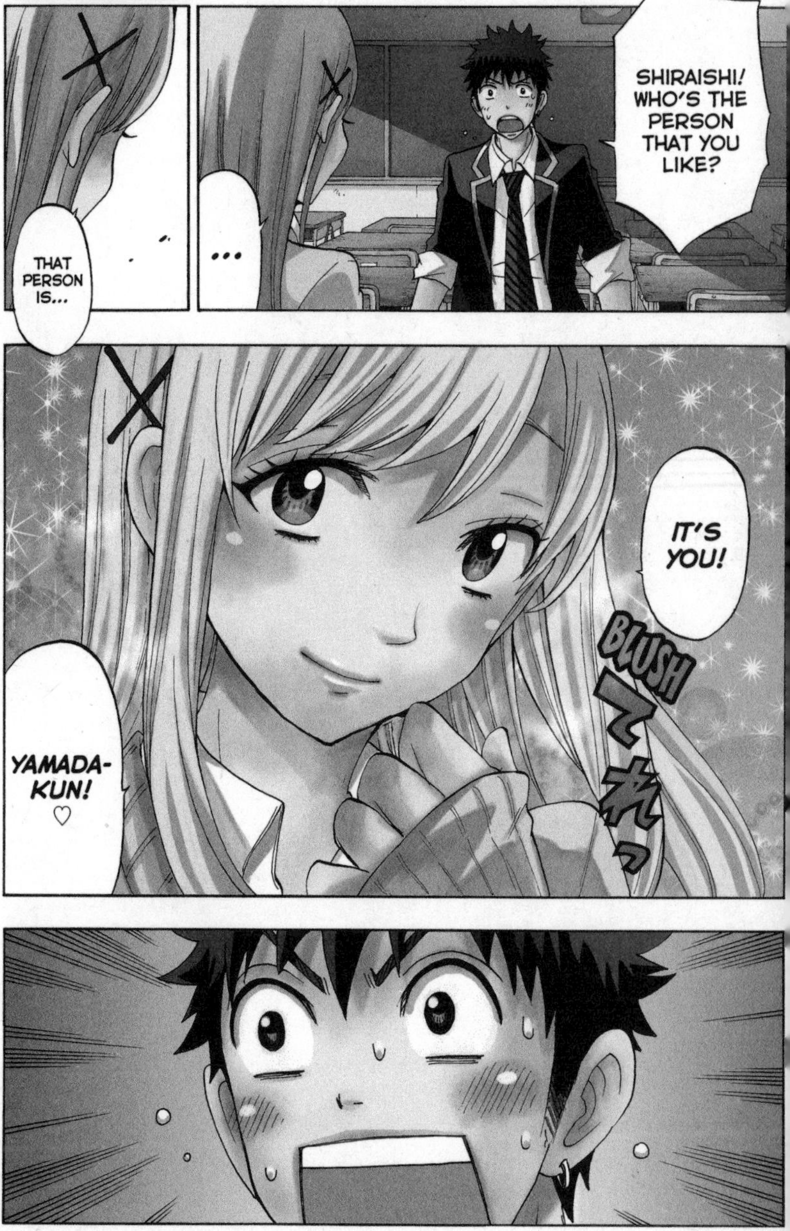
SHIRAISHI! WHO'S THE PERSON THAT YOU LIKE?
...
THAT PERSON IS...
IT'S YOU!
BLUSH
てれっ
YAMADA-KUN! ♡

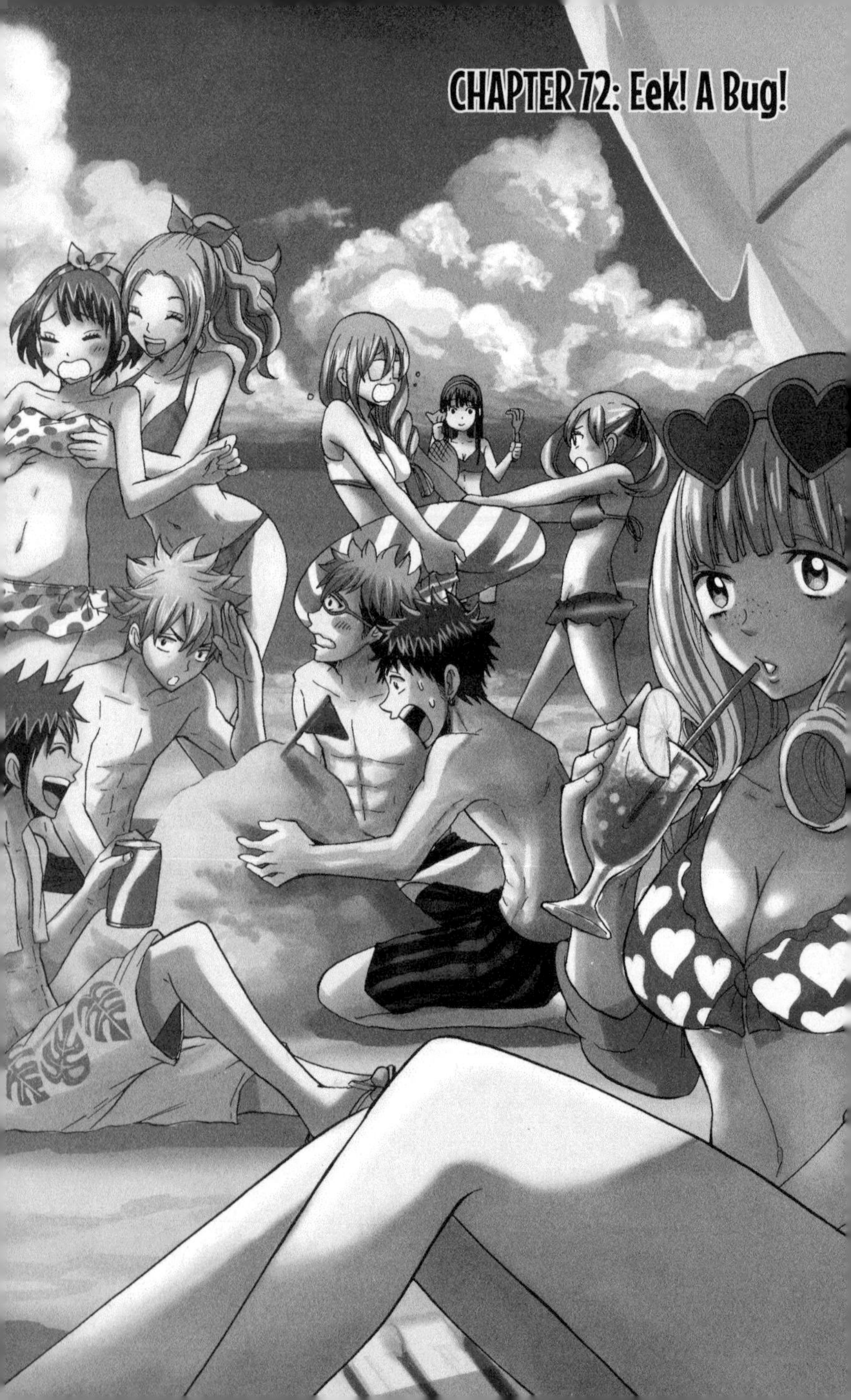
CHAPTER 72: Eek! A Bug!

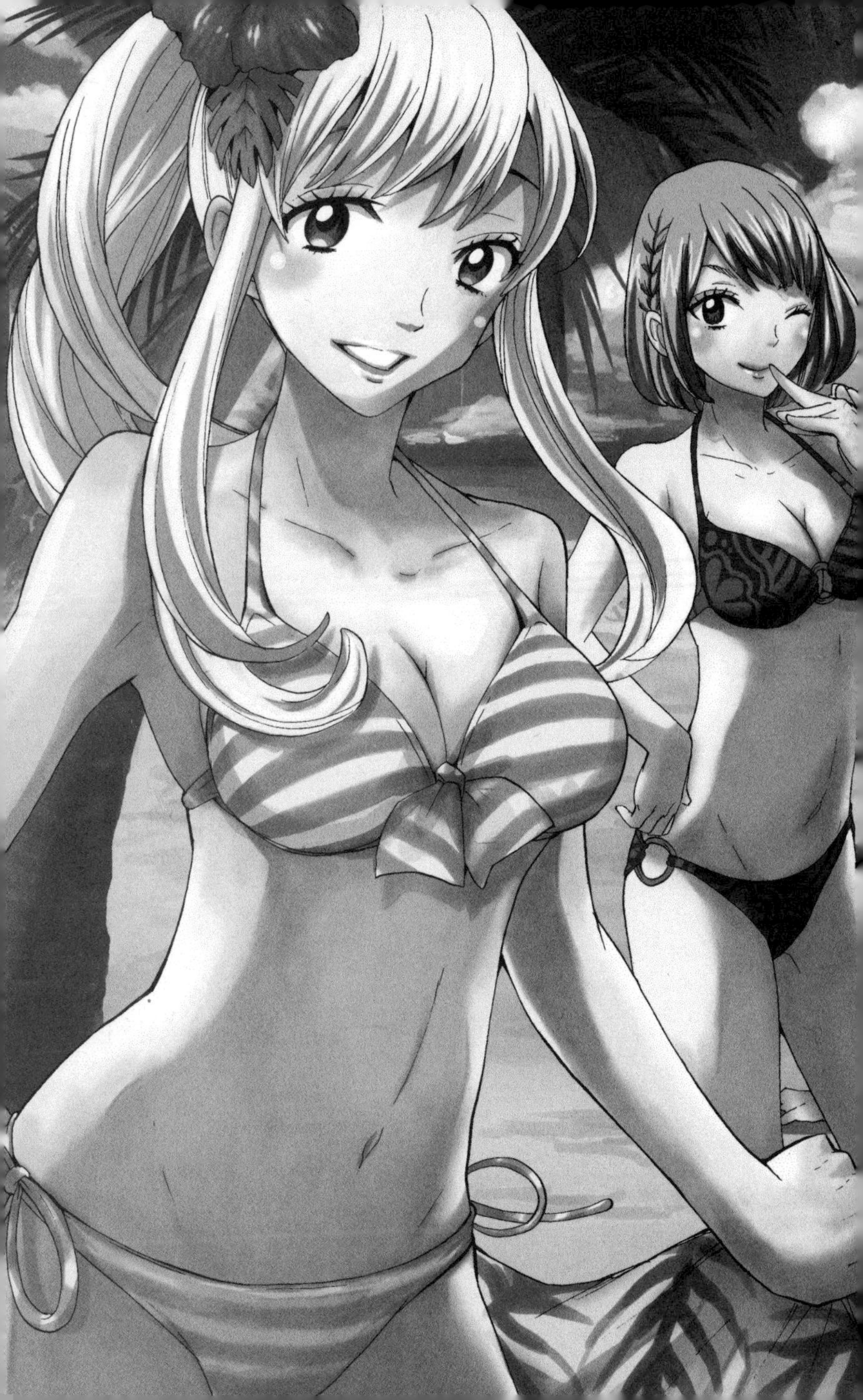

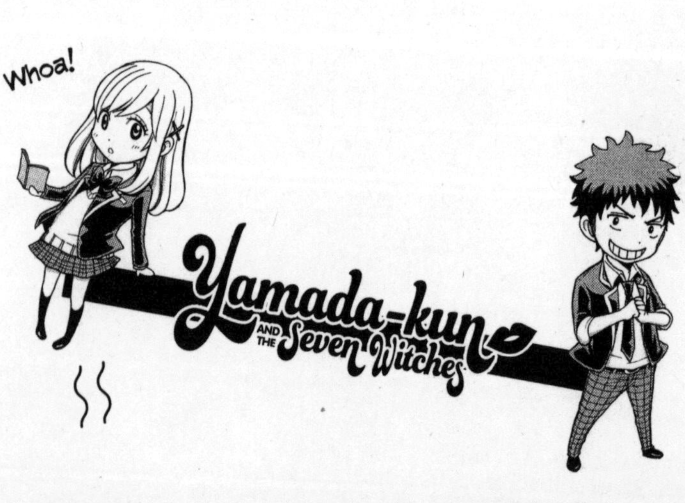
Whoa!
Yamada-kun AND THE Seven Witches

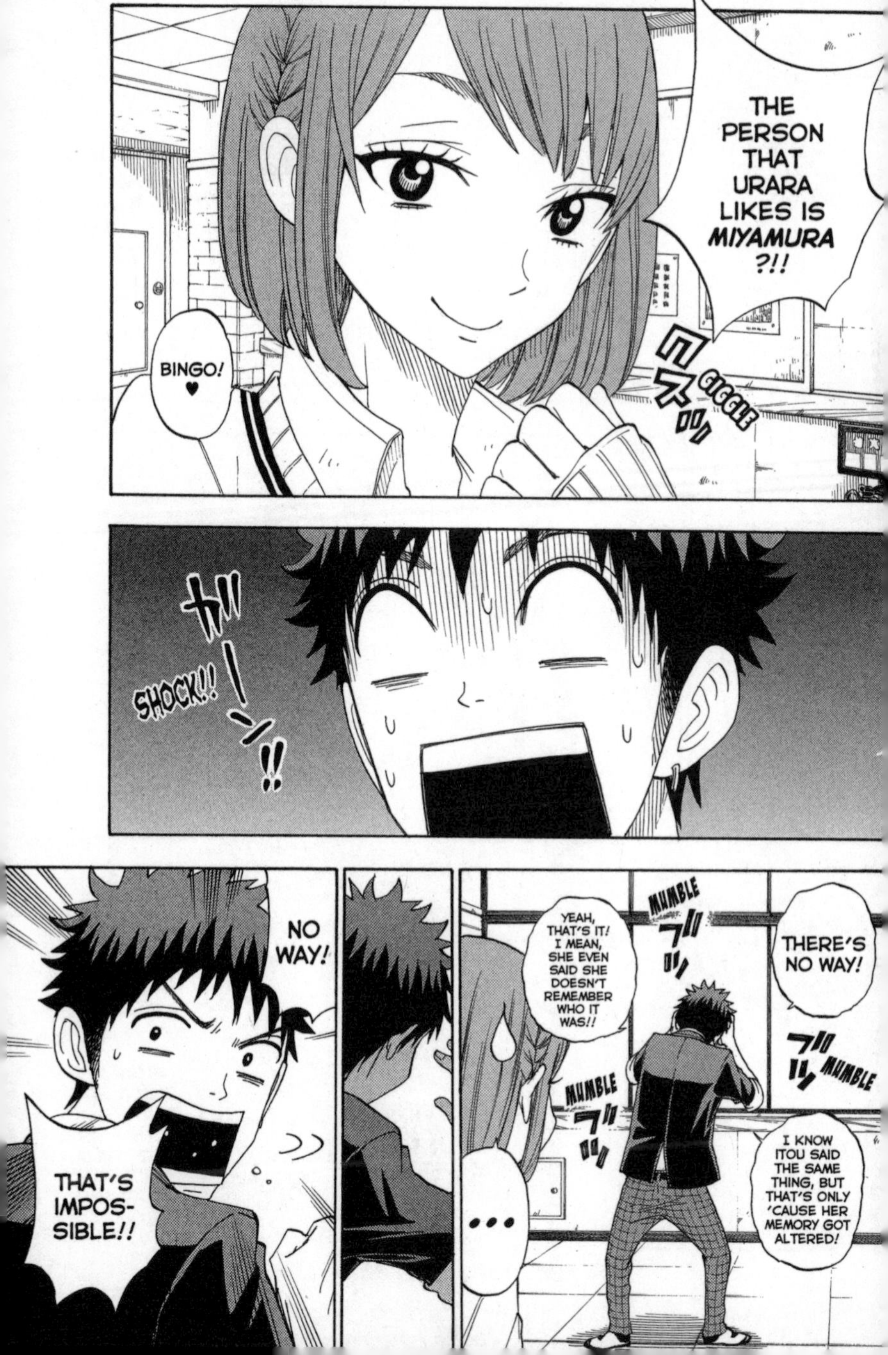
THE PERSON THAT URARA LIKES IS MIYAMURA ?!!
GIGGLE
BINGO! ♥
SHOCK!!
THERE'S NO WAY!
MUMBLE
YEAH, THAT'S IT! I MEAN, SHE EVEN SAID SHE DOESN'T REMEMBER WHO IT WAS!!
MUMBLE
MUMBLE
I KNOW ITOU SAID THE SAME THING, BUT THAT'S ONLY 'CAUSE HER MEMORY GOT ALTERED!
...
NO WAY!
THAT'S IMPOS-SIBLE!!

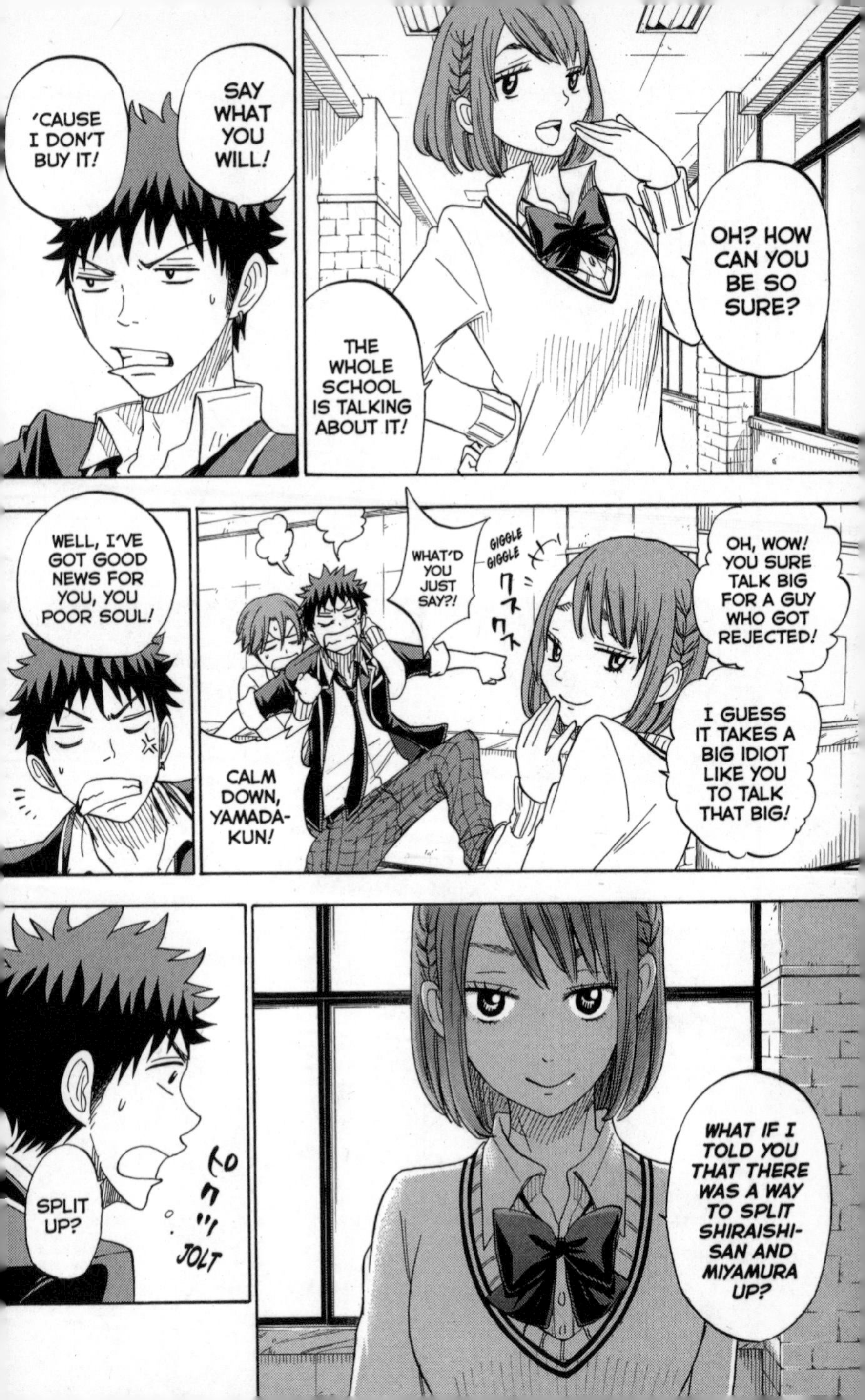
OH? HOW CAN YOU BE SO SURE?
THE WHOLE SCHOOL IS TALKING ABOUT IT!
SAY WHAT YOU WILL!
'CAUSE I DON'T BUY IT!
OH, WOW! YOU SURE TALK BIG FOR A GUY WHO GOT REJECTED!
I GUESS IT TAKES A BIG IDIOT LIKE YOU TO TALK THAT BIG!
GIGGLE GIGGLE
WHAT'D YOU JUST SAY?!
CALM DOWN, YAMADA-KUN!
WELL, I'VE GOT GOOD NEWS FOR YOU, YOU POOR SOUL!
WHAT IF I TOLD YOU THAT THERE WAS A WAY TO SPLIT SHIRAISHI-SAN AND MIYAMURA UP?
JOLT
SPLIT UP?

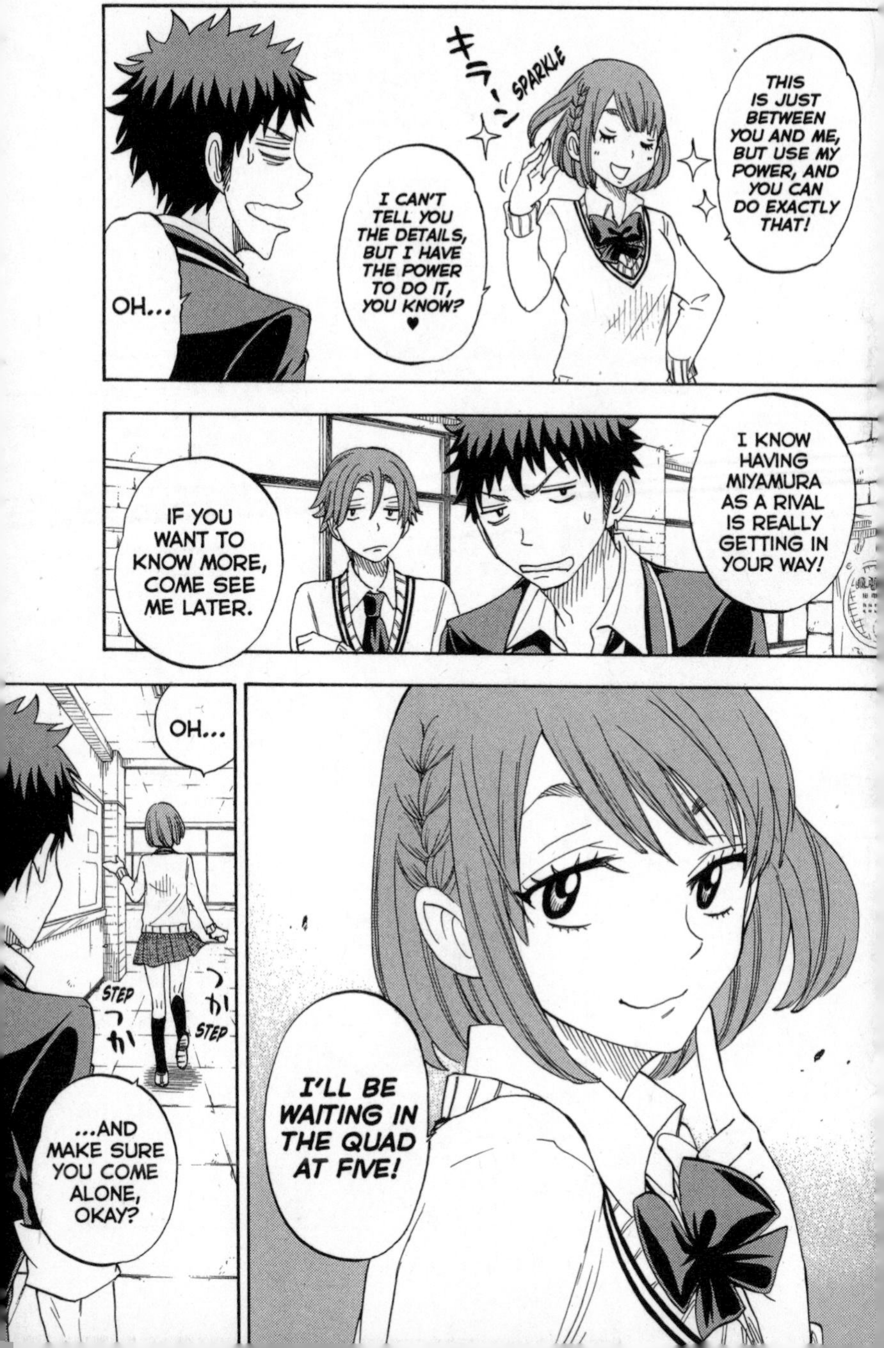
THIS IS JUST BETWEEN YOU AND ME, BUT USE MY POWER, AND YOU CAN DO EXACTLY THAT!
キラーン
SPARKLE
I CAN'T TELL YOU THE DETAILS, BUT I HAVE THE POWER TO DO IT, YOU KNOW? ♥
OH...
I KNOW HAVING MIYAMURA AS A RIVAL IS REALLY GETTING IN YOUR WAY!
IF YOU WANT TO KNOW MORE, COME SEE ME LATER.
I'LL BE WAITING IN THE QUAD AT FIVE!
OH...
つか
STEP
つか
STEP
...AND MAKE SURE YOU COME ALONE, OKAY?

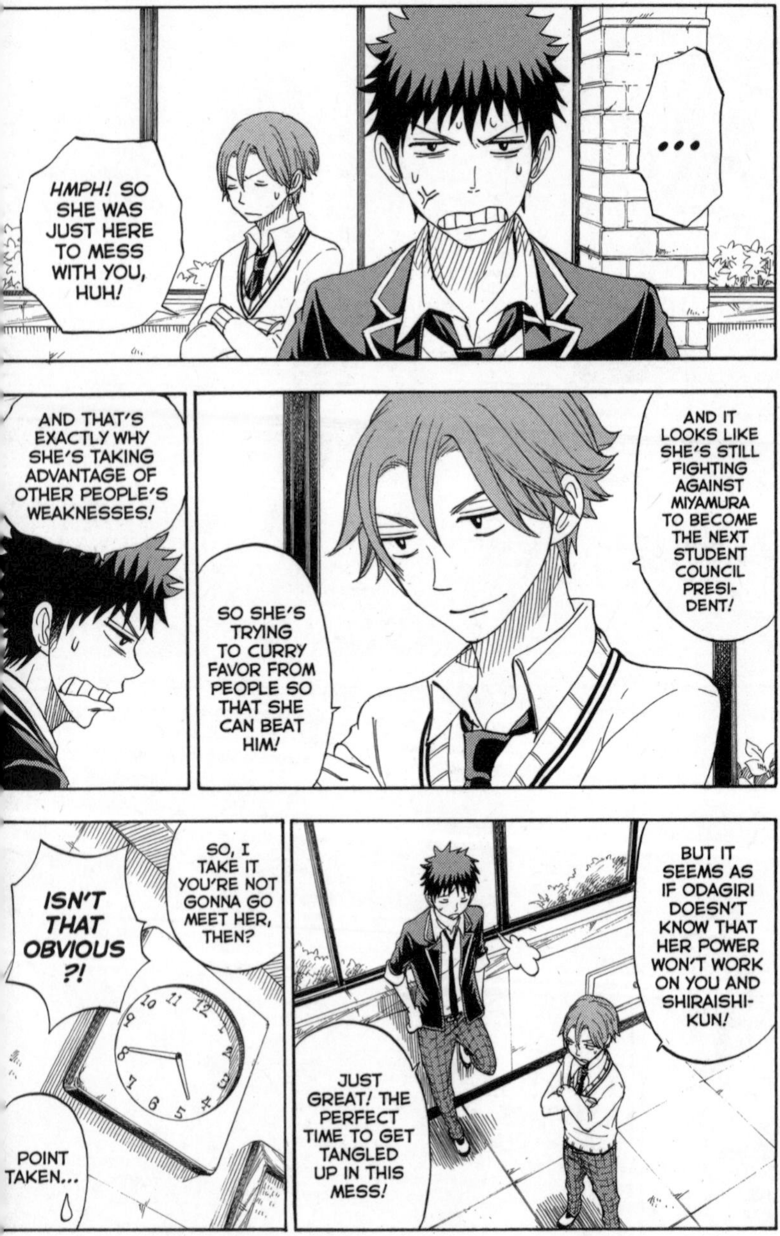
...
HMPH! SO SHE WAS JUST HERE TO MESS WITH YOU, HUH!
AND IT LOOKS LIKE SHE'S STILL FIGHTING AGAINST MIYAMURA TO BECOME THE NEXT STUDENT COUNCIL PRESI-DENT!
SO SHE'S TRYING TO CURRY FAVOR FROM PEOPLE SO THAT SHE CAN BEAT HIM!
AND THAT'S EXACTLY WHY SHE'S TAKING ADVANTAGE OF OTHER PEOPLE'S WEAKNESSES!
BUT IT SEEMS AS IF ODAGIRI DOESN'T KNOW THAT HER POWER WON'T WORK ON YOU AND SHIRAISHI-KUN!
JUST GREAT! THE PERFECT TIME TO GET TANGLED UP IN THIS MESS!
SO, I TAKE IT YOU'RE NOT GONNA GO MEET HER, THEN?
ISN'T THAT OBVIOUS?!
POINT TAKEN...

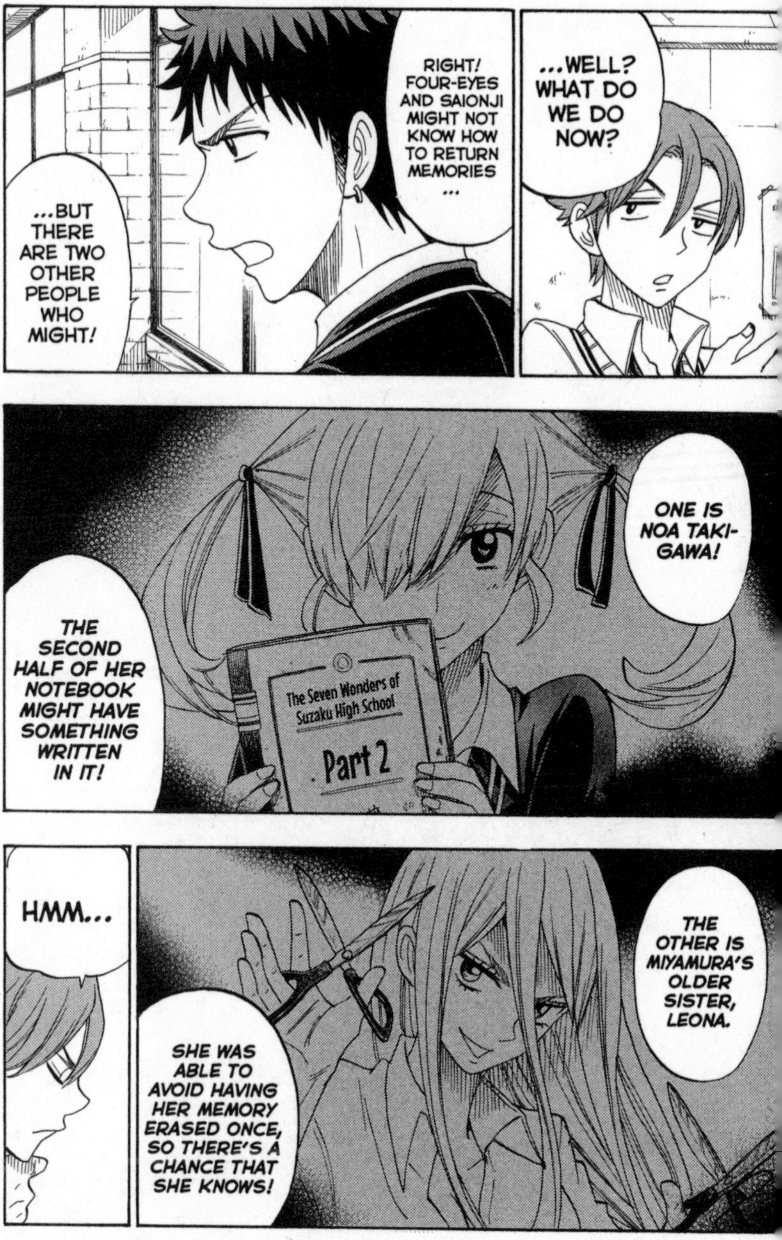
...WELL? WHAT DO WE DO NOW?
RIGHT! FOUR-EYES AND SAIONJI MIGHT NOT KNOW HOW TO RETURN MEMORIES ...
...BUT THERE ARE TWO OTHER PEOPLE WHO MIGHT!
ONE IS NOA TAKI-GAWA!
THE SECOND HALF OF HER NOTEBOOK MIGHT HAVE SOMETHING WRITTEN IN IT!
The Seven Wonders of Suzaku High School
Part 2
THE OTHER IS MIYAMURA'S OLDER SISTER, LEONA.
SHE WAS ABLE TO AVOID HAVING HER MEMORY ERASED ONCE, SO THERE'S A CHANCE THAT SHE KNOWS!
HMM...

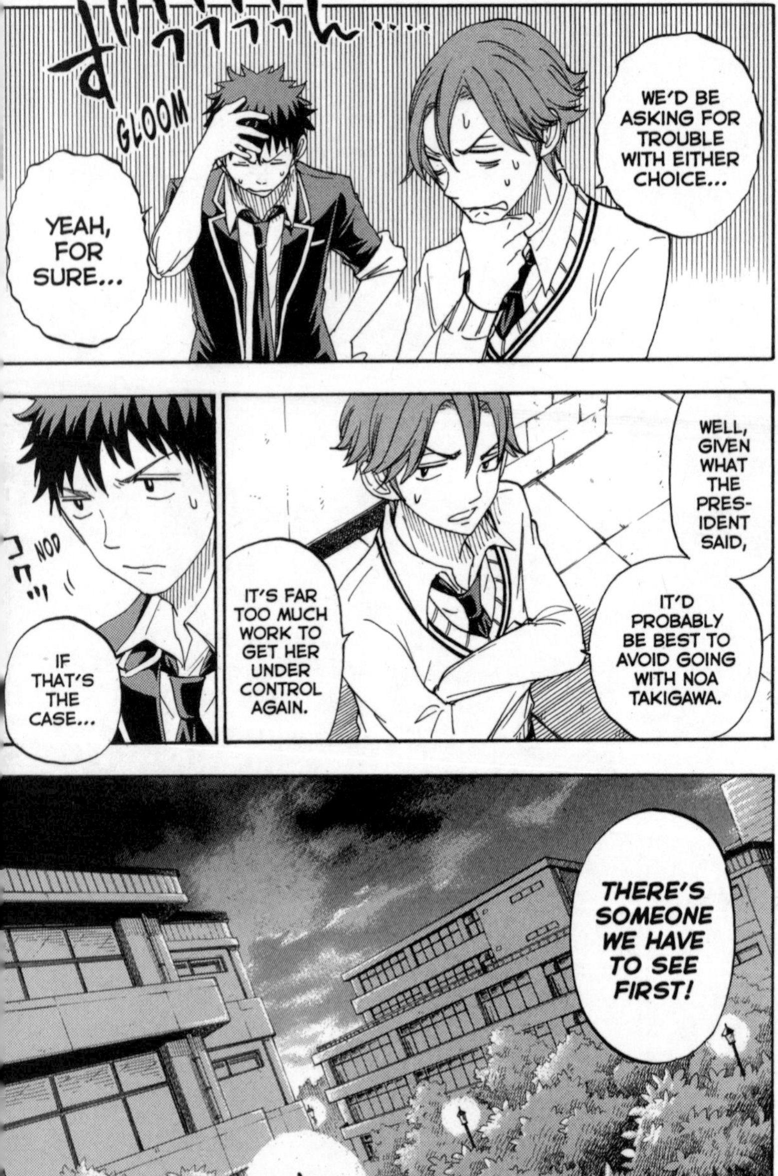
WE'D BE ASKING FOR TROUBLE WITH EITHER CHOICE...
GLOOM
YEAH, FOR SURE...
WELL, GIVEN WHAT THE PRES-IDENT SAID,
IT'D PROBABLY BE BEST TO AVOID GOING WITH NOA TAKIGAWA.
IT'S FAR TOO MUCH WORK TO GET HER UNDER CONTROL AGAIN.
NOD
IF THAT'S THE CASE...
THERE'S SOMEONE WE HAVE TO SEE FIRST!

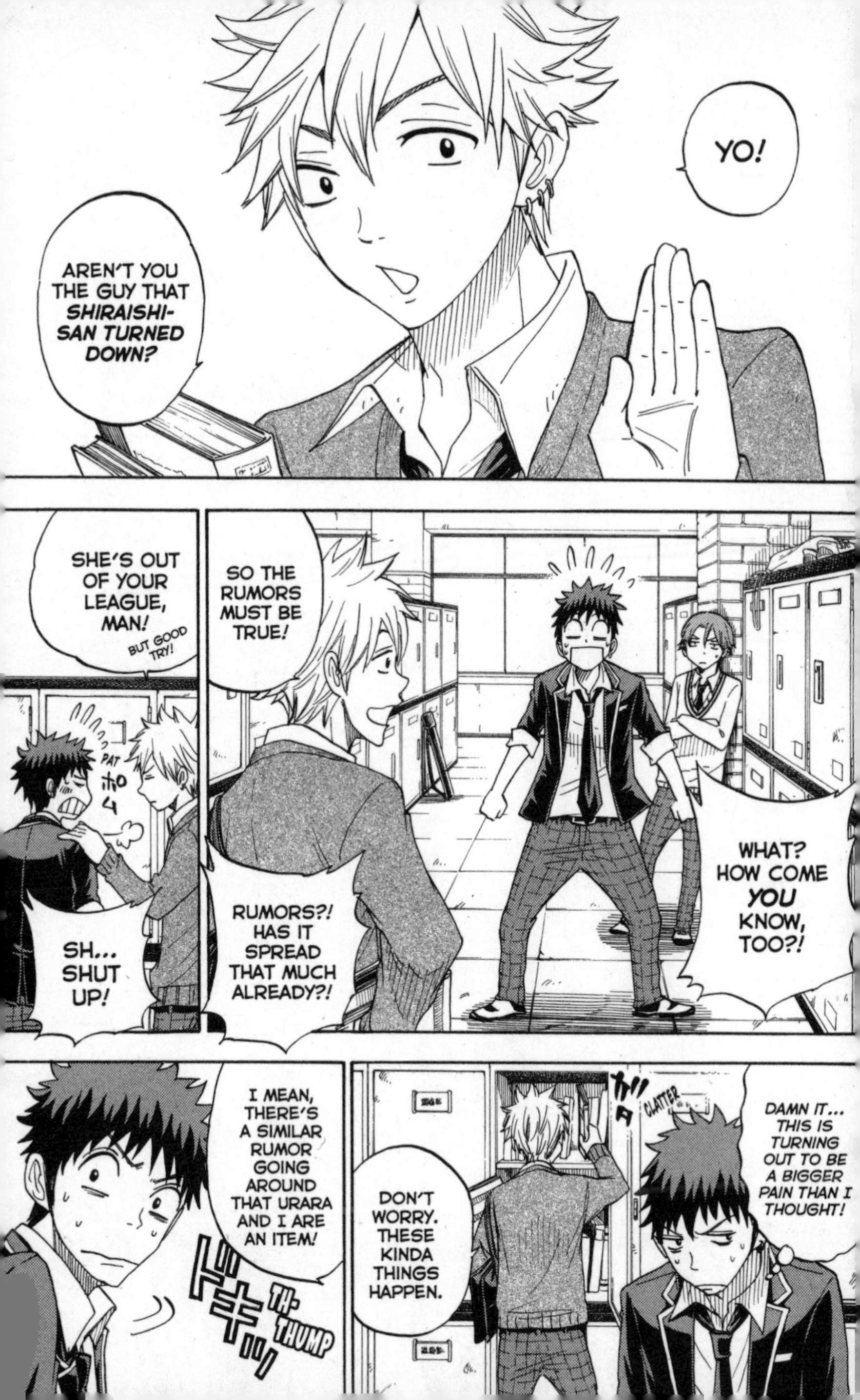
YO!
AREN'T YOU THE GUY THAT SHIRAISHI-SAN TURNED DOWN?
SO THE RUMORS MUST BE TRUE!
WHAT? HOW COME YOU KNOW, TOO?!
RUMORS?! HAS IT SPREAD THAT MUCH ALREADY?!
SHE'S OUT OF YOUR LEAGUE, MAN!
BUT GOOD TRY!
PAT
SH... SHUT UP!
DAMN IT... THIS IS TURNING OUT TO BE A BIGGER PAIN THAN I THOUGHT!
CLATTER
DON'T WORRY. THESE KINDA THINGS HAPPEN.
I MEAN, THERE'S A SIMILAR RUMOR GOING AROUND THAT URARA AND I ARE AN ITEM!
TH-THUMP

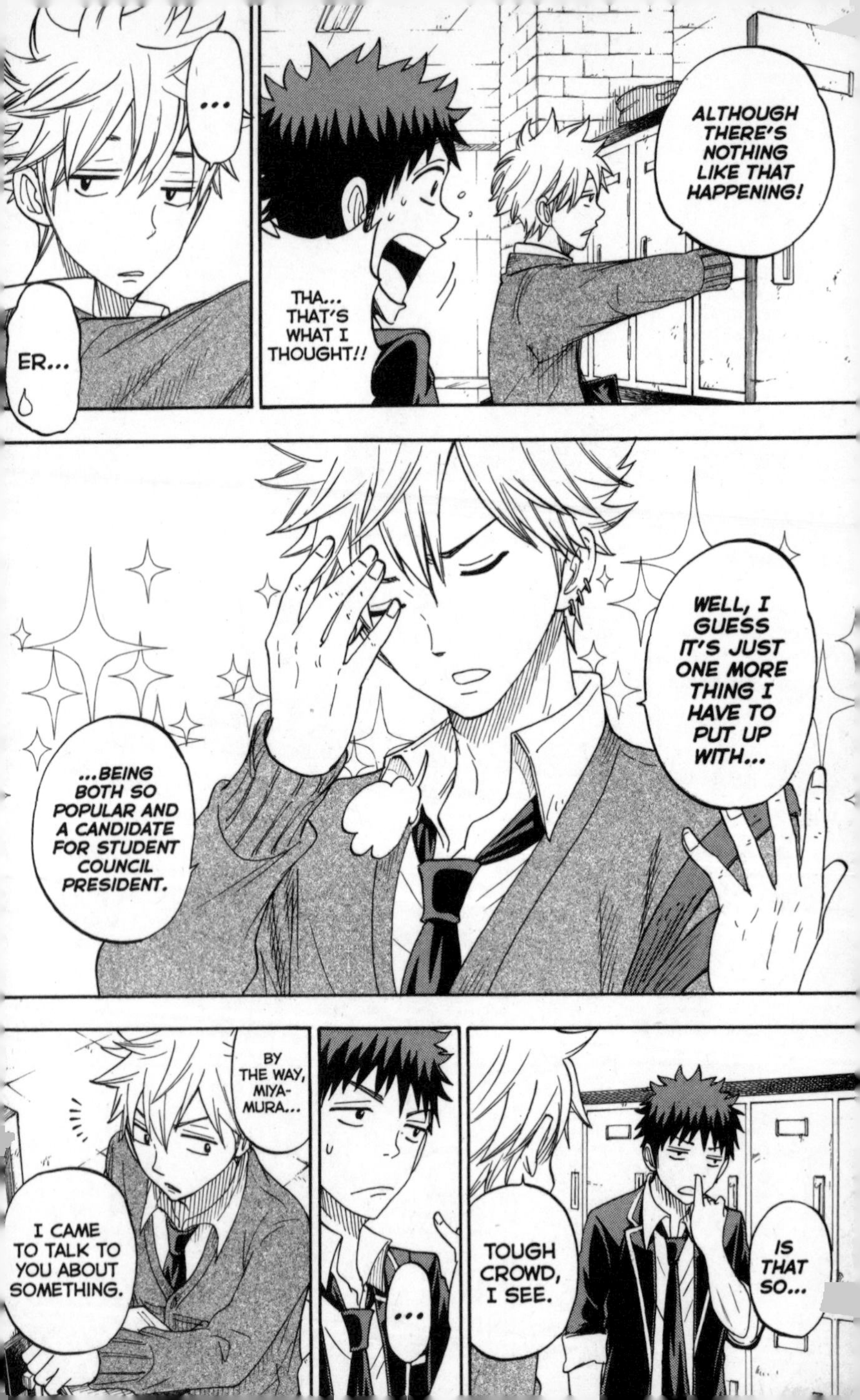
ALTHOUGH THERE'S NOTHING LIKE THAT HAPPENING!
THA... THAT'S WHAT I THOUGHT!!
...
ER...
WELL, I GUESS IT'S JUST ONE MORE THING I HAVE TO PUT UP WITH...
...BEING BOTH SO POPULAR AND A CANDIDATE FOR STUDENT COUNCIL PRESIDENT.
IS THAT SO...
TOUGH CROWD, I SEE.
...
BY THE WAY, MIYA-MURA...
I CAME TO TALK TO YOU ABOUT SOMETHING.

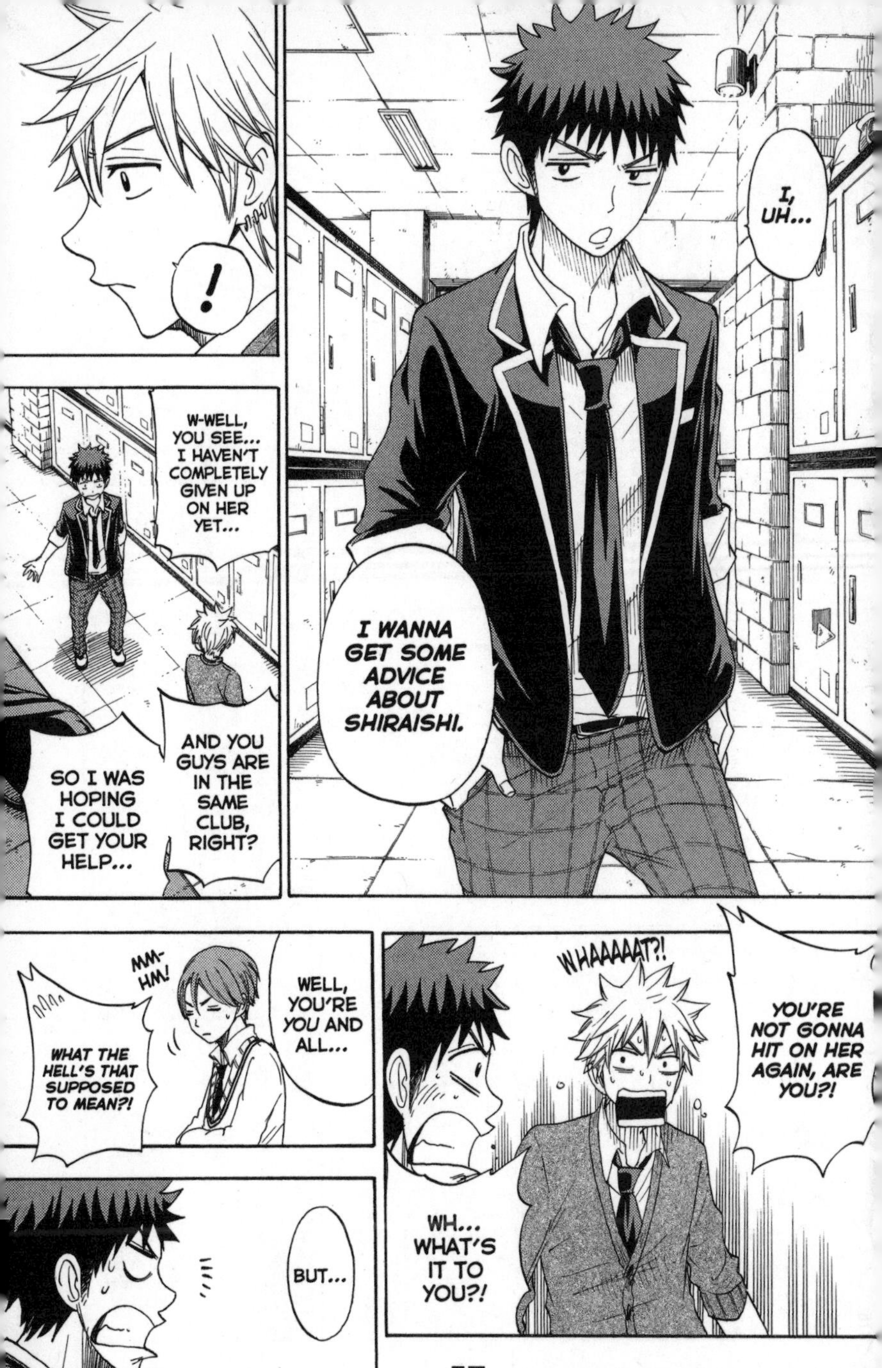
I, UH...
I WANNA GET SOME ADVICE ABOUT SHIRAISHI.
!
W-WELL, YOU SEE... I HAVEN'T COMPLETELY GIVEN UP ON HER YET...
AND YOU GUYS ARE IN THE SAME CLUB, RIGHT?
SO I WAS HOPING I COULD GET YOUR HELP...
YOU'RE NOT GONNA HIT ON HER AGAIN, ARE YOU?!
WHAAAAAT?!
WH... WHAT'S IT TO YOU?!
WELL, YOU'RE YOU AND ALL...
MM-HM!
WHAT THE HELL'S THAT SUPPOSED TO MEAN?!
BUT...

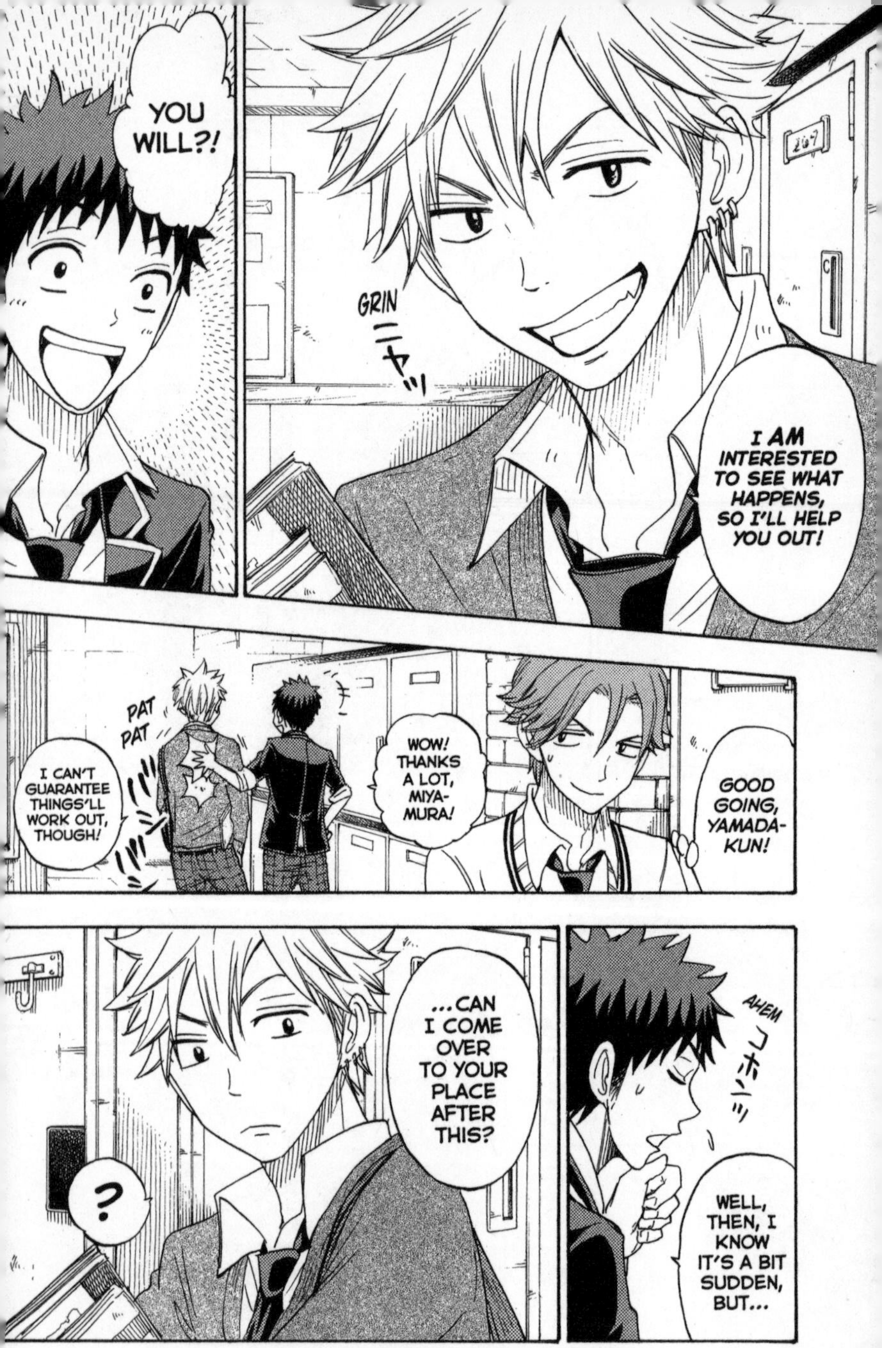
I AM INTERESTED TO SEE WHAT HAPPENS, SO I'LL HELP YOU OUT!
GRIN
ニヤッ
YOU WILL?!
GOOD GOING, YAMADA-KUN!
WOW! THANKS A LOT, MIYA-MURA!
PAT PAT
I CAN'T GUARANTEE THINGS'LL WORK OUT, THOUGH!
AHEM
コホンッ
WELL, THEN, I KNOW IT'S A BIT SUDDEN, BUT...
...CAN I COME OVER TO YOUR PLACE AFTER THIS?
?

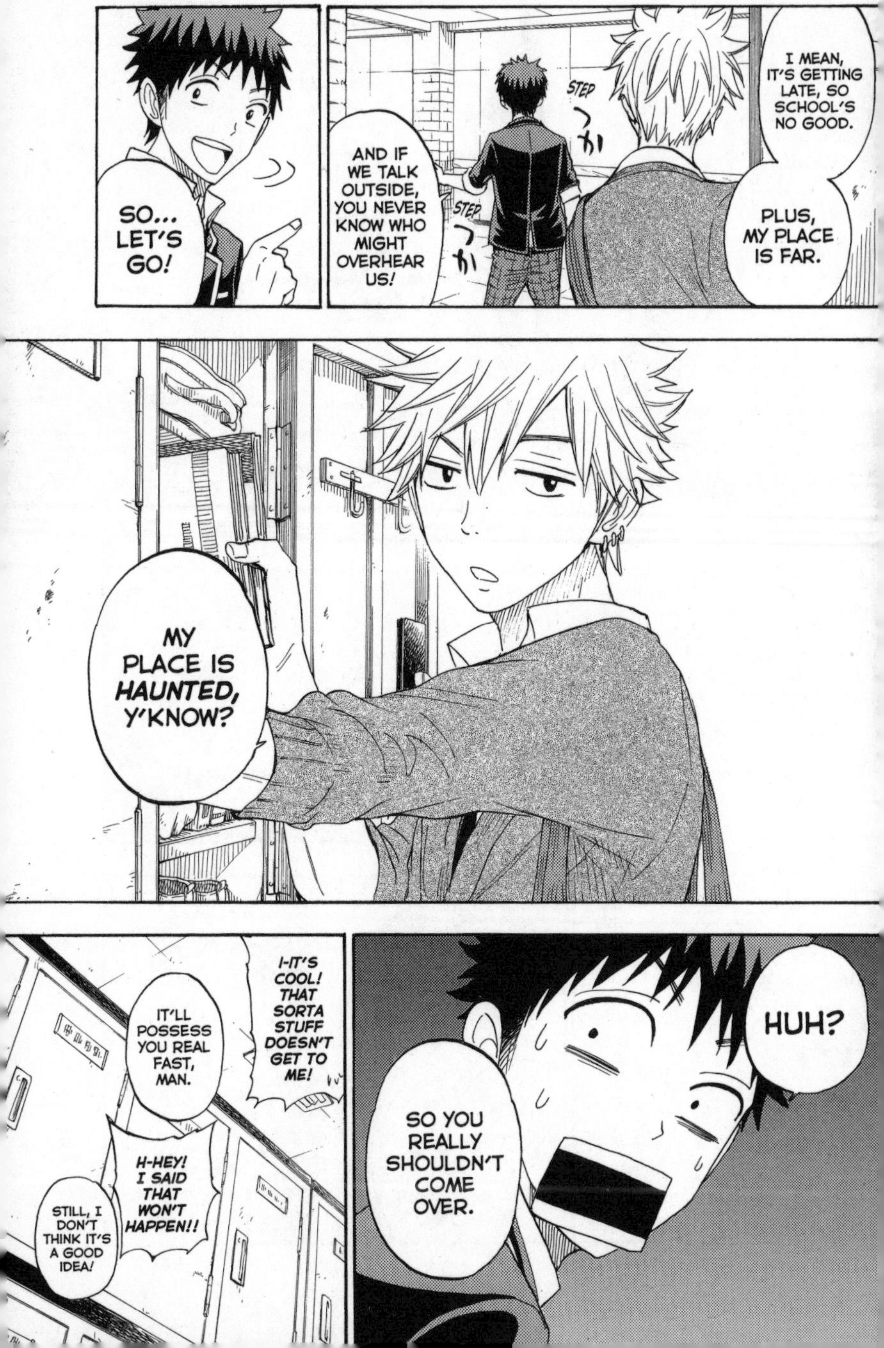
I MEAN, IT'S GETTING LATE, SO SCHOOL'S NO GOOD.
PLUS, MY PLACE IS FAR.
STEP つか
STEP つか
AND IF WE TALK OUTSIDE, YOU NEVER KNOW WHO MIGHT OVERHEAR US!
SO... LET'S GO!
MY PLACE IS *HAUNTED,* Y'KNOW?
HUH?
SO YOU REALLY SHOULDN'T COME OVER.
I-IT'S COOL! THAT SORTA STUFF DOESN'T GET TO ME!
IT'LL POSSESS YOU REAL FAST, MAN.
H-HEY! I SAID THAT WON'T HAPPEN!!
STILL, I DON'T THINK IT'S A GOOD IDEA!

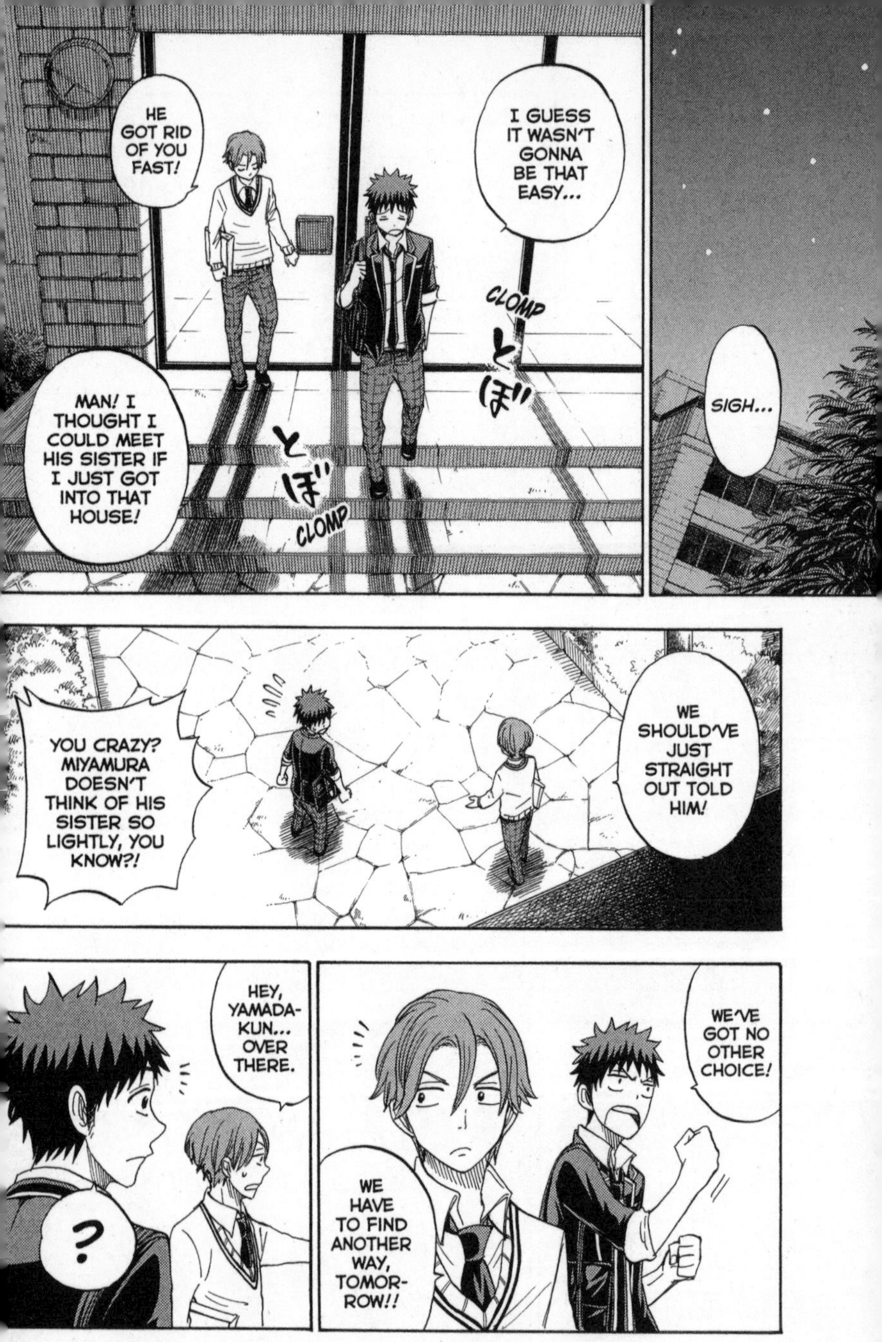
SIGH...
I GUESS IT WASN'T GONNA BE THAT EASY...
HE GOT RID OF YOU FAST!
CLOMP
とぼ
MAN! I THOUGHT I COULD MEET HIS SISTER IF I JUST GOT INTO THAT HOUSE!
とぼ
CLOMP
WE SHOULD'VE JUST STRAIGHT OUT TOLD HIM!
YOU CRAZY? MIYAMURA DOESN'T THINK OF HIS SISTER SO LIGHTLY, YOU KNOW?!
WE'VE GOT NO OTHER CHOICE!
WE HAVE TO FIND ANOTHER WAY, TOMORROW!!
HEY, YAMADA-KUN... OVER THERE.
?

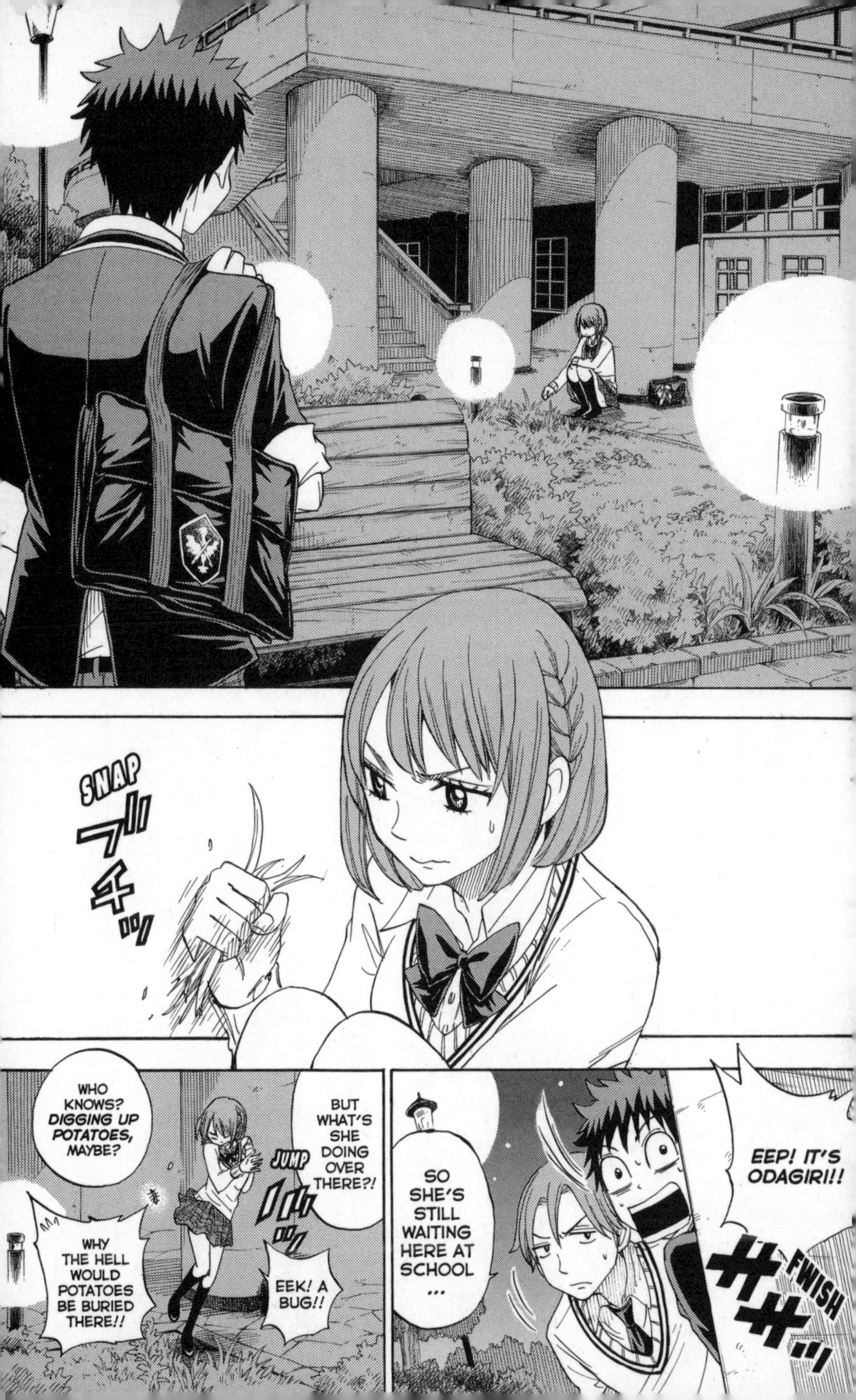
SNAP
EEP! IT'S ODAGIRI!!
FWISH
SO SHE'S STILL WAITING HERE AT SCHOOL ...
BUT WHAT'S SHE DOING OVER THERE?!
WHO KNOWS? DIGGING UP POTATOES, MAYBE?
JUMP
EEK! A BUG!!
WHY THE HELL WOULD POTATOES BE BURIED THERE!!

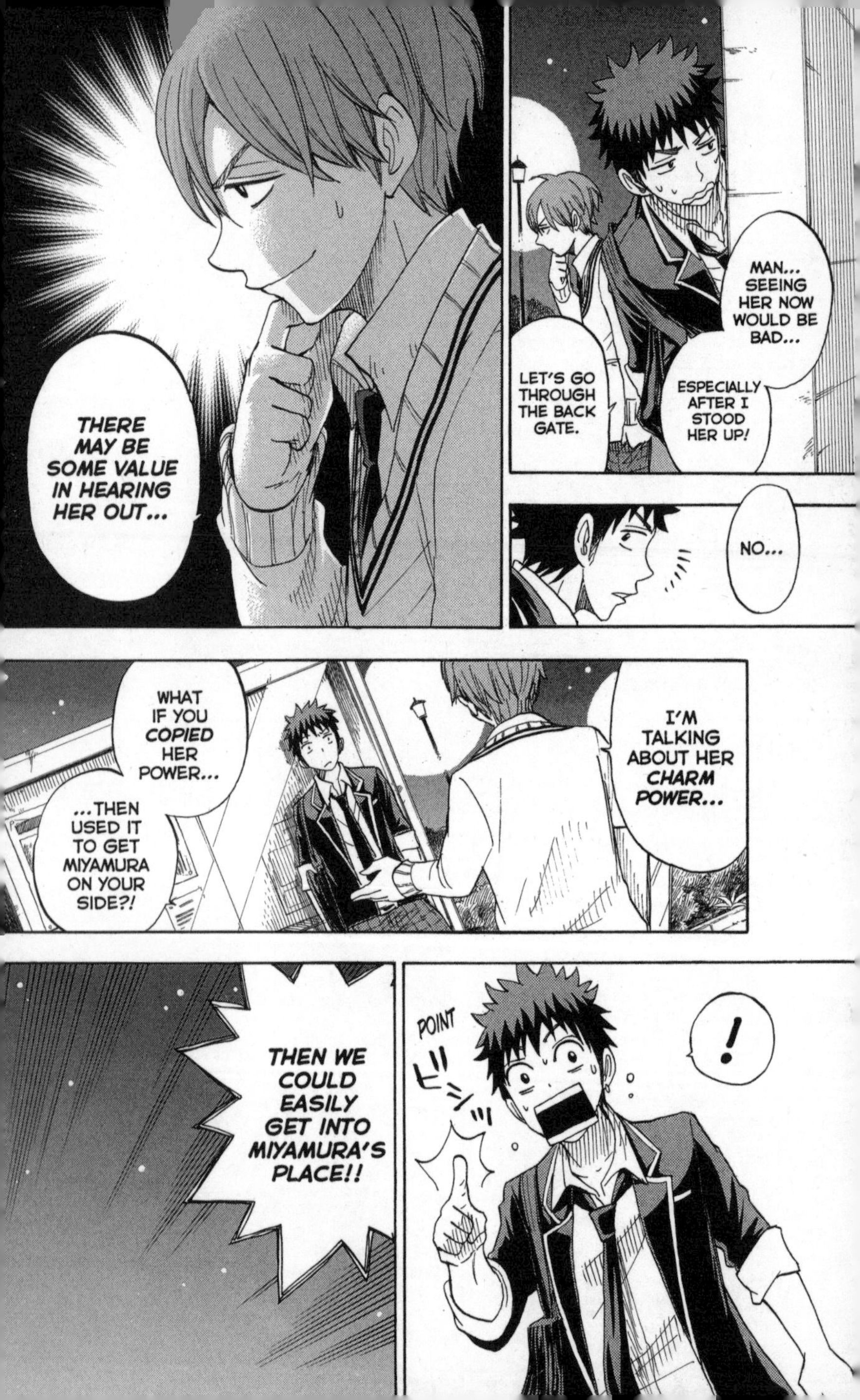
MAN... SEEING HER NOW WOULD BE BAD...
ESPECIALLY AFTER I STOOD HER UP!
LET'S GO THROUGH THE BACK GATE.
NO...
THERE MAY BE SOME VALUE IN HEARING HER OUT...
I'M TALKING ABOUT HER CHARM POWER...
WHAT IF YOU COPIED HER POWER...
...THEN USED IT TO GET MIYAMURA ON YOUR SIDE?!
!
POINT
ビシッ
THEN WE COULD EASILY GET INTO MIYAMURA'S PLACE!!

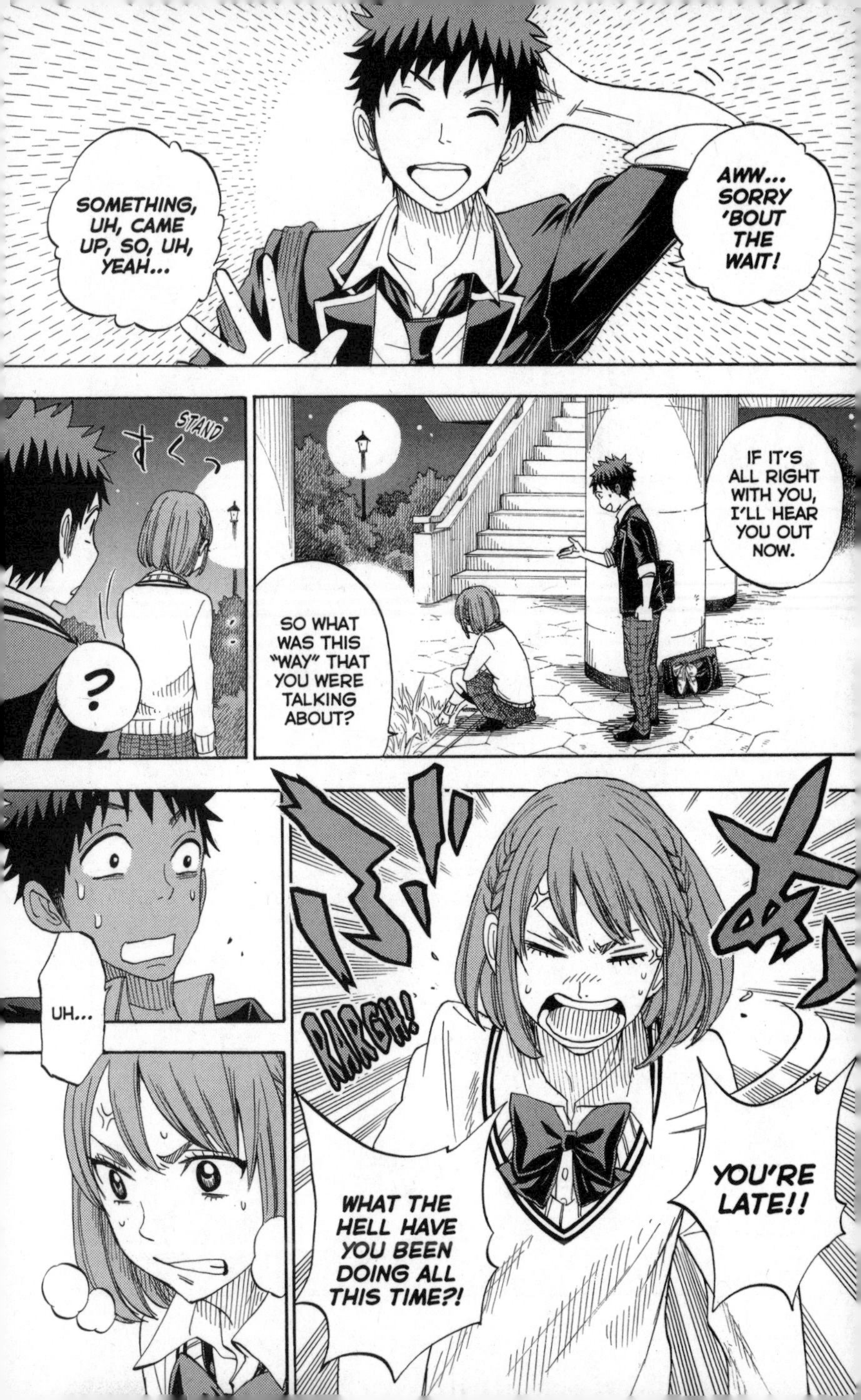
AWW... SORRY 'BOUT THE WAIT!
SOMETHING, UH, CAME UP, SO, UH, YEAH...
IF IT'S ALL RIGHT WITH YOU, I'LL HEAR YOU OUT NOW.
SO WHAT WAS THIS "WAY" THAT YOU WERE TALKING ABOUT?
STAND
すくっ
?
YOU'RE LATE!!
WHAT THE HELL HAVE YOU BEEN DOING ALL THIS TIME?!
RAARGH!!
UH...

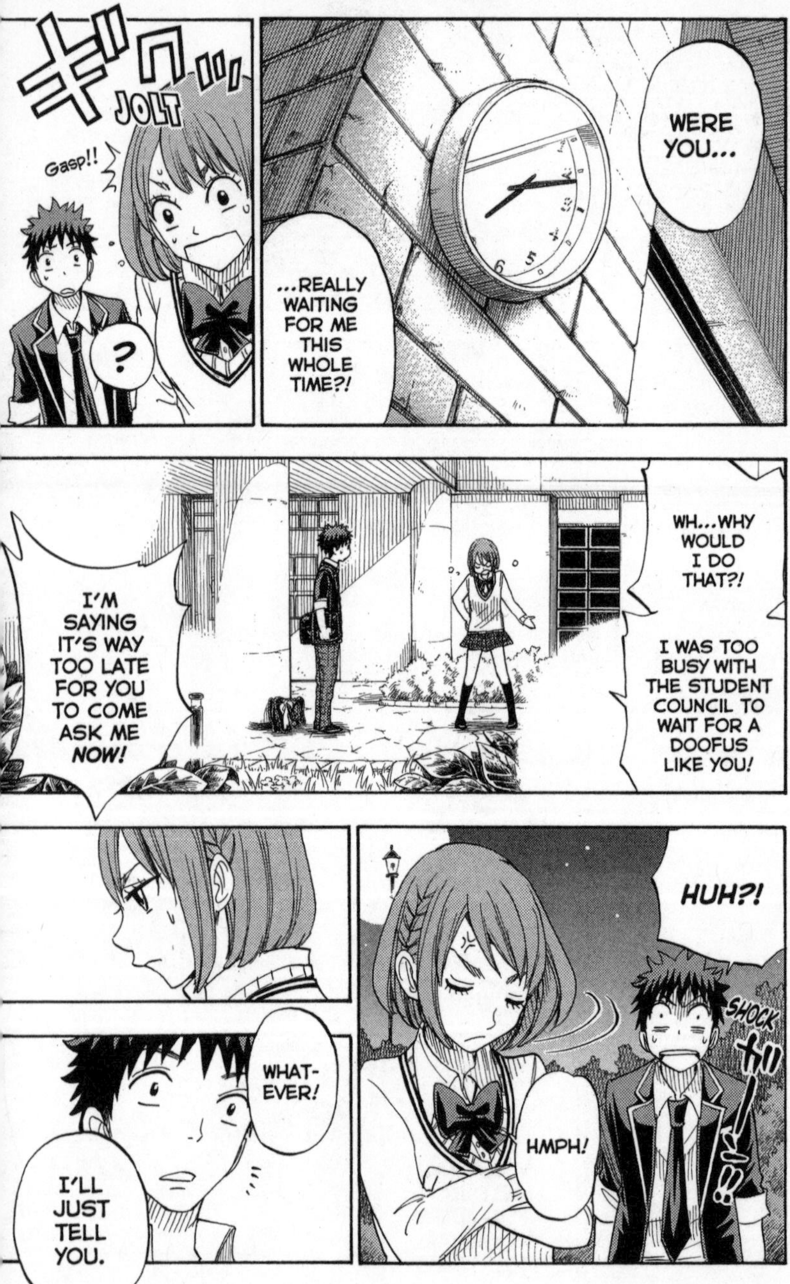
WERE YOU...
...REALLY WAITING FOR ME THIS WHOLE TIME?!
JOLT
Gasp!!
?
WH...WHY WOULD I DO THAT?!
I WAS TOO BUSY WITH THE STUDENT COUNCIL TO WAIT FOR A DOOFUS LIKE YOU!
I'M SAYING IT'S WAY TOO LATE FOR YOU TO COME ASK ME *NOW!*
HUH?!
SHOCK
HMPH!
WHAT-EVER!
I'LL JUST TELL YOU.

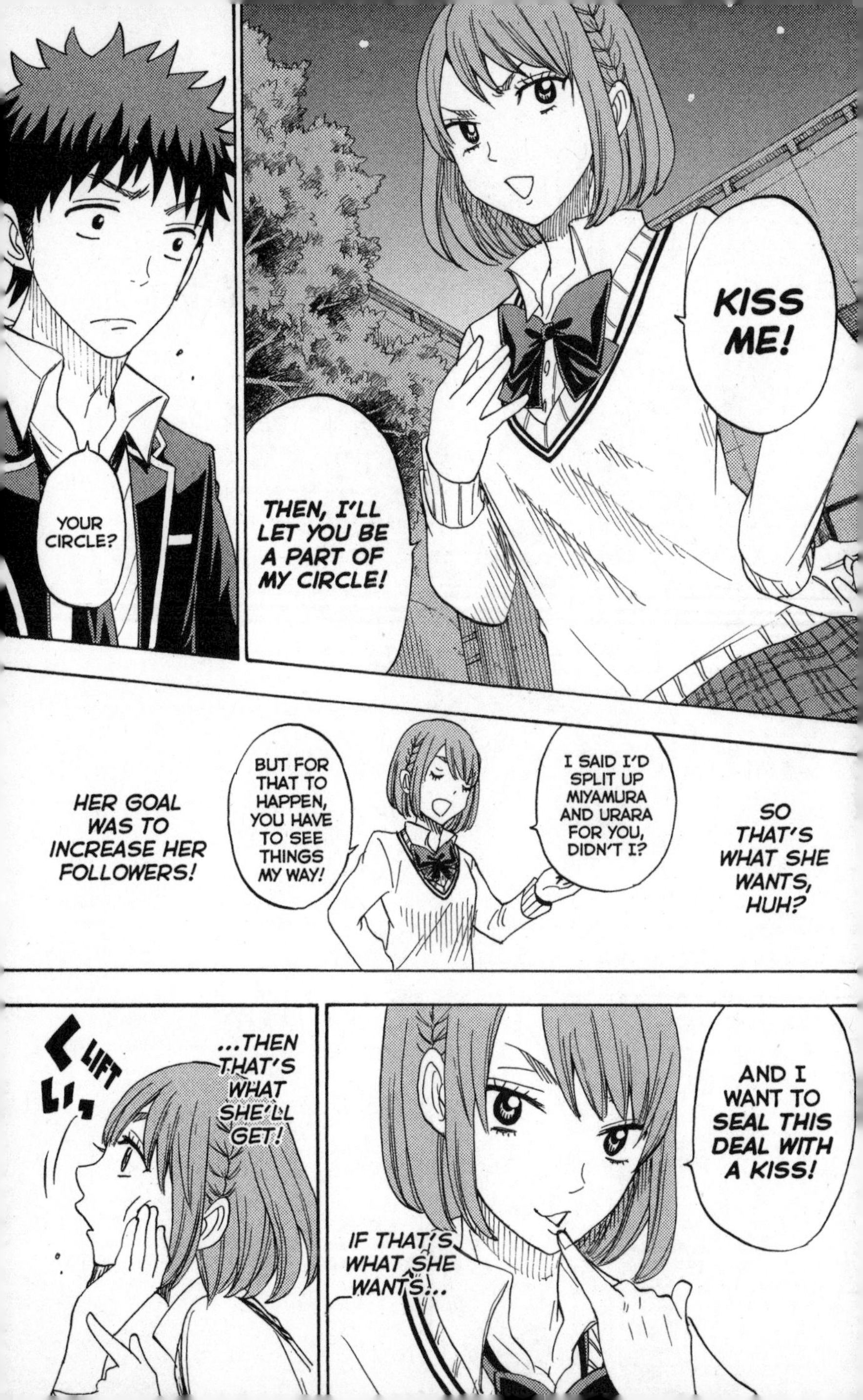
KISS ME!
THEN, I'LL LET YOU BE A PART OF MY CIRCLE!
YOUR CIRCLE?
SO THAT'S WHAT SHE WANTS, HUH?
I SAID I'D SPLIT UP MIYAMURA AND URARA FOR YOU, DIDN'T I?
BUT FOR THAT TO HAPPEN, YOU HAVE TO SEE THINGS MY WAY!
HER GOAL WAS TO INCREASE HER FOLLOWERS!
AND I WANT TO SEAL THIS DEAL WITH A KISS!
IF THAT'S WHAT SHE WANTS...
...THEN THAT'S WHAT SHE'LL GET!
LIFT

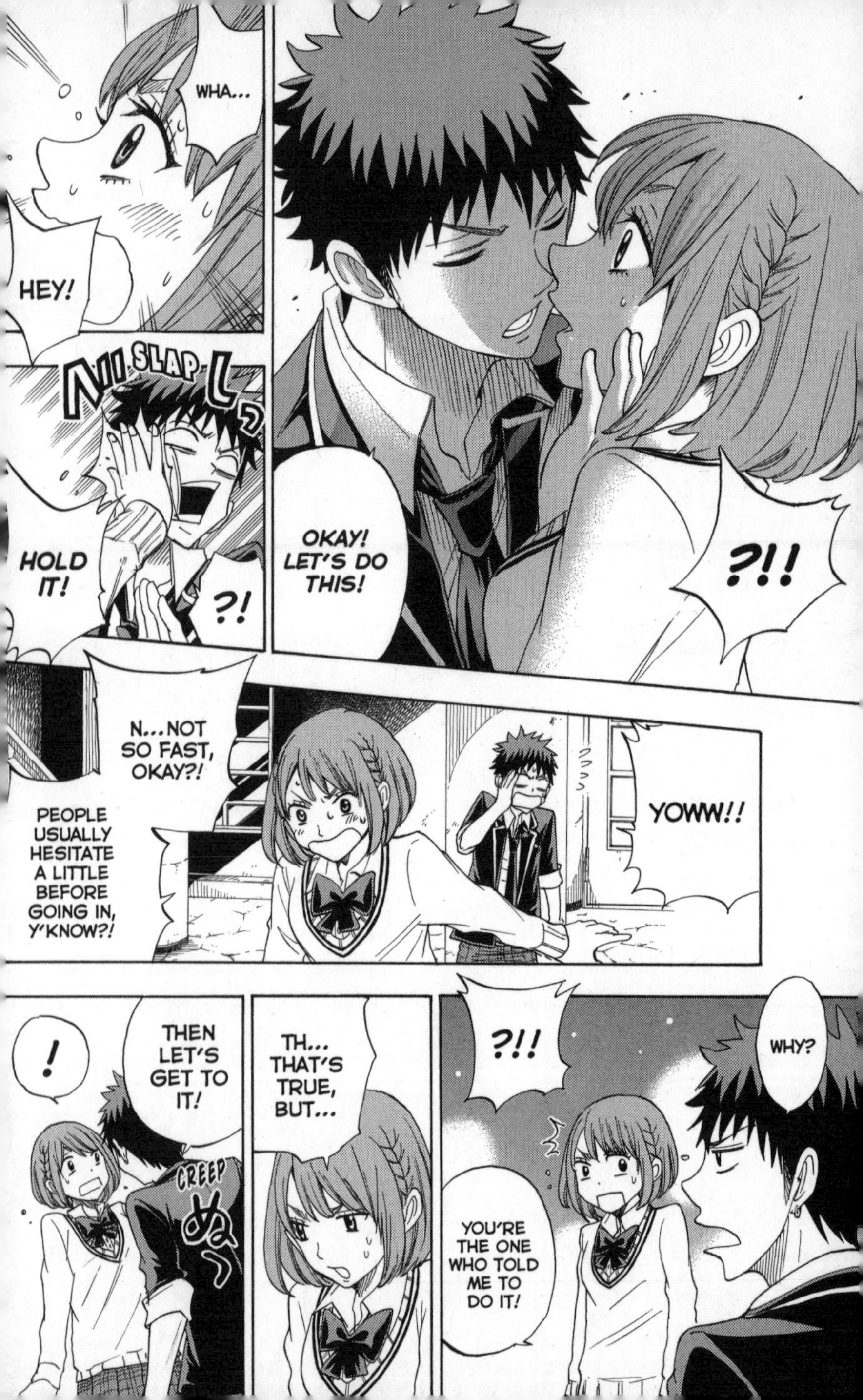
...
OKAY! LET'S DO THIS!
?!!
WHA...
HEY!
SLAP
?!
HOLD IT!
YOWW!!
N...NOT SO FAST, OKAY?!
PEOPLE USUALLY HESITATE A LITTLE BEFORE GOING IN, Y'KNOW?!
WHY?
?!!
YOU'RE THE ONE WHO TOLD ME TO DO IT!
TH... THAT'S TRUE, BUT...
THEN LET'S GET TO IT!
!
CREEP

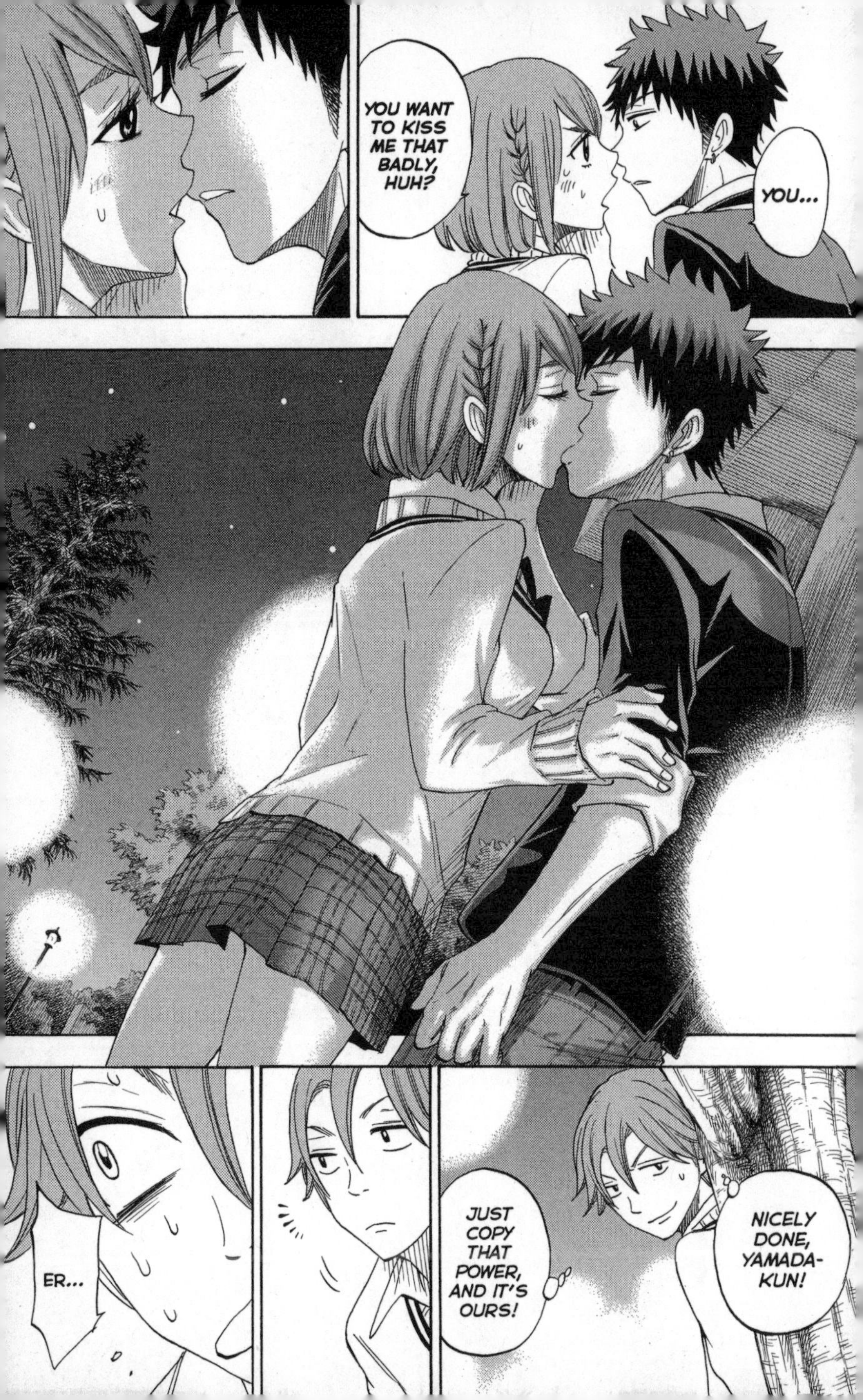
YOU...
YOU WANT TO KISS ME THAT BADLY, HUH?
NICELY DONE, YAMADA-KUN!
JUST COPY THAT POWER, AND IT'S OURS!
ER...

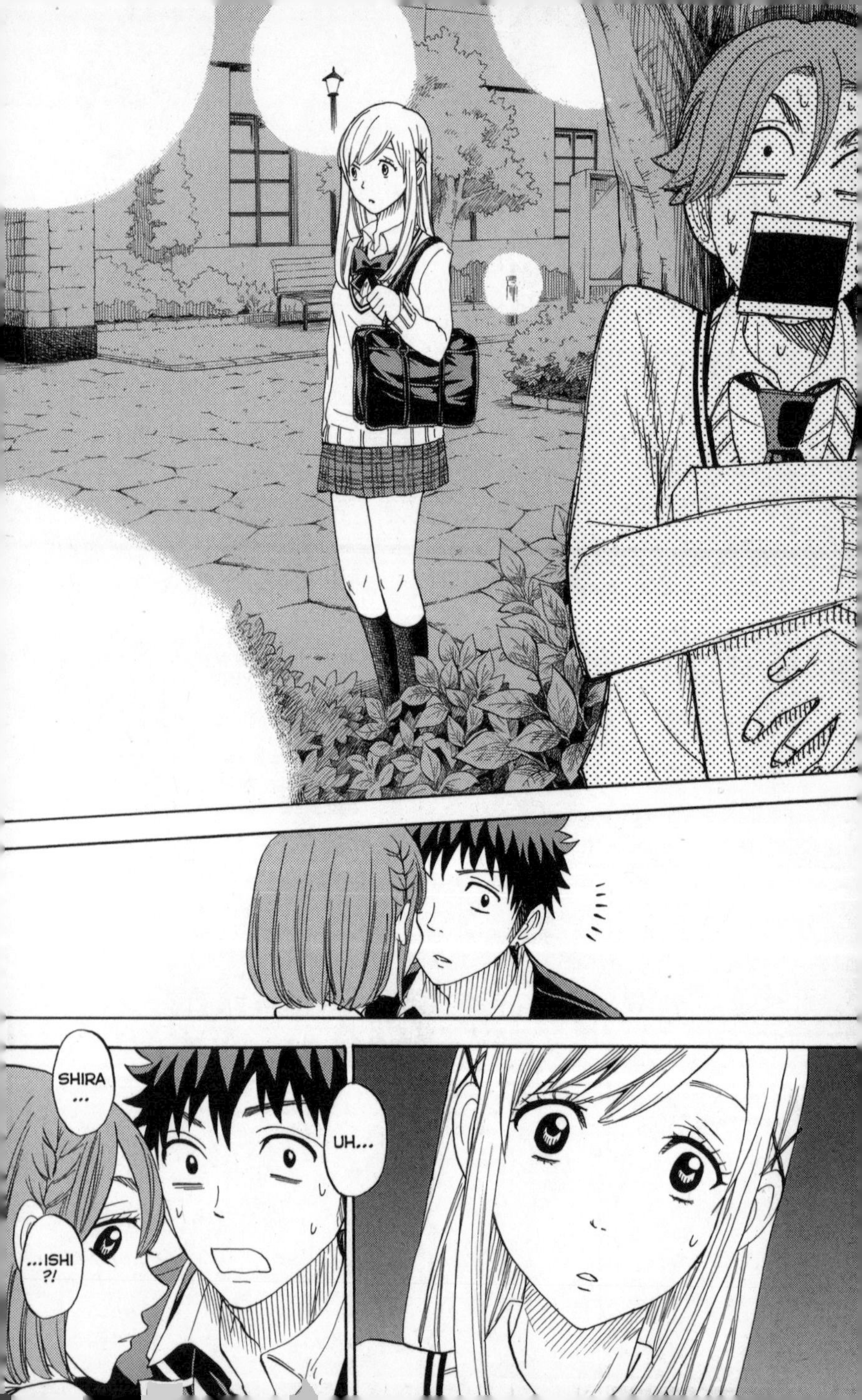
SHIRA...
UH...
...ISHI?!

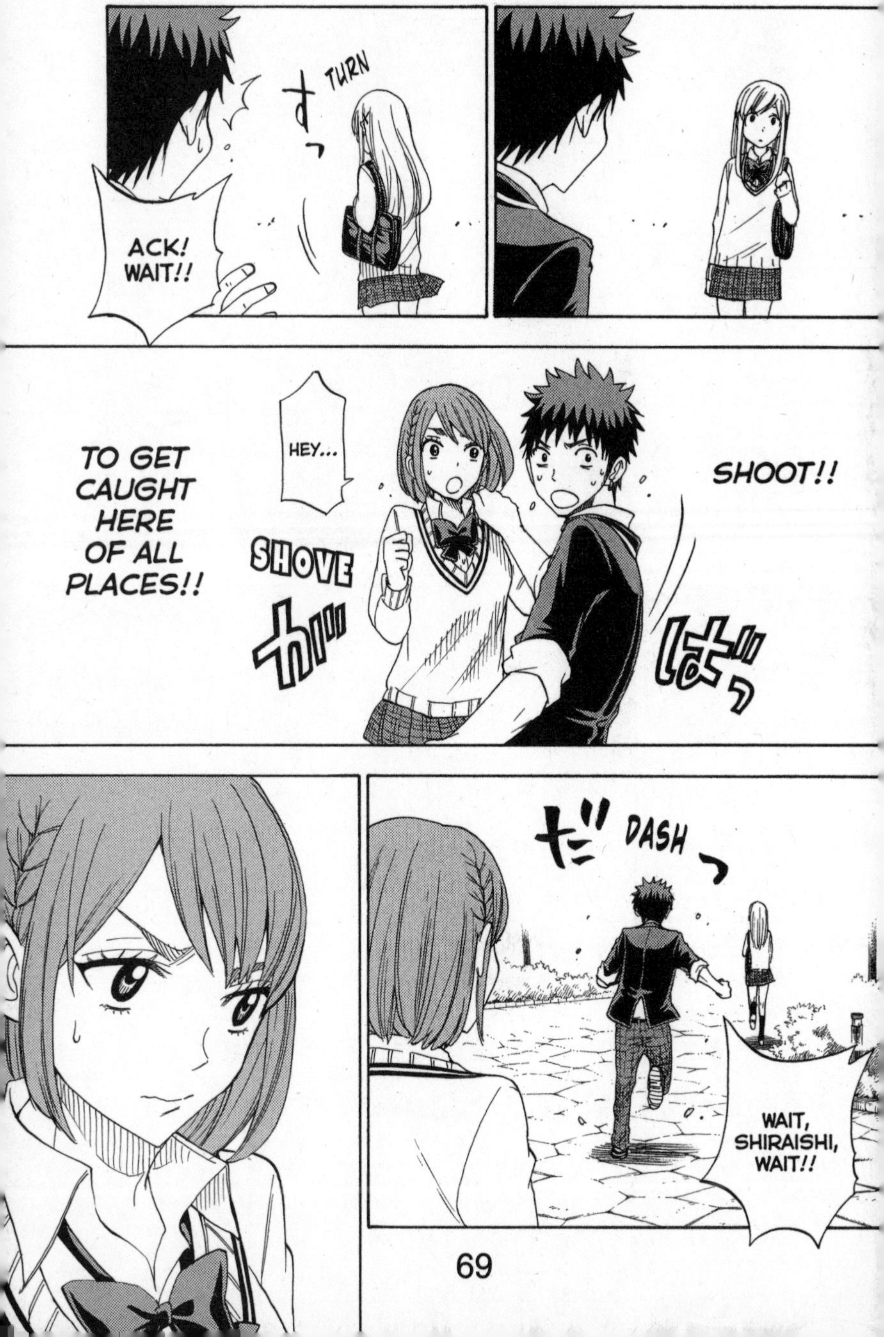
...
...
すっ
TURN
...
ACK! WAIT!!
SHOOT!!
はっ
HEY...
SHOVE
TO GET CAUGHT HERE OF ALL PLACES!!
DASH
WAIT, SHIRAISHI, WAIT!!

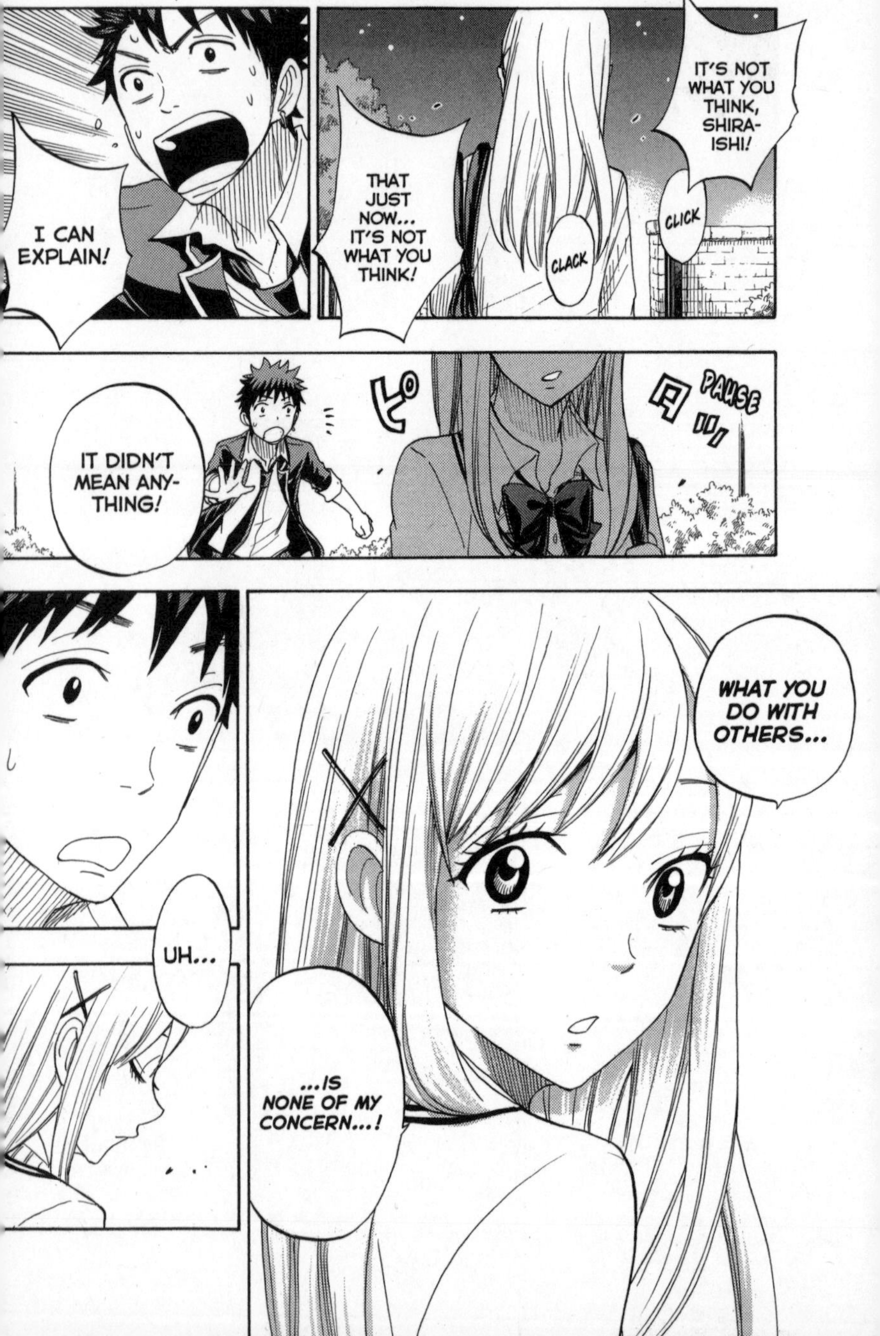
IT'S NOT WHAT YOU THINK, SHIRA-ISHI!
CLICK
CLACK
THAT JUST NOW... IT'S NOT WHAT YOU THINK!
I CAN EXPLAIN!
PAUSE
IT DIDN'T MEAN ANY-THING!
WHAT YOU DO WITH OTHERS...
...IS NONE OF MY CONCERN...!
UH...

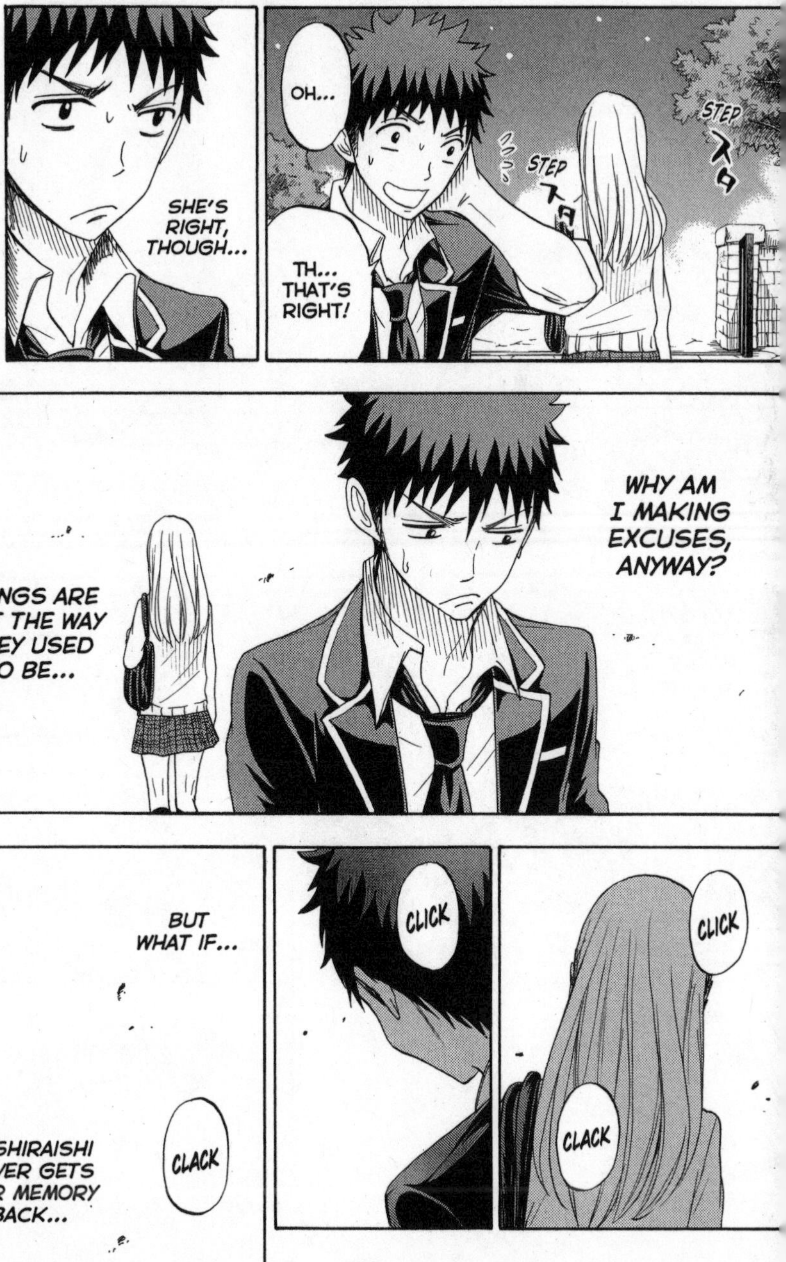
STEP
スタ
STEP
スタ
OH...
TH... THAT'S RIGHT!
SHE'S RIGHT, THOUGH...
WHY AM I MAKING EXCUSES, ANYWAY?
THINGS ARE NOT THE WAY THEY USED TO BE...
CLICK
CLACK
CLICK
BUT WHAT IF...
CLACK
...SHIRAISHI NEVER GETS HER MEMORY BACK...

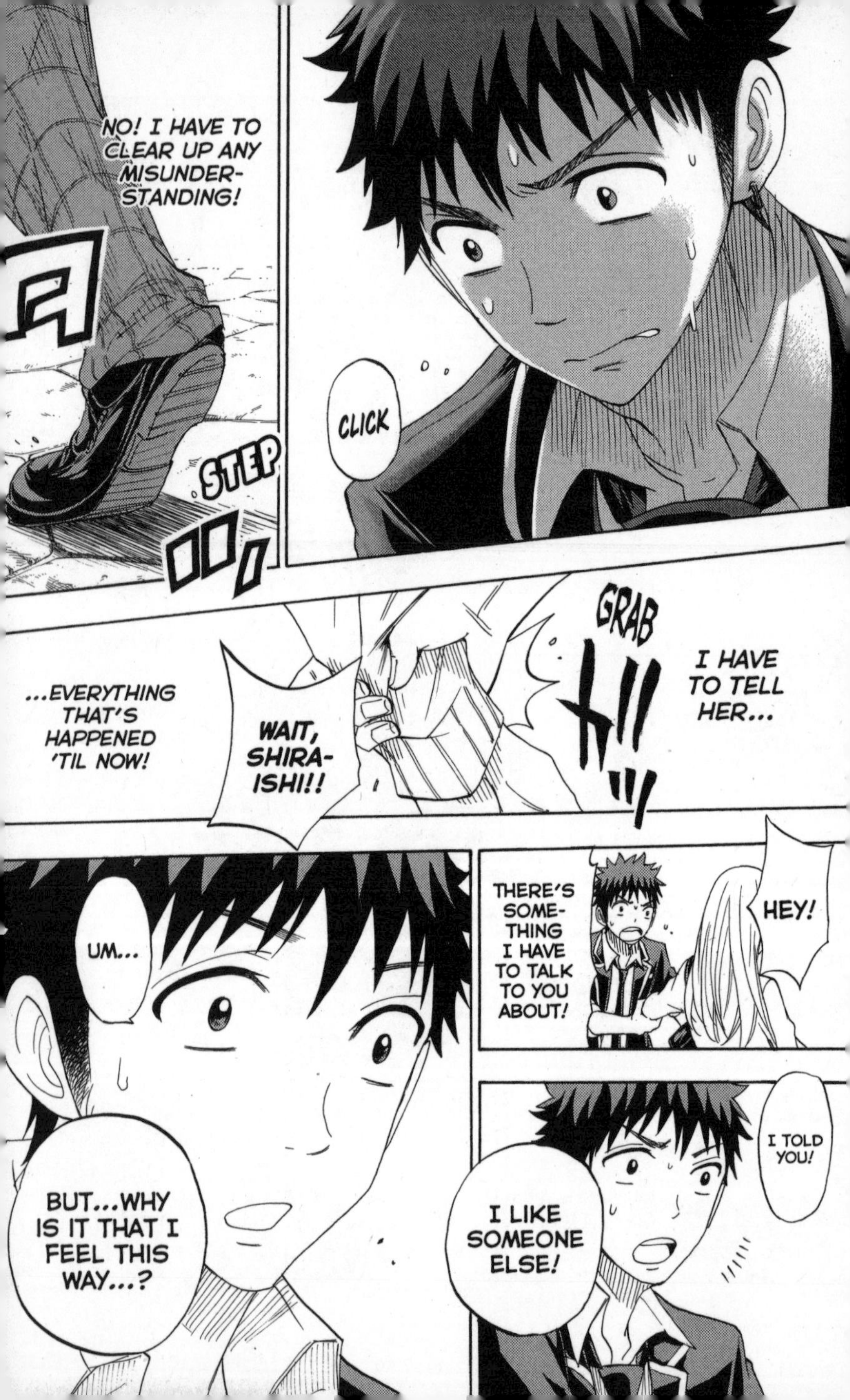
CLICK
NO! I HAVE TO CLEAR UP ANY MISUNDER-STANDING!
STEP
I HAVE TO TELL HER...
GRAB
WAIT, SHIRA-ISHI!!
...EVERYTHING THAT'S HAPPENED 'TIL NOW!
HEY!
THERE'S SOME-THING I HAVE TO TALK TO YOU ABOUT!
I TOLD YOU!
I LIKE SOMEONE ELSE!
UM...
BUT...WHY IS IT THAT I FEEL THIS WAY...?

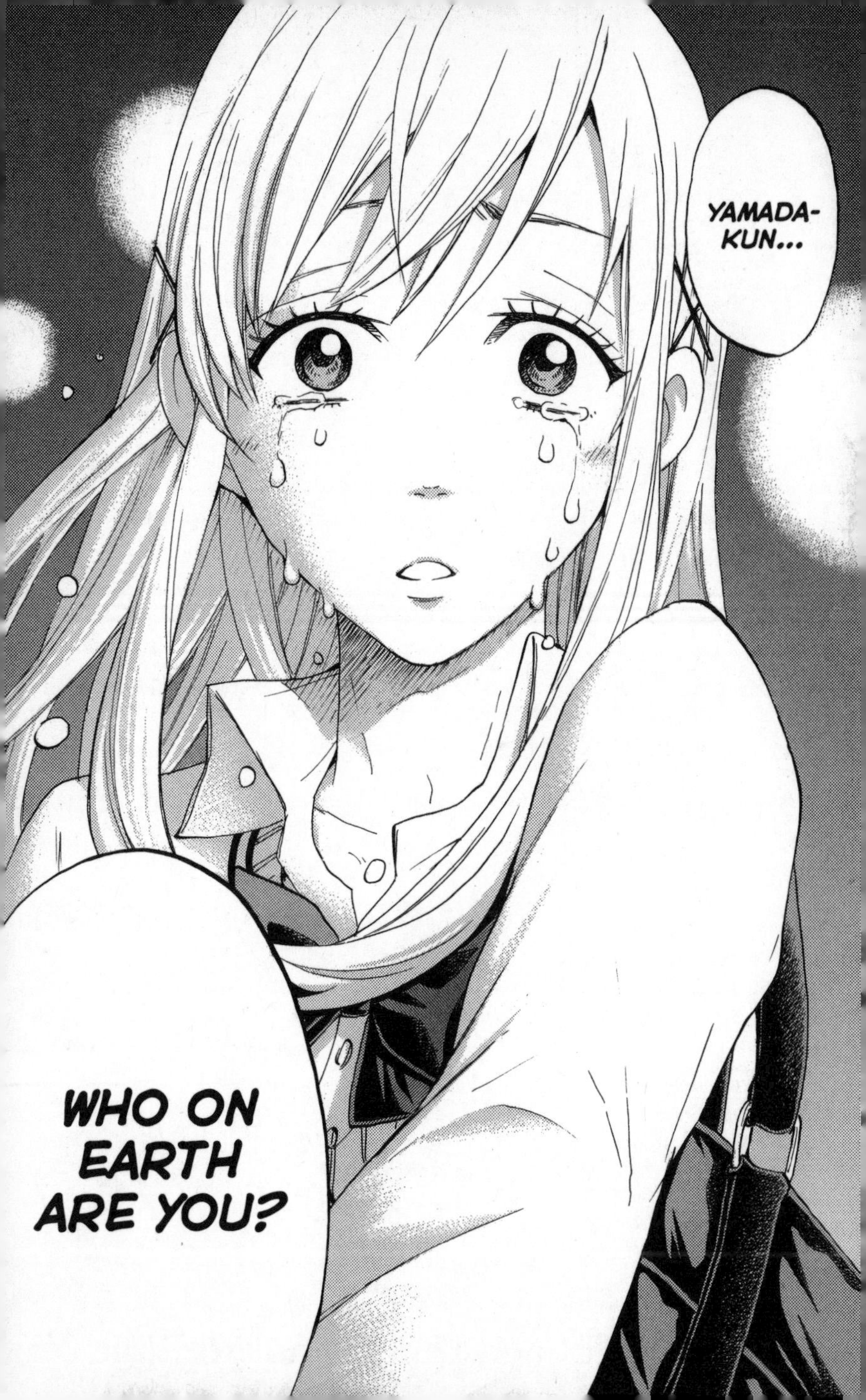
YAMADA-KUN...
WHO ON EARTH ARE YOU?

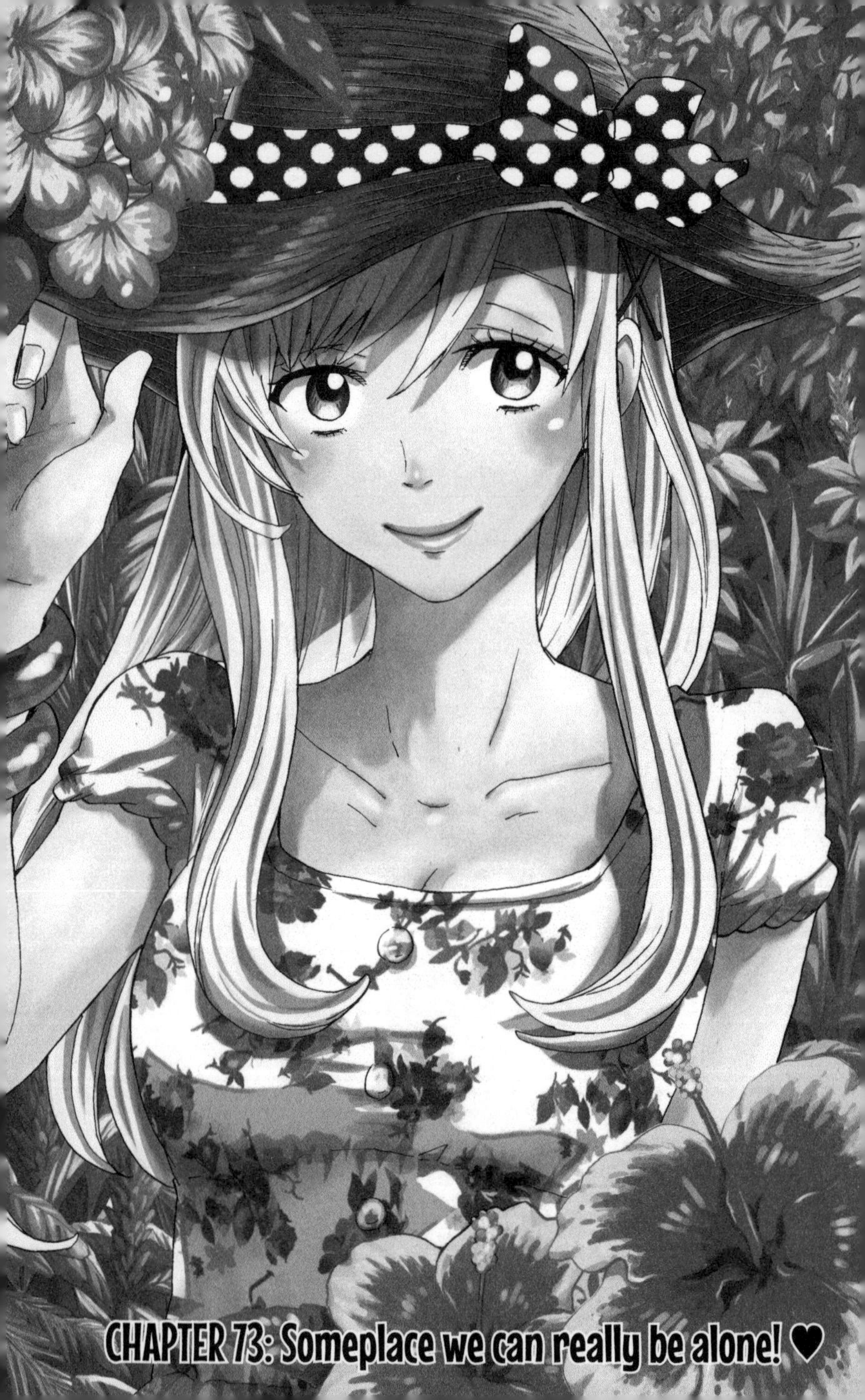

CHAPTER 73: Someplace we can really be alone! ♥

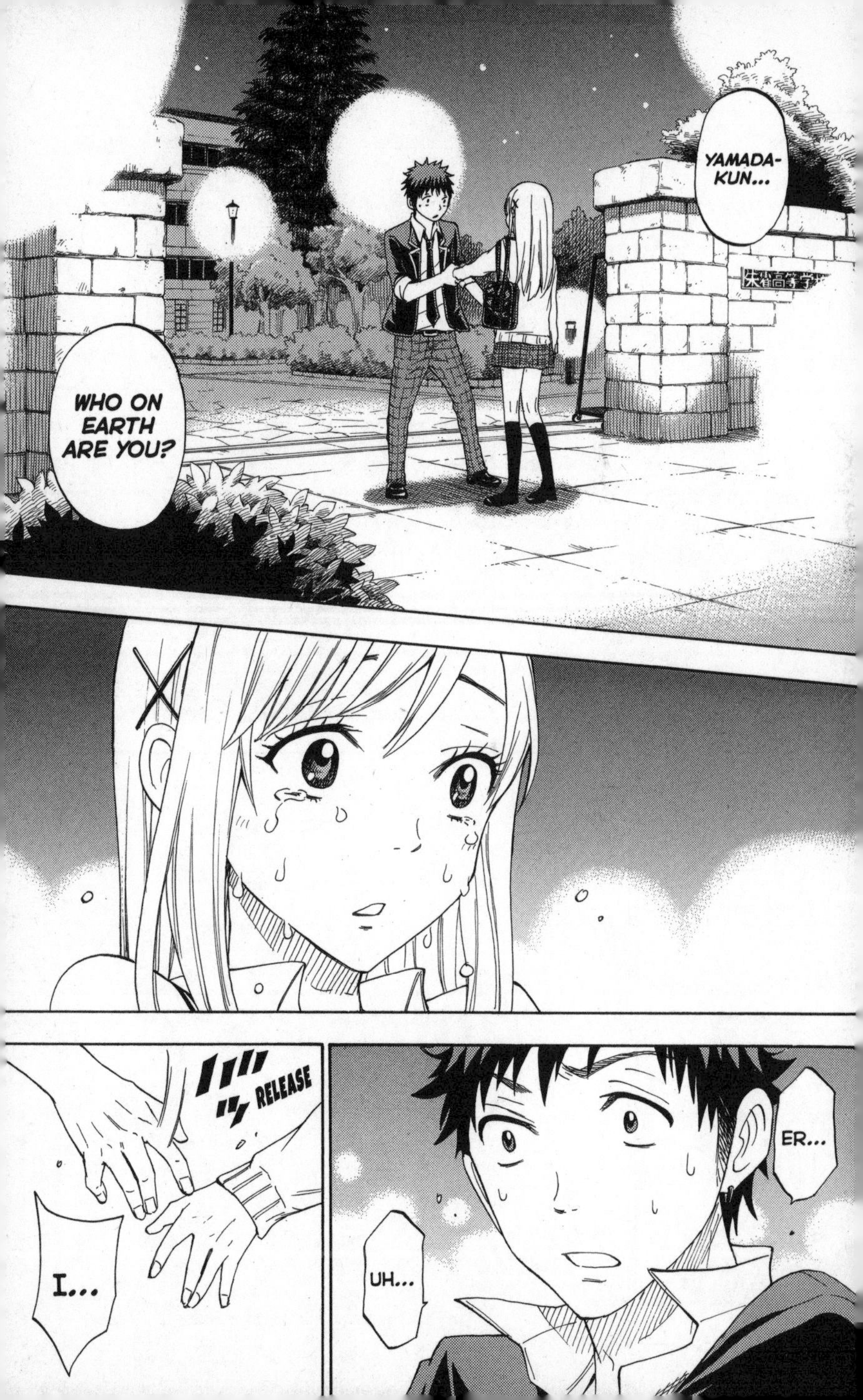
YAMADA-KUN...
WHO ON EARTH ARE YOU?
ER...
UH...
RELEASE
I...

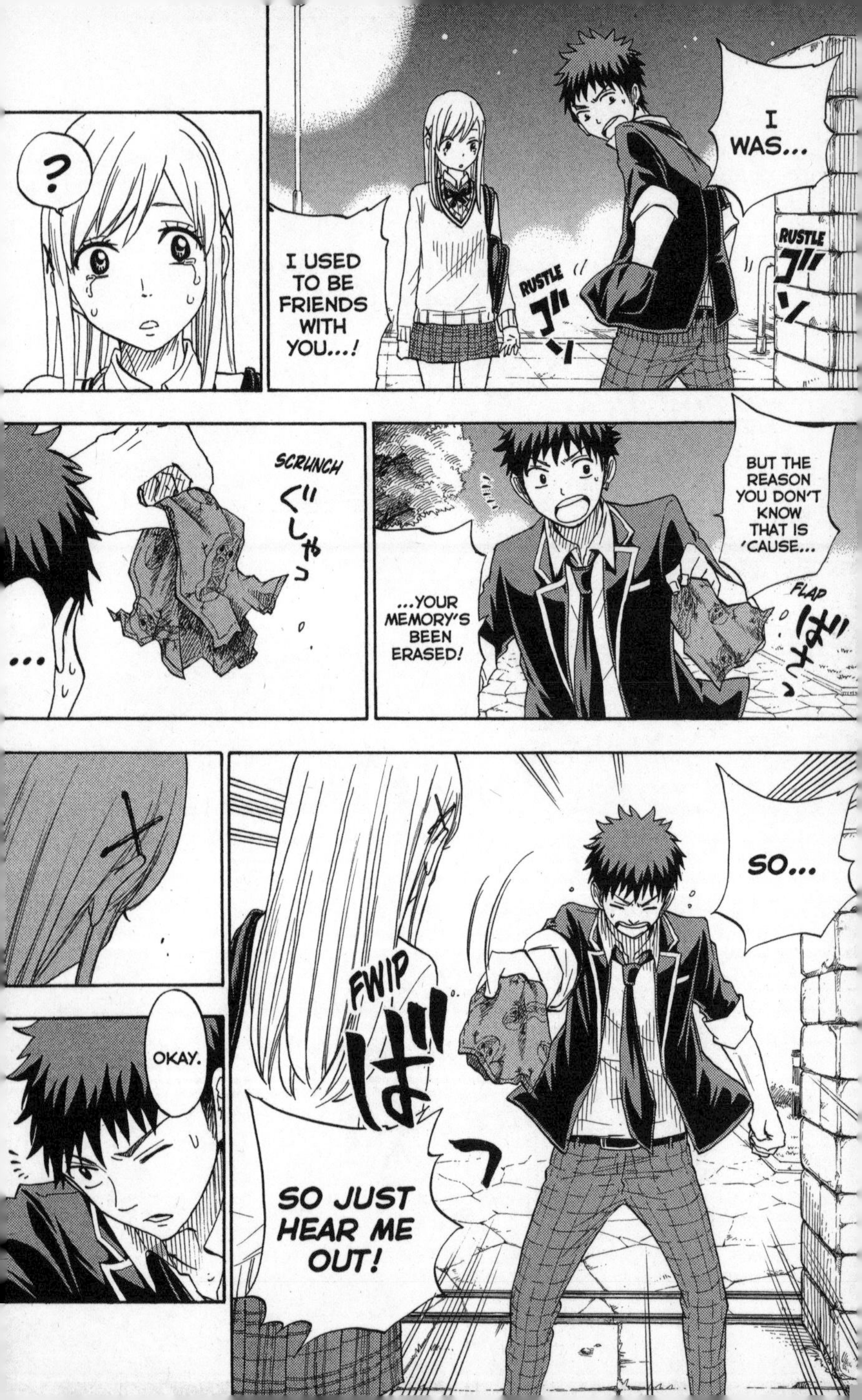
I WAS...
RUSTLE
ゴソ
I USED TO BE FRIENDS WITH YOU...!
RUSTLE
ゴソ
?
BUT THE REASON YOU DON'T KNOW THAT IS 'CAUSE...
FLAP
ばさっ
...YOUR MEMORY'S BEEN ERASED!
SCRUNCH
ぐしゃっ
...
SO...
FWIP
ばっ
SO JUST HEAR ME OUT!
OKAY.

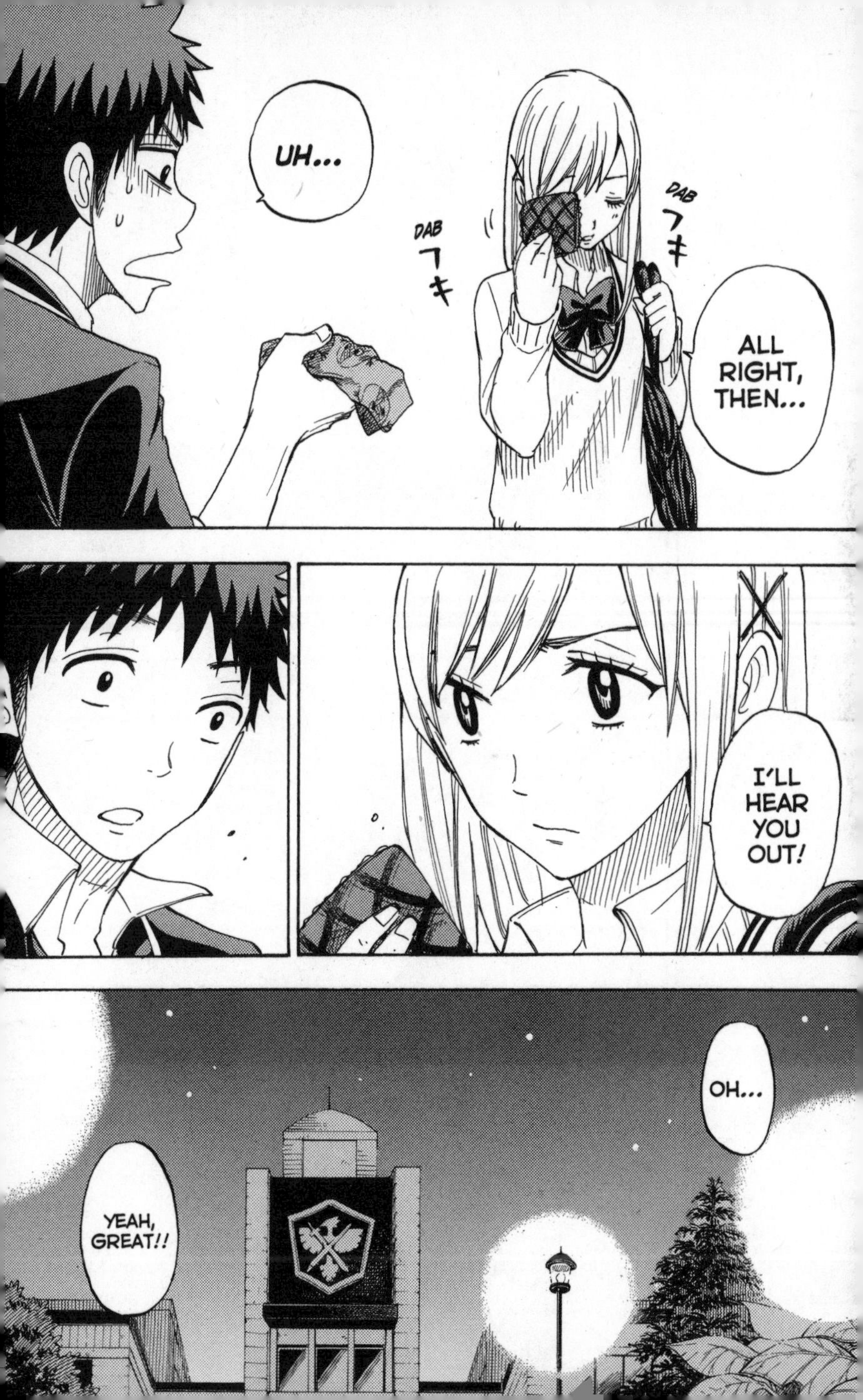
DAB
フキ
DAB
フキ
ALL RIGHT, THEN...
UH...
I'LL HEAR YOU OUT!
OH...
YEAH, GREAT!!

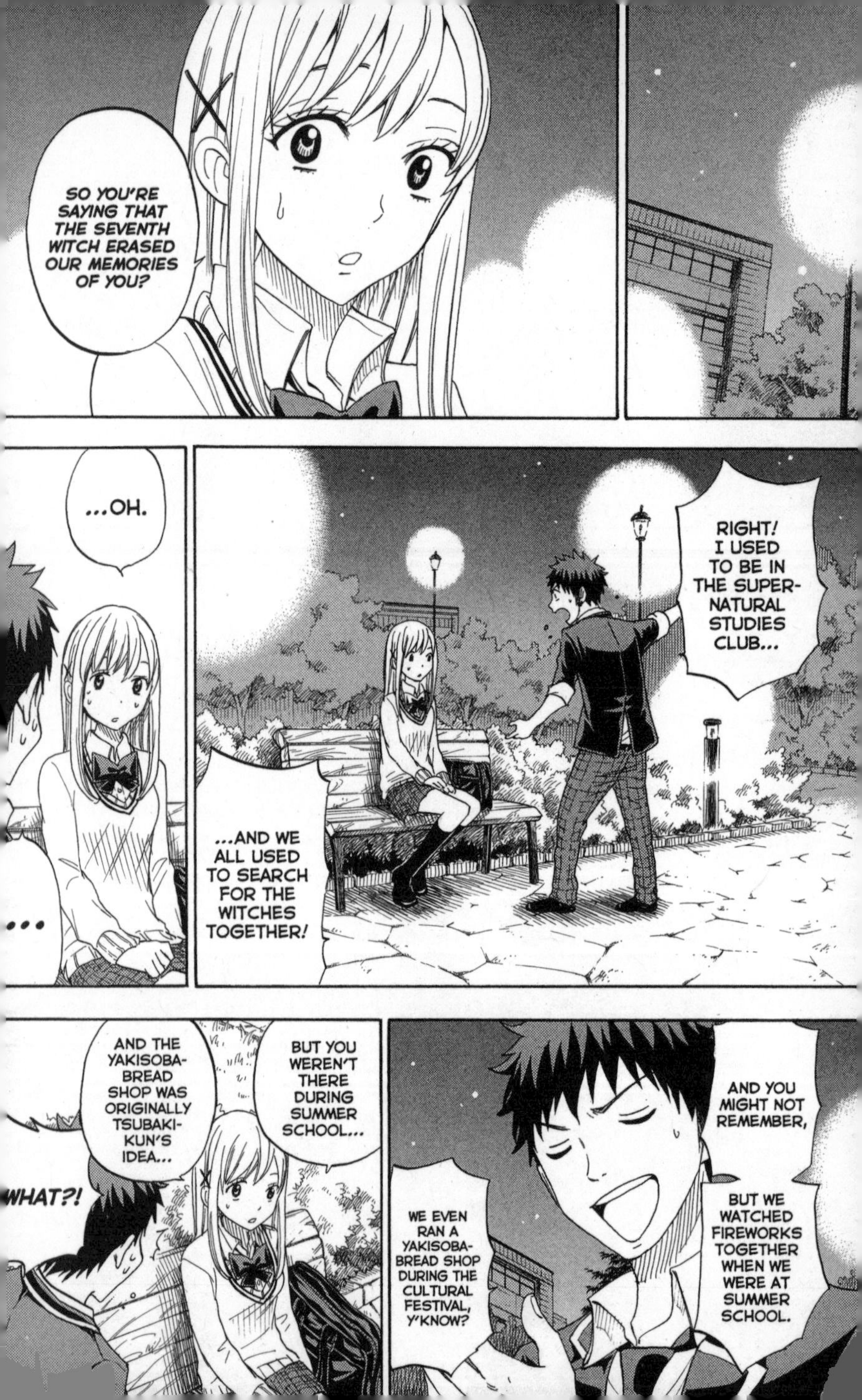
SO YOU'RE SAYING THAT THE SEVENTH WITCH ERASED OUR MEMORIES OF YOU?
RIGHT! I USED TO BE IN THE SUPER-NATURAL STUDIES CLUB...
...AND WE ALL USED TO SEARCH FOR THE WITCHES TOGETHER!
...OH.
...
AND YOU MIGHT NOT REMEMBER,
BUT WE WATCHED FIREWORKS TOGETHER WHEN WE WERE AT SUMMER SCHOOL.
WE EVEN RAN A YAKISOBA-BREAD SHOP DURING THE CULTURAL FESTIVAL, Y'KNOW?
BUT YOU WEREN'T THERE DURING SUMMER SCHOOL...
AND THE YAKISOBA-BREAD SHOP WAS ORIGINALLY TSUBAKI-KUN'S IDEA...
WHAT?!

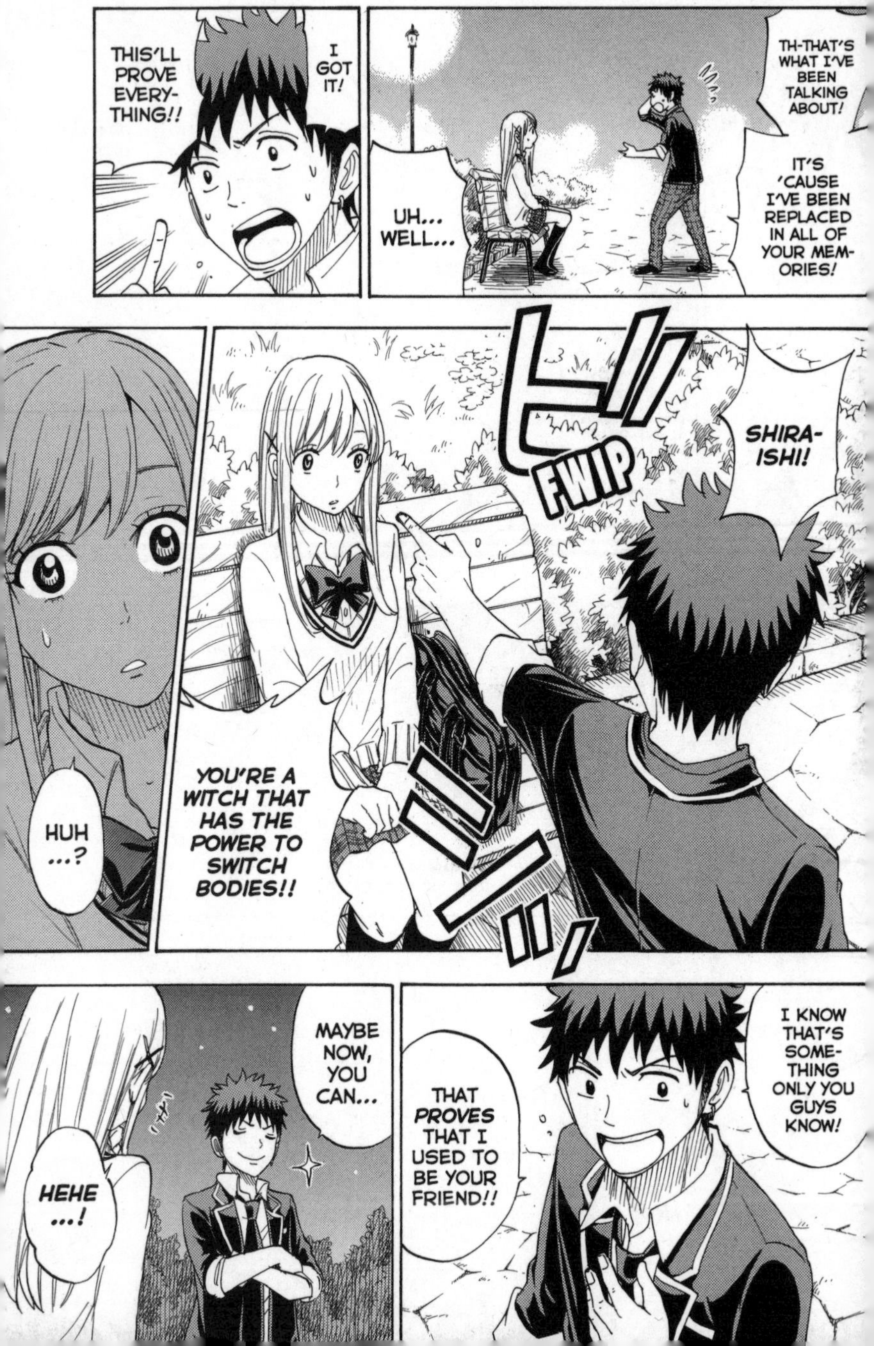
TH-THAT'S WHAT I'VE BEEN TALKING ABOUT!
IT'S 'CAUSE I'VE BEEN REPLACED IN ALL OF YOUR MEMORIES!
UH... WELL...
I GOT IT!
THIS'LL PROVE EVERYTHING!!
SHIRAISHI!
FWIP
YOU'RE A WITCH THAT HAS THE POWER TO SWITCH BODIES!!
HUH ...?
I KNOW THAT'S SOMETHING ONLY YOU GUYS KNOW!
THAT PROVES THAT I USED TO BE YOUR FRIEND!!
MAYBE NOW, YOU CAN...
HEHE ...!

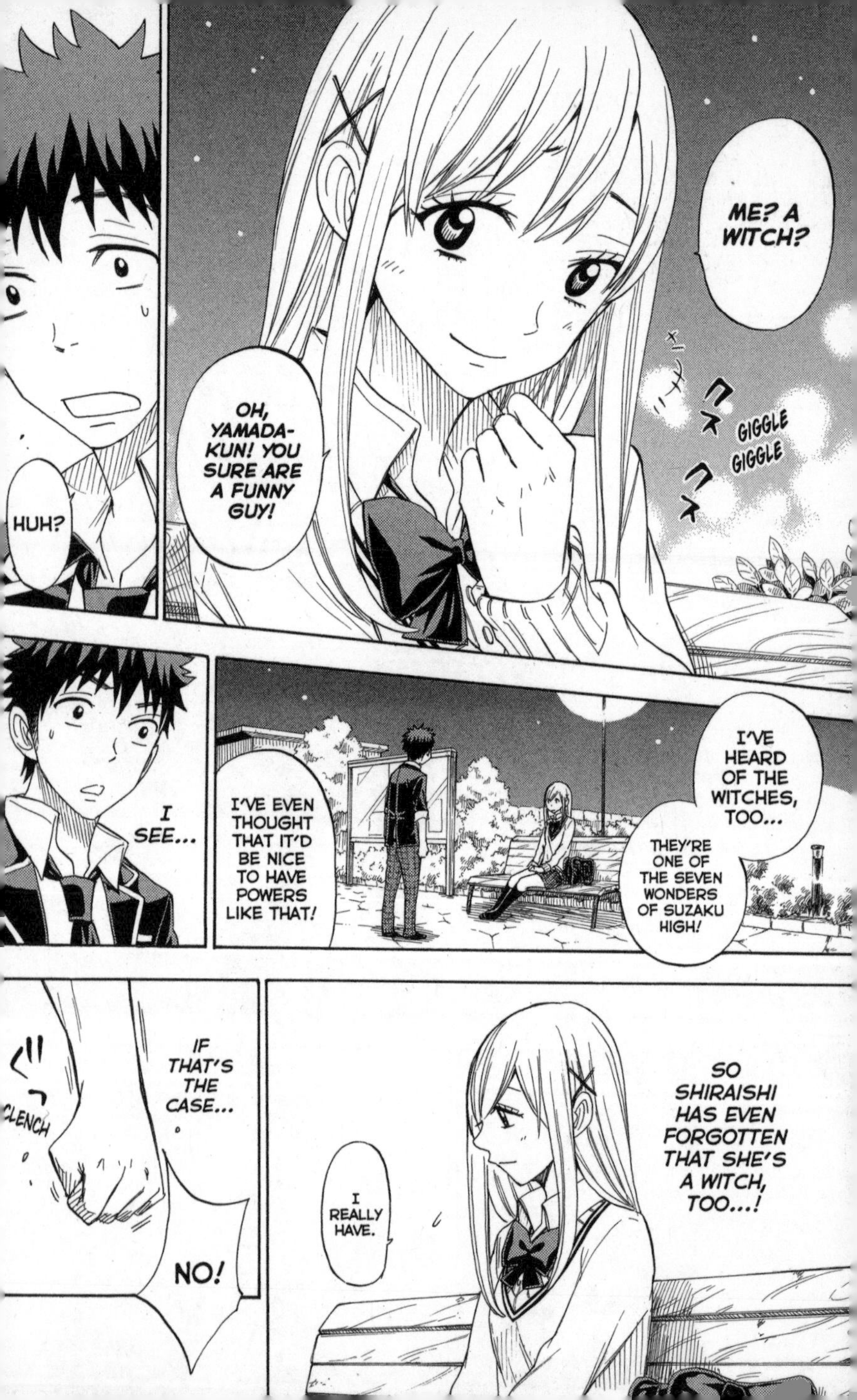
ME? A WITCH?
クス クス
GIGGLE GIGGLE
OH, YAMADA-KUN! YOU SURE ARE A FUNNY GUY!
HUH?
I'VE HEARD OF THE WITCHES, TOO...
THEY'RE ONE OF THE SEVEN WONDERS OF SUZAKU HIGH!
I'VE EVEN THOUGHT THAT IT'D BE NICE TO HAVE POWERS LIKE THAT!
I SEE...
SO SHIRAISHI HAS EVEN FORGOTTEN THAT SHE'S A WITCH, TOO...!
I REALLY HAVE.
IF THAT'S THE CASE...
CLENCH
NO!

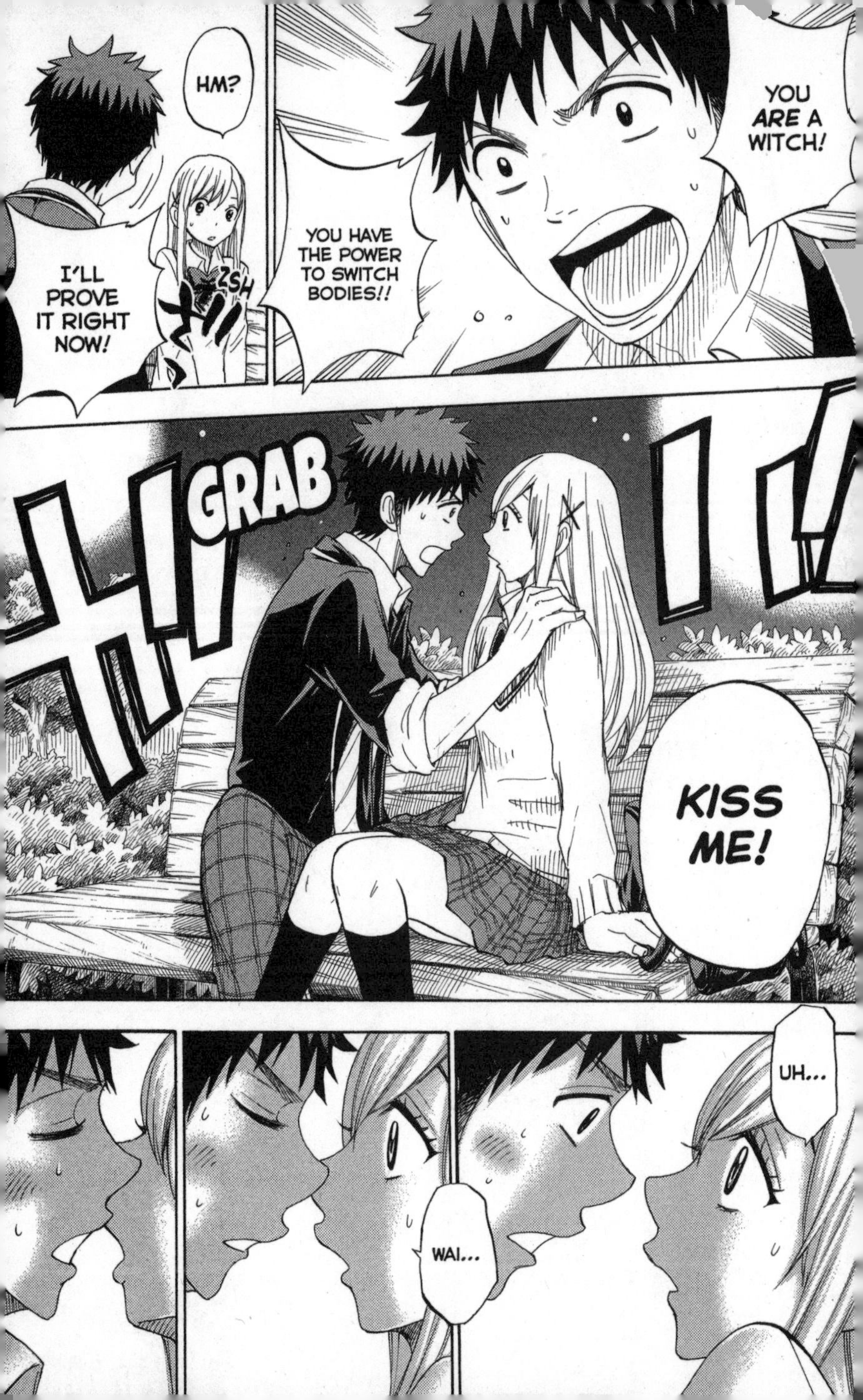
YOU ARE A WITCH!
YOU HAVE THE POWER TO SWITCH BODIES!!
HM?
ZSH
I'LL PROVE IT RIGHT NOW!
GRAB
KISS ME!
UH...
WAI...

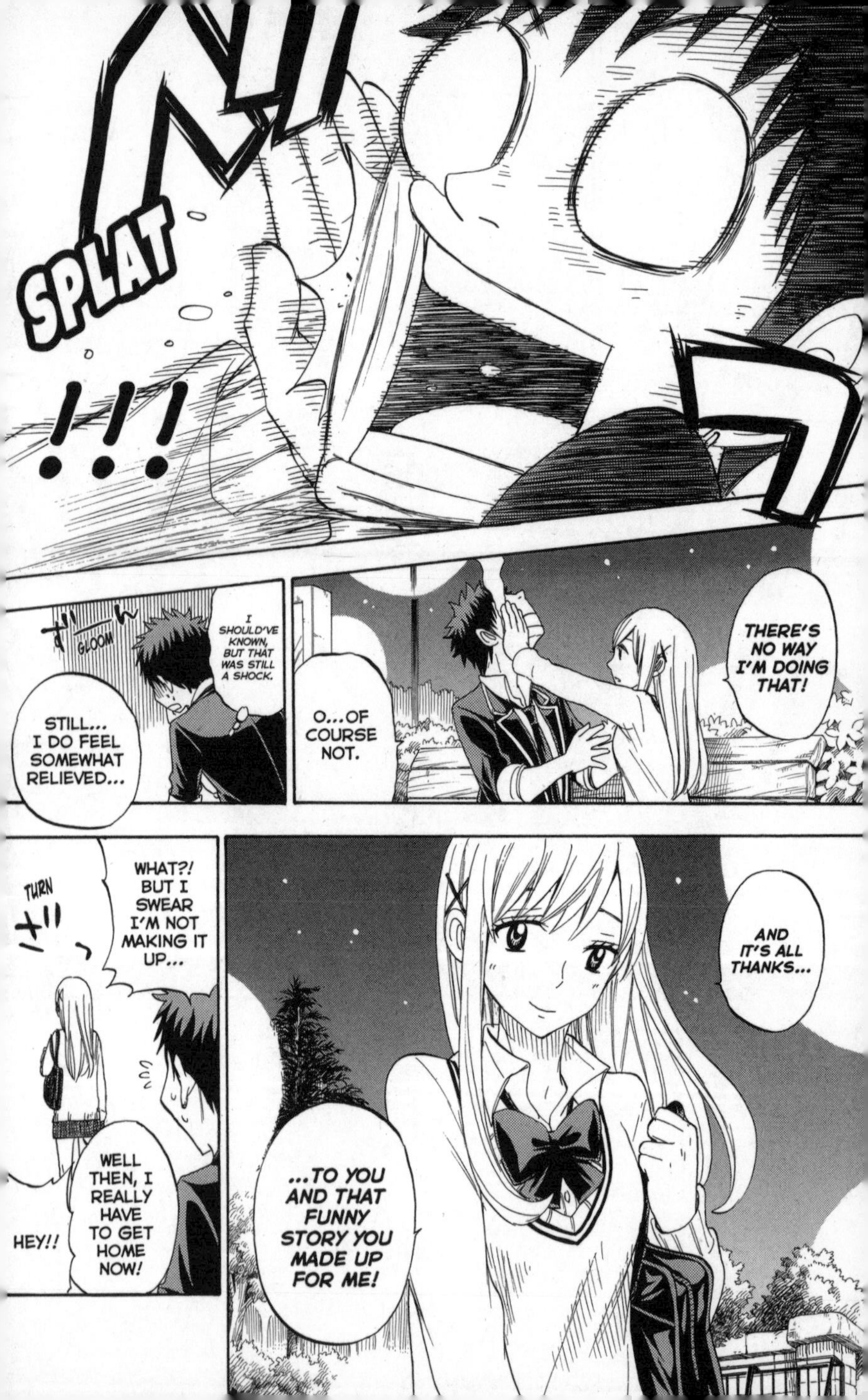
SPLAT
!!!
THERE'S NO WAY I'M DOING THAT!
O...OF COURSE NOT.
I SHOULD'VE KNOWN, BUT THAT WAS STILL A SHOCK.
GLOOM
STILL... I DO FEEL SOMEWHAT RELIEVED...
AND IT'S ALL THANKS...
...TO YOU AND THAT FUNNY STORY YOU MADE UP FOR ME!
WHAT?! BUT I SWEAR I'M NOT MAKING IT UP...
TURN
WELL THEN, I REALLY HAVE TO GET HOME NOW!
HEY!!

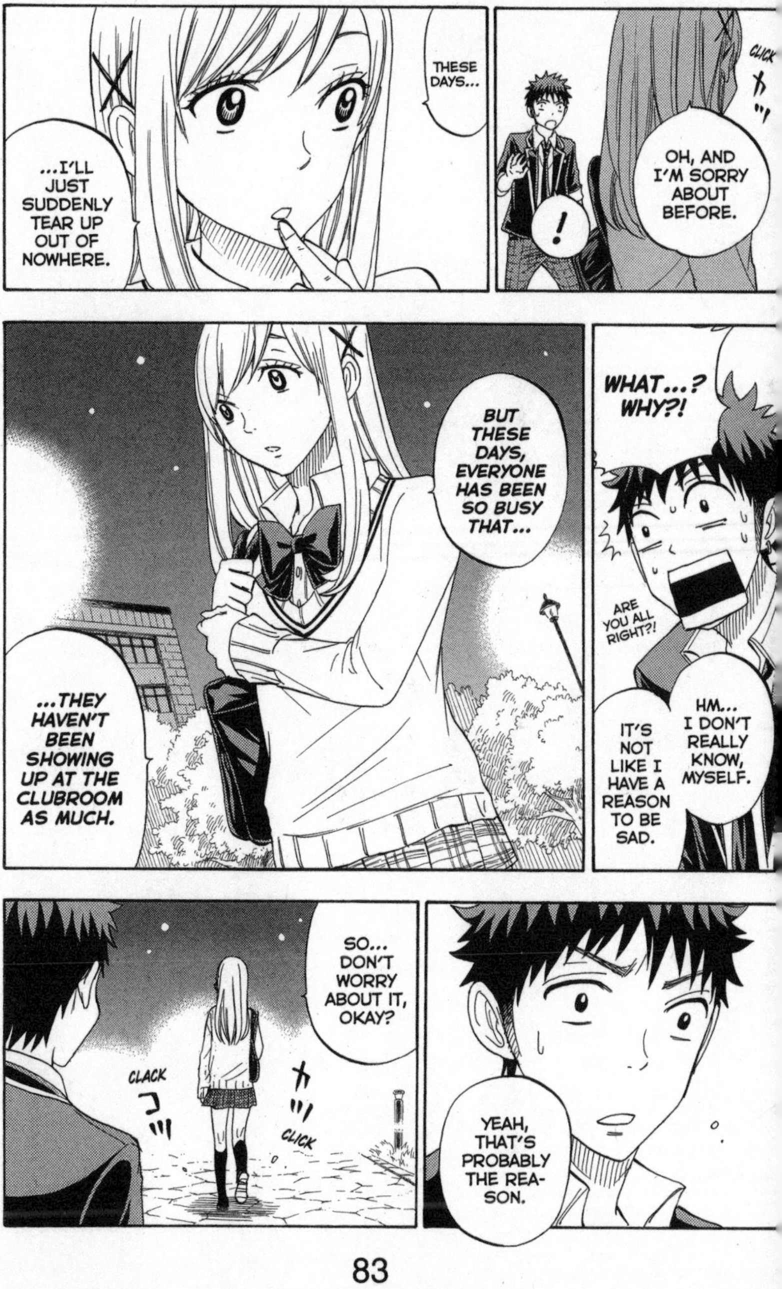
CLICK
OH, AND I'M SORRY ABOUT BEFORE.
!
THESE DAYS...
...I'LL JUST SUDDENLY TEAR UP OUT OF NOWHERE.
WHAT...? WHY?!
ARE YOU ALL RIGHT?!
HM... I DON'T REALLY KNOW, MYSELF.
IT'S NOT LIKE I HAVE A REASON TO BE SAD.
BUT THESE DAYS, EVERYONE HAS BEEN SO BUSY THAT...
...THEY HAVEN'T BEEN SHOWING UP AT THE CLUBROOM AS MUCH.
YEAH, THAT'S PROBABLY THE REA-SON.
SO... DON'T WORRY ABOUT IT, OKAY?
CLACK
CLICK

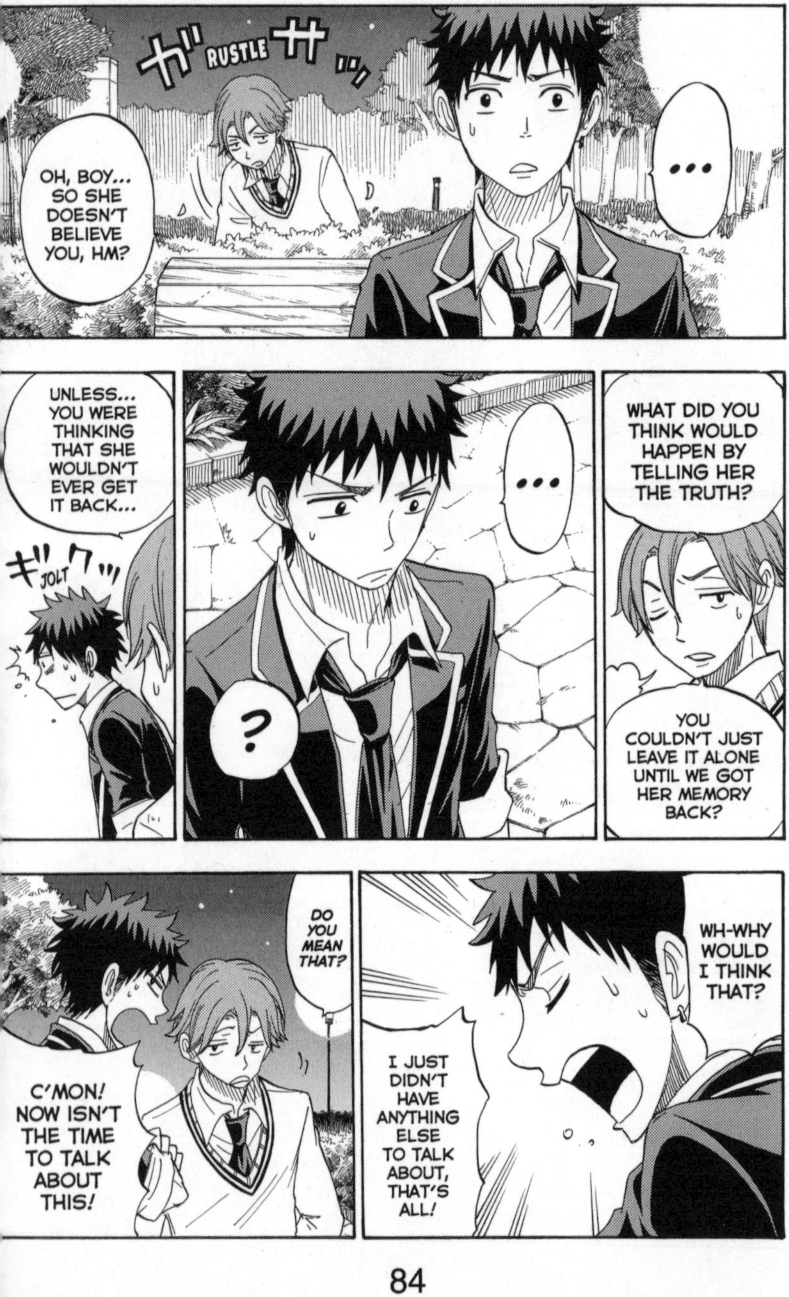
...
RUSTLE
OH, BOY... SO SHE DOESN'T BELIEVE YOU, HM?
WHAT DID YOU THINK WOULD HAPPEN BY TELLING HER THE TRUTH?
YOU COULDN'T JUST LEAVE IT ALONE UNTIL WE GOT HER MEMORY BACK?
...
?
UNLESS... YOU WERE THINKING THAT SHE WOULDN'T EVER GET IT BACK...
JOLT
WH-WHY WOULD I THINK THAT?
I JUST DIDN'T HAVE ANYTHING ELSE TO TALK ABOUT, THAT'S ALL!
DO YOU MEAN THAT?
C'MON! NOW ISN'T THE TIME TO TALK ABOUT THIS!

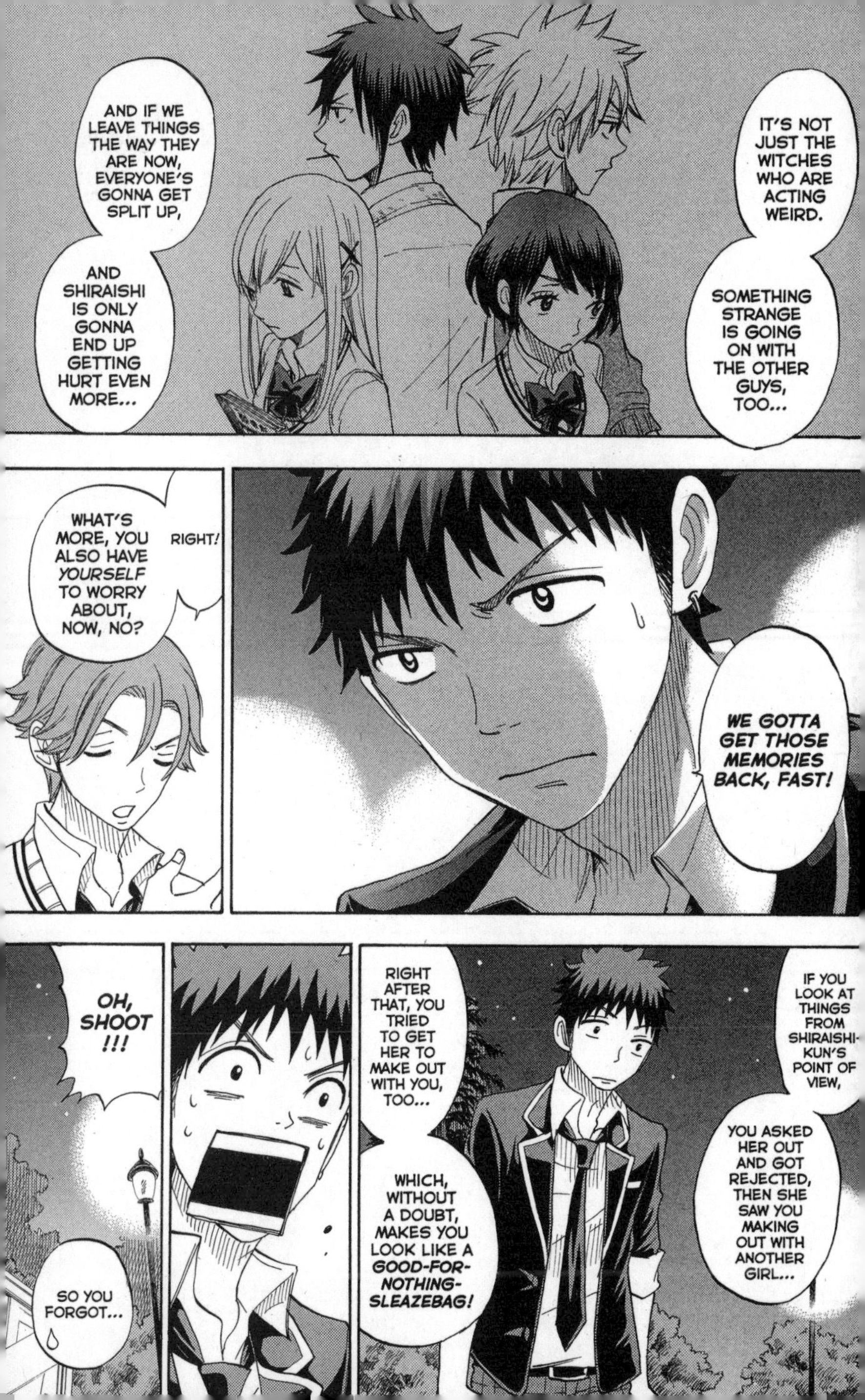
IT'S NOT JUST THE WITCHES WHO ARE ACTING WEIRD.
SOMETHING STRANGE IS GOING ON WITH THE OTHER GUYS, TOO...
AND IF WE LEAVE THINGS THE WAY THEY ARE NOW, EVERYONE'S GONNA GET SPLIT UP,
AND SHIRAISHI IS ONLY GONNA END UP GETTING HURT EVEN MORE...
WE GOTTA GET THOSE MEMORIES BACK, FAST!
WHAT'S MORE, YOU ALSO HAVE *YOURSELF* TO WORRY ABOUT, NOW, NO?
RIGHT!
IF YOU LOOK AT THINGS FROM SHIRAISHI-KUN'S POINT OF VIEW,
YOU ASKED HER OUT AND GOT REJECTED, THEN SHE SAW YOU MAKING OUT WITH ANOTHER GIRL...
RIGHT AFTER THAT, YOU TRIED TO GET HER TO MAKE OUT WITH YOU, TOO...
WHICH, WITHOUT A DOUBT, MAKES YOU LOOK LIKE A *GOOD-FOR-NOTHING-SLEAZEBAG!*
OH, SHOOT!!!
SO YOU FORGOT...

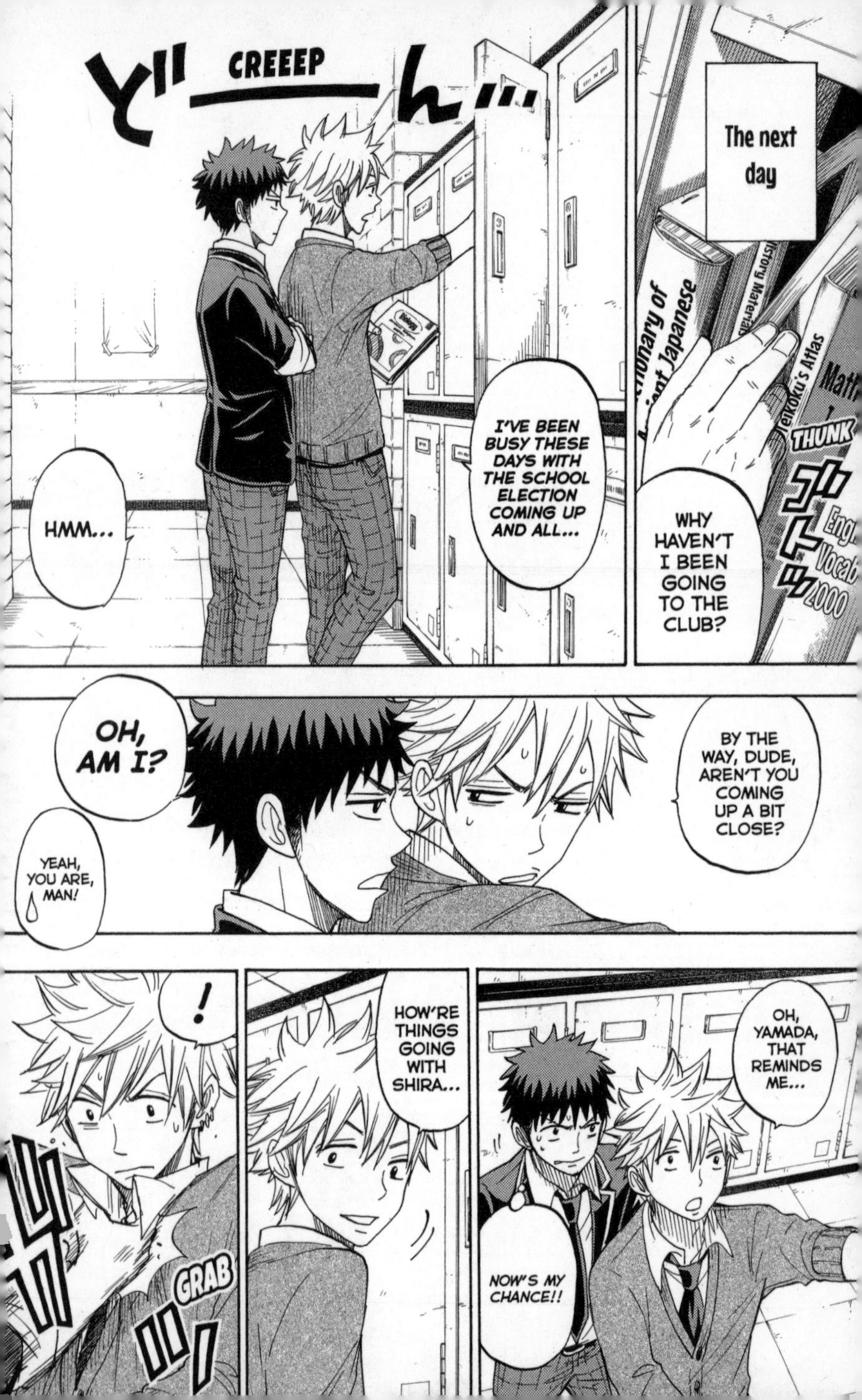
The next day
WHY HAVEN'T I BEEN GOING TO THE CLUB?
THUNK
CREEEP
I'VE BEEN BUSY THESE DAYS WITH THE SCHOOL ELECTION COMING UP AND ALL...
HMM...
BY THE WAY, DUDE, AREN'T YOU COMING UP A BIT CLOSE?
OH, AM I?
YEAH, YOU ARE, MAN!
OH, YAMADA, THAT REMINDS ME...
NOW'S MY CHANCE!!
HOW'RE THINGS GOING WITH SHIRA...
!
GRAB

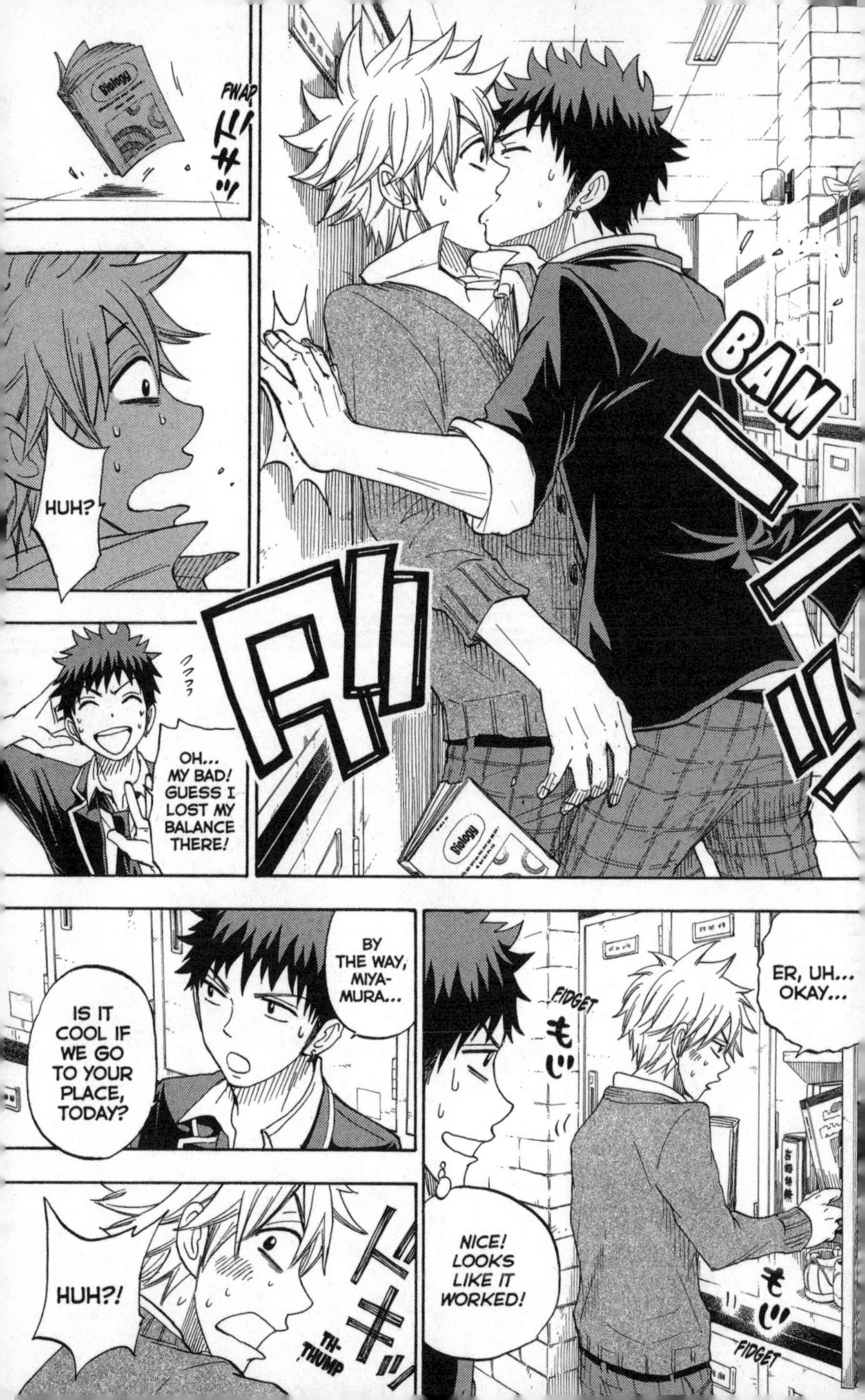
BAM
FWAP
HUH?
OH... MY BAD! GUESS I LOST MY BALANCE THERE!
ER, UH... OKAY...
FIDGET
NICE! LOOKS LIKE IT WORKED!
FIDGET
BY THE WAY, MIYA-MURA...
IS IT COOL IF WE GO TO YOUR PLACE, TODAY?
HUH?!
TH-THUMP

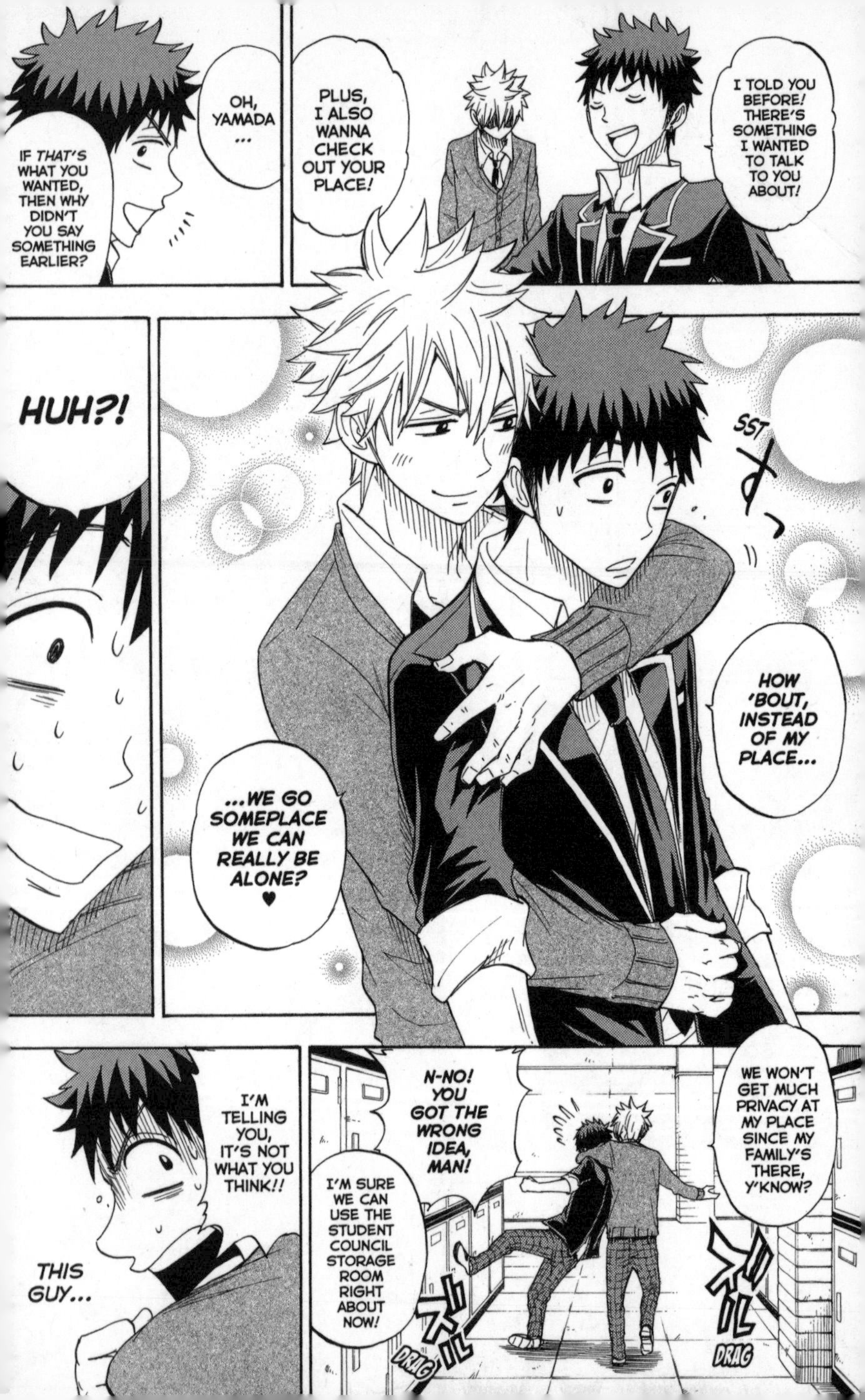
I TOLD YOU BEFORE! THERE'S SOMETHING I WANTED TO TALK TO YOU ABOUT!
PLUS, I ALSO WANNA CHECK OUT YOUR PLACE!
OH, YAMADA...
IF *THAT'S* WHAT YOU WANTED, THEN WHY DIDN'T YOU SAY SOMETHING EARLIER?
SST
HOW 'BOUT, INSTEAD OF MY PLACE...
...WE GO SOMEPLACE WE CAN REALLY BE ALONE? ♥
HUH?!
WE WON'T GET MUCH PRIVACY AT MY PLACE SINCE MY FAMILY'S THERE, Y'KNOW?
N-NO! YOU GOT THE WRONG IDEA, MAN!
I'M SURE WE CAN USE THE STUDENT COUNCIL STORAGE ROOM RIGHT ABOUT NOW!
DRAG
DRAG
I'M TELLING YOU, IT'S NOT WHAT YOU THINK!!
THIS GUY...

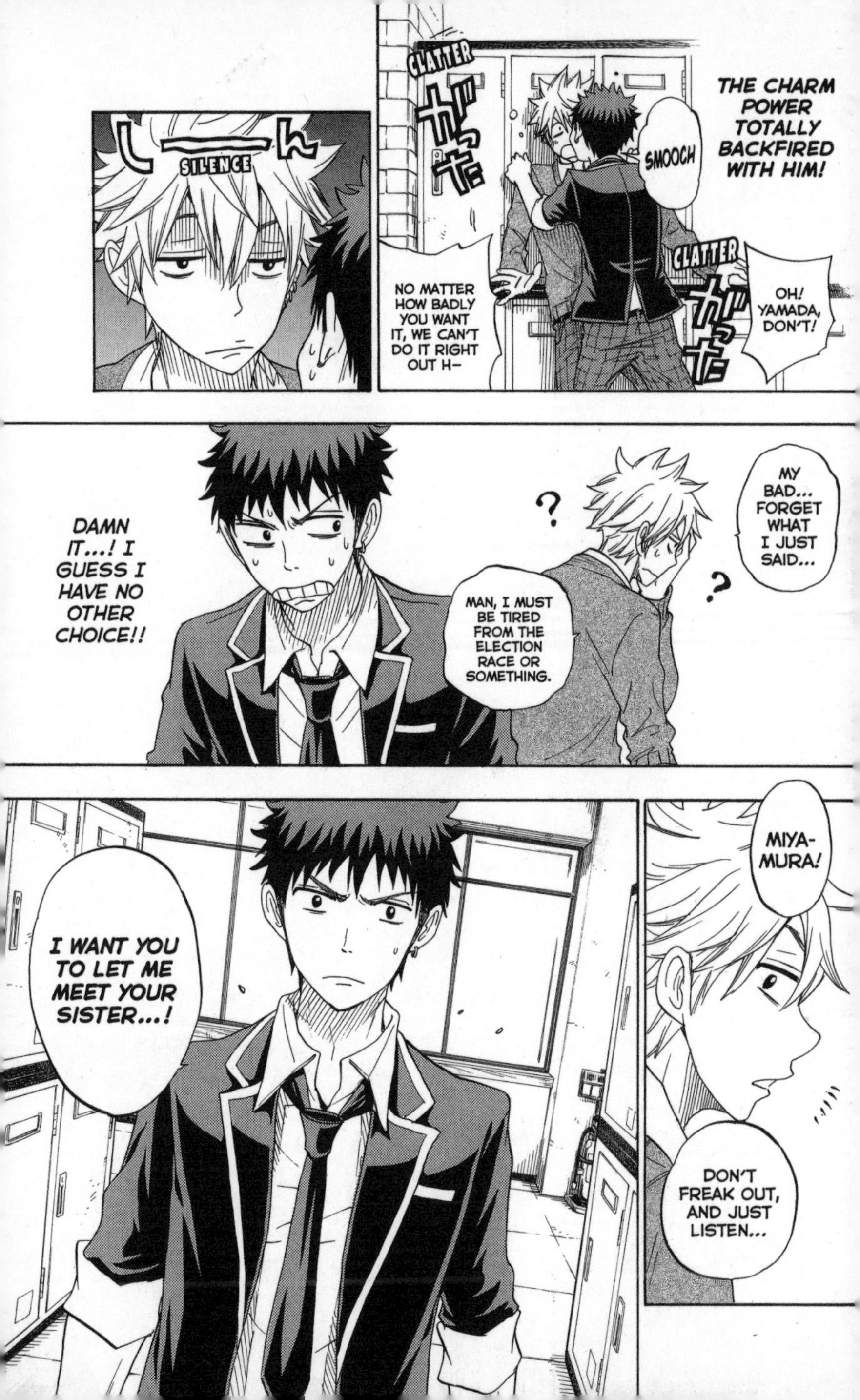
THE CHARM POWER TOTALLY BACKFIRED WITH HIM!
SMOOCH
CLATTER
OH! YAMADA, DON'T!
CLATTER
NO MATTER HOW BADLY YOU WANT IT, WE CAN'T DO IT RIGHT OUT H–
SILENCE
MY BAD... FORGET WHAT I JUST SAID...
MAN, I MUST BE TIRED FROM THE ELECTION RACE OR SOMETHING.
DAMN IT...! I GUESS I HAVE NO OTHER CHOICE!!
MIYA-MURA!
DON'T FREAK OUT, AND JUST LISTEN...
I WANT YOU TO LET ME MEET YOUR SISTER...!

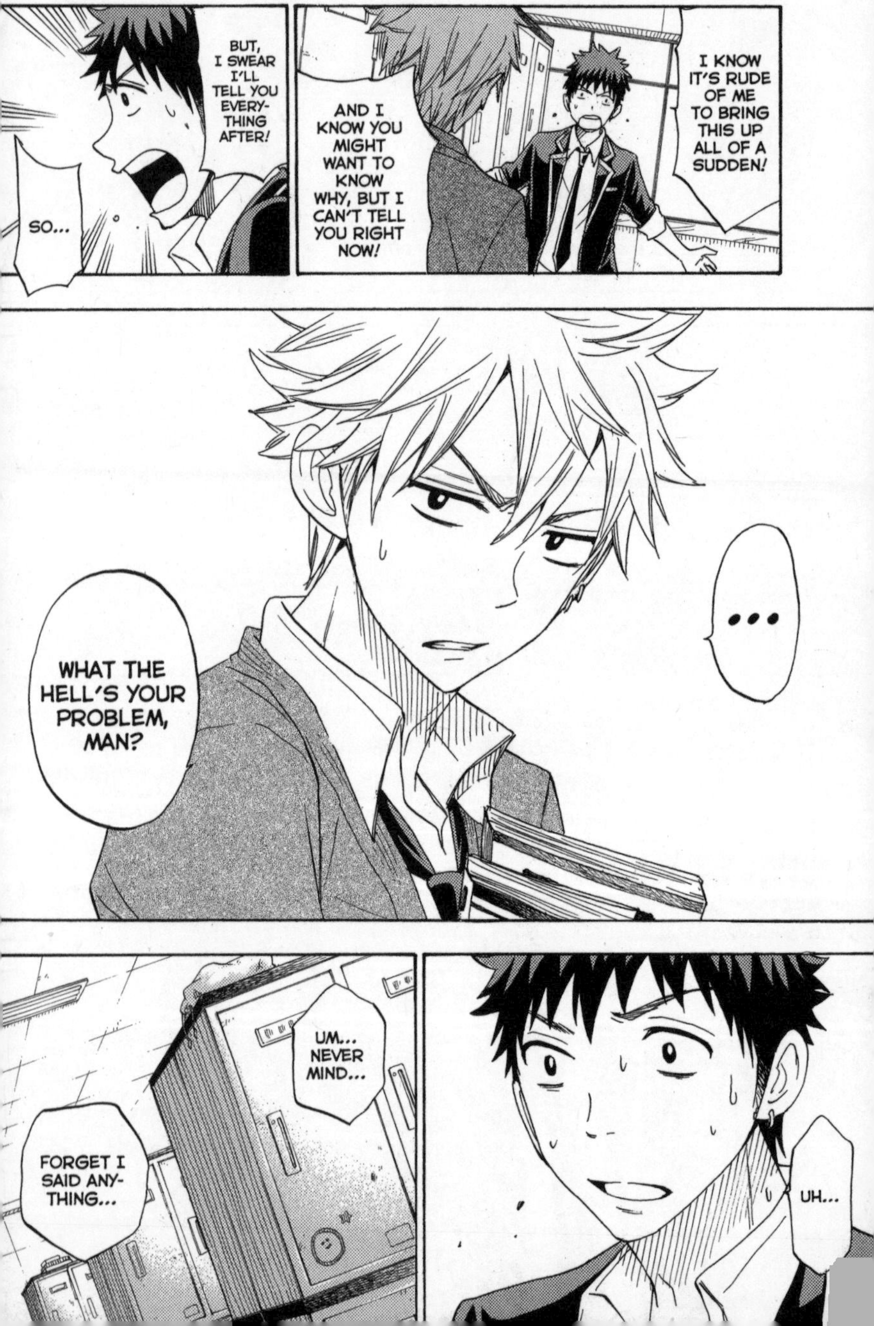
I KNOW IT'S RUDE OF ME TO BRING THIS UP ALL OF A SUDDEN!
AND I KNOW YOU MIGHT WANT TO KNOW WHY, BUT I CAN'T TELL YOU RIGHT NOW!
BUT, I SWEAR I'LL TELL YOU EVERY-THING AFTER!
SO...
...
WHAT THE HELL'S YOUR PROBLEM, MAN?
UH...
UM... NEVER MIND...
FORGET I SAID ANY-THING...

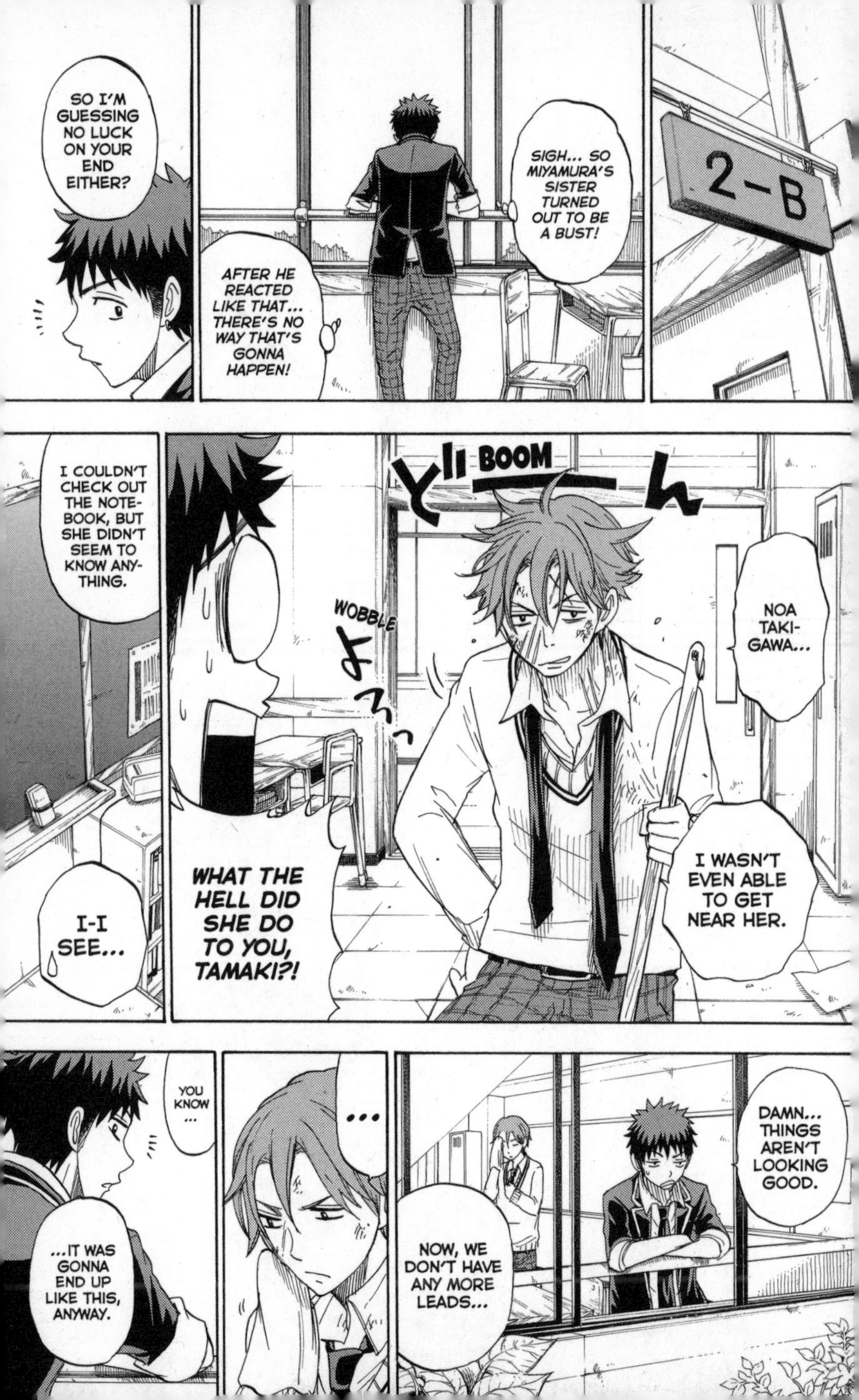
SIGH... SO MIYAMURA'S SISTER TURNED OUT TO BE A BUST!
AFTER HE REACTED LIKE THAT... THERE'S NO WAY THAT'S GONNA HAPPEN!
SO I'M GUESSING NO LUCK ON YOUR END EITHER?
BOOM
NOA TAKI-GAWA...
I WASN'T EVEN ABLE TO GET NEAR HER.
WOBBLE
WHAT THE HELL DID SHE DO TO YOU, TAMAKI?!
I COULDN'T CHECK OUT THE NOTE-BOOK, BUT SHE DIDN'T SEEM TO KNOW ANY-THING.
I-I SEE...
DAMN... THINGS AREN'T LOOKING GOOD.
NOW, WE DON'T HAVE ANY MORE LEADS...
...
YOU KNOW ...
...IT WAS GONNA END UP LIKE THIS, ANYWAY.

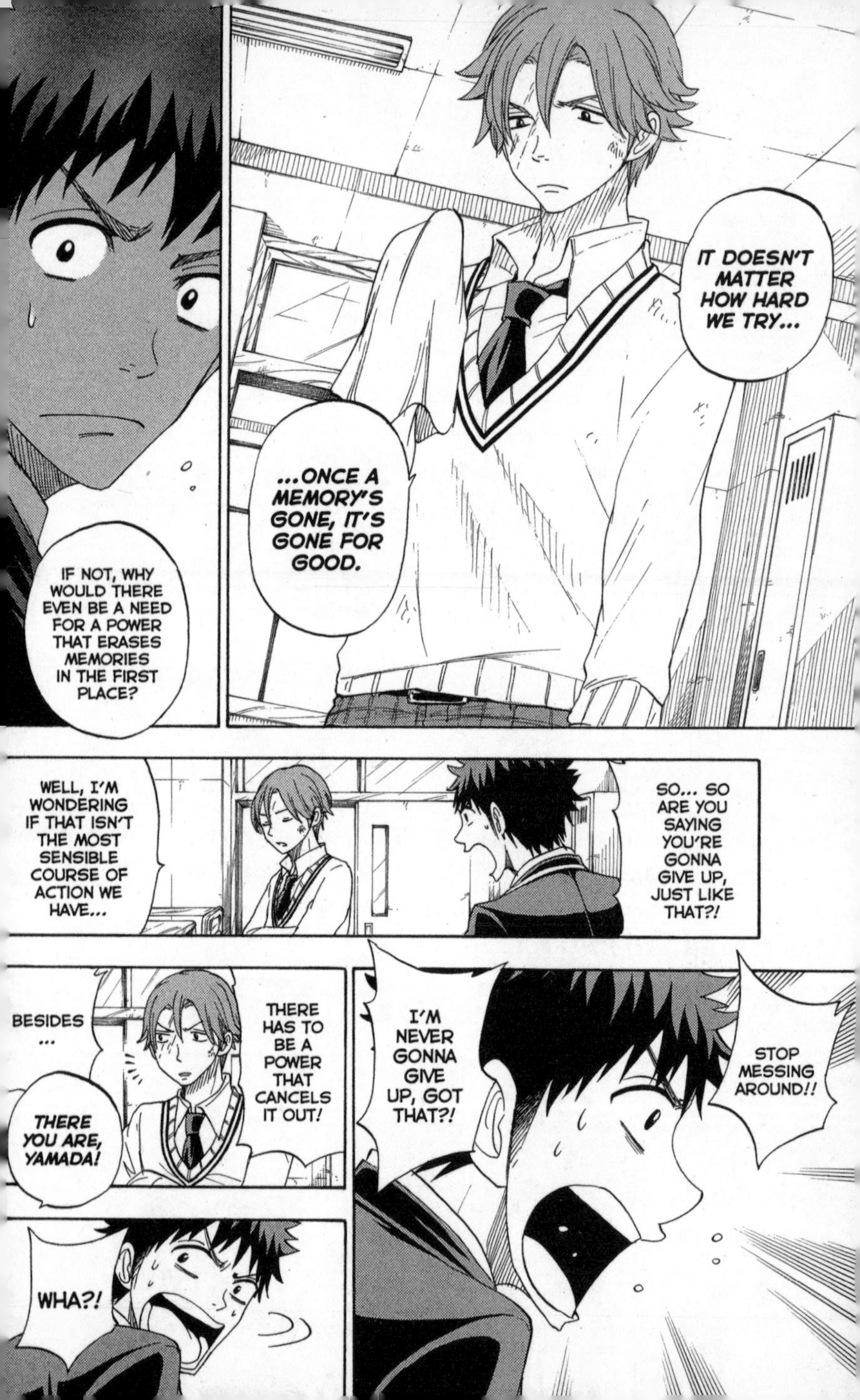
IT DOESN'T MATTER HOW HARD WE TRY...
...ONCE A MEMORY'S GONE, IT'S GONE FOR GOOD.
IF NOT, WHY WOULD THERE EVEN BE A NEED FOR A POWER THAT ERASES MEMORIES IN THE FIRST PLACE?
SO... SO ARE YOU SAYING YOU'RE GONNA GIVE UP, JUST LIKE THAT?!
WELL, I'M WONDERING IF THAT ISN'T THE MOST SENSIBLE COURSE OF ACTION WE HAVE...
STOP MESSING AROUND!!
I'M NEVER GONNA GIVE UP, GOT THAT?!
THERE HAS TO BE A POWER THAT CANCELS IT OUT!
BESIDES...
THERE YOU ARE, YAMADA!
WHA?!

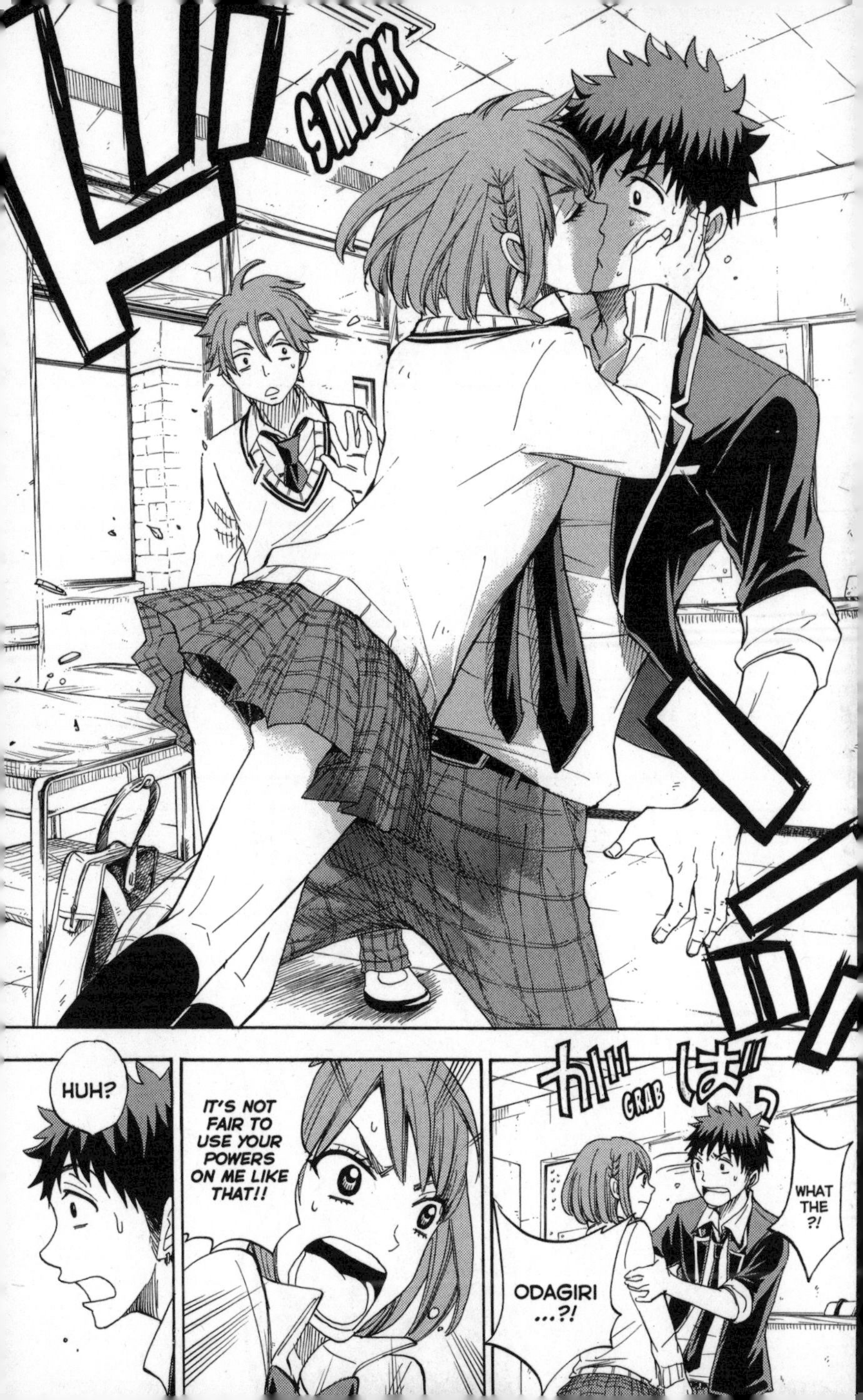
SMACK
GRAB
WHAT THE ?!
ODAGIRI ...?!
IT'S NOT FAIR TO USE YOUR POWERS ON ME LIKE THAT!!
HUH?

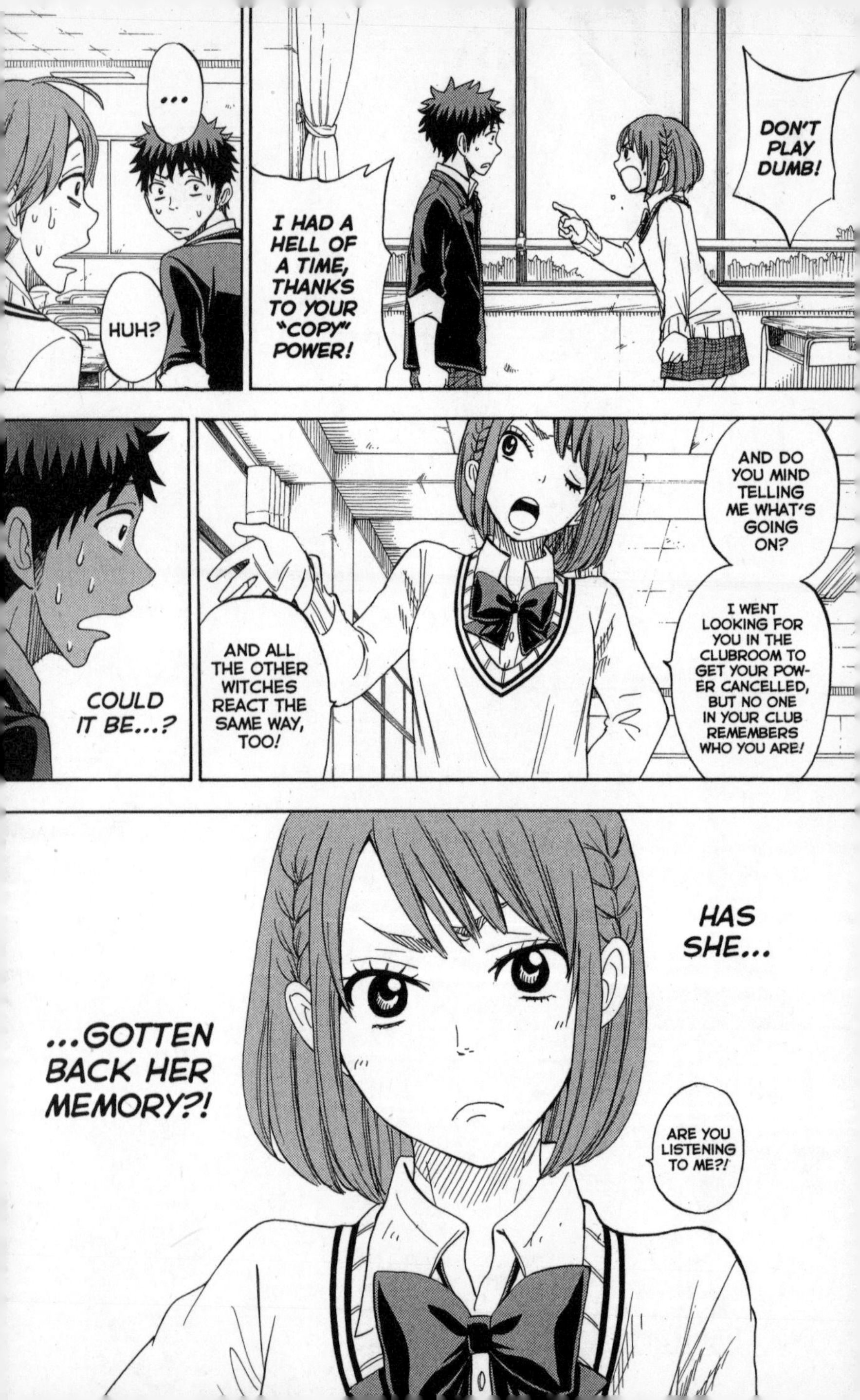
DON'T PLAY DUMB!
I HAD A HELL OF A TIME, THANKS TO YOUR "COPY" POWER!
...
HUH?
AND DO YOU MIND TELLING ME WHAT'S GOING ON?
I WENT LOOKING FOR YOU IN THE CLUBROOM TO GET YOUR POW-ER CANCELLED, BUT NO ONE IN YOUR CLUB REMEMBERS WHO YOU ARE!
AND ALL THE OTHER WITCHES REACT THE SAME WAY, TOO!
COULD IT BE...?
HAS SHE...
...GOTTEN BACK HER MEMORY?!
ARE YOU LISTENING TO ME?!

CHAPTER 74: You're a real creep!

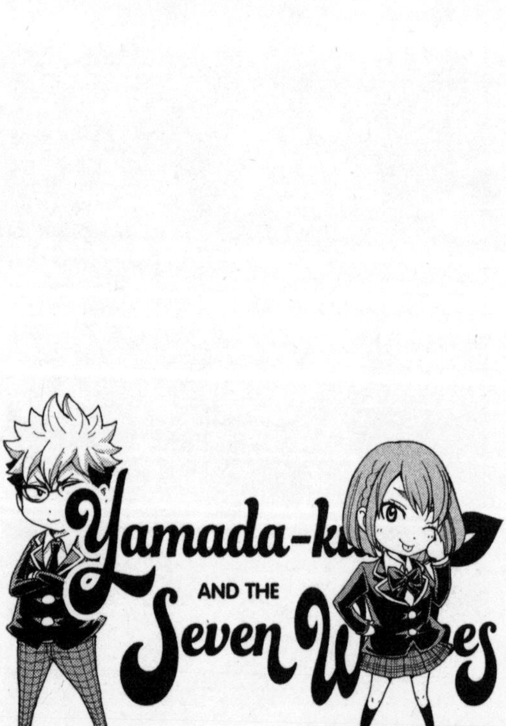
AND THE

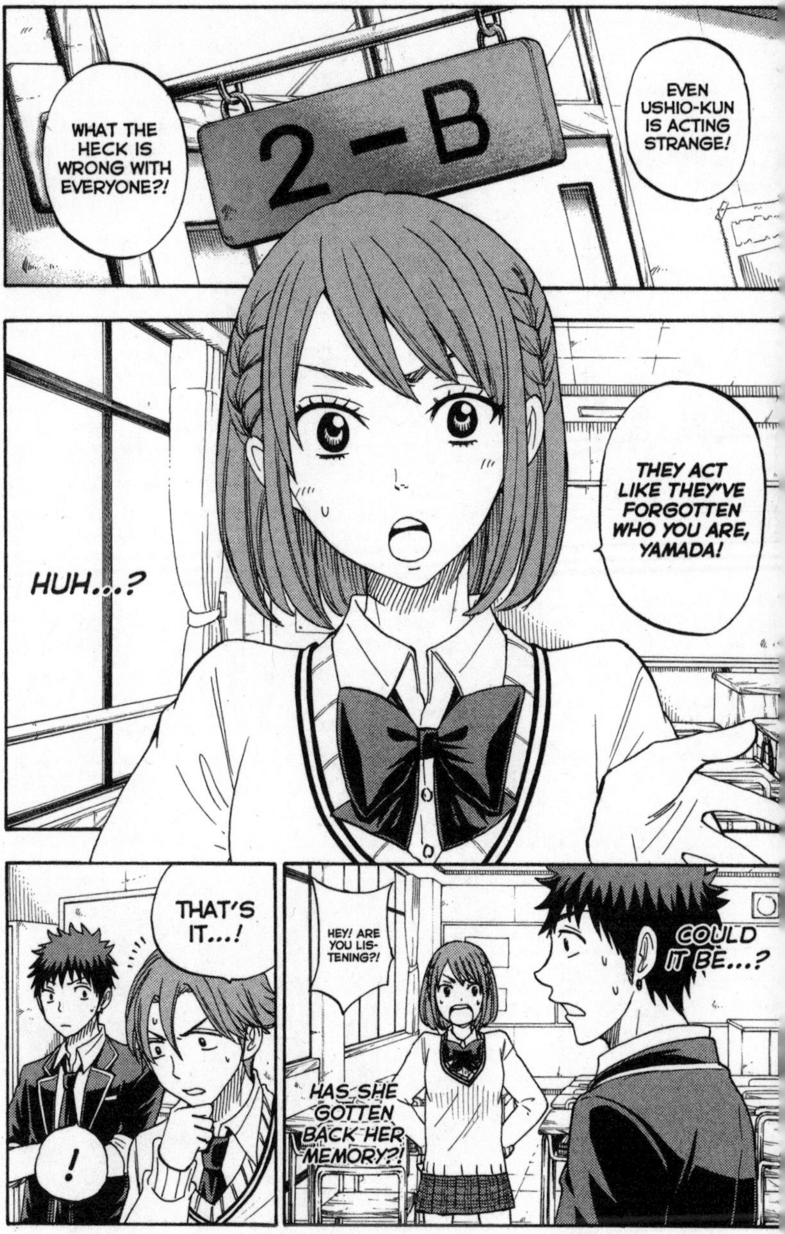
EVEN USHIO-KUN IS ACTING STRANGE!
WHAT THE HECK IS WRONG WITH EVERYONE?!
2-B
THEY ACT LIKE THEY'VE FORGOTTEN WHO YOU ARE, YAMADA!
HUH...?
COULD IT BE...?
HEY! ARE YOU LIS-TENING?!
HAS SHE GOTTEN BACK HER MEMORY?!
THAT'S IT...!
!

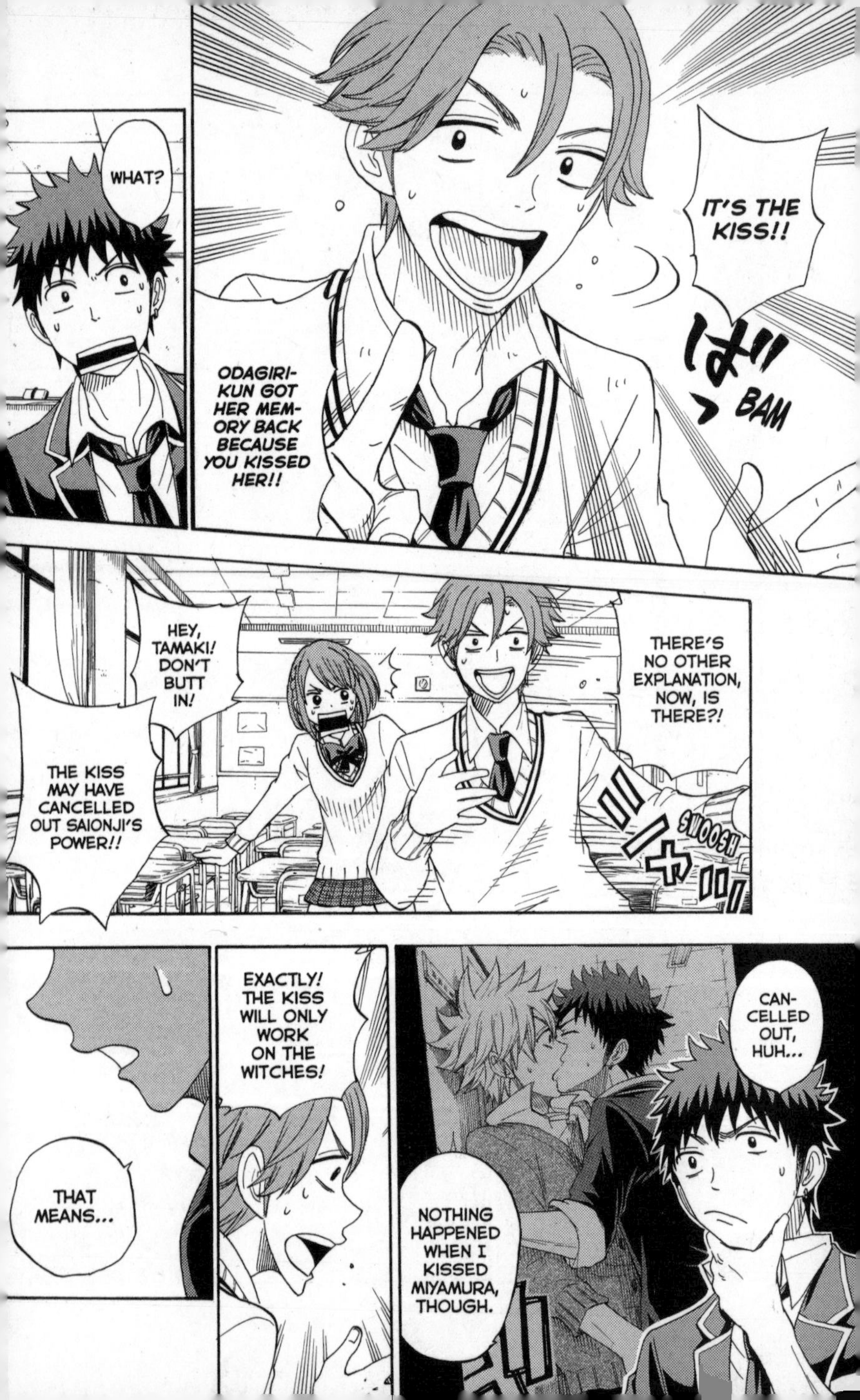

IT'S THE KISS!!
BAM
ODAGIRI-KUN GOT HER MEMORY BACK BECAUSE YOU KISSED HER!!
WHAT?
THERE'S NO OTHER EXPLANATION, NOW, IS THERE?!
SWOOSH
HEY, TAMAKI! DON'T BUTT IN!
THE KISS MAY HAVE CANCELLED OUT SAIONJI'S POWER!!
CAN-CELLED OUT, HUH...
NOTHING HAPPENED WHEN I KISSED MIYAMURA, THOUGH.
EXACTLY! THE KISS WILL ONLY WORK ON THE WITCHES!
THAT MEANS...

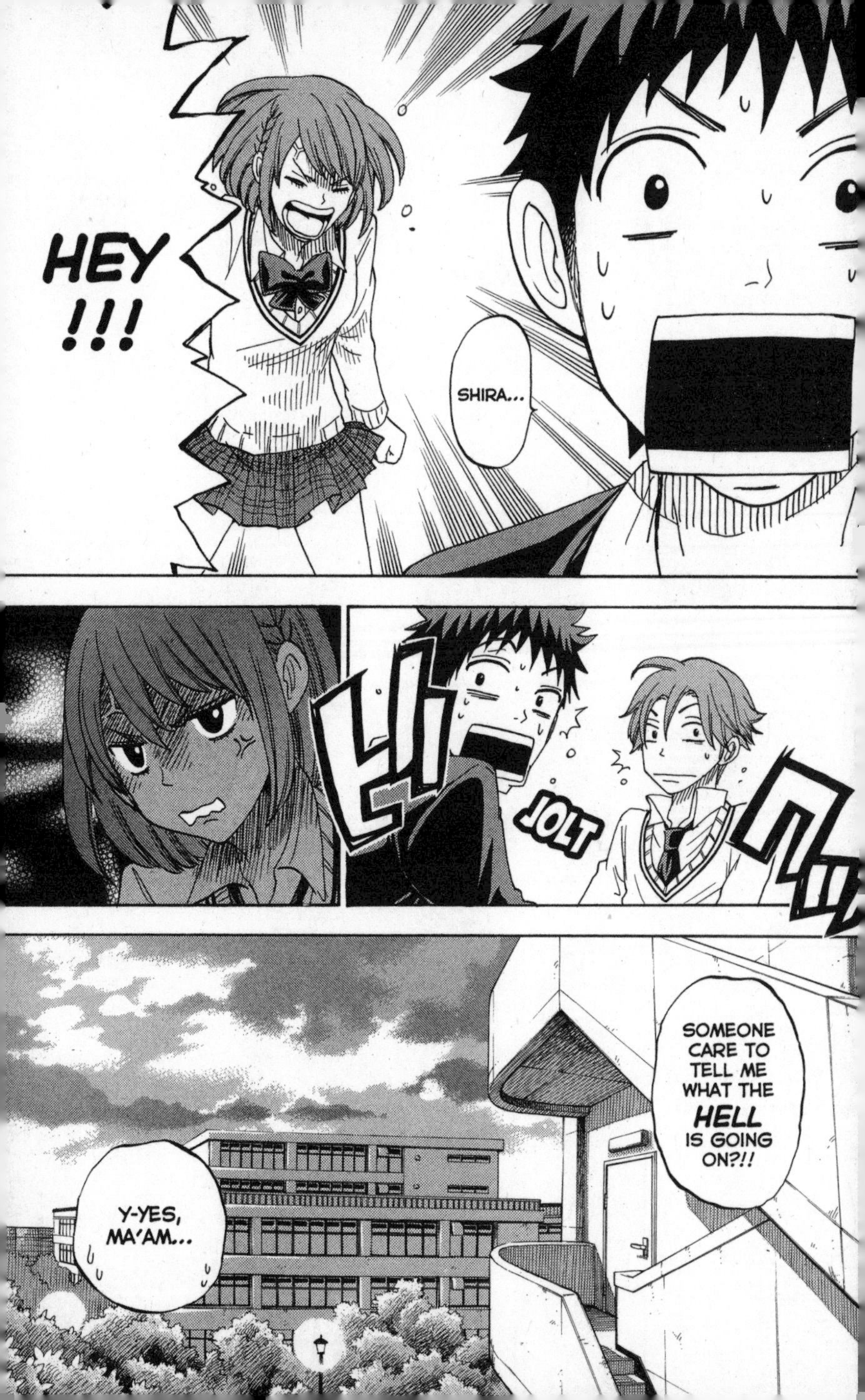
SHIRA...
HEY !!!
JOLT
SOMEONE CARE TO TELL ME WHAT THE HELL IS GOING ON?!!
Y-YES, MA'AM...

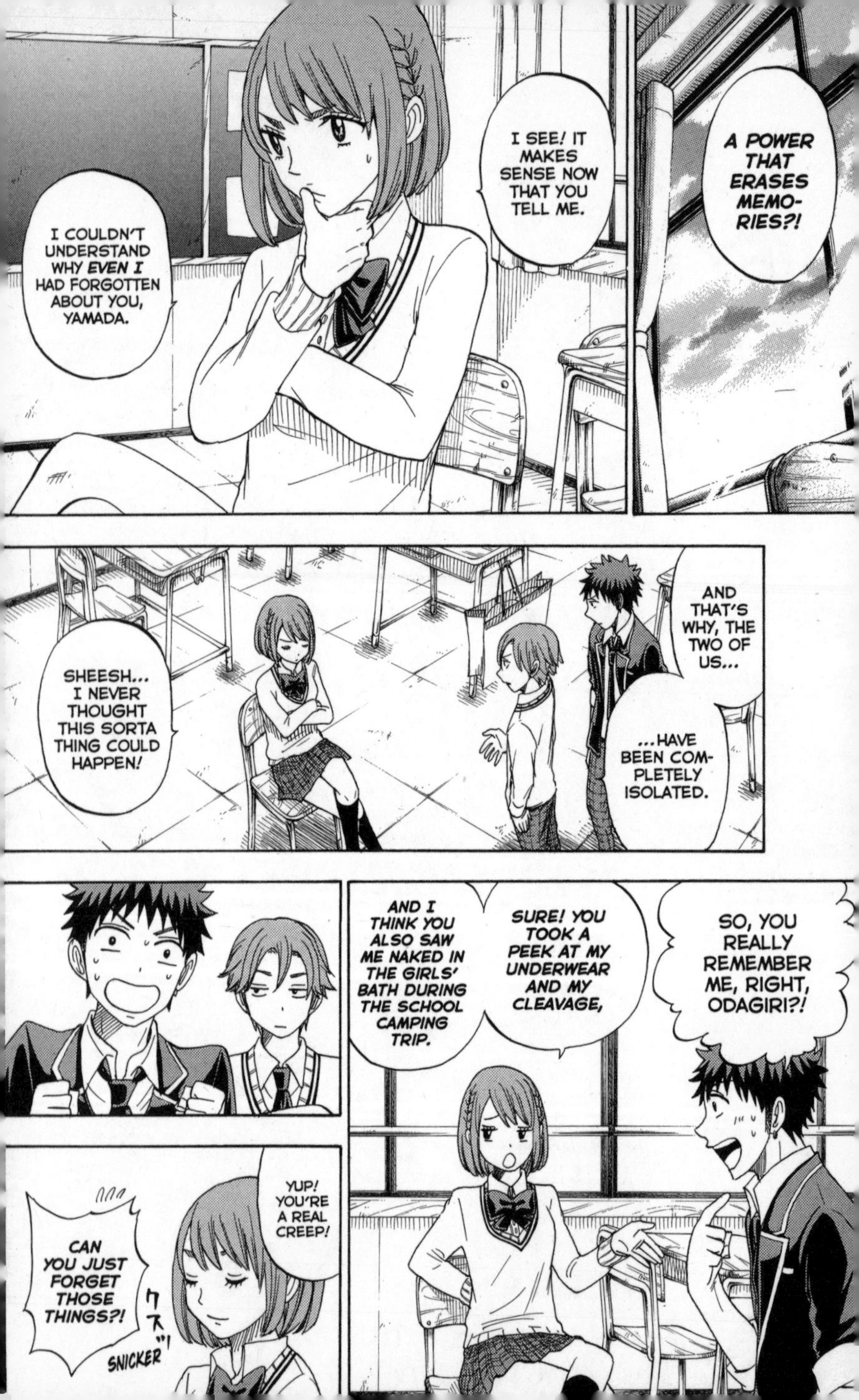
A POWER THAT ERASES MEMORIES?!
I SEE! IT MAKES SENSE NOW THAT YOU TELL ME.
I COULDN'T UNDERSTAND WHY *EVEN I* HAD FORGOTTEN ABOUT YOU, YAMADA.
AND THAT'S WHY, THE TWO OF US...
...HAVE BEEN COMPLETELY ISOLATED.
SHEESH... I NEVER THOUGHT THIS SORTA THING COULD HAPPEN!
SO, YOU REALLY REMEMBER ME, RIGHT, ODAGIRI?!
SURE! YOU TOOK A PEEK AT MY UNDERWEAR AND MY CLEAVAGE,
AND I THINK YOU ALSO SAW ME NAKED IN THE GIRLS' BATH DURING THE SCHOOL CAMPING TRIP.
YUP! YOU'RE A REAL CREEP!
CAN YOU JUST FORGET THOSE THINGS?!
クスッ
SNICKER

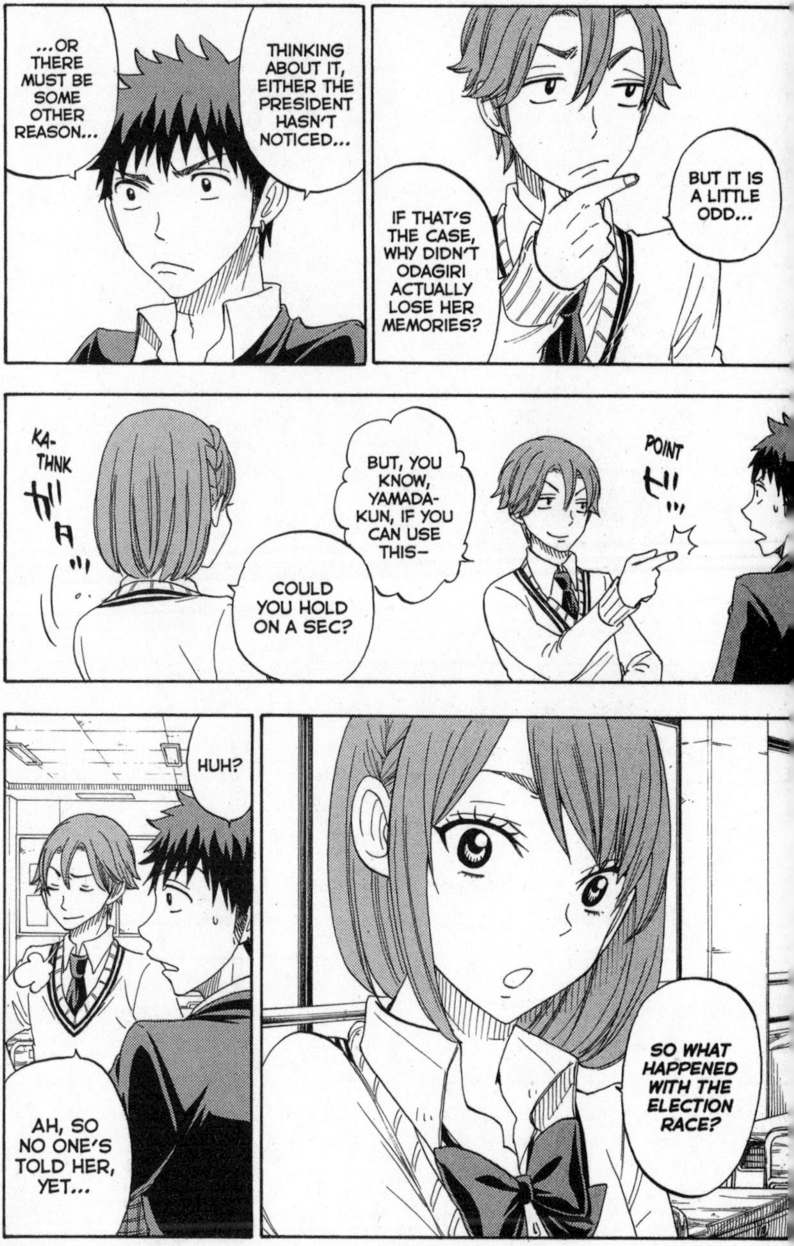
BUT IT IS A LITTLE ODD...
IF THAT'S THE CASE, WHY DIDN'T ODAGIRI ACTUALLY LOSE HER MEMORIES?
THINKING ABOUT IT, EITHER THE PRESIDENT HASN'T NOTICED...
...OR THERE MUST BE SOME OTHER REASON...
POINT
BUT, YOU KNOW, YAMADA-KUN, IF YOU CAN USE THIS–
COULD YOU HOLD ON A SEC?
KA-THNK
SO WHAT HAPPENED WITH THE ELECTION RACE?
HUH?
AH, SO NO ONE'S TOLD HER, YET...

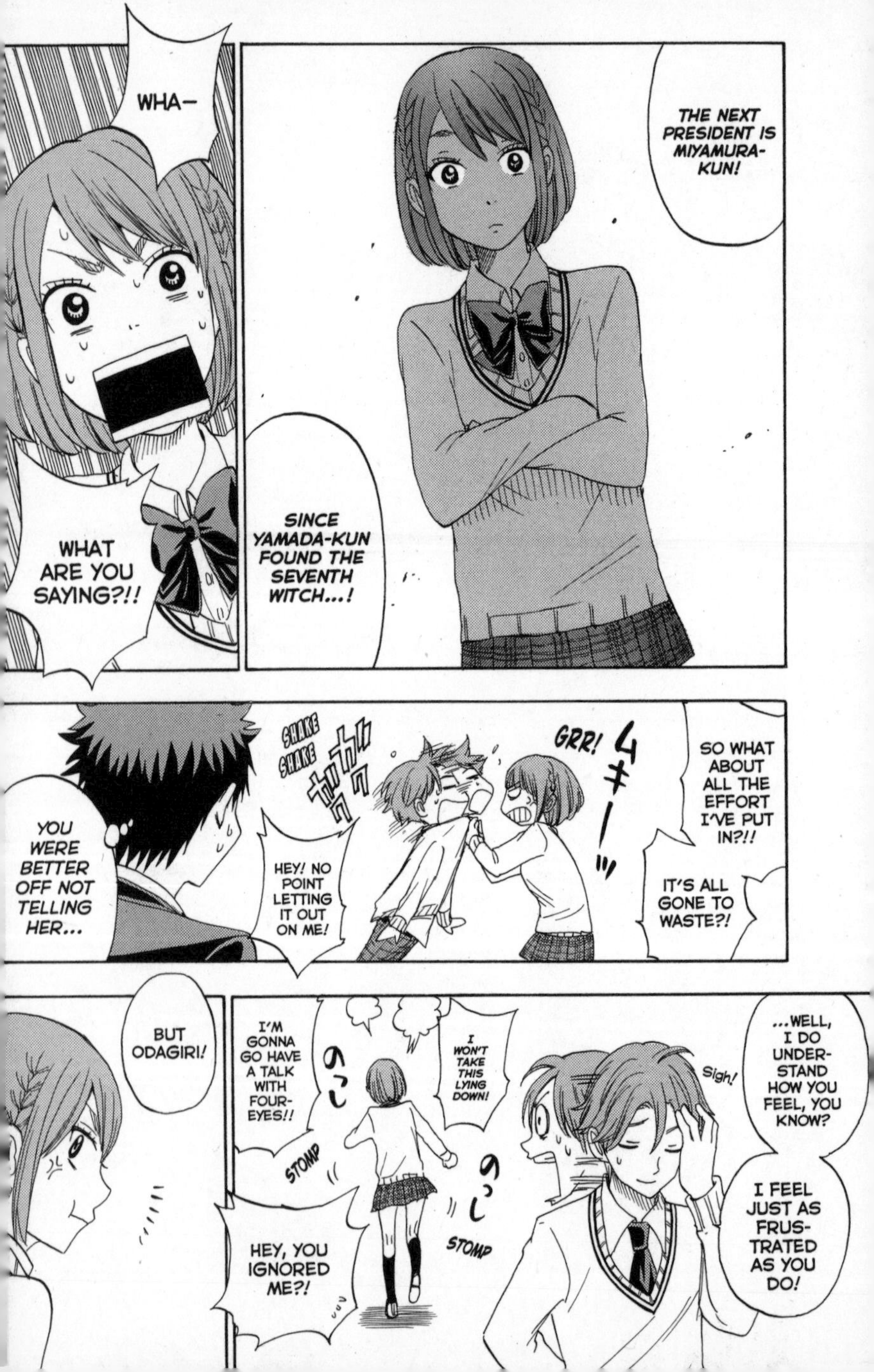
THE NEXT PRESIDENT IS MIYAMURA-KUN!
SINCE YAMADA-KUN FOUND THE SEVENTH WITCH...!
WHA—
WHAT ARE YOU SAYING?!!
GRR!
ムキー!
SO WHAT ABOUT ALL THE EFFORT I'VE PUT IN?!!
IT'S ALL GONE TO WASTE?!
SHAKE SHAKE
HEY! NO POINT LETTING IT OUT ON ME!
YOU WERE BETTER OFF NOT TELLING HER...
...WELL, I DO UNDERSTAND HOW YOU FEEL, YOU KNOW?
Sigh!
I FEEL JUST AS FRUSTRATED AS YOU DO!
I WON'T TAKE THIS LYING DOWN!
I'M GONNA GO HAVE A TALK WITH FOUR-EYES!!
STOMP
STOMP
HEY, YOU IGNORED ME?!
BUT ODAGIRI!

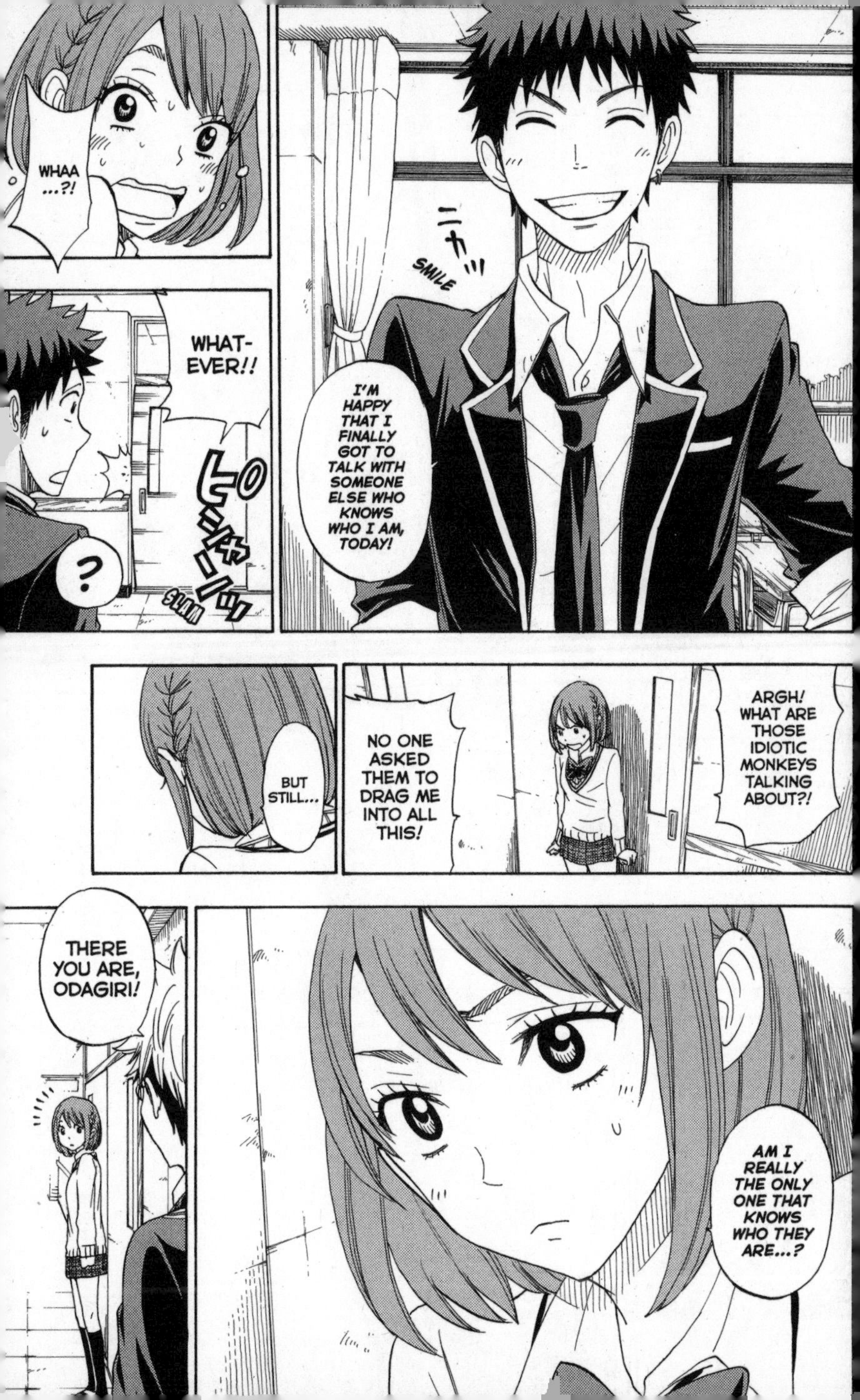
ニカッ
SMILE
I'M HAPPY THAT I FINALLY GOT TO TALK WITH SOMEONE ELSE WHO KNOWS WHO I AM, TODAY!
WHAA ...?!
WHAT-EVER!!
SLAM
?
ARGH! WHAT ARE THOSE IDIOTIC MONKEYS TALKING ABOUT?!
NO ONE ASKED THEM TO DRAG ME INTO ALL THIS!
BUT STILL...
AM I REALLY THE ONLY ONE THAT KNOWS WHO THEY ARE...?
THERE YOU ARE, ODAGIRI!

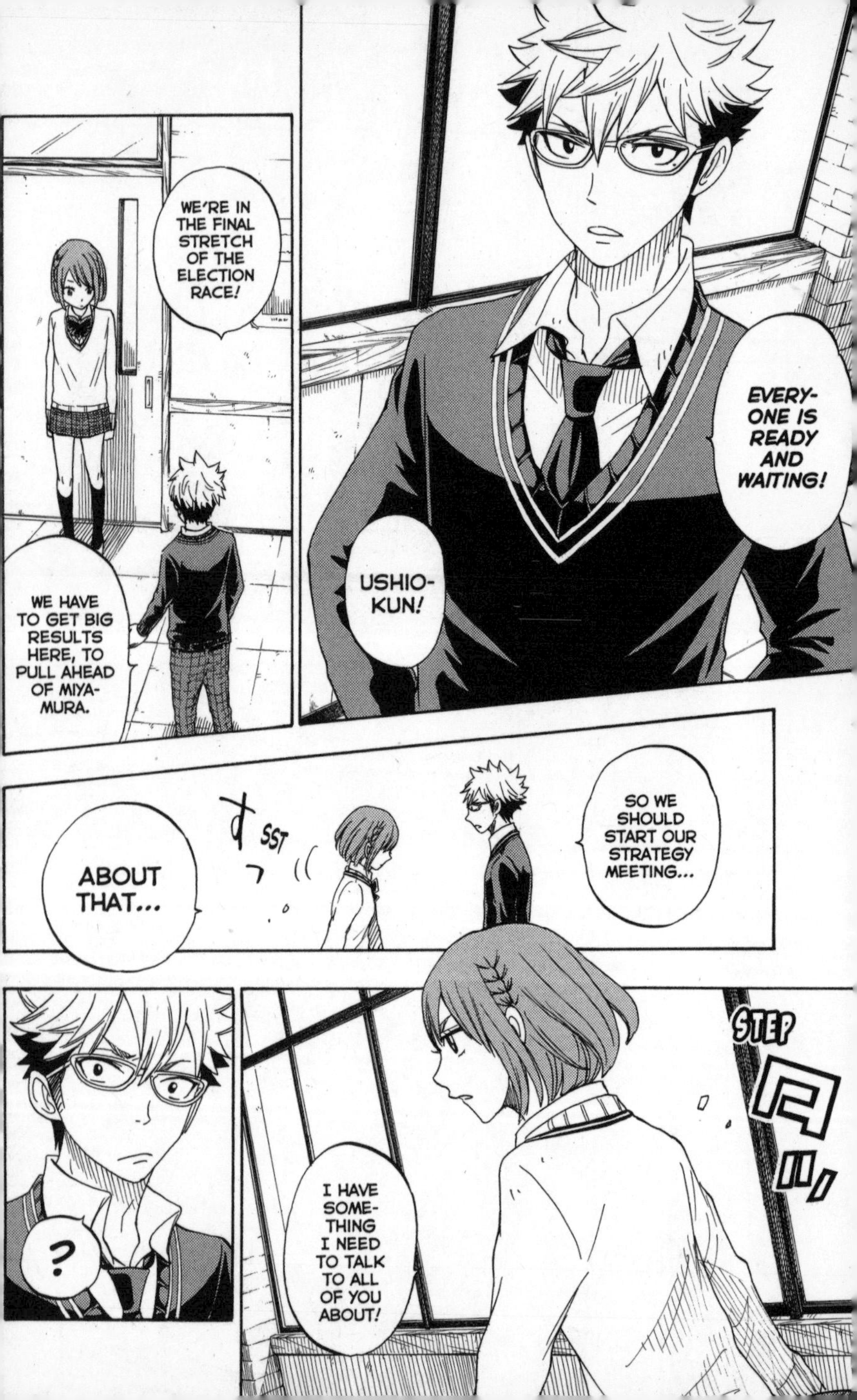
EVERY-ONE IS READY AND WAITING!
USHIO-KUN!
WE'RE IN THE FINAL STRETCH OF THE ELECTION RACE!
WE HAVE TO GET BIG RESULTS HERE, TO PULL AHEAD OF MIYA-MURA.
SO WE SHOULD START OUR STRATEGY MEETING...
SST
ABOUT THAT...
STEP
I HAVE SOME-THING I NEED TO TALK TO ALL OF YOU ABOUT!
?

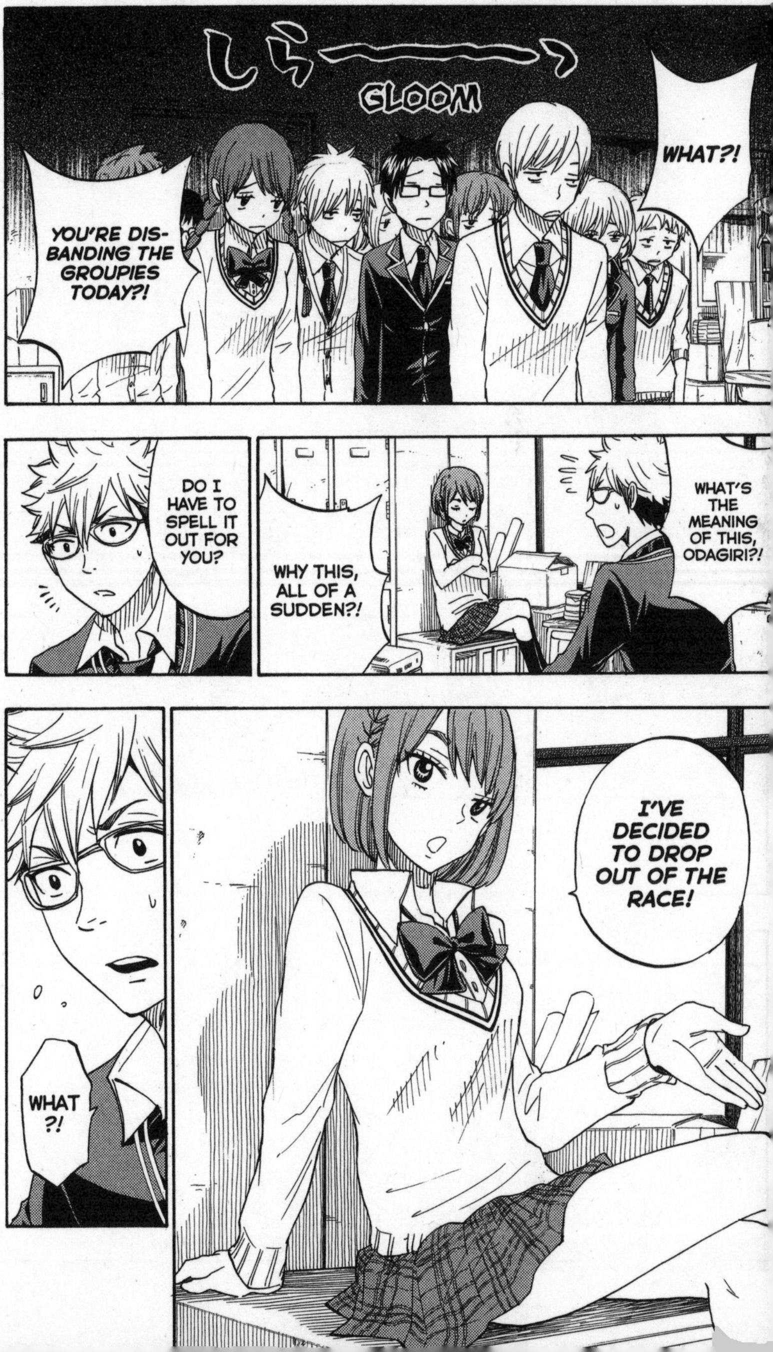
しらーーーっ
GLOOM
WHAT?!
YOU'RE DIS-BANDING THE GROUPIES TODAY?!
WHAT'S THE MEANING OF THIS, ODAGIRI?!
WHY THIS, ALL OF A SUDDEN?!
DO I HAVE TO SPELL IT OUT FOR YOU?
I'VE DECIDED TO DROP OUT OF THE RACE!
WHAT ?!

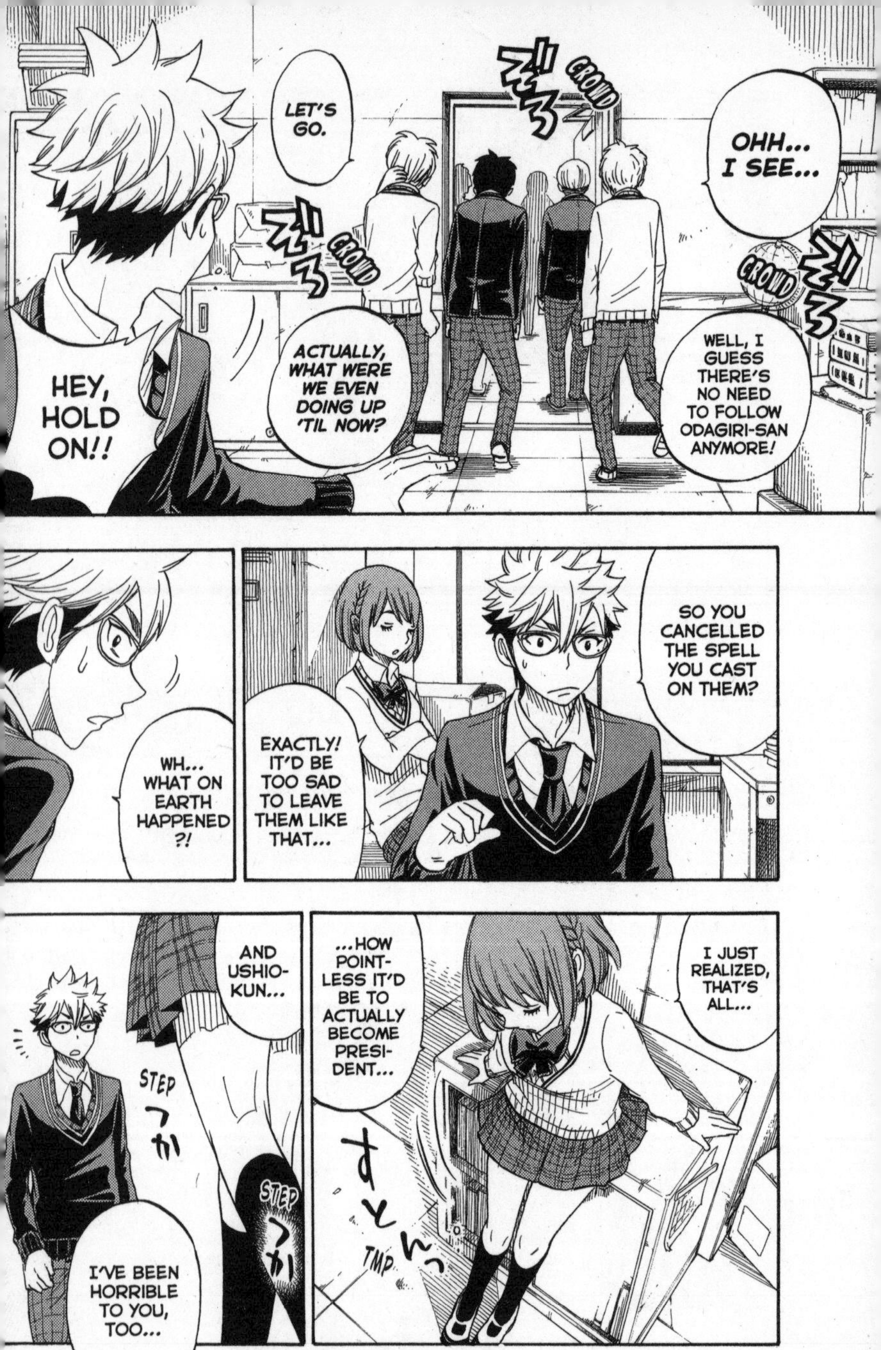
CROWD
OHH... I SEE...
WELL, I GUESS THERE'S NO NEED TO FOLLOW ODAGIRI-SAN ANYMORE!
CROWD
LET'S GO.
CROWD
ACTUALLY, WHAT WERE WE EVEN DOING UP 'TIL NOW?
HEY, HOLD ON!!
SO YOU CANCELLED THE SPELL YOU CAST ON THEM?
EXACTLY! IT'D BE TOO SAD TO LEAVE THEM LIKE THAT...
WH... WHAT ON EARTH HAPPENED?!
I JUST REALIZED, THAT'S ALL...
...HOW POINTLESS IT'D BE TO ACTUALLY BECOME PRESIDENT...
すとんっ
TMP
AND USHIO-KUN...
STEP
つか
STEP
つか
I'VE BEEN HORRIBLE TO YOU, TOO...

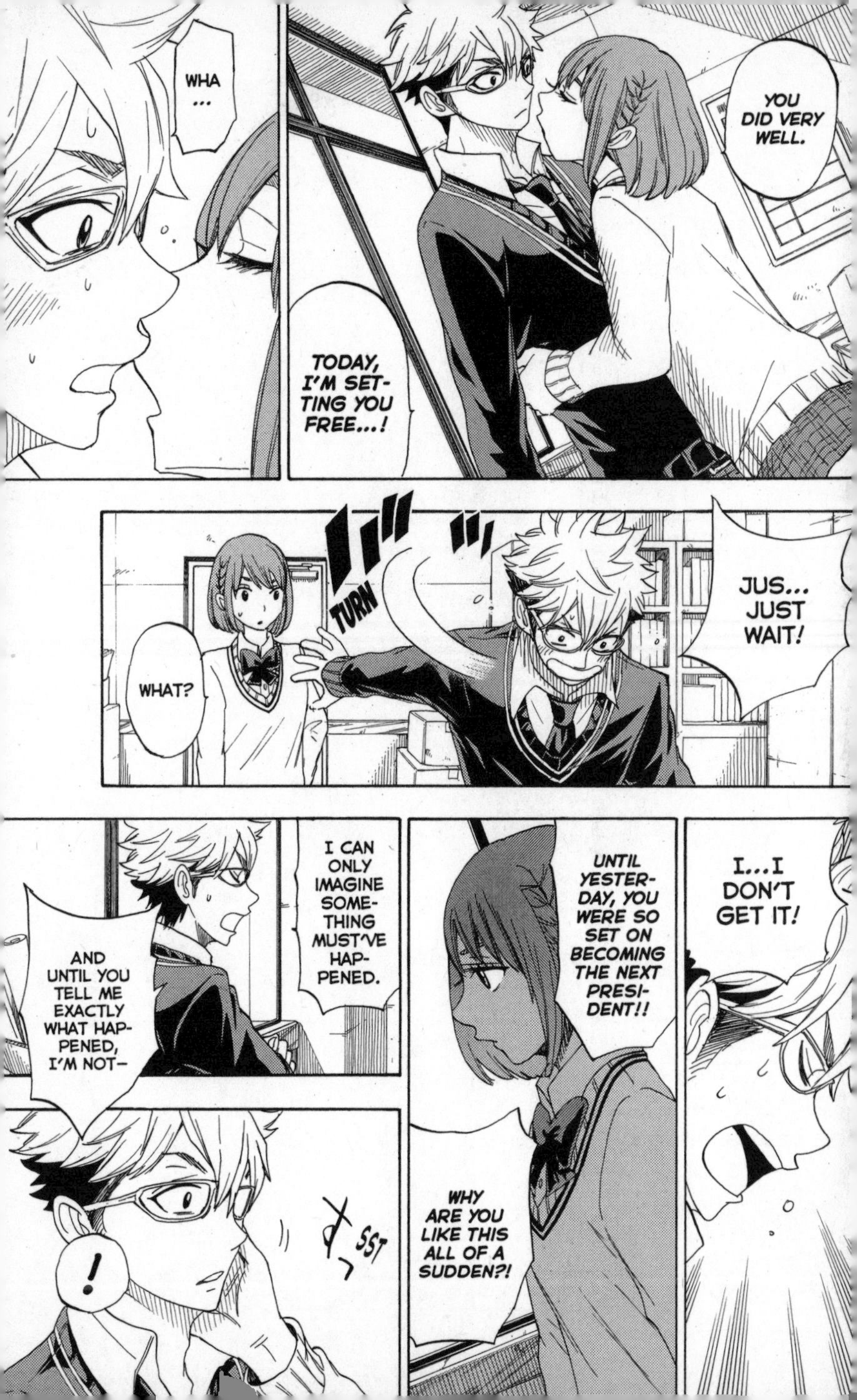
YOU DID VERY WELL.
TODAY, I'M SET-TING YOU FREE...!
WHA ...
JUS... JUST WAIT!
TURN
WHAT?
I...I DON'T GET IT!
UNTIL YESTER-DAY, YOU WERE SO SET ON BECOMING THE NEXT PRESI-DENT!!
WHY ARE YOU LIKE THIS ALL OF A SUDDEN?!
I CAN ONLY IMAGINE SOME-THING MUST'VE HAP-PENED.
AND UNTIL YOU TELL ME EXACTLY WHAT HAP-PENED, I'M NOT—
SST
!

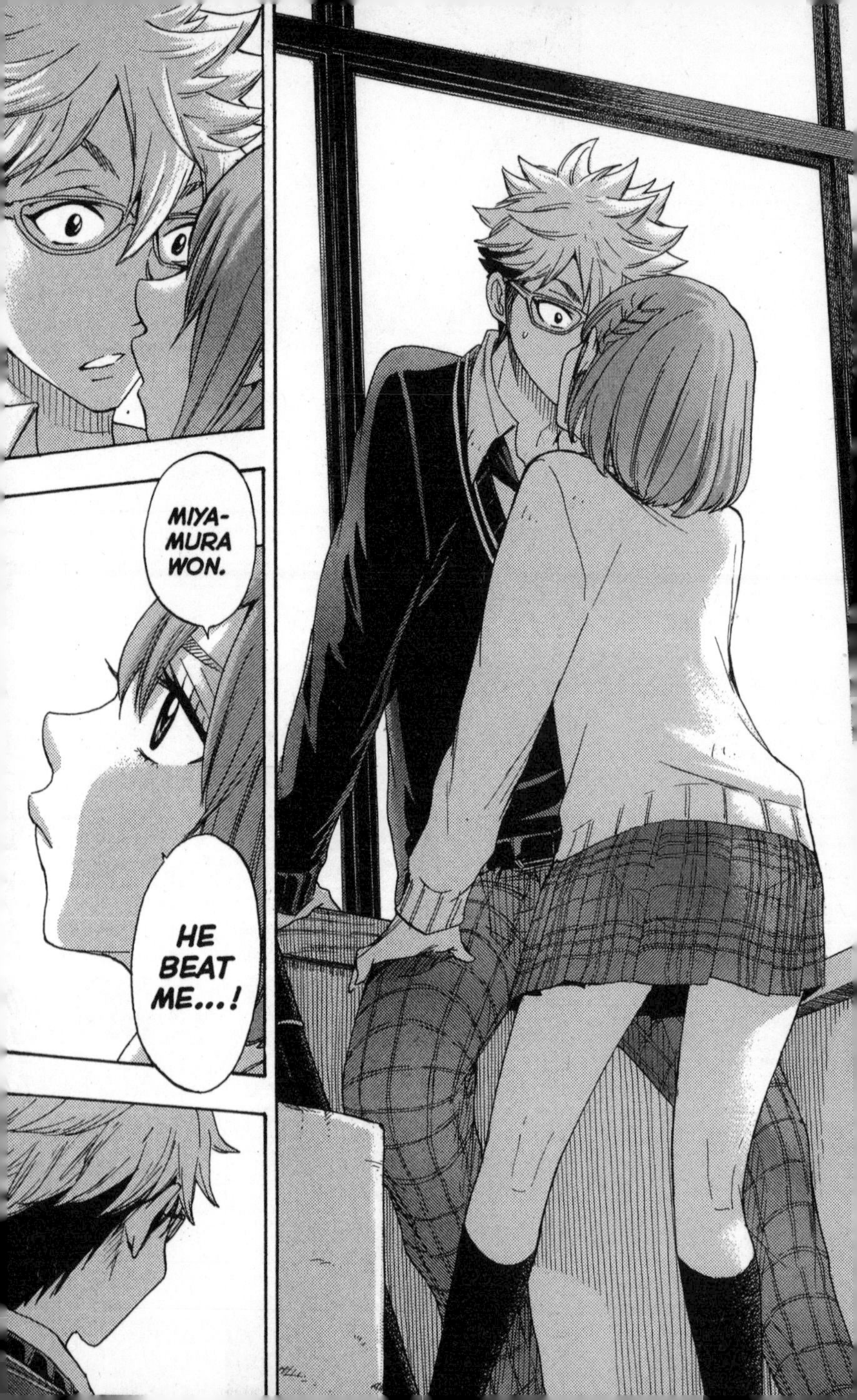
MIYA-MURA WON.
HE BEAT ME...!

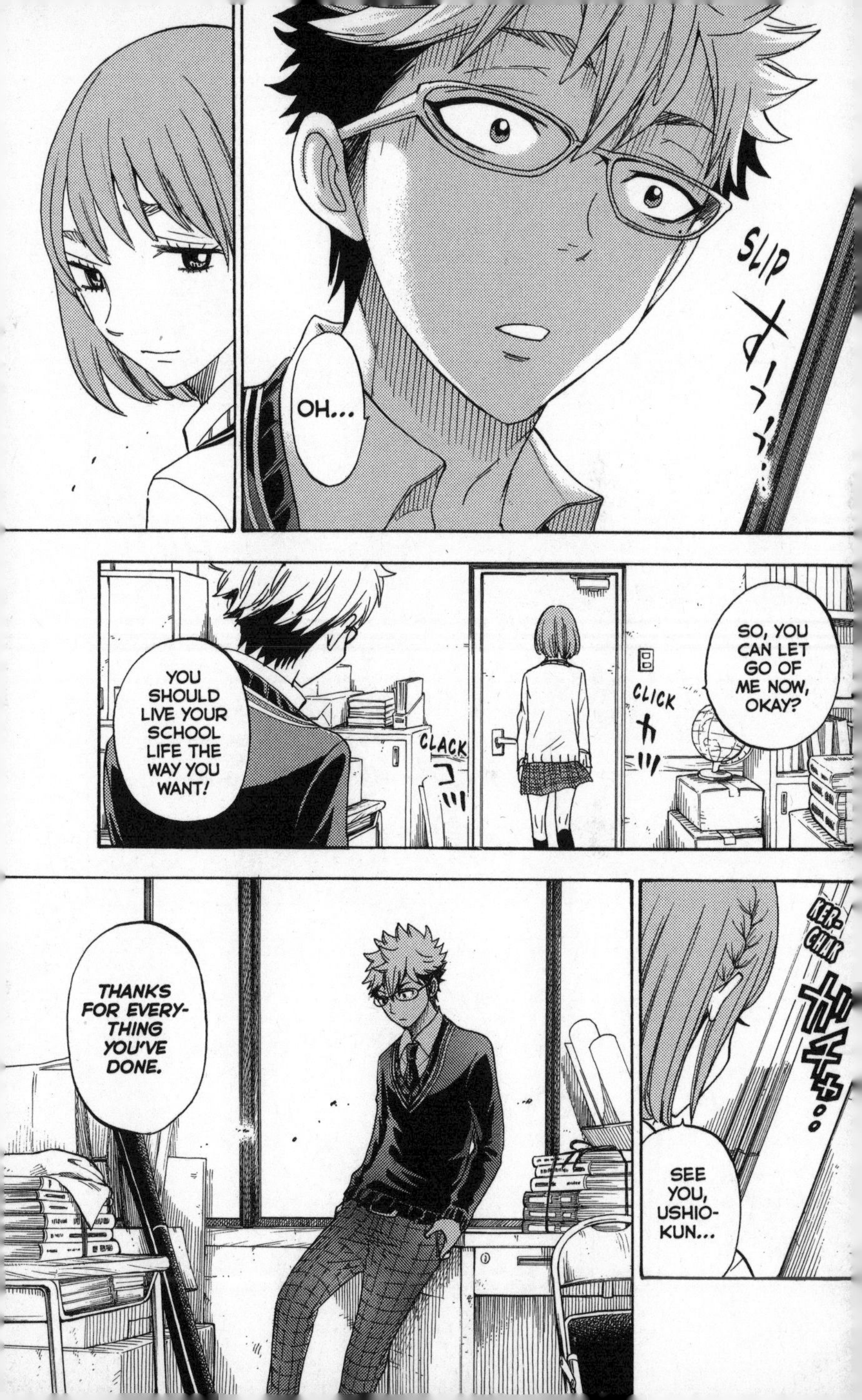
SLIP
OH...
SO, YOU CAN LET GO OF ME NOW, OKAY?
CLICK
CLACK
YOU SHOULD LIVE YOUR SCHOOL LIFE THE WAY YOU WANT!
KER-CHAK
SEE YOU, USHIO-KUN...
THANKS FOR EVERY-THING YOU'VE DONE.

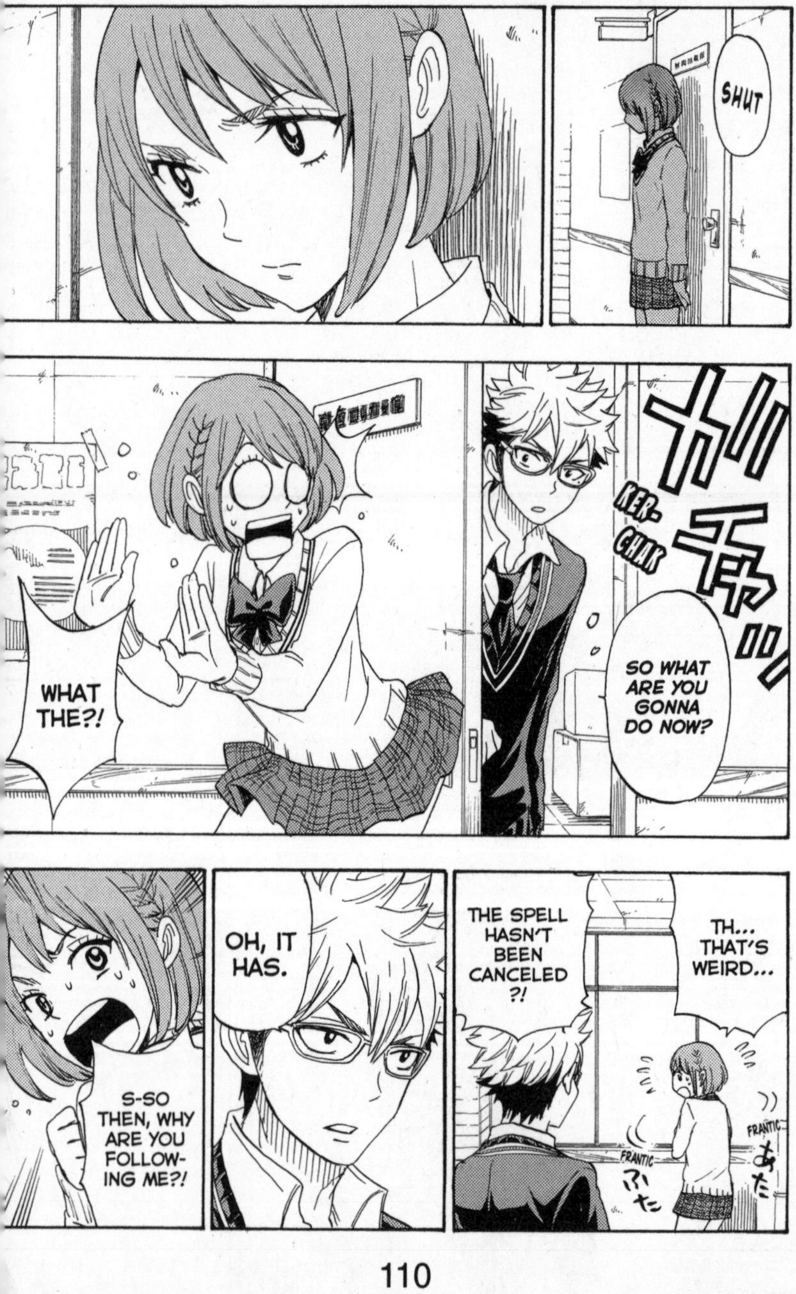
SHUT
ガチャッ
KER-CHAK
SO WHAT ARE YOU GONNA DO NOW?
WHAT THE?!
TH... THAT'S WEIRD...
THE SPELL HASN'T BEEN CANCELED ?!
FRANTIC
あた
FRANTIC
ふた
OH, IT HAS.
S-SO THEN, WHY ARE YOU FOLLOW-ING ME?!

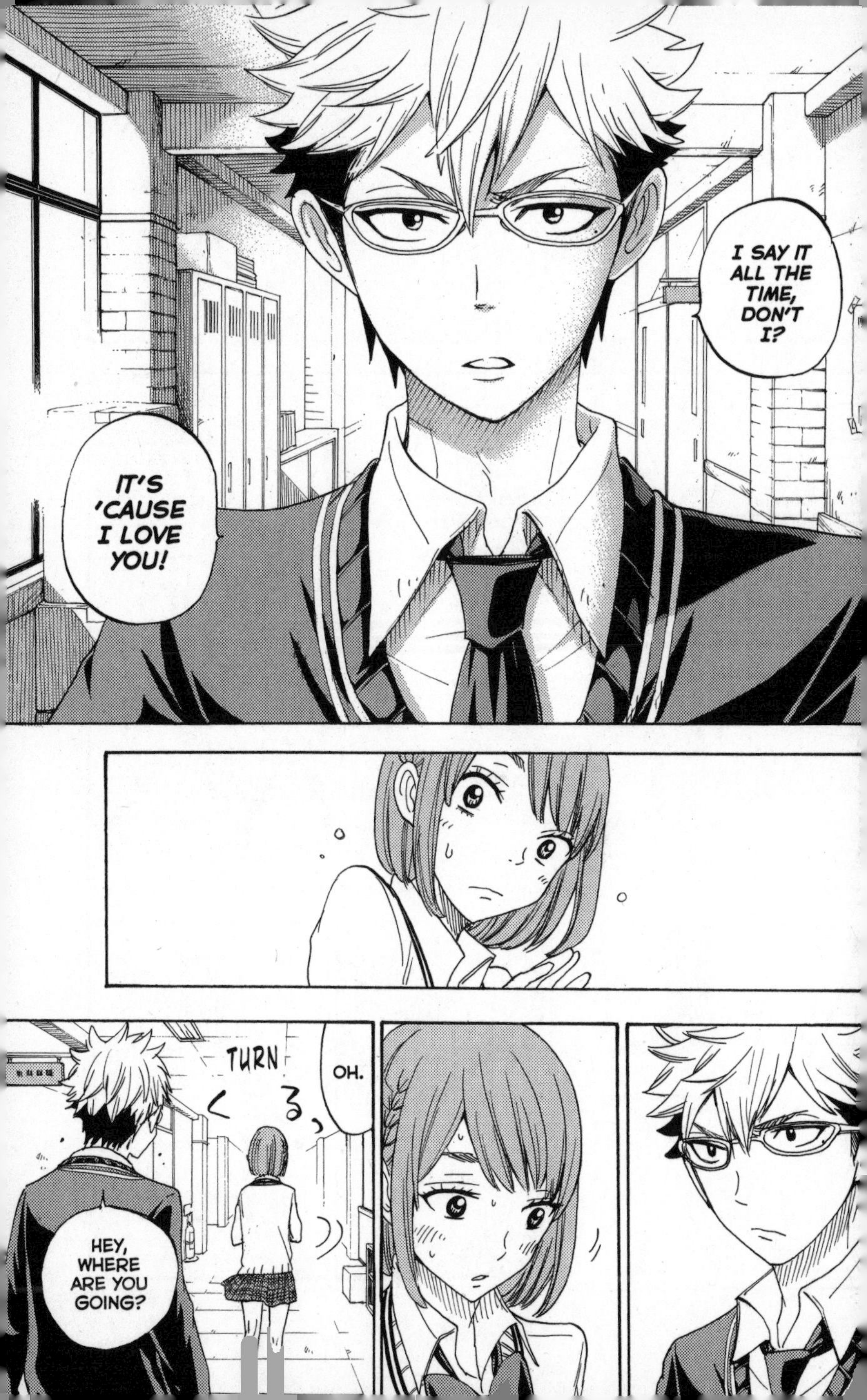
I SAY IT ALL THE TIME, DON'T I?
IT'S 'CAUSE I LOVE YOU!
OH.
TURN
くる
HEY, WHERE ARE YOU GOING?

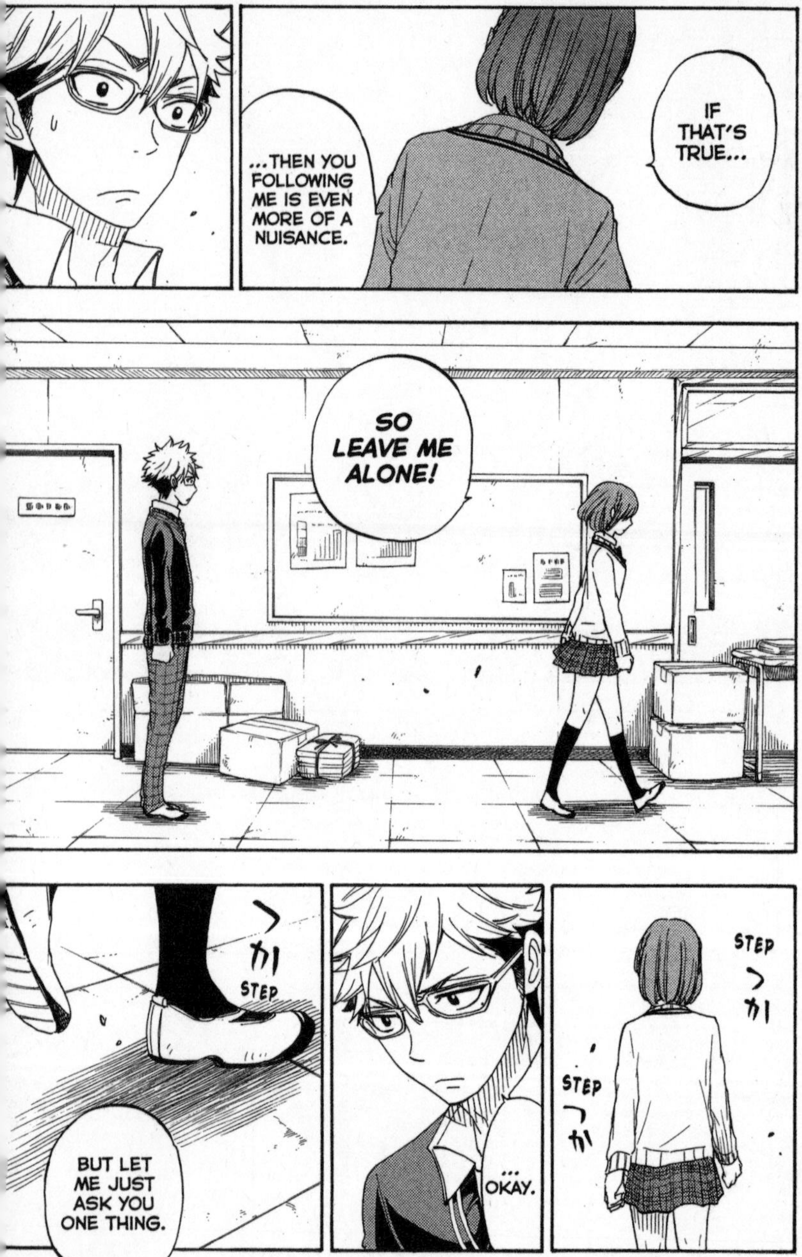
IF THAT'S TRUE...
...THEN YOU FOLLOWING ME IS EVEN MORE OF A NUISANCE.
SO LEAVE ME ALONE!
STEP
つか
STEP
つか
...OKAY.
つか
STEP
BUT LET ME JUST ASK YOU ONE THING.

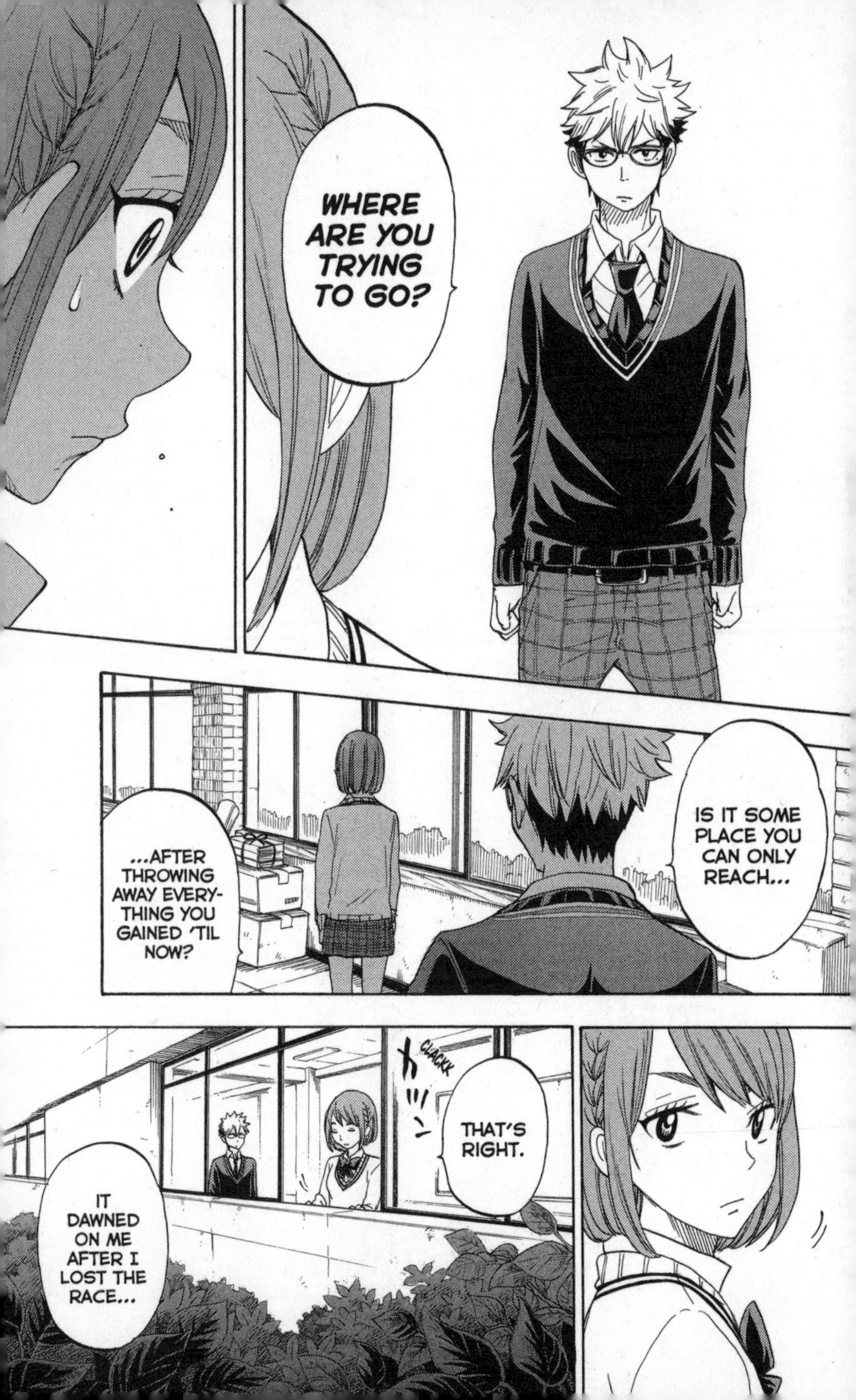
WHERE ARE YOU TRYING TO GO?
IS IT SOME PLACE YOU CAN ONLY REACH...
...AFTER THROWING AWAY EVERY-THING YOU GAINED 'TIL NOW?
CLACKK
THAT'S RIGHT.
IT DAWNED ON ME AFTER I LOST THE RACE...

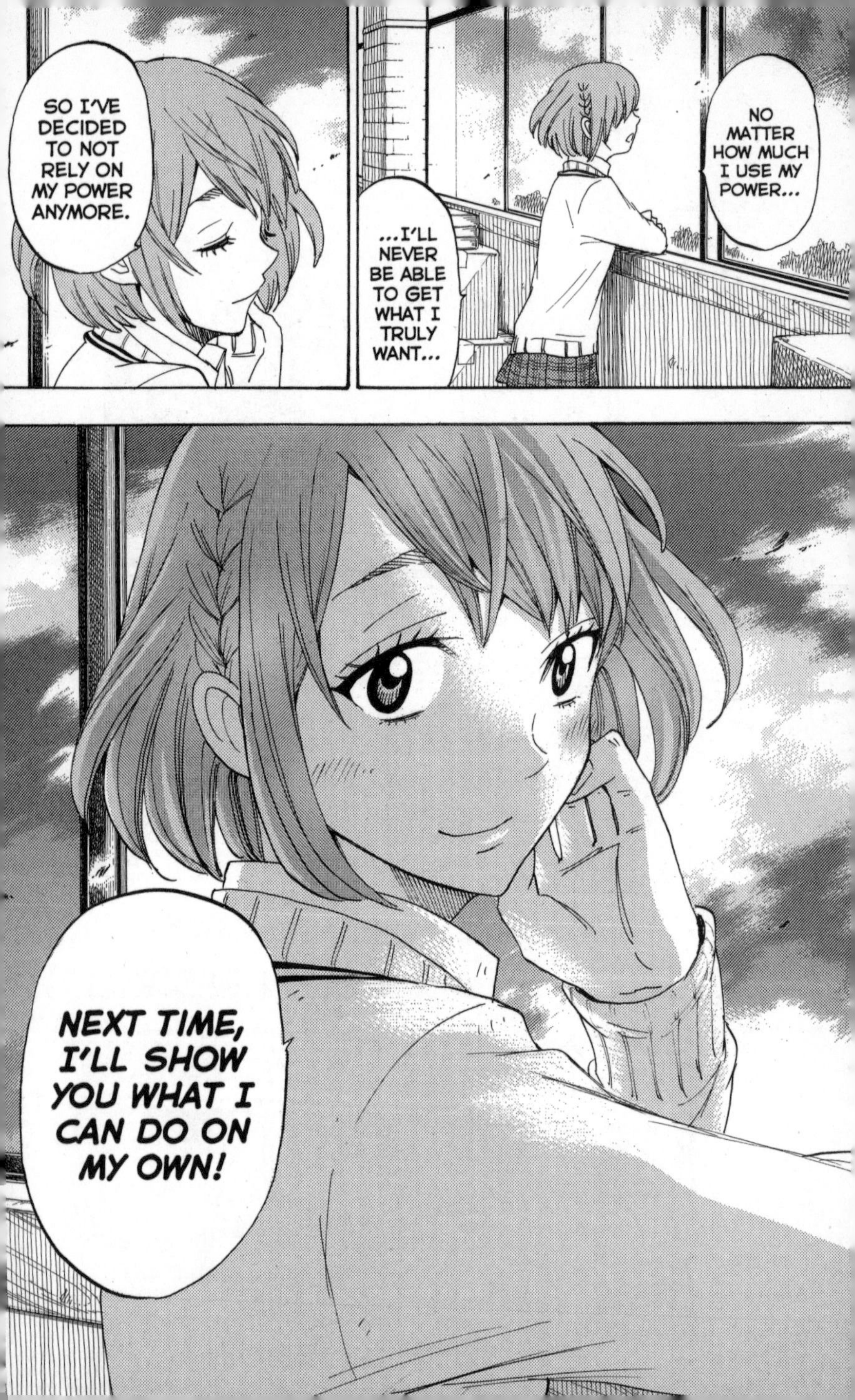
NO MATTER HOW MUCH I USE MY POWER...
...I'LL NEVER BE ABLE TO GET WHAT I TRULY WANT...
SO I'VE DECIDED TO NOT RELY ON MY POWER ANYMORE.
NEXT TIME, I'LL SHOW YOU WHAT I CAN DO ON MY OWN!

SO, I'M SORRY, BUT...

...I CAN'T TAKE YOU ALONG WITH ME ANY-MORE...!

...I SEE.

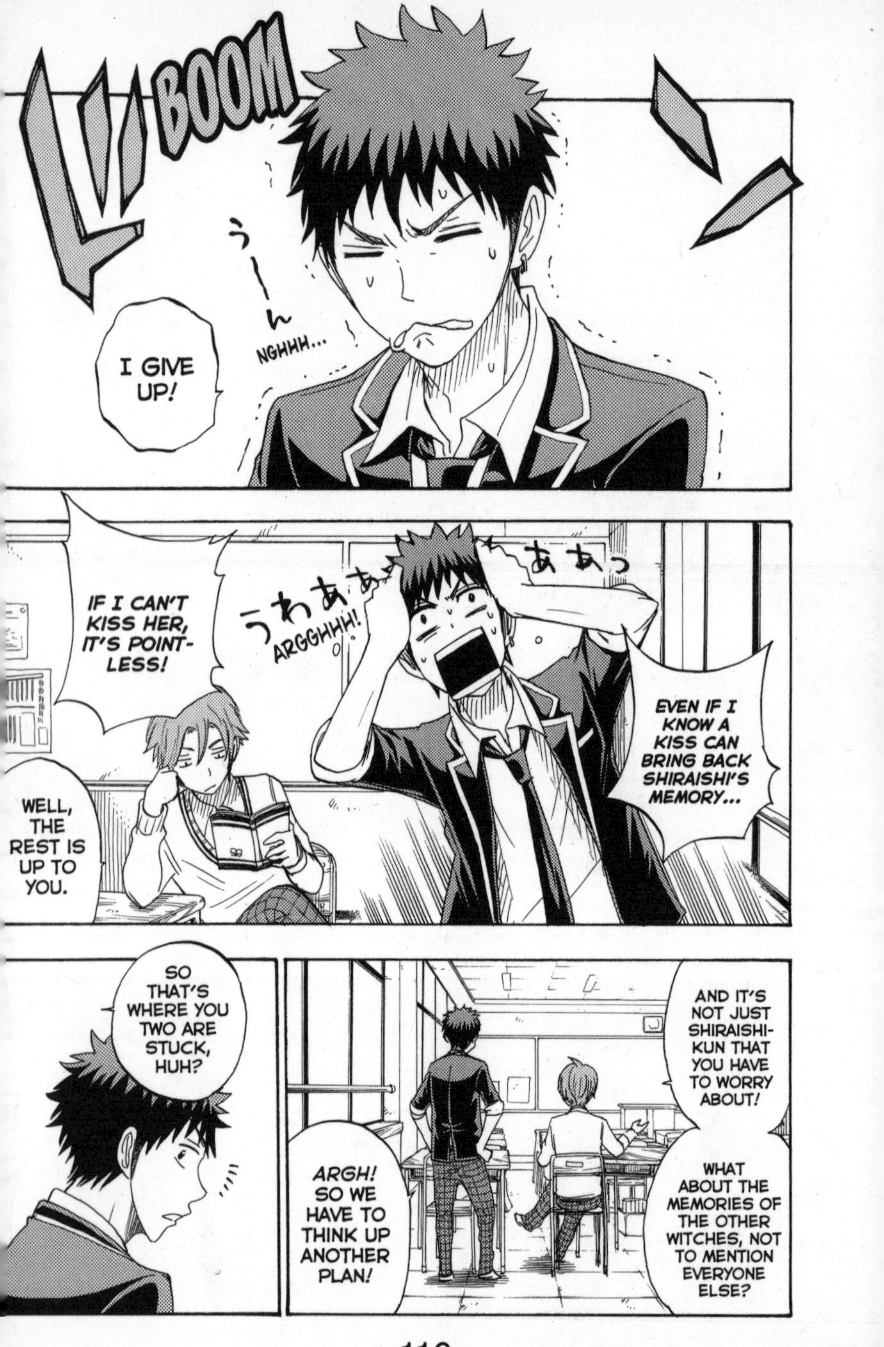
BOOM
うーん
NGHHH...
I GIVE UP!
うわあああっ
ARGGHHH!
EVEN IF I KNOW A KISS CAN BRING BACK SHIRAISHI'S MEMORY...
IF I CAN'T KISS HER, IT'S POINTLESS!
WELL, THE REST IS UP TO YOU.
AND IT'S NOT JUST SHIRAISHI-KUN THAT YOU HAVE TO WORRY ABOUT!
WHAT ABOUT THE MEMORIES OF THE OTHER WITCHES, NOT TO MENTION EVERYONE ELSE?
ARGH! SO WE HAVE TO THINK UP ANOTHER PLAN!
SO THAT'S WHERE YOU TWO ARE STUCK, HUH?

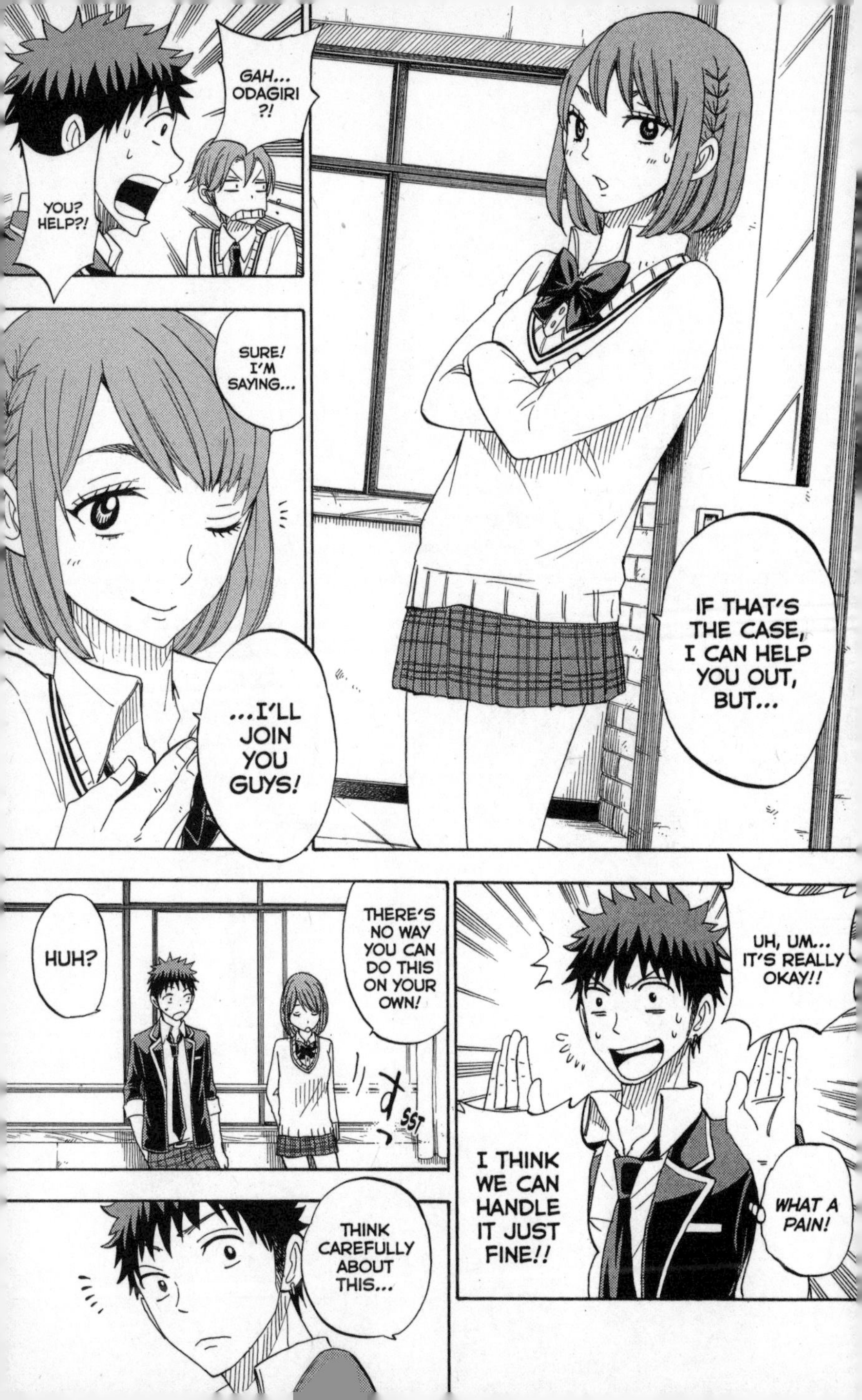
IF THAT'S THE CASE, I CAN HELP YOU OUT, BUT...
GAH... ODAGIRI ?!
YOU? HELP?!
SURE! I'M SAYING...
...I'LL JOIN YOU GUYS!
UH, UM... IT'S REALLY OKAY!!
WHAT A PAIN!
I THINK WE CAN HANDLE IT JUST FINE!!
THERE'S NO WAY YOU CAN DO THIS ON YOUR OWN!
す SST
HUH?
THINK CAREFULLY ABOUT THIS...

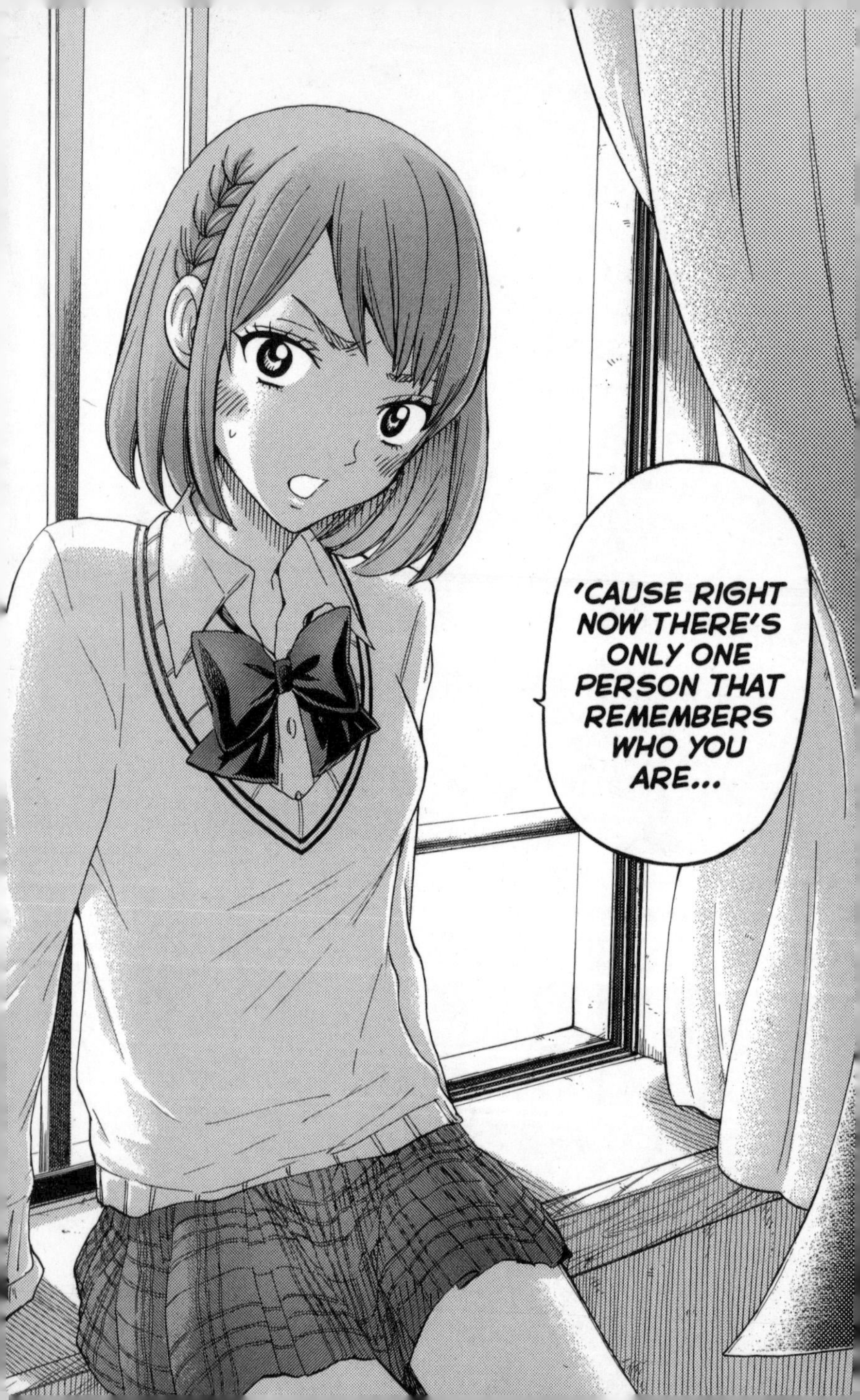
'CAUSE RIGHT NOW THERE'S ONLY ONE PERSON THAT REMEMBERS WHO YOU ARE...

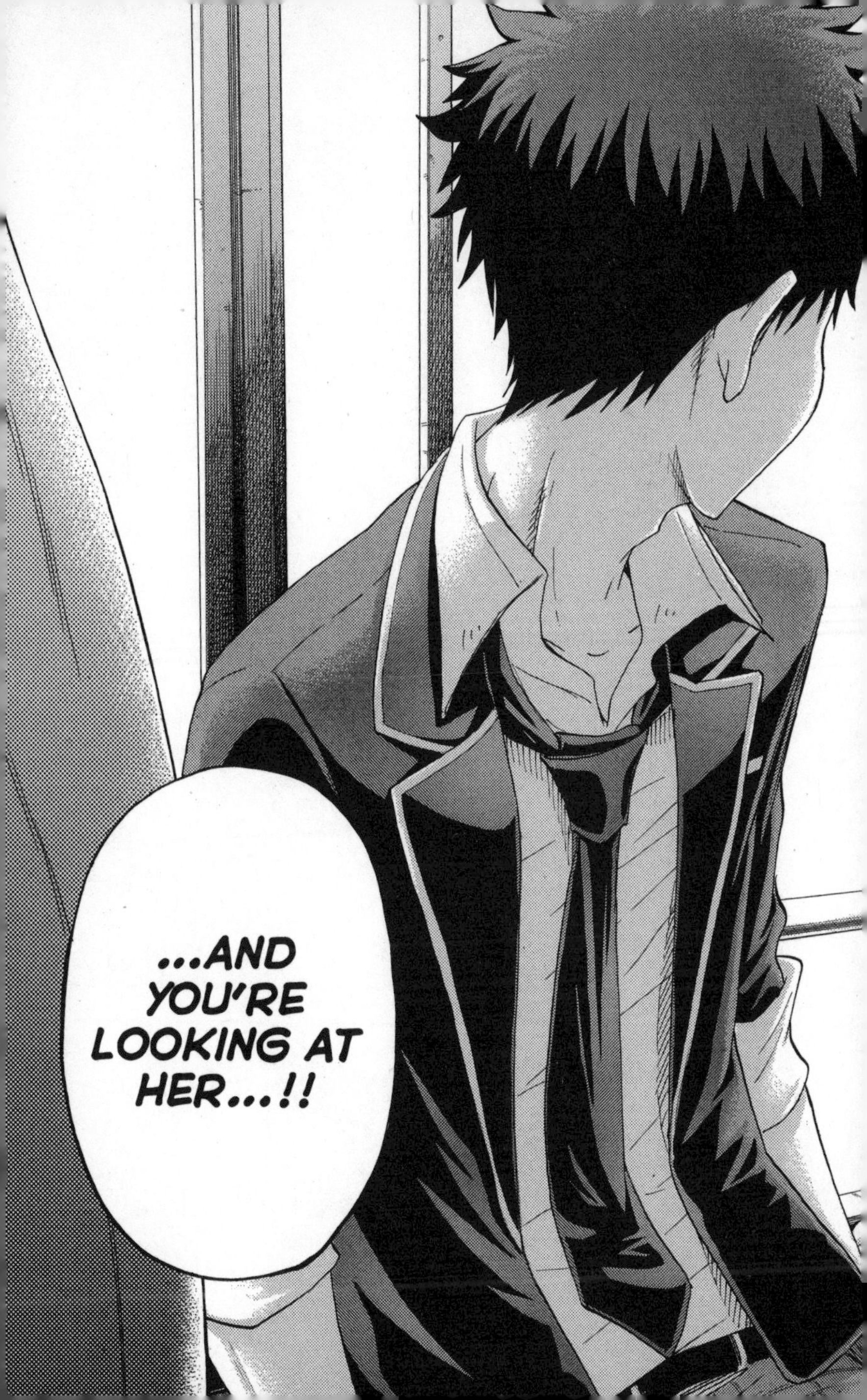
...AND YOU'RE LOOKING AT HER...!!

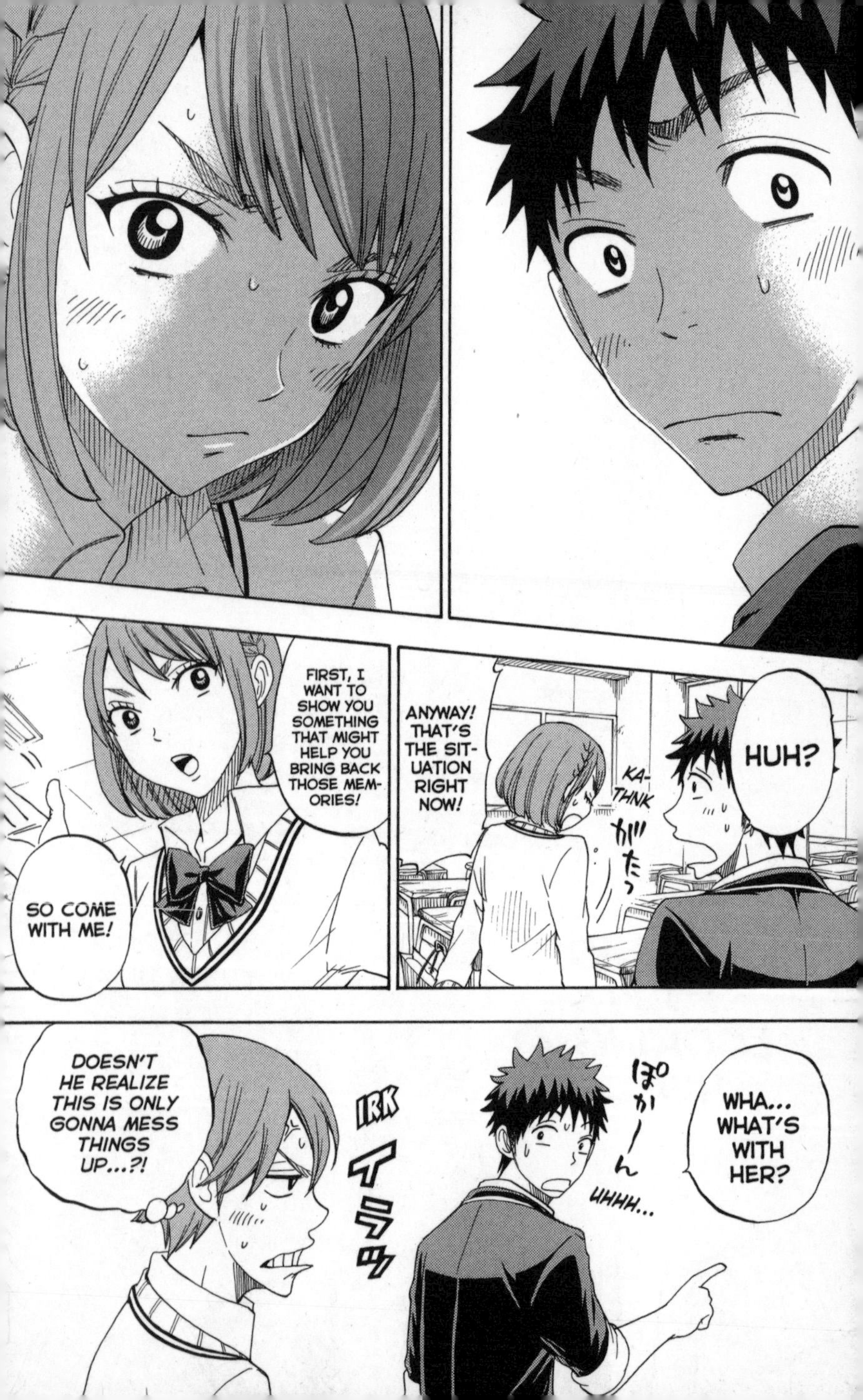
HUH?
ANYWAY! THAT'S THE SITUATION RIGHT NOW!
KA-THNK
がたっ
FIRST, I WANT TO SHOW YOU SOMETHING THAT MIGHT HELP YOU BRING BACK THOSE MEMORIES!
SO COME WITH ME!
WHA... WHAT'S WITH HER?
ぽか〜ん
UHHH...
IRK
イラッ
DOESN'T HE REALIZE THIS IS ONLY GONNA MESS THINGS UP...?!

Chapter 75: It's like a dream, isn't it?

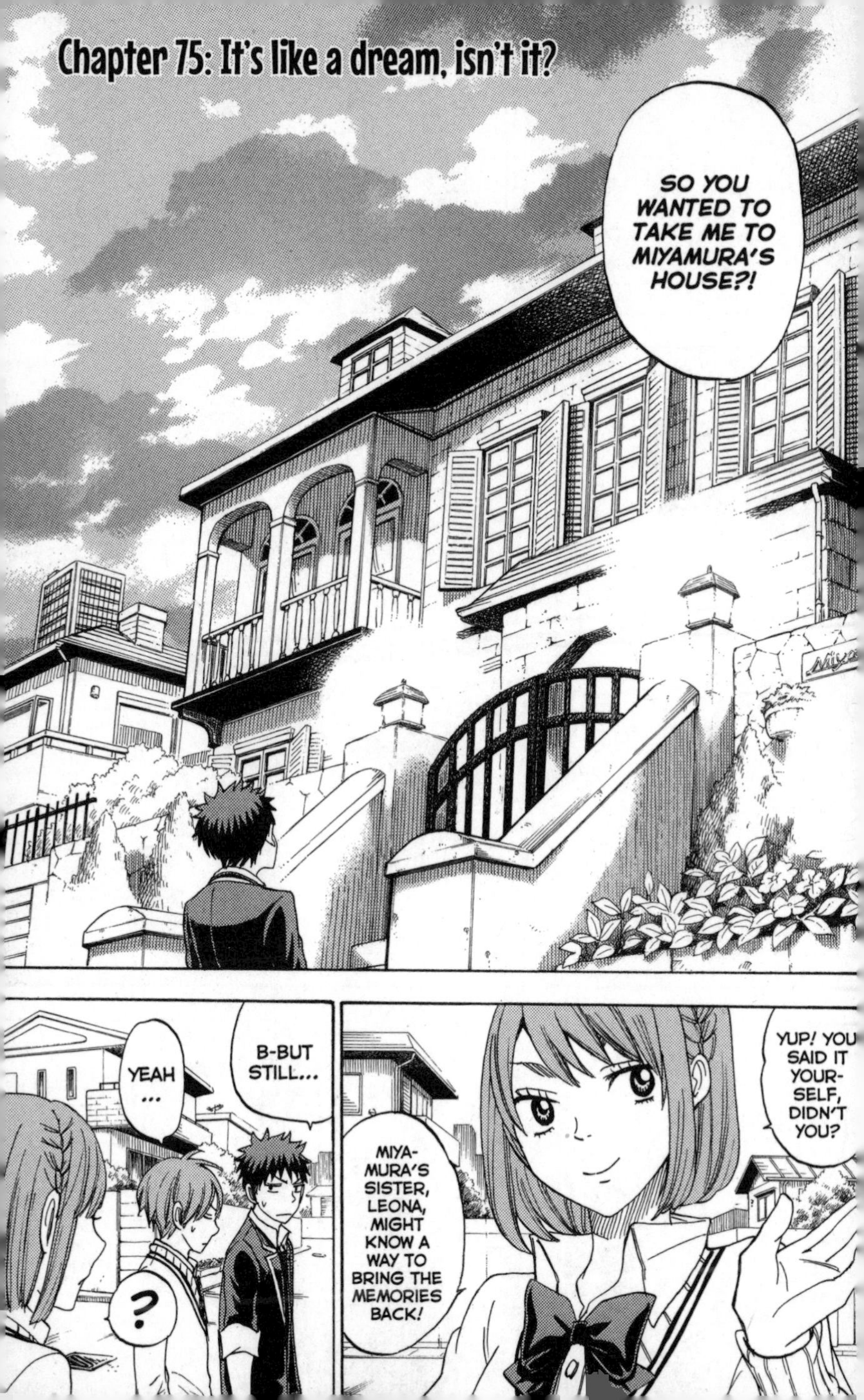
SO YOU WANTED TO TAKE ME TO MIYAMURA'S HOUSE?!
YUP! YOU SAID IT YOURSELF, DIDN'T YOU?
MIYAMURA'S SISTER, LEONA, MIGHT KNOW A WAY TO BRING THE MEMORIES BACK!
B-BUT STILL...
YEAH ...
?

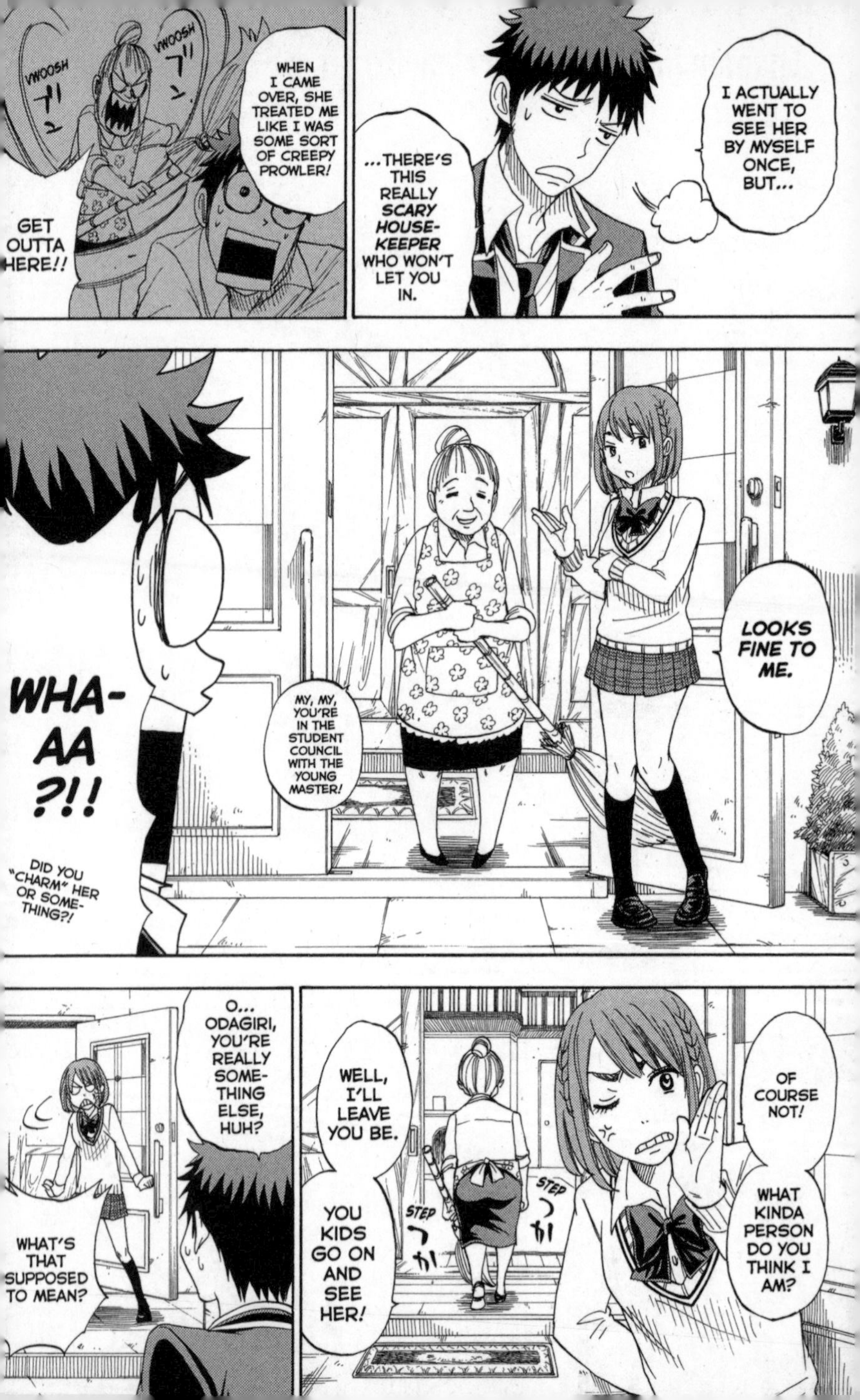
I ACTUALLY WENT TO SEE HER BY MYSELF ONCE, BUT...
...THERE'S THIS REALLY SCARY HOUSE-KEEPER WHO WON'T LET YOU IN.
WHEN I CAME OVER, SHE TREATED ME LIKE I WAS SOME SORT OF CREEPY PROWLER!
VWOOSH
VWOOSH
GET OUTTA HERE!!
LOOKS FINE TO ME.
MY, MY, YOU'RE IN THE STUDENT COUNCIL WITH THE YOUNG MASTER!
WHA-AA?!!
DID YOU "CHARM" HER OR SOME-THING?!
OF COURSE NOT!
WHAT KINDA PERSON DO YOU THINK I AM?
WELL, I'LL LEAVE YOU BE.
YOU KIDS GO ON AND SEE HER!
STEP
STEP
O... ODAGIRI, YOU'RE REALLY SOME-THING ELSE, HUH?
WHAT'S THAT SUPPOSED TO MEAN?

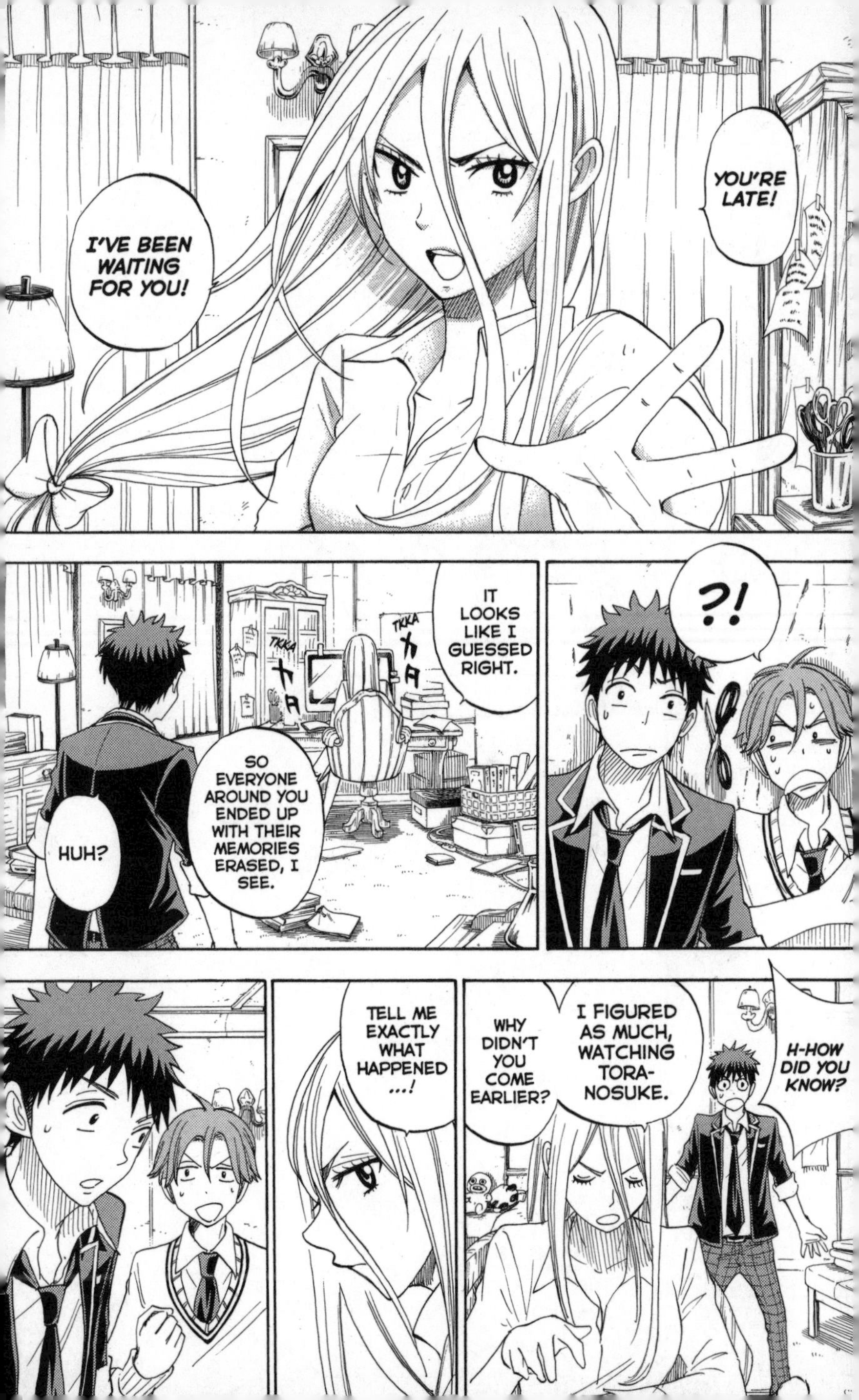
YOU'RE LATE!
I'VE BEEN WAITING FOR YOU!
?!
IT LOOKS LIKE I GUESSED RIGHT.
TKKA
TKKA
SO EVERYONE AROUND YOU ENDED UP WITH THEIR MEMORIES ERASED, I SEE.
HUH?
H-HOW DID YOU KNOW?
I FIGURED AS MUCH, WATCHING TORA-NOSUKE.
WHY DIDN'T YOU COME EARLIER?
TELL ME EXACTLY WHAT HAPPENED ...!

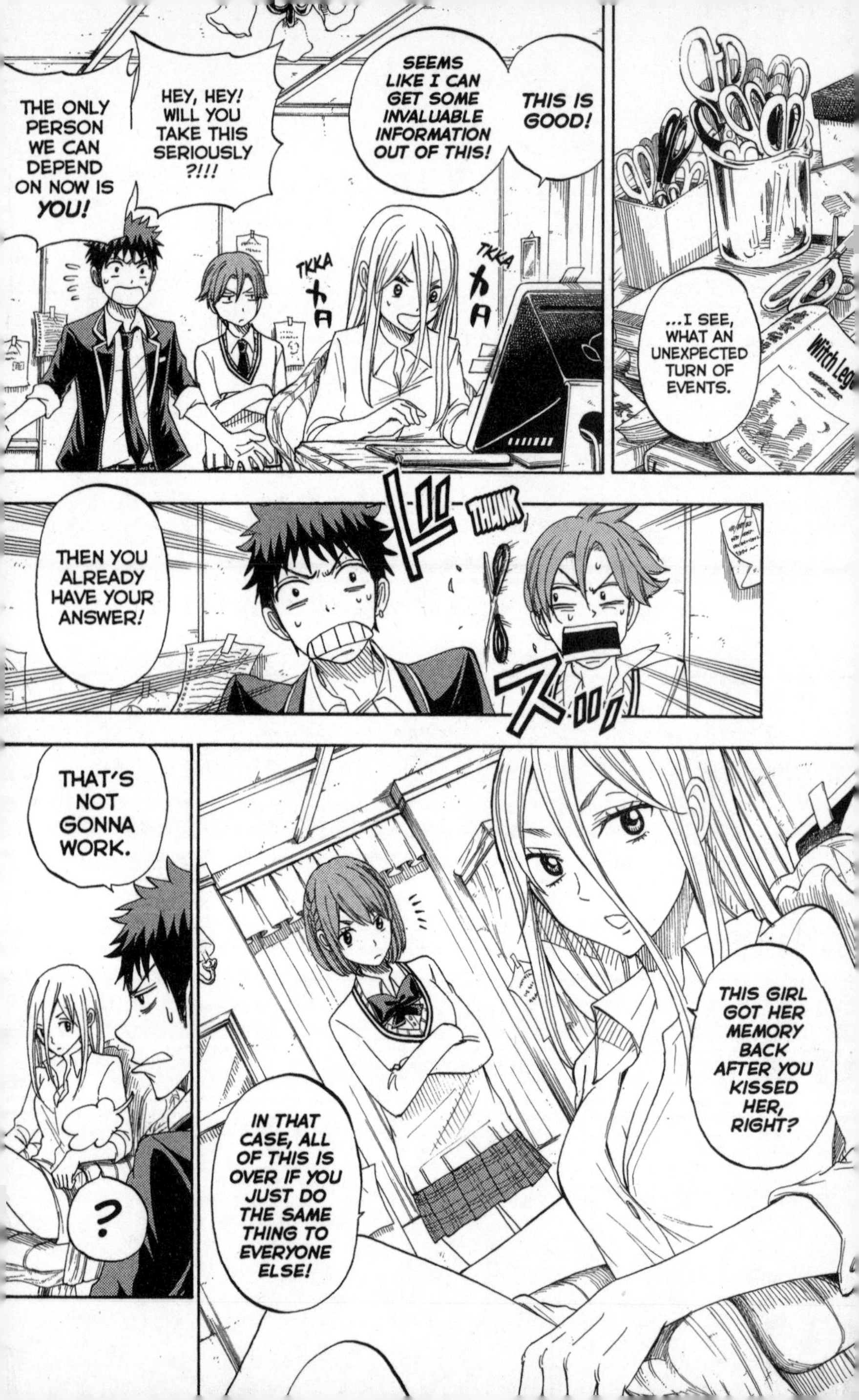
...I SEE, WHAT AN UNEXPECTED TURN OF EVENTS.
THIS IS GOOD!
SEEMS LIKE I CAN GET SOME INVALUABLE INFORMATION OUT OF THIS!
TKKA
TKKA
HEY, HEY! WILL YOU TAKE THIS SERIOUSLY?!!!
THE ONLY PERSON WE CAN DEPEND ON NOW IS YOU!
THUNK
THEN YOU ALREADY HAVE YOUR ANSWER!
THIS GIRL GOT HER MEMORY BACK AFTER YOU KISSED HER, RIGHT?
IN THAT CASE, ALL OF THIS IS OVER IF YOU JUST DO THE SAME THING TO EVERYONE ELSE!
THAT'S NOT GONNA WORK.
?

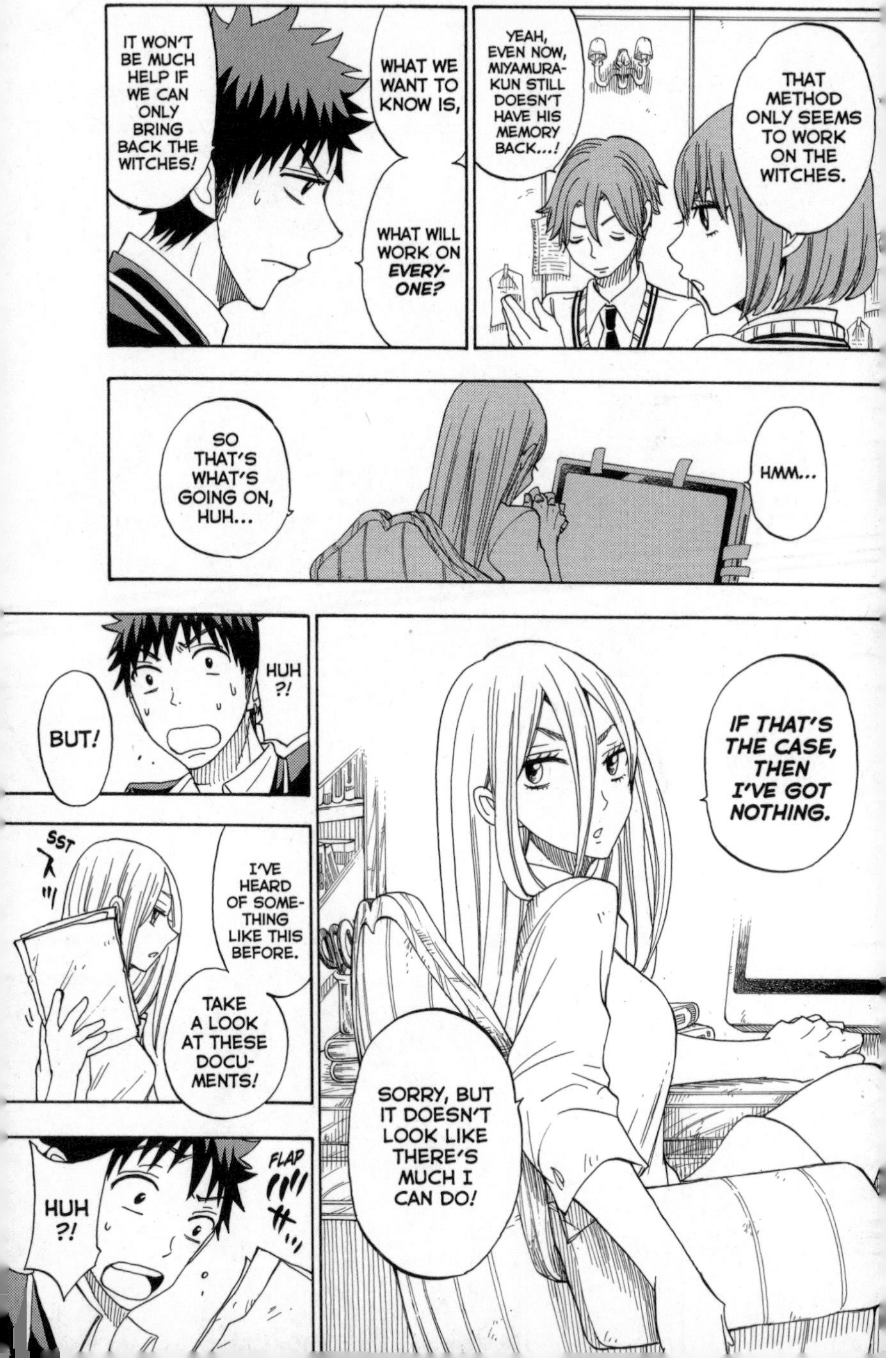
THAT METHOD ONLY SEEMS TO WORK ON THE WITCHES.
YEAH, EVEN NOW, MIYAMURA-KUN STILL DOESN'T HAVE HIS MEMORY BACK...!
WHAT WE WANT TO KNOW IS,
WHAT WILL WORK ON *EVERY-ONE?*
IT WON'T BE MUCH HELP IF WE CAN ONLY BRING BACK THE WITCHES!
HMM...
SO THAT'S WHAT'S GOING ON, HUH...
IF THAT'S THE CASE, THEN I'VE GOT NOTHING.
SORRY, BUT IT DOESN'T LOOK LIKE THERE'S MUCH I CAN DO!
HUH ?!
BUT!
SST
I'VE HEARD OF SOME-THING LIKE THIS BEFORE.
TAKE A LOOK AT THESE DOCU-MENTS!
FLAP
HUH ?!

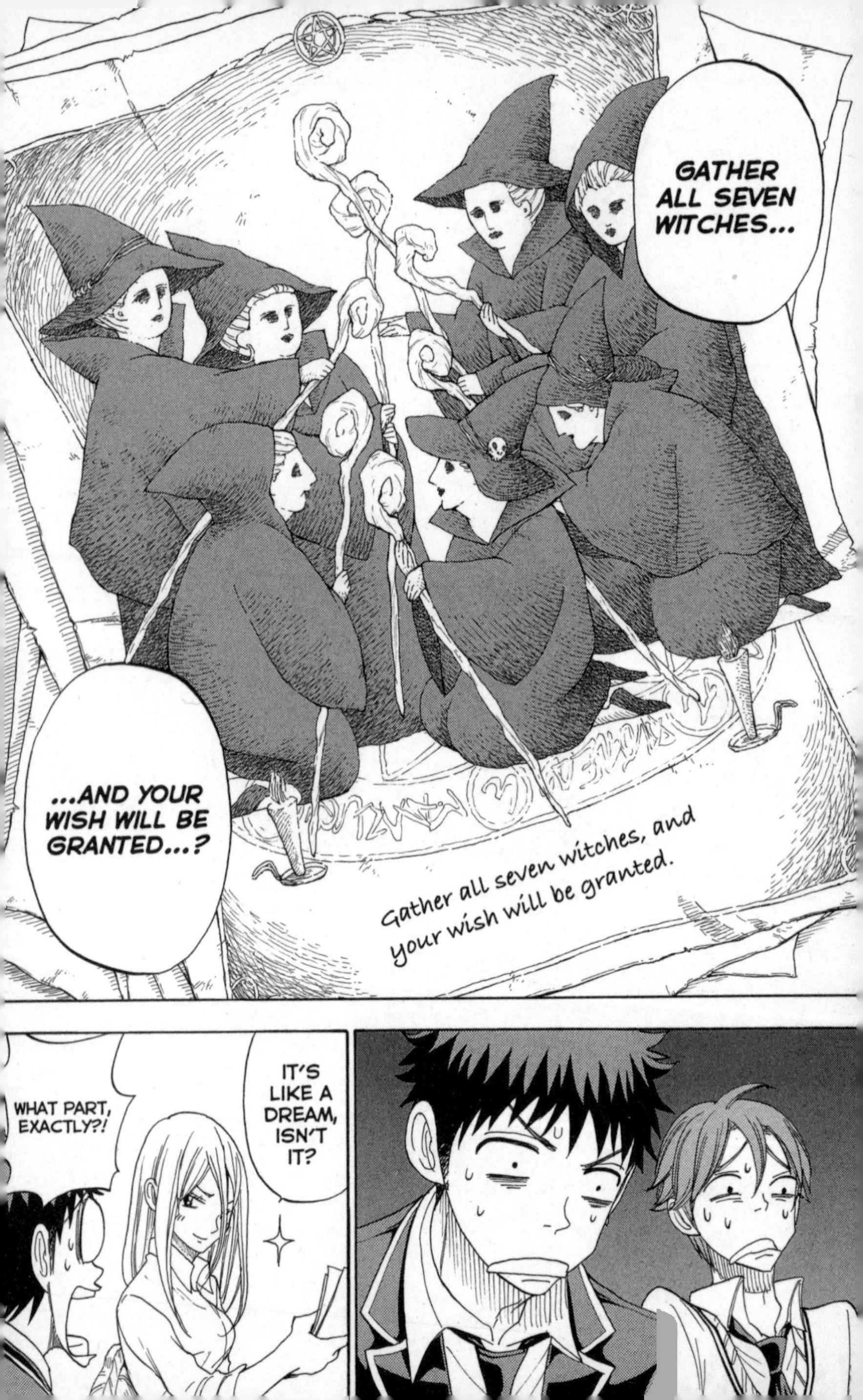
GATHER ALL SEVEN WITCHES...
Gather all seven witches, and your wish will be granted.
...AND YOUR WISH WILL BE GRANTED...?
IT'S LIKE A DREAM, ISN'T IT?
WHAT PART, EXACTLY?!

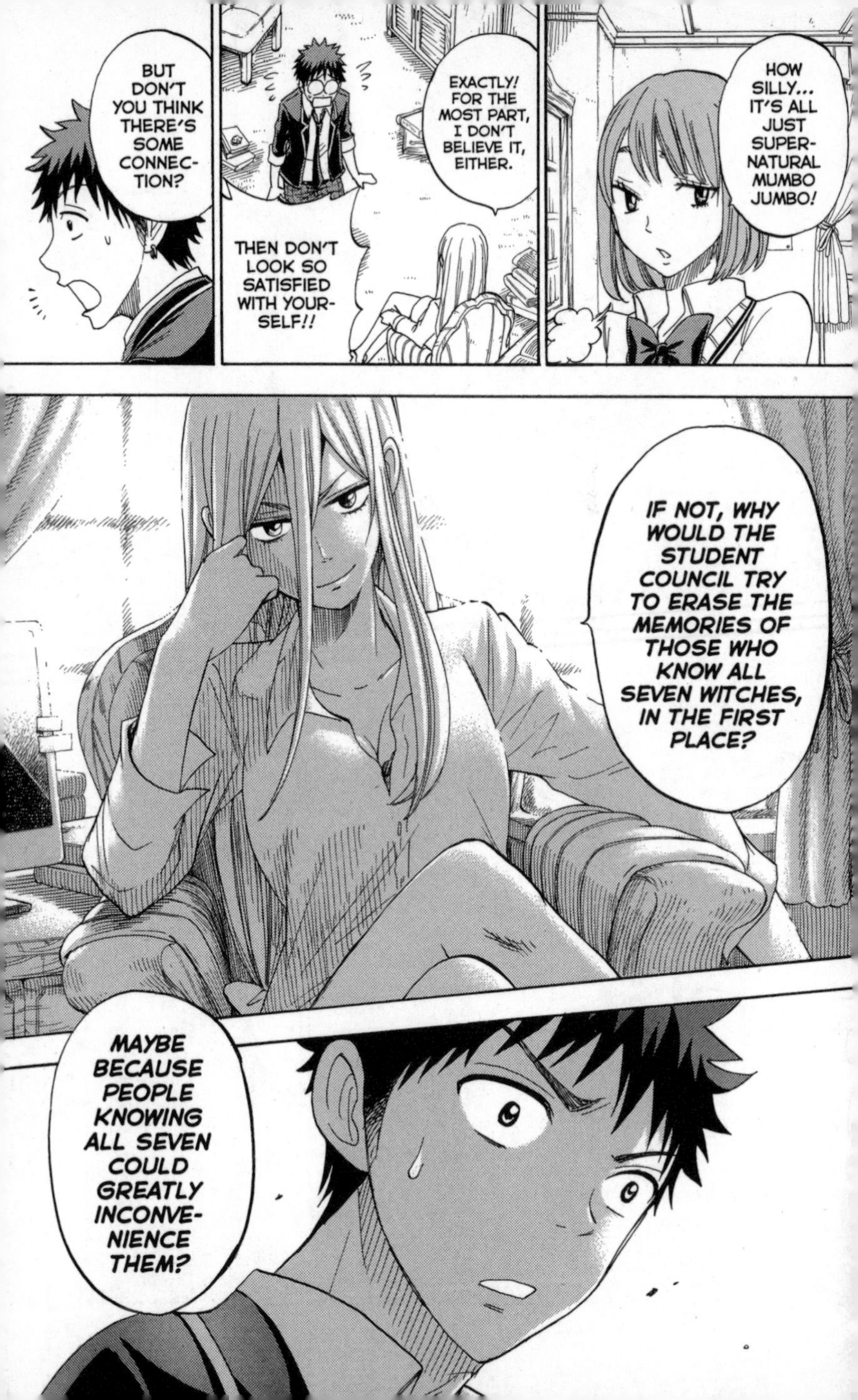
HOW SILLY... IT'S ALL JUST SUPER-NATURAL MUMBO JUMBO!
EXACTLY! FOR THE MOST PART, I DON'T BELIEVE IT, EITHER.
THEN DON'T LOOK SO SATISFIED WITH YOUR-SELF!!
BUT DON'T YOU THINK THERE'S SOME CONNEC-TION?
IF NOT, WHY WOULD THE STUDENT COUNCIL TRY TO ERASE THE MEMORIES OF THOSE WHO KNOW ALL SEVEN WITCHES, IN THE FIRST PLACE?
MAYBE BECAUSE PEOPLE KNOWING ALL SEVEN COULD GREATLY INCONVE-NIENCE THEM?

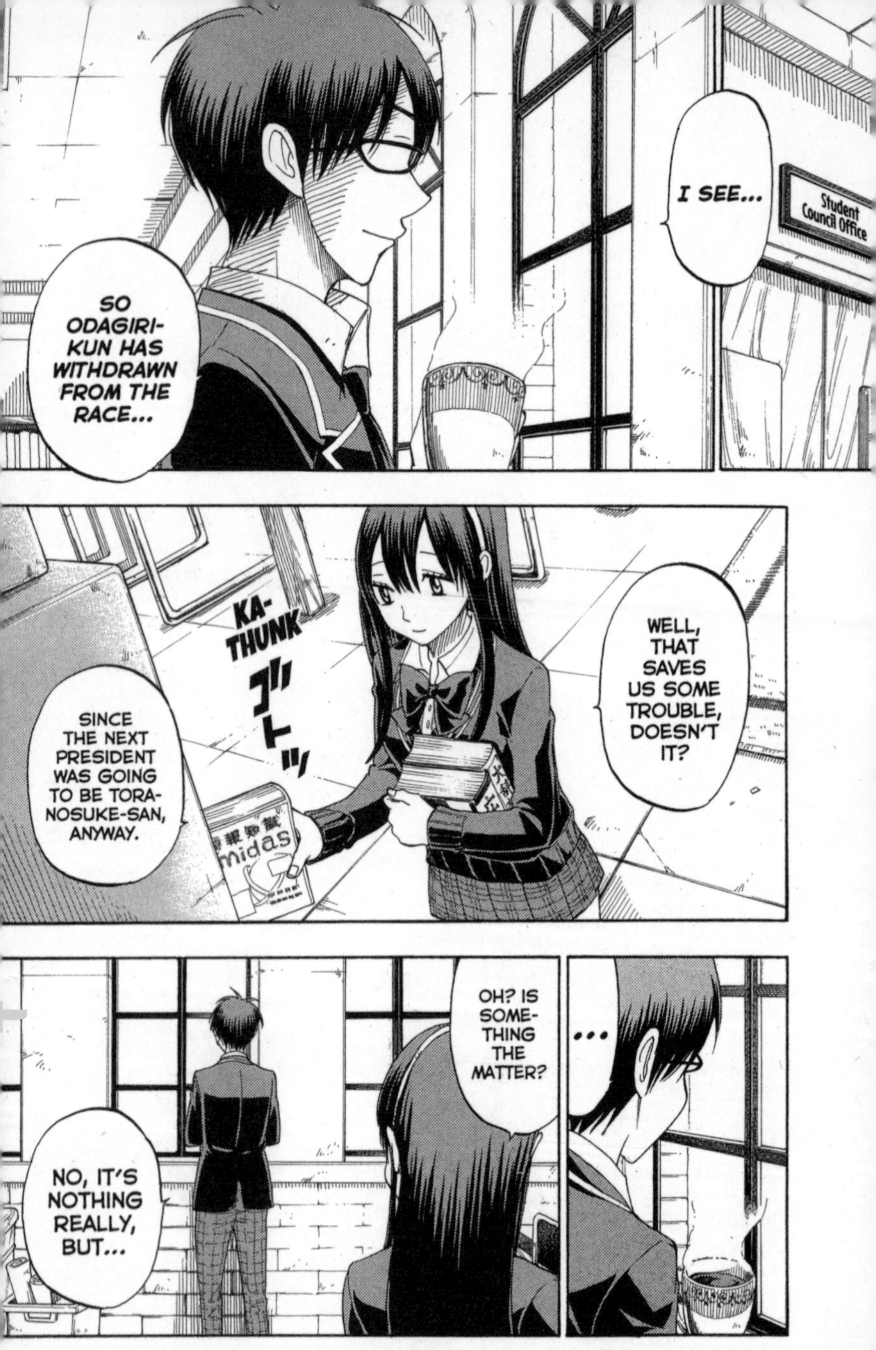
I SEE...
Student Council Office
SO ODAGIRI-KUN HAS WITHDRAWN FROM THE RACE...
WELL, THAT SAVES US SOME TROUBLE, DOESN'T IT?
KA-THUNK
ゴトッ
SINCE THE NEXT PRESIDENT WAS GOING TO BE TORA-NOSUKE-SAN, ANYWAY.
...
OH? IS SOME-THING THE MATTER?
NO, IT'S NOTHING REALLY, BUT...

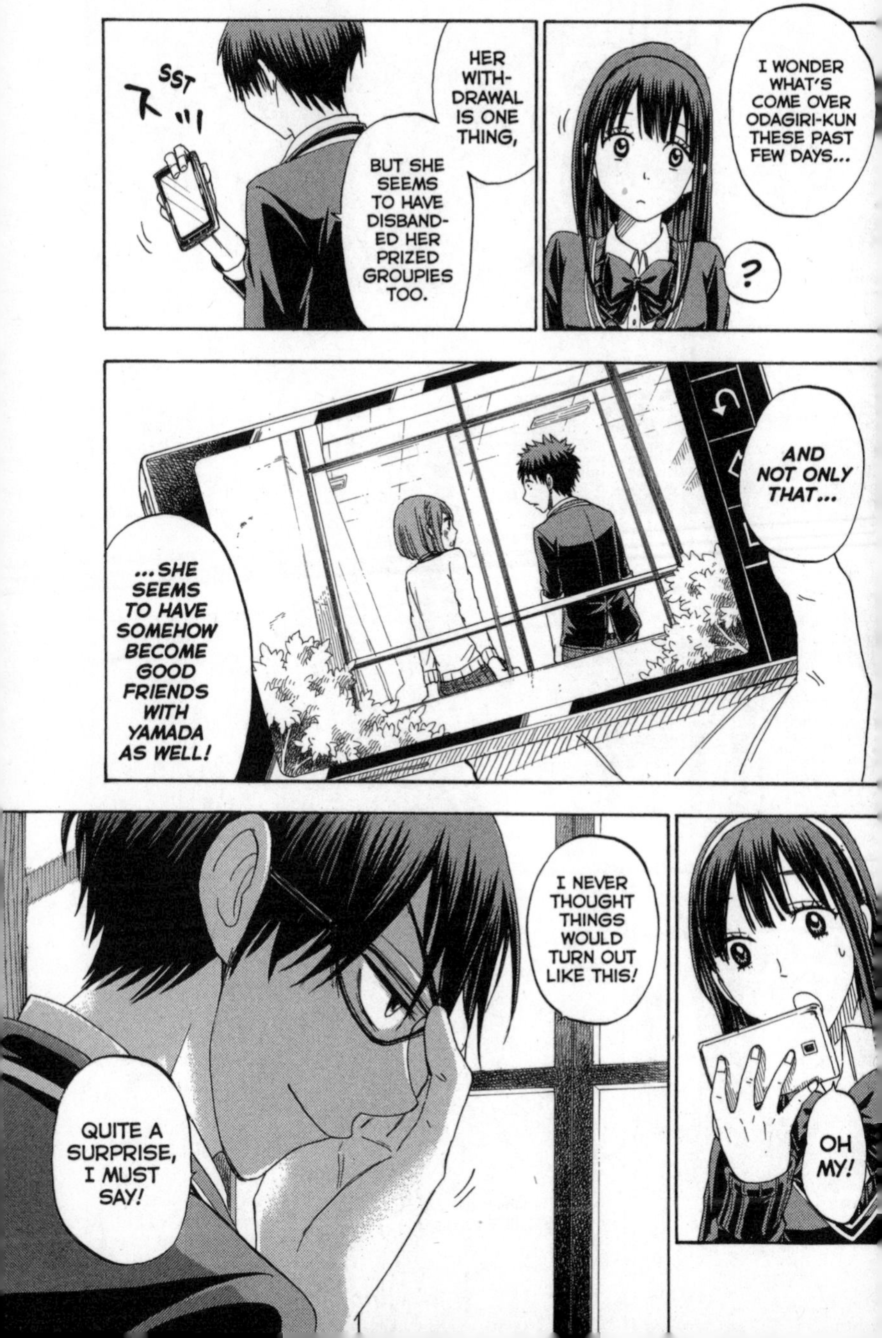
I WONDER WHAT'S COME OVER ODAGIRI-KUN THESE PAST FEW DAYS...
?
HER WITH-DRAWAL IS ONE THING,
BUT SHE SEEMS TO HAVE DISBAND-ED HER PRIZED GROUPIES TOO.
SST
スッ
AND NOT ONLY THAT...
...SHE SEEMS TO HAVE SOMEHOW BECOME GOOD FRIENDS WITH YAMADA AS WELL!
OH MY!
I NEVER THOUGHT THINGS WOULD TURN OUT LIKE THIS!
QUITE A SURPRISE, I MUST SAY!

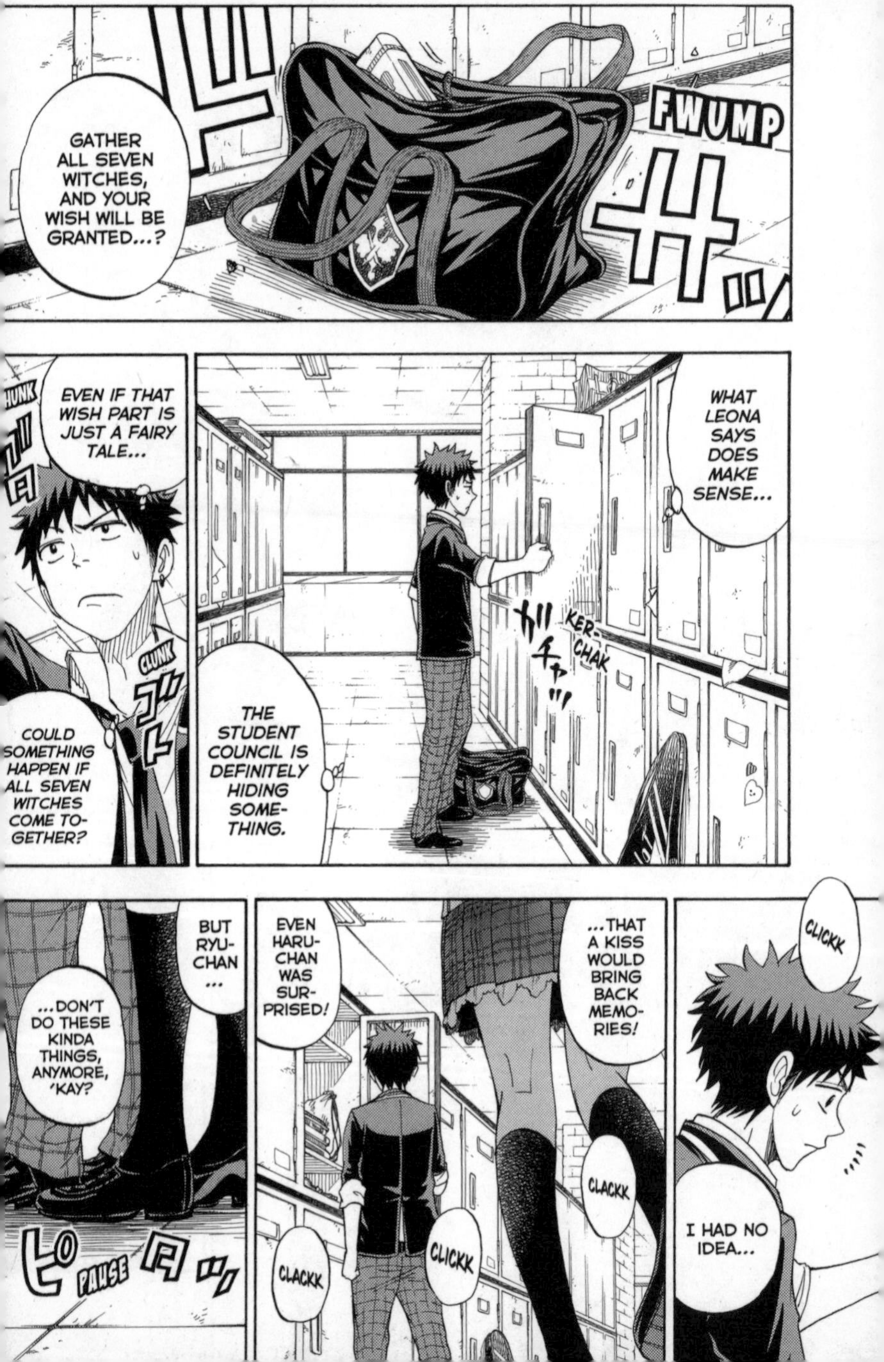
FWUMP
GATHER ALL SEVEN WITCHES, AND YOUR WISH WILL BE GRANTED...?
WHAT LEONA SAYS DOES MAKE SENSE...
KER-CHAK
THE STUDENT COUNCIL IS DEFINITELY HIDING SOME-THING.
HUNK
EVEN IF THAT WISH PART IS JUST A FAIRY TALE...
CLUNK
COULD SOMETHING HAPPEN IF ALL SEVEN WITCHES COME TO-GETHER?
CLICKK
I HAD NO IDEA...
...THAT A KISS WOULD BRING BACK MEMO-RIES!
EVEN HARU-CHAN WAS SUR-PRISED!
CLACKK
CLICKK
CLACKK
BUT RYU-CHAN...
...DON'T DO THESE KINDA THINGS, ANYMORE, 'KAY?
PAUSE

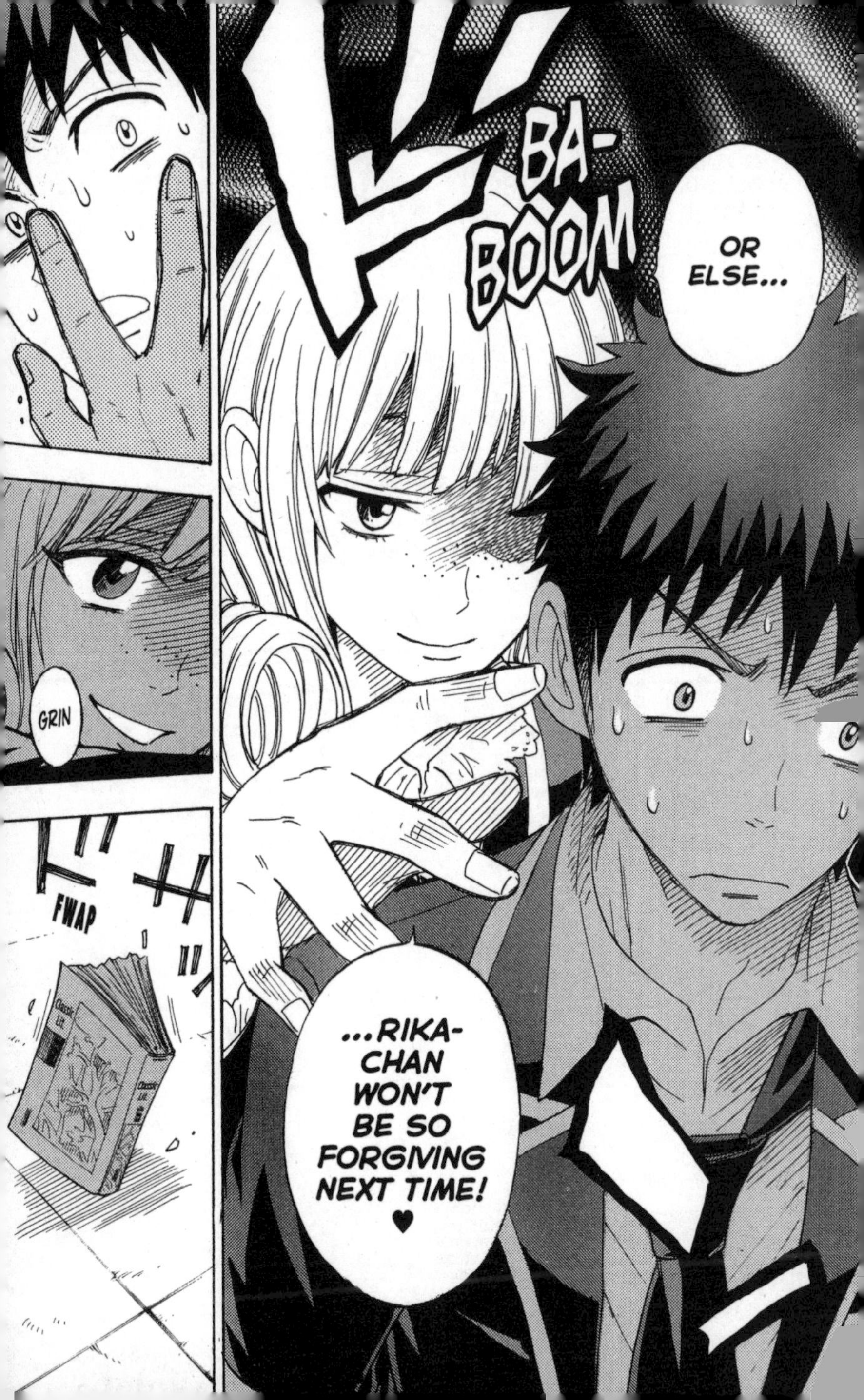
BA-BOOM
OR ELSE...
...RIKA-CHAN WON'T BE SO FORGIVING NEXT TIME! ♥
GRIN
FWAP

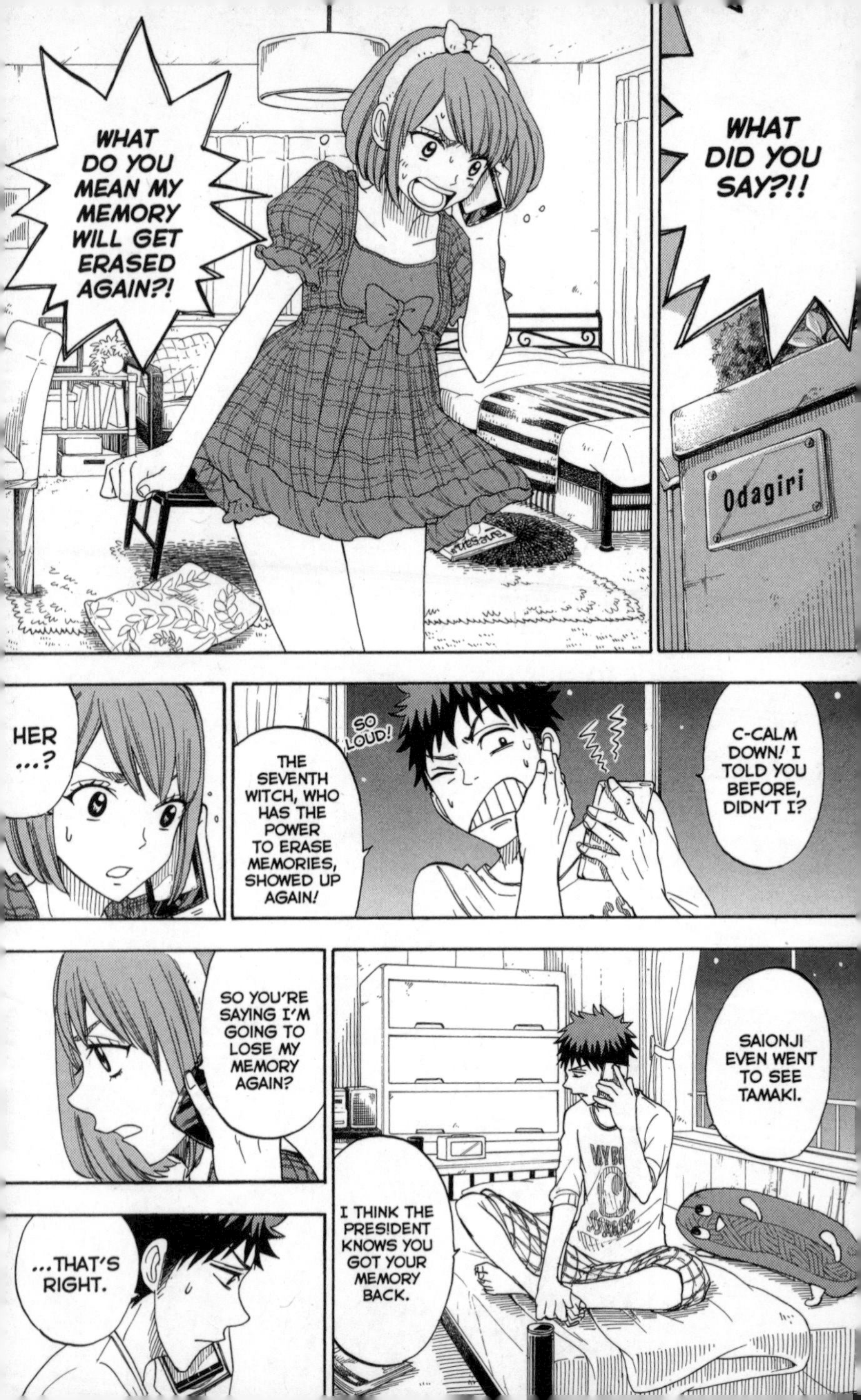
WHAT DID YOU SAY?!!
Odagiri
WHAT DO YOU MEAN MY MEMORY WILL GET ERASED AGAIN?!
C-CALM DOWN! I TOLD YOU BEFORE, DIDN'T I?
SO LOUD!
THE SEVENTH WITCH, WHO HAS THE POWER TO ERASE MEMORIES, SHOWED UP AGAIN!
HER ...?
SAIONJI EVEN WENT TO SEE TAMAKI.
I THINK THE PRESIDENT KNOWS YOU GOT YOUR MEMORY BACK.
SO YOU'RE SAYING I'M GOING TO LOSE MY MEMORY AGAIN?
...THAT'S RIGHT.

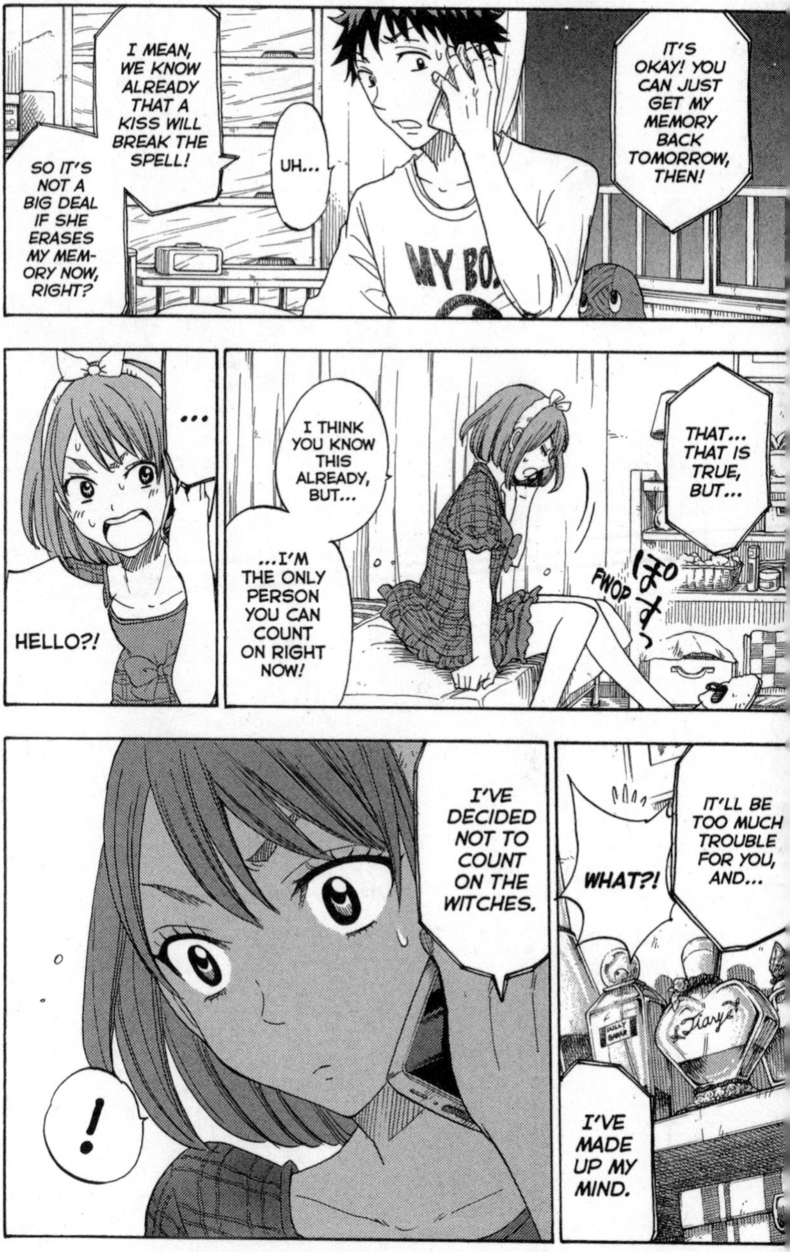
IT'S OKAY! YOU CAN JUST GET MY MEMORY BACK TOMORROW, THEN!
UH...
I MEAN, WE KNOW ALREADY THAT A KISS WILL BREAK THE SPELL!
SO IT'S NOT A BIG DEAL IF SHE ERASES MY MEMORY NOW, RIGHT?
THAT... THAT IS TRUE, BUT...
FWOP
ぽすっ
I THINK YOU KNOW THIS ALREADY, BUT...
...I'M THE ONLY PERSON YOU CAN COUNT ON RIGHT NOW!
...
HELLO?!
IT'LL BE TOO MUCH TROUBLE FOR YOU, AND...
WHAT?!
I'VE MADE UP MY MIND.
I'VE DECIDED NOT TO COUNT ON THE WITCHES.
!

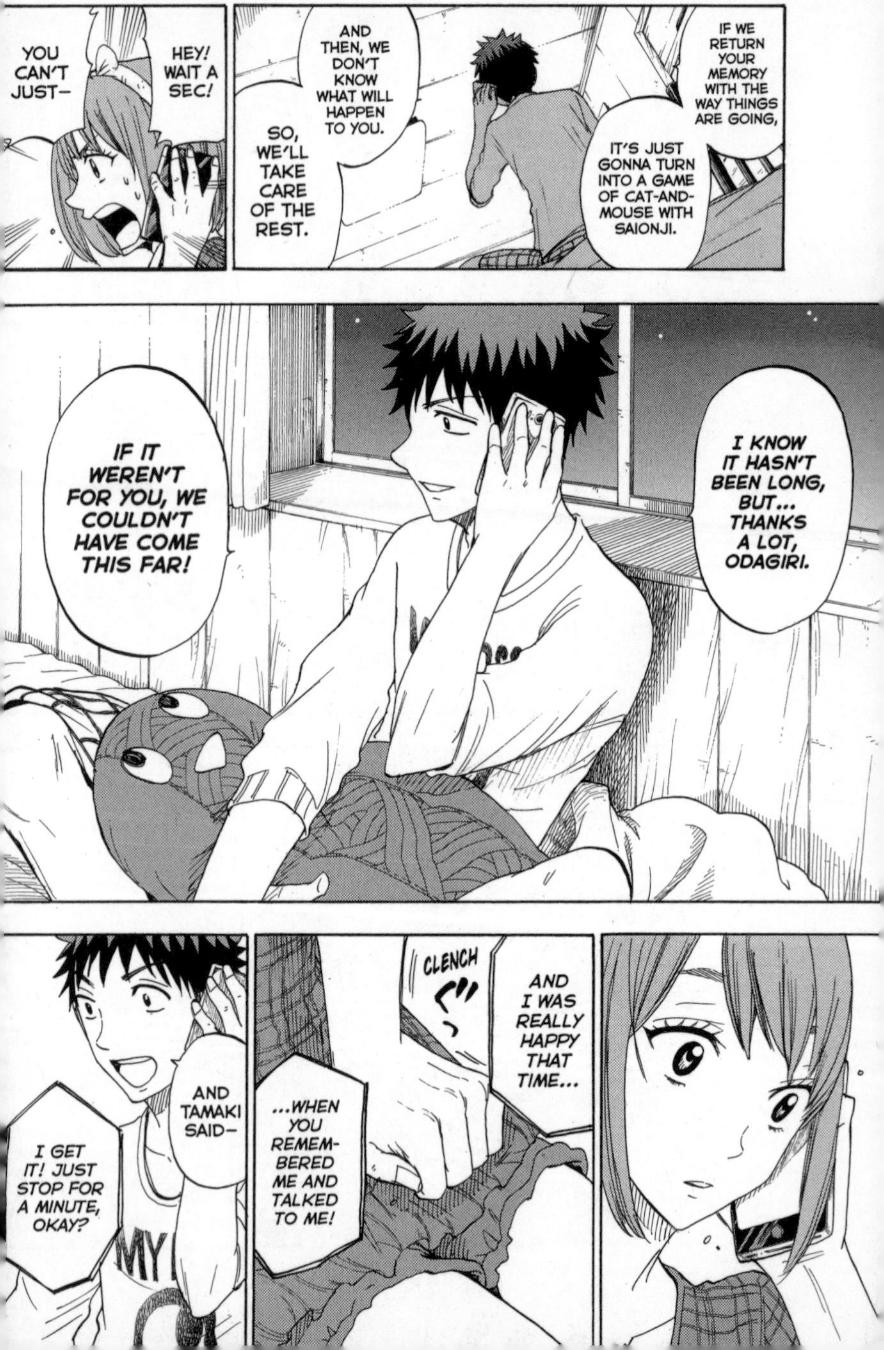
IF WE RETURN YOUR MEMORY WITH THE WAY THINGS ARE GOING,
IT'S JUST GONNA TURN INTO A GAME OF CAT-AND-MOUSE WITH SAIONJI.
AND THEN, WE DON'T KNOW WHAT WILL HAPPEN TO YOU.
SO, WE'LL TAKE CARE OF THE REST.
HEY! WAIT A SEC!
YOU CAN'T JUST–
I KNOW IT HASN'T BEEN LONG, BUT... THANKS A LOT, ODAGIRI.
IF IT WEREN'T FOR YOU, WE COULDN'T HAVE COME THIS FAR!
AND I WAS REALLY HAPPY THAT TIME...
CLENCH
...WHEN YOU REMEMBERED ME AND TALKED TO ME!
AND TAMAKI SAID–
I GET IT! JUST STOP FOR A MINUTE, OKAY?

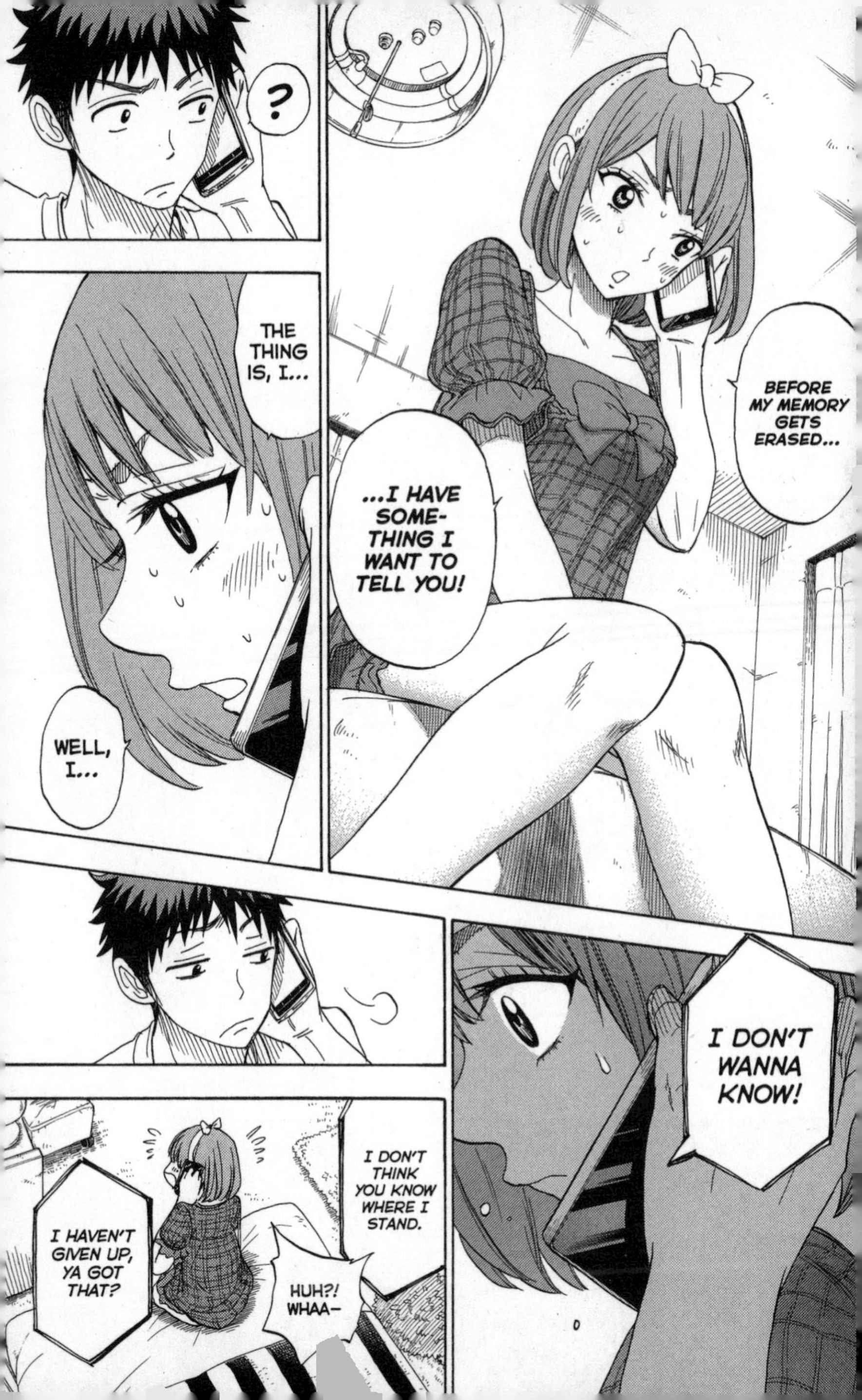
BEFORE MY MEMORY GETS ERASED...
...I HAVE SOME-THING I WANT TO TELL YOU!
?
THE THING IS, I...
WELL, I...
I DON'T WANNA KNOW!
I DON'T THINK YOU KNOW WHERE I STAND.
HUH?! WHAA–
I HAVEN'T GIVEN UP, YA GOT THAT?

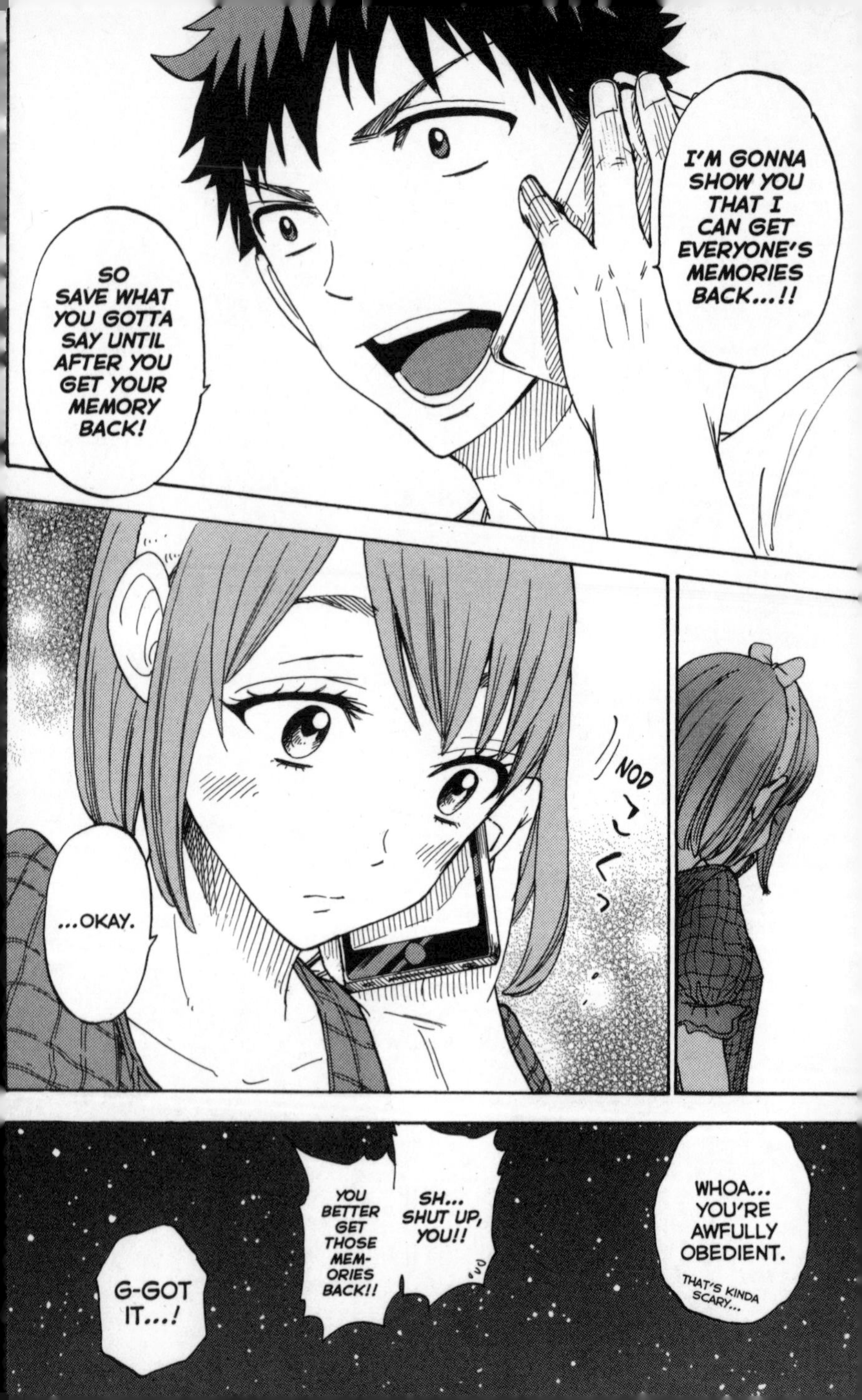
I'M GONNA SHOW YOU THAT I CAN GET EVERYONE'S MEMORIES BACK...!!
SO SAVE WHAT YOU GOTTA SAY UNTIL AFTER YOU GET YOUR MEMORY BACK!
NOD
...OKAY.
WHOA... YOU'RE AWFULLY OBEDIENT.
THAT'S KINDA SCARY...
SH... SHUT UP, YOU!!
YOU BETTER GET THOSE MEM-ORIES BACK!!
G-GOT IT...!

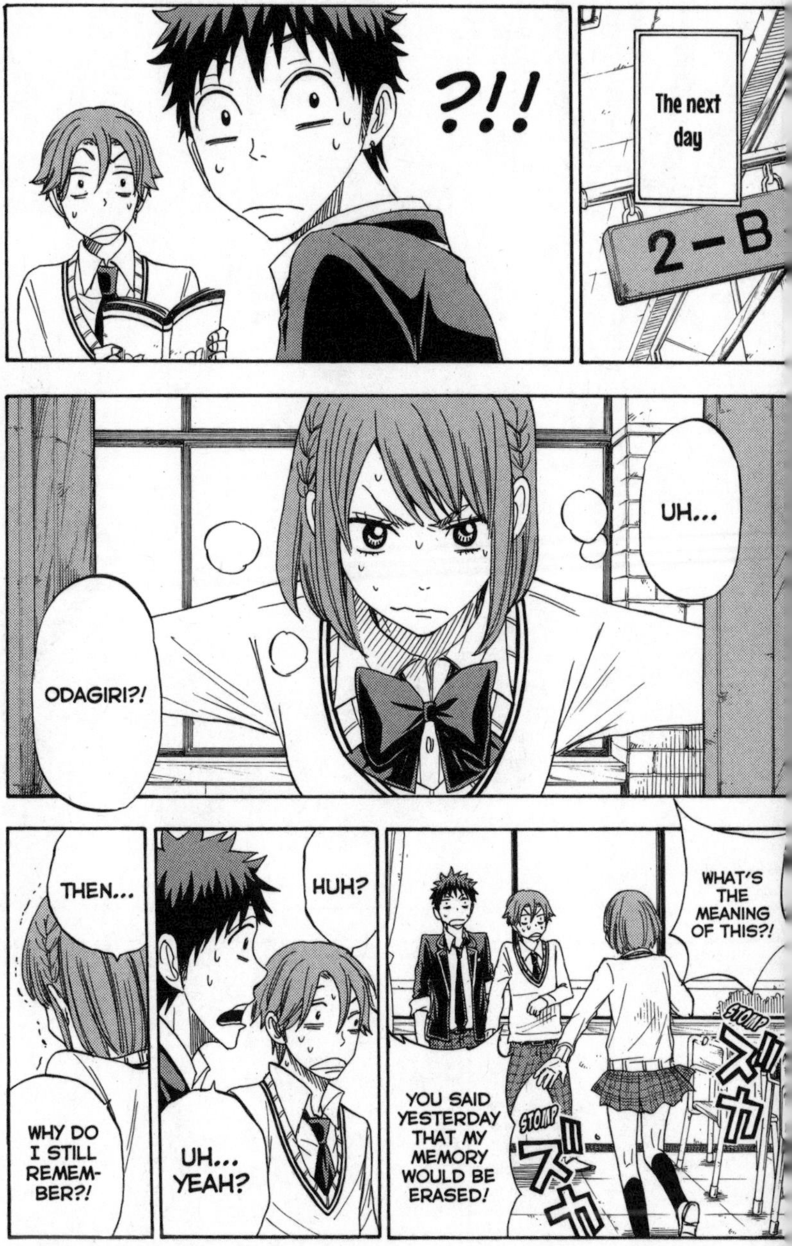
The next day
2-B
?!!
UH...
ODAGIRI?!
WHAT'S THE MEANING OF THIS?!
STOMP
YOU SAID YESTERDAY THAT MY MEMORY WOULD BE ERASED!
STOMP
HUH?
UH... YEAH?
THEN...
WHY DO I STILL REMEMBER?!

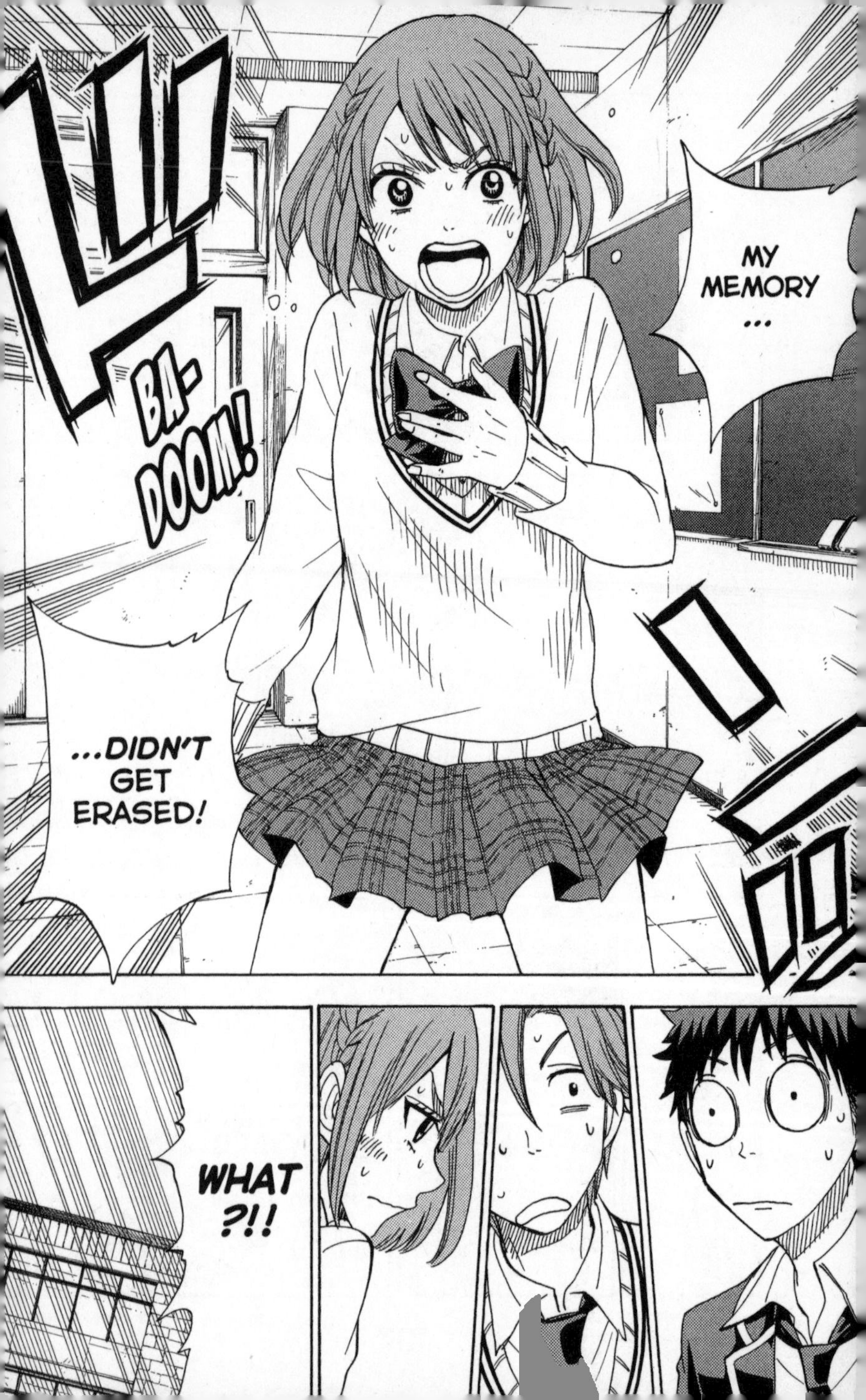
MY MEMORY ...
BA-DOOM!
...DIDN'T GET ERASED!
WHAT ?!!

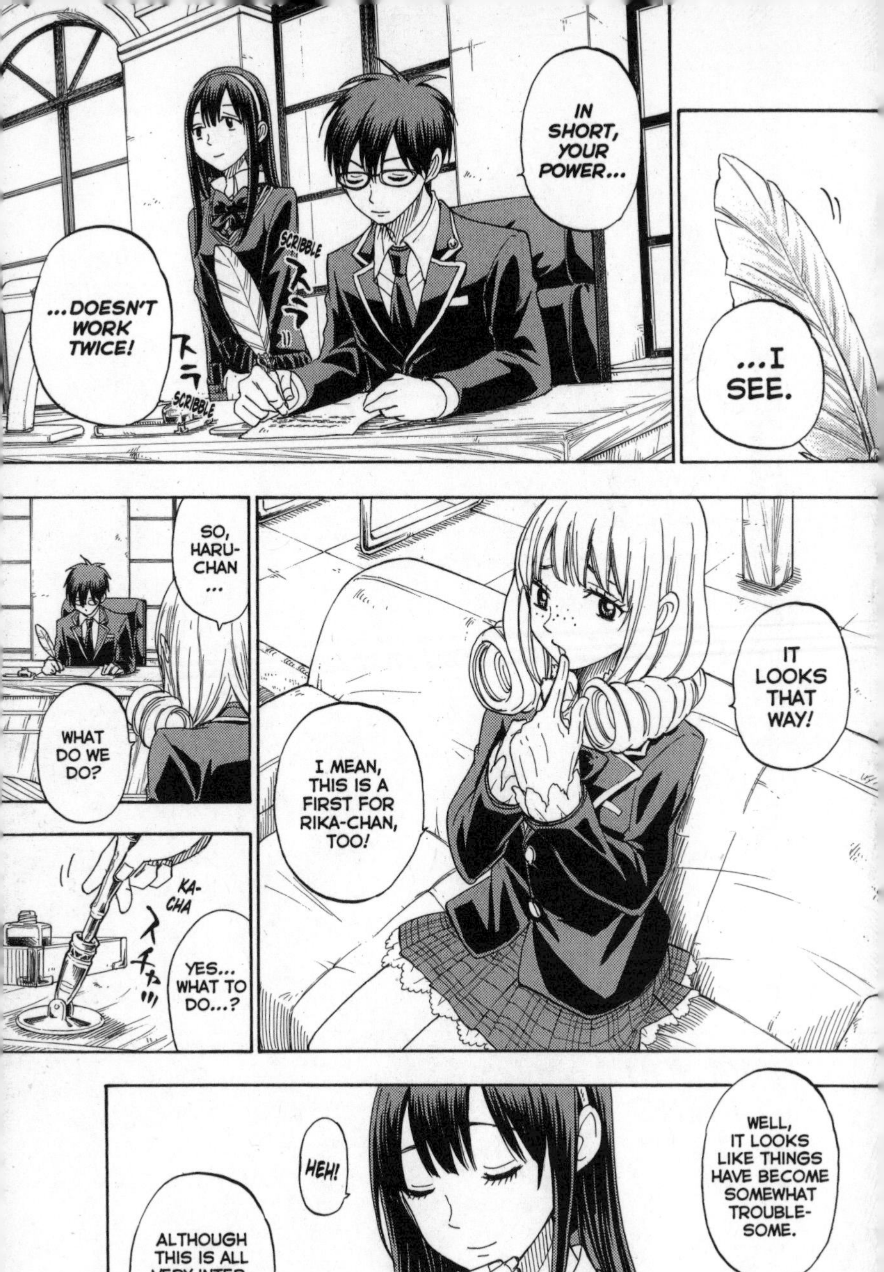
...I SEE.
IN SHORT, YOUR POWER...
SCRIBBLE
SCRIBBLE
...DOESN'T WORK TWICE!
IT LOOKS THAT WAY!
I MEAN, THIS IS A FIRST FOR RIKA-CHAN, TOO!
SO, HARU-CHAN ...
WHAT DO WE DO?
KA-CHA
YES... WHAT TO DO...?
WELL, IT LOOKS LIKE THINGS HAVE BECOME SOMEWHAT TROUBLE-SOME.
HEH!
ALTHOUGH THIS IS ALL VERY INTER-ESTING...

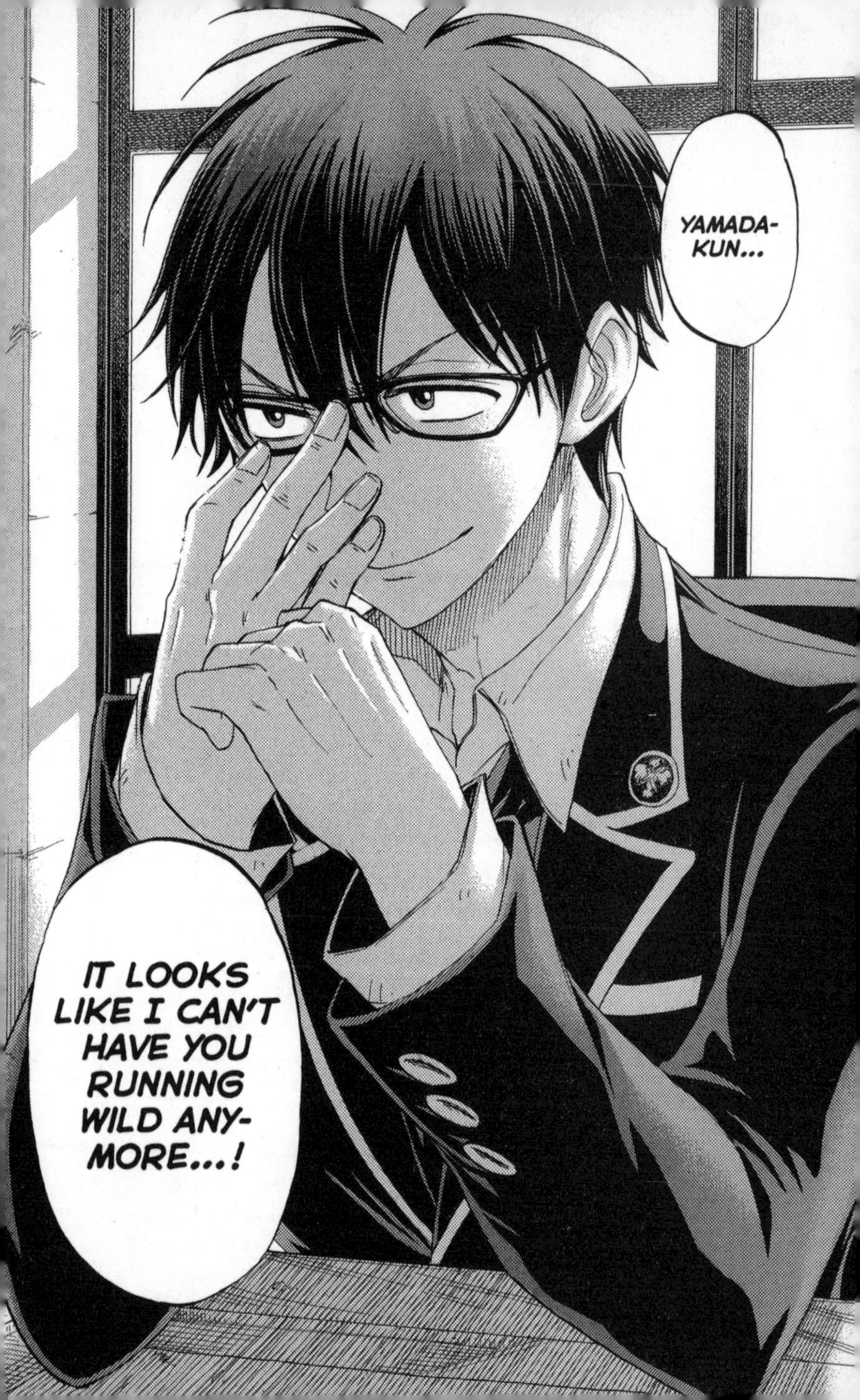
YAMADA-KUN...
IT LOOKS LIKE I CAN'T HAVE YOU RUNNING WILD ANYMORE...!

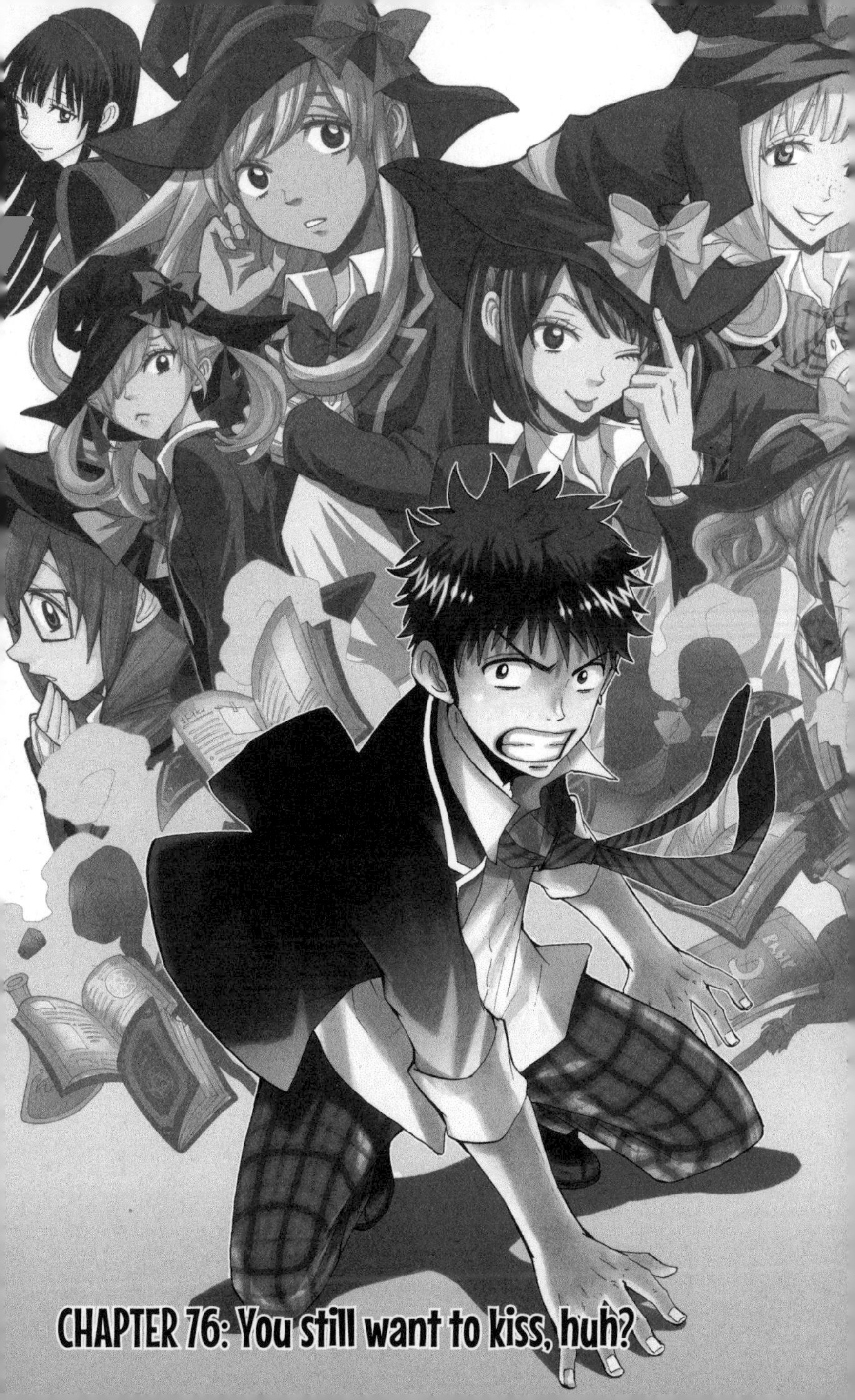
CHAPTER 76: You still want to kiss, huh?

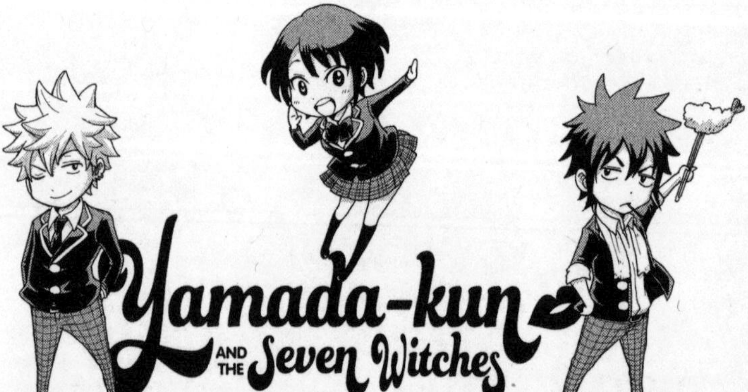
Yamada-kun
AND THE Seven Witches

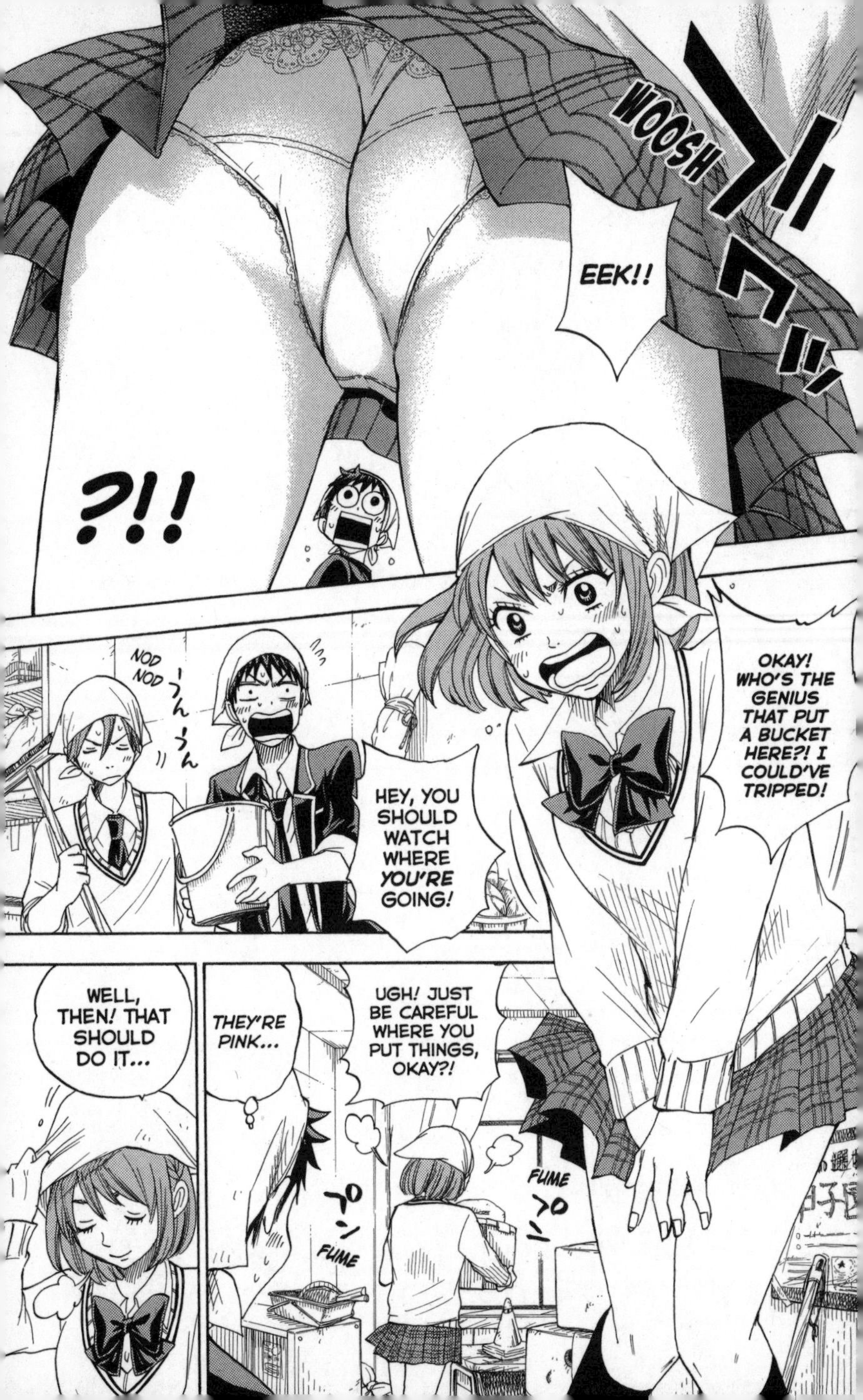
WOOSH
EEK!!
?!!
OKAY! WHO'S THE GENIUS THAT PUT A BUCKET HERE?! I COULD'VE TRIPPED!
HEY, YOU SHOULD WATCH WHERE YOU'RE GOING!
NOD NOD
UGH! JUST BE CAREFUL WHERE YOU PUT THINGS, OKAY?!
FUME
FUME
THEY'RE PINK...
WELL, THEN! THAT SHOULD DO IT...

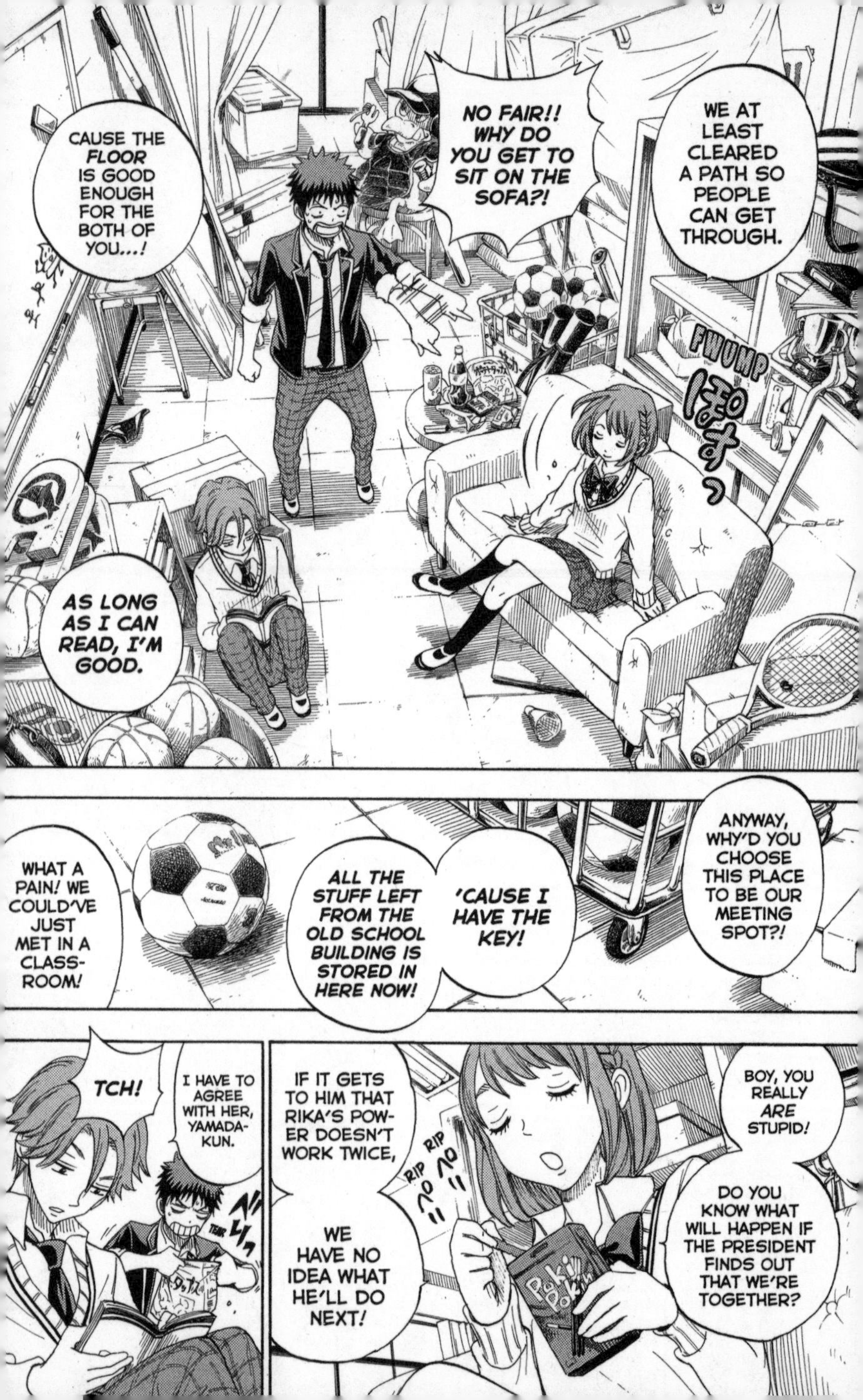

WE AT LEAST CLEARED A PATH SO PEOPLE CAN GET THROUGH.
FWUMP
NO FAIR!! WHY DO YOU GET TO SIT ON THE SOFA?!
CAUSE THE FLOOR IS GOOD ENOUGH FOR THE BOTH OF YOU...!
AS LONG AS I CAN READ, I'M GOOD.
ANYWAY, WHY'D YOU CHOOSE THIS PLACE TO BE OUR MEETING SPOT?!
'CAUSE I HAVE THE KEY!
ALL THE STUFF LEFT FROM THE OLD SCHOOL BUILDING IS STORED IN HERE NOW!
WHAT A PAIN! WE COULD'VE JUST MET IN A CLASS-ROOM!
BOY, YOU REALLY ARE STUPID!
DO YOU KNOW WHAT WILL HAPPEN IF THE PRESIDENT FINDS OUT THAT WE'RE TOGETHER?
RIP RIP
IF IT GETS TO HIM THAT RIKA'S POW-ER DOESN'T WORK TWICE,
WE HAVE NO IDEA WHAT HE'LL DO NEXT!
I HAVE TO AGREE WITH HER, YAMADA-KUN.
TEAR
TCH!

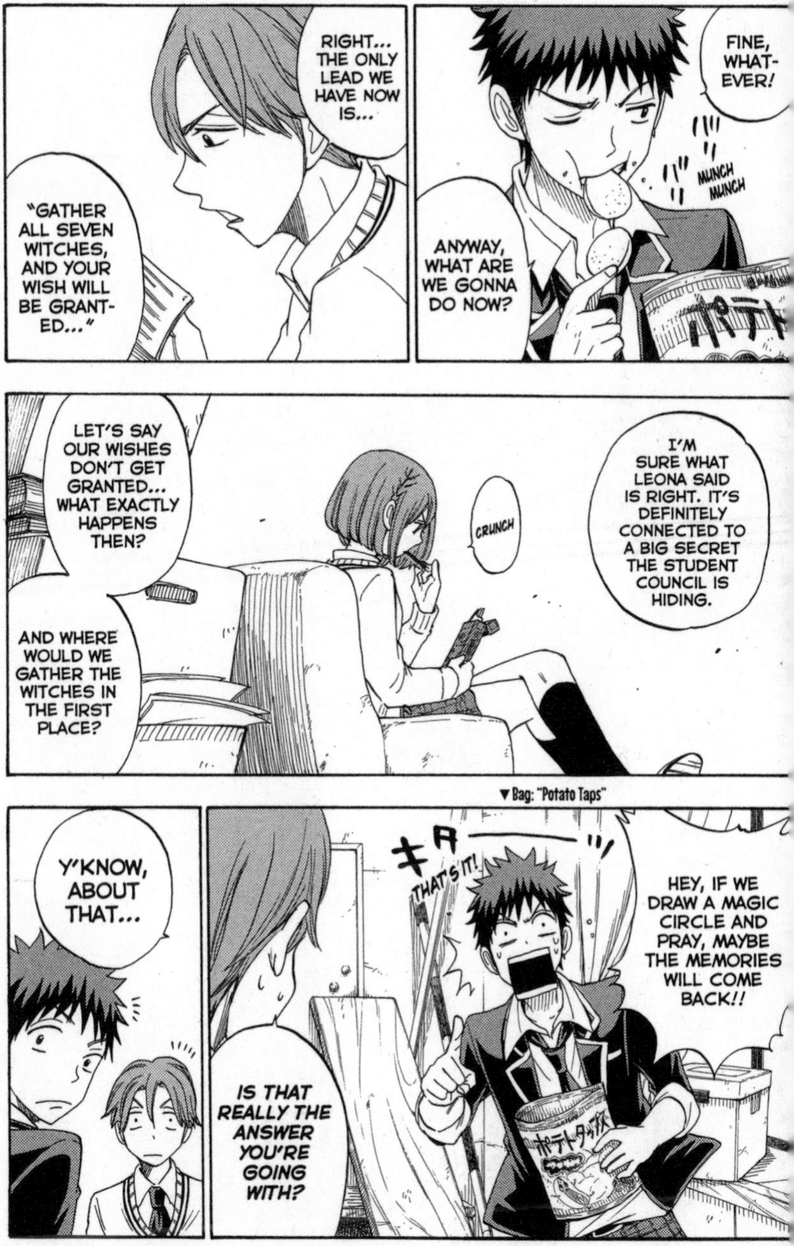
FINE, WHATEVER!
MUNCH MUNCH
ANYWAY, WHAT ARE WE GONNA DO NOW?
RIGHT... THE ONLY LEAD WE HAVE NOW IS...
"GATHER ALL SEVEN WITCHES, AND YOUR WISH WILL BE GRANTED..."
I'M SURE WHAT LEONA SAID IS RIGHT. IT'S DEFINITELY CONNECTED TO A BIG SECRET THE STUDENT COUNCIL IS HIDING.
CRUNCH
LET'S SAY OUR WISHES DON'T GET GRANTED... WHAT EXACTLY HAPPENS THEN?
AND WHERE WOULD WE GATHER THE WITCHES IN THE FIRST PLACE?
▼Bag: "Potato Taps"
THAT'S IT!
HEY, IF WE DRAW A MAGIC CIRCLE AND PRAY, MAYBE THE MEMORIES WILL COME BACK!!
IS THAT REALLY THE ANSWER YOU'RE GOING WITH?
Y'KNOW, ABOUT THAT...

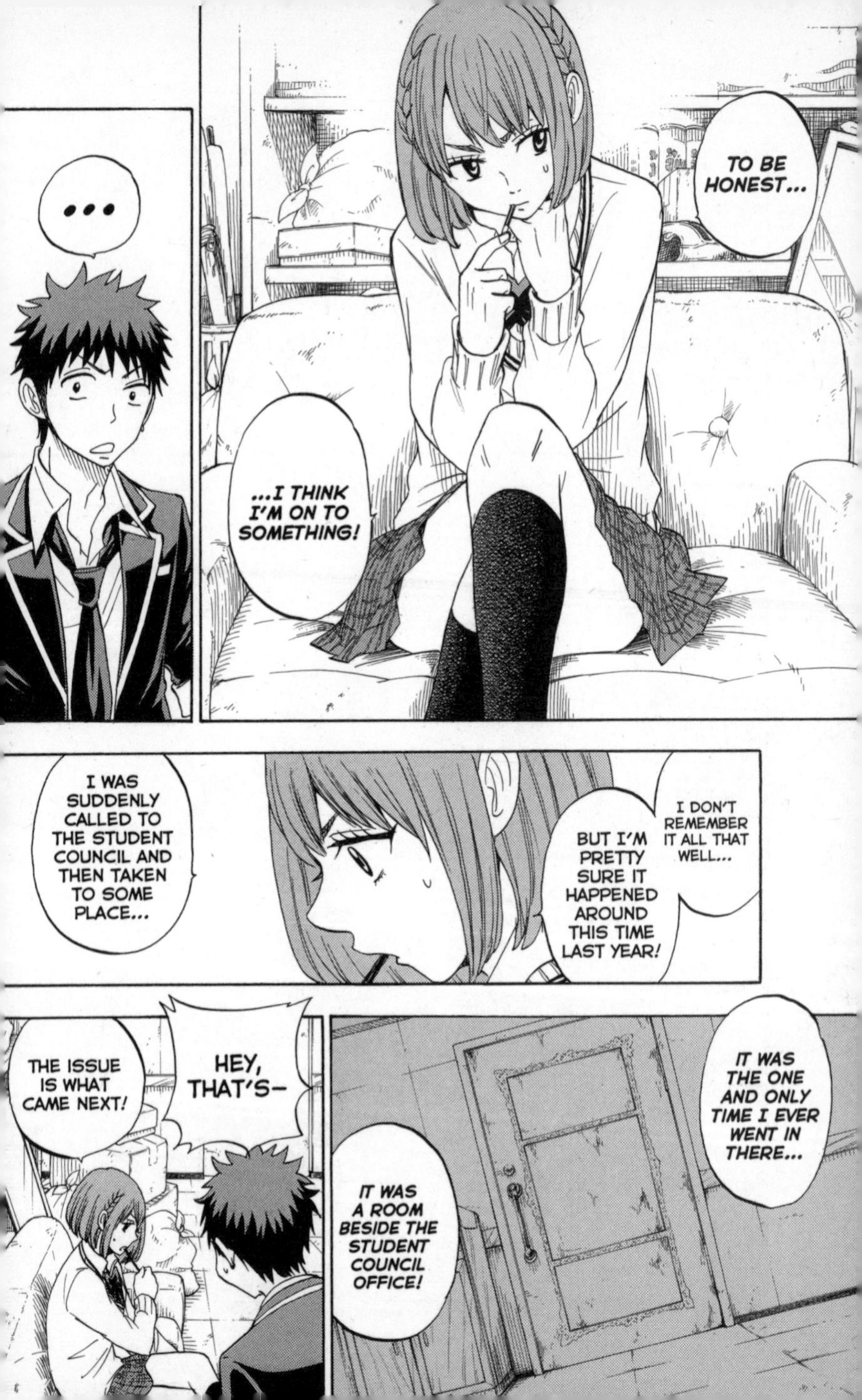
TO BE HONEST...
...I THINK I'M ON TO SOMETHING!
...
I DON'T REMEMBER IT ALL THAT WELL...
BUT I'M PRETTY SURE IT HAPPENED AROUND THIS TIME LAST YEAR!
I WAS SUDDENLY CALLED TO THE STUDENT COUNCIL AND THEN TAKEN TO SOME PLACE...
IT WAS THE ONE AND ONLY TIME I EVER WENT IN THERE...
IT WAS A ROOM BESIDE THE STUDENT COUNCIL OFFICE!
HEY, THAT'S—
THE ISSUE IS WHAT CAME NEXT!

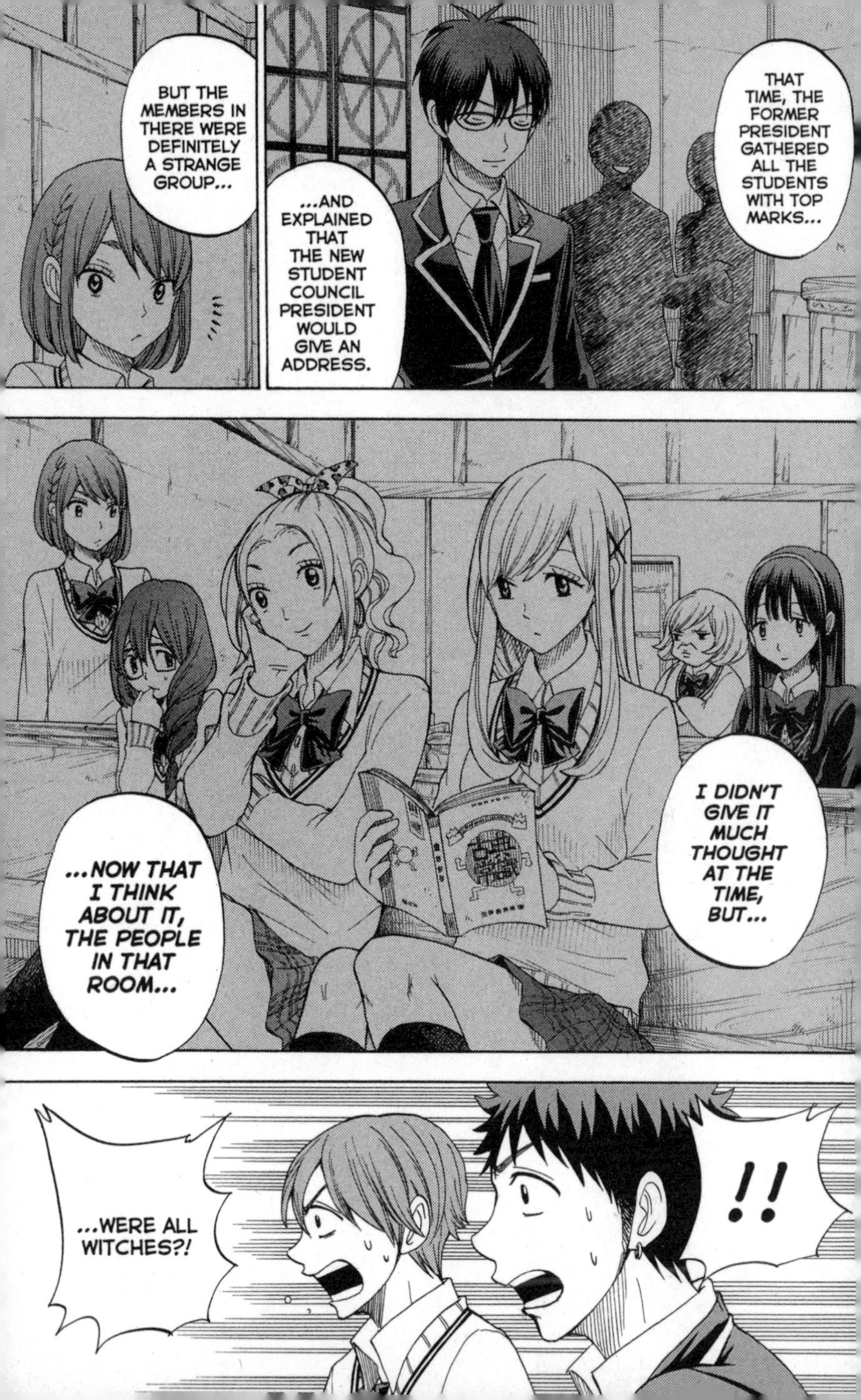
THAT TIME, THE FORMER PRESIDENT GATHERED ALL THE STUDENTS WITH TOP MARKS...
...AND EXPLAINED THAT THE NEW STUDENT COUNCIL PRESIDENT WOULD GIVE AN ADDRESS.
BUT THE MEMBERS IN THERE WERE DEFINITELY A STRANGE GROUP...
I DIDN'T GIVE IT MUCH THOUGHT AT THE TIME, BUT...
...NOW THAT I THINK ABOUT IT, THE PEOPLE IN THAT ROOM...
!!
...WERE ALL WITCHES?!

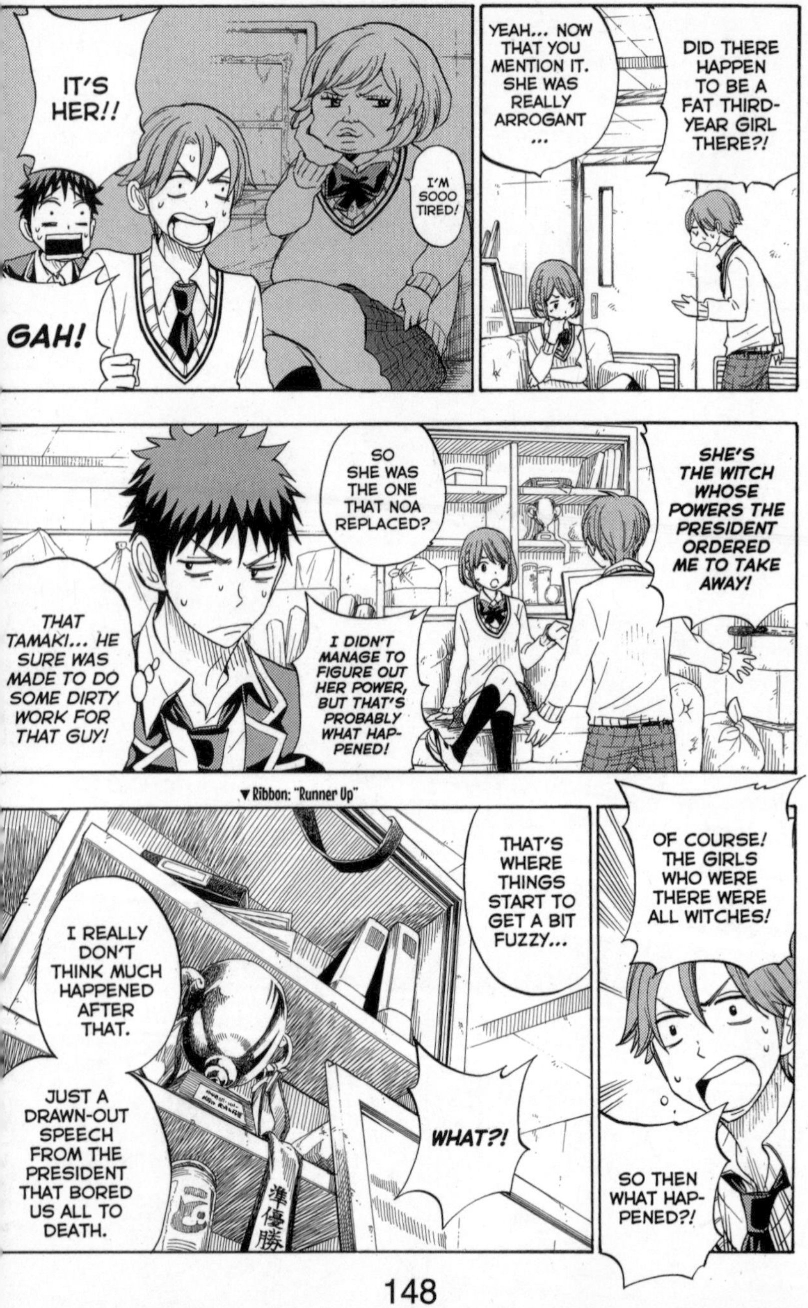
DID THERE HAPPEN TO BE A FAT THIRD-YEAR GIRL THERE?!
YEAH... NOW THAT YOU MENTION IT. SHE WAS REALLY ARROGANT ...
IT'S HER!!
I'M SOOO TIRED!
GAH!
SHE'S THE WITCH WHOSE POWERS THE PRESIDENT ORDERED ME TO TAKE AWAY!
SO SHE WAS THE ONE THAT NOA REPLACED?
I DIDN'T MANAGE TO FIGURE OUT HER POWER, BUT THAT'S PROBABLY WHAT HAPPENED!
THAT TAMAKI... HE SURE WAS MADE TO DO SOME DIRTY WORK FOR THAT GUY!
▼Ribbon: "Runner Up"
OF COURSE! THE GIRLS WHO WERE THERE WERE ALL WITCHES!
SO THEN WHAT HAPPENED?!
THAT'S WHERE THINGS START TO GET A BIT FUZZY...
WHAT?!
I REALLY DON'T THINK MUCH HAPPENED AFTER THAT.
JUST A DRAWN-OUT SPEECH FROM THE PRESIDENT THAT BORED US ALL TO DEATH.
準優勝

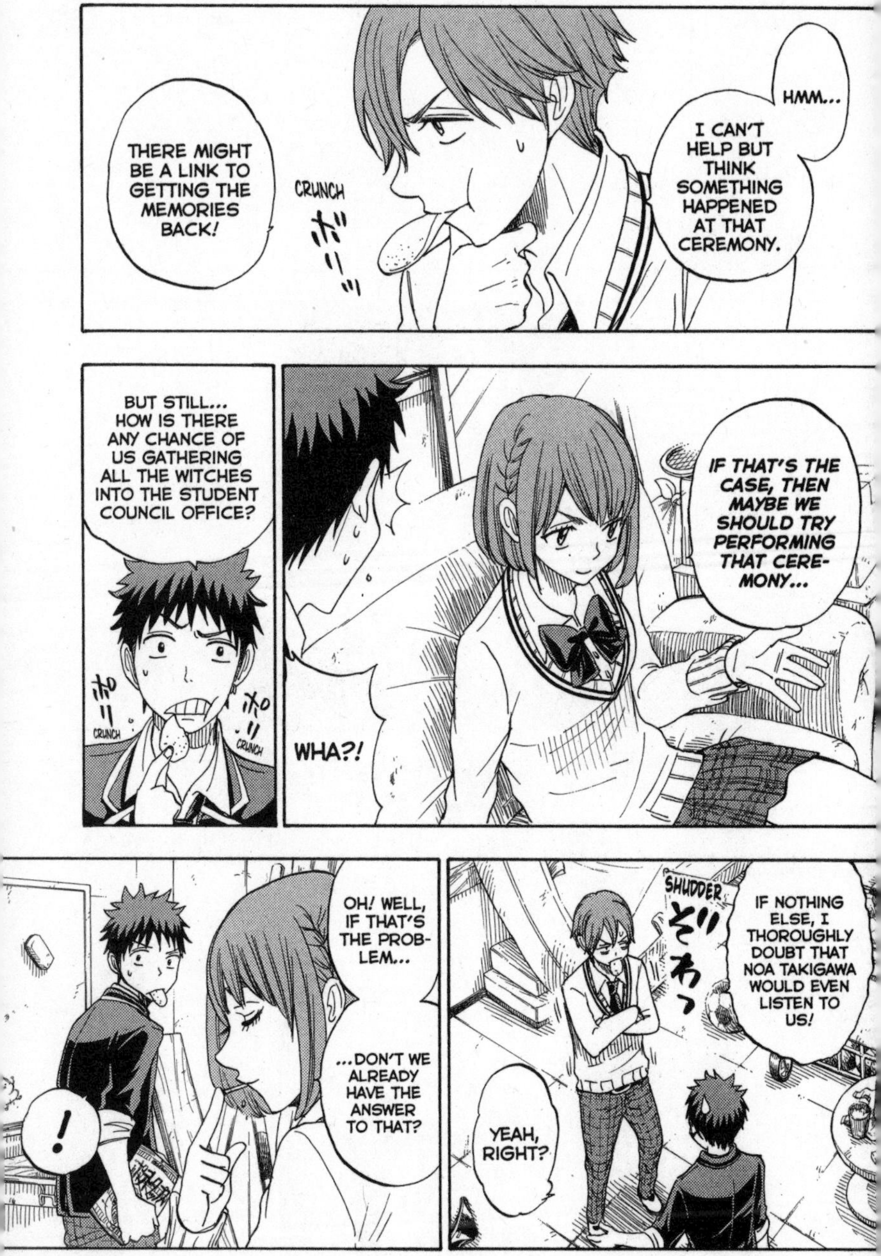
HMM...
I CAN'T HELP BUT THINK SOMETHING HAPPENED AT THAT CEREMONY.
CRUNCH
THERE MIGHT BE A LINK TO GETTING THE MEMORIES BACK!
IF THAT'S THE CASE, THEN MAYBE WE SHOULD TRY PERFORMING THAT CERE-MONY...
WHA?!
BUT STILL... HOW IS THERE ANY CHANCE OF US GATHERING ALL THE WITCHES INTO THE STUDENT COUNCIL OFFICE?
CRUNCH
CRUNCH
SHUDDER
IF NOTHING ELSE, I THOROUGHLY DOUBT THAT NOA TAKIGAWA WOULD EVEN LISTEN TO US!
YEAH, RIGHT?
OH! WELL, IF THAT'S THE PROB-LEM...
...DON'T WE ALREADY HAVE THE ANSWER TO THAT?
!

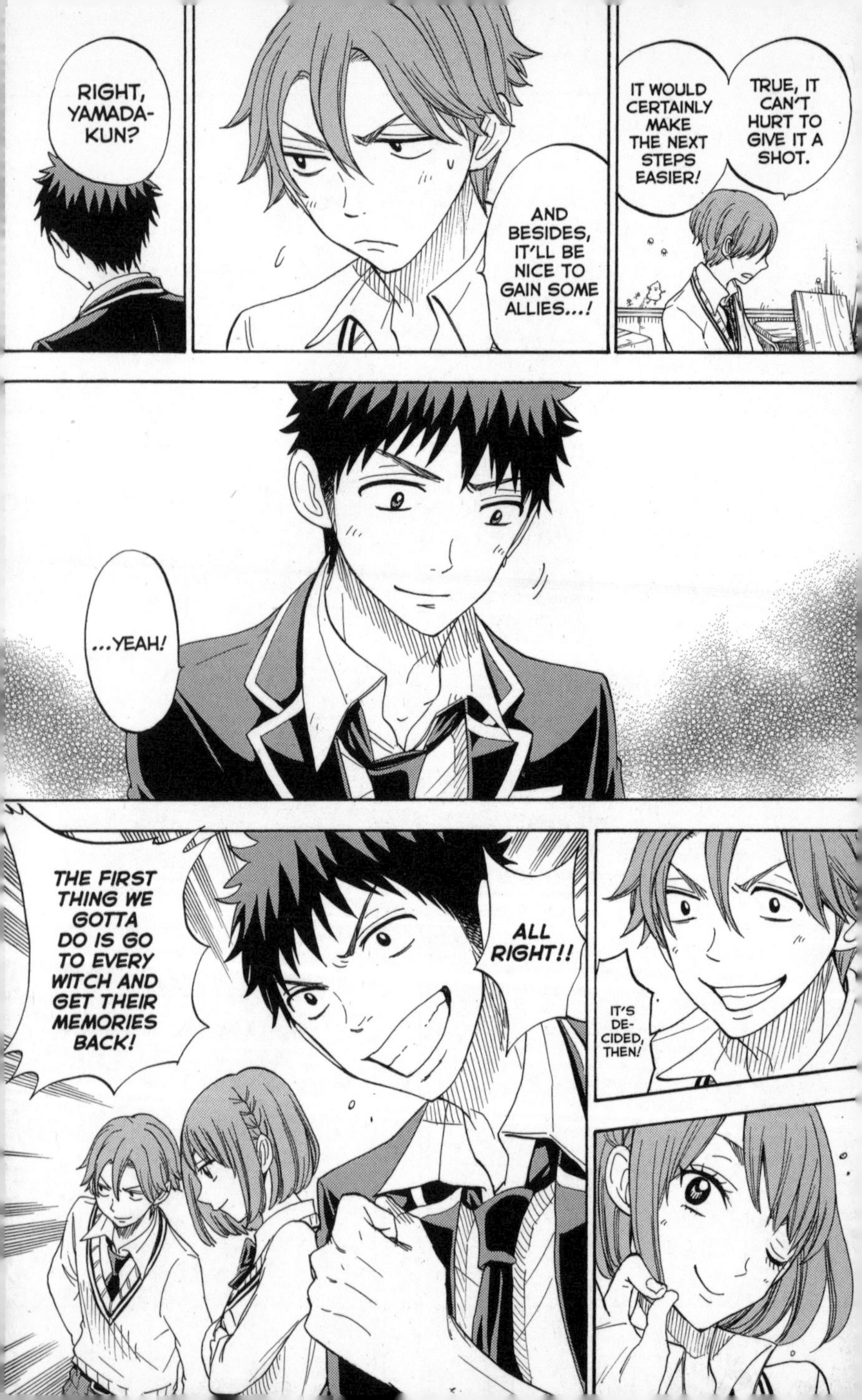
TRUE, IT CAN'T HURT TO GIVE IT A SHOT.
IT WOULD CERTAINLY MAKE THE NEXT STEPS EASIER!
AND BESIDES, IT'LL BE NICE TO GAIN SOME ALLIES...!
RIGHT, YAMADA-KUN?
...YEAH!
IT'S DE-CIDED, THEN!
ALL RIGHT!!
THE FIRST THING WE GOTTA DO IS GO TO EVERY WITCH AND GET THEIR MEMORIES BACK!

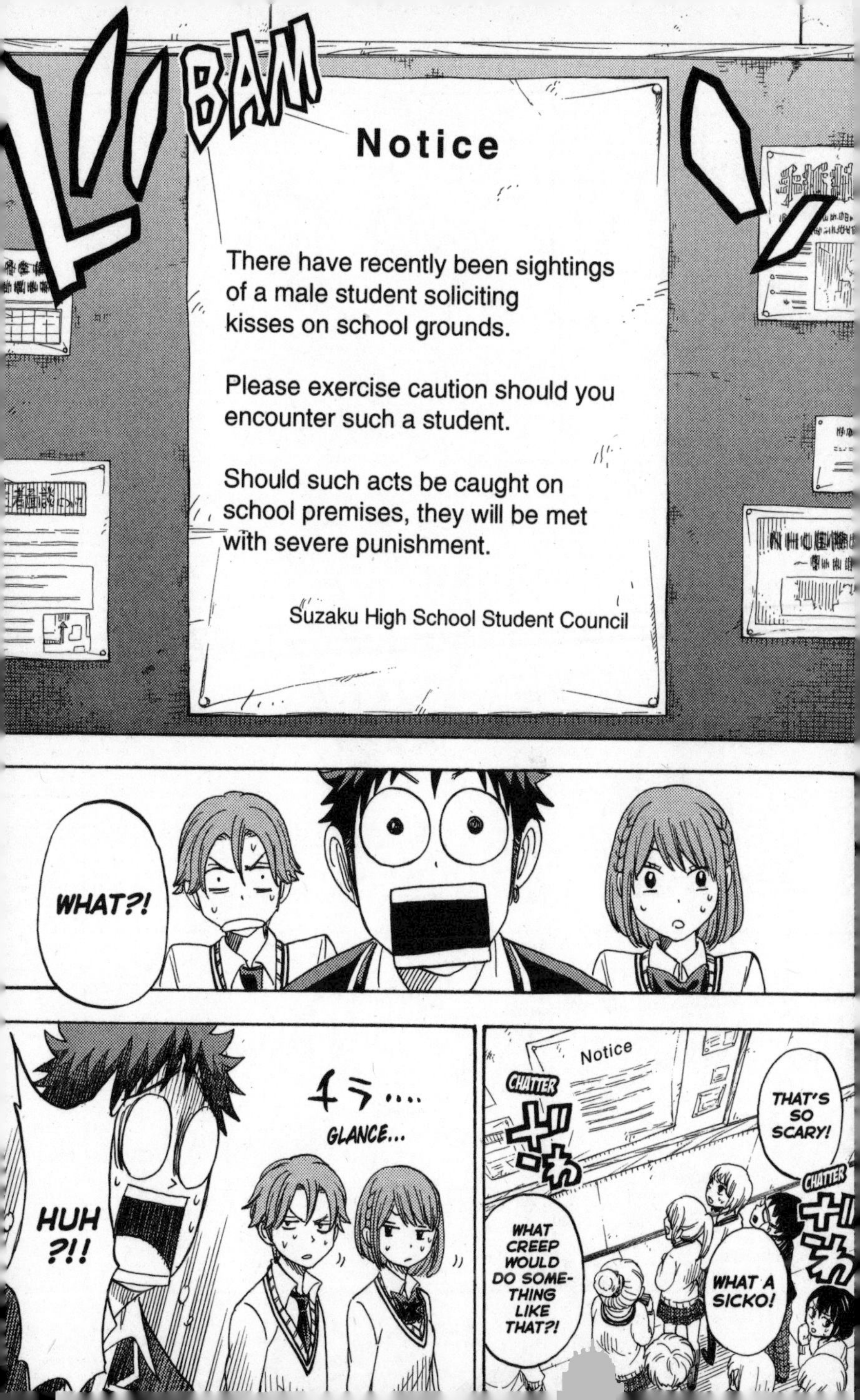
BAM
Notice
There have recently been sightings of a male student soliciting kisses on school grounds.
Please exercise caution should you encounter such a student.
Should such acts be caught on school premises, they will be met with severe punishment.
Suzaku High School Student Council
WHAT?!
THAT'S SO SCARY!
CHATTER
WHAT A SICKO!
Notice
CHATTER
WHAT CREEP WOULD DO SOME-THING LIKE THAT?!
GLANCE...
HUH ?!!

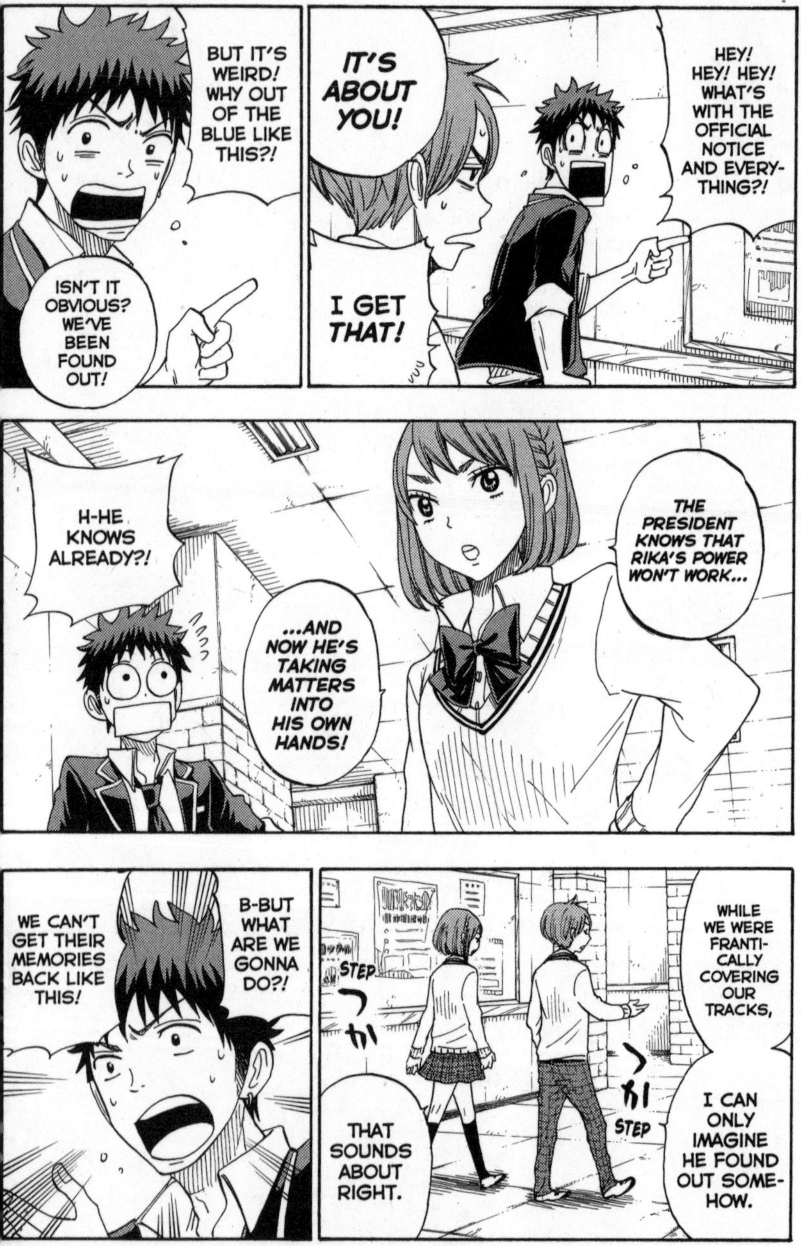
HEY! HEY! HEY! WHAT'S WITH THE OFFICIAL NOTICE AND EVERY-THING?!
IT'S ABOUT YOU!
I GET THAT!
BUT IT'S WEIRD! WHY OUT OF THE BLUE LIKE THIS?!
ISN'T IT OBVIOUS? WE'VE BEEN FOUND OUT!
THE PRESIDENT KNOWS THAT RIKA'S POWER WON'T WORK...
...AND NOW HE'S TAKING MATTERS INTO HIS OWN HANDS!
H-HE KNOWS ALREADY?!
WHILE WE WERE FRANTI-CALLY COVERING OUR TRACKS,
I CAN ONLY IMAGINE HE FOUND OUT SOME-HOW.
STEP
STEP
THAT SOUNDS ABOUT RIGHT.
B-BUT WHAT ARE WE GONNA DO?!
WE CAN'T GET THEIR MEMORIES BACK LIKE THIS!

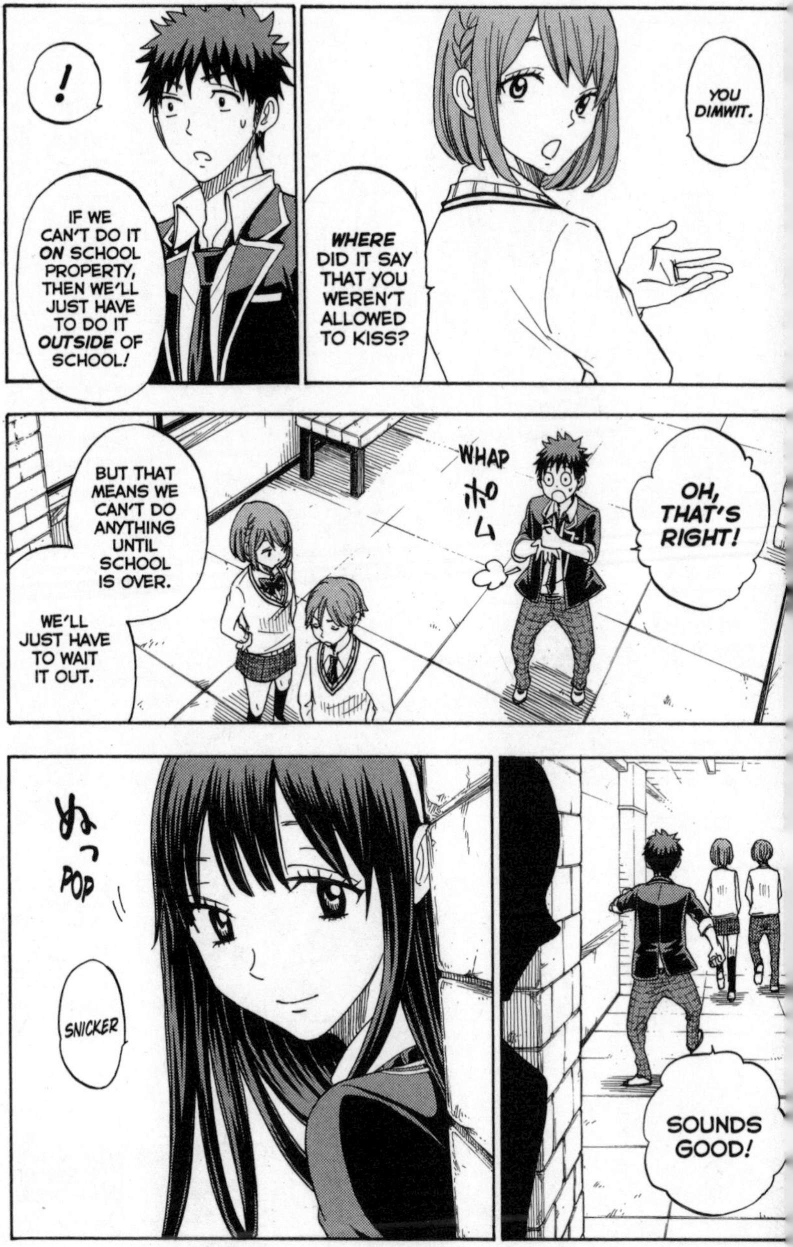
YOU DIMWIT.
WHERE DID IT SAY THAT YOU WEREN'T ALLOWED TO KISS?
!
IF WE CAN'T DO IT ON SCHOOL PROPERTY, THEN WE'LL JUST HAVE TO DO IT OUTSIDE OF SCHOOL!
OH, THAT'S RIGHT!
WHAP
ポム
BUT THAT MEANS WE CAN'T DO ANYTHING UNTIL SCHOOL IS OVER.
WE'LL JUST HAVE TO WAIT IT OUT.
SOUNDS GOOD!
ぬっ
POP
SNICKER

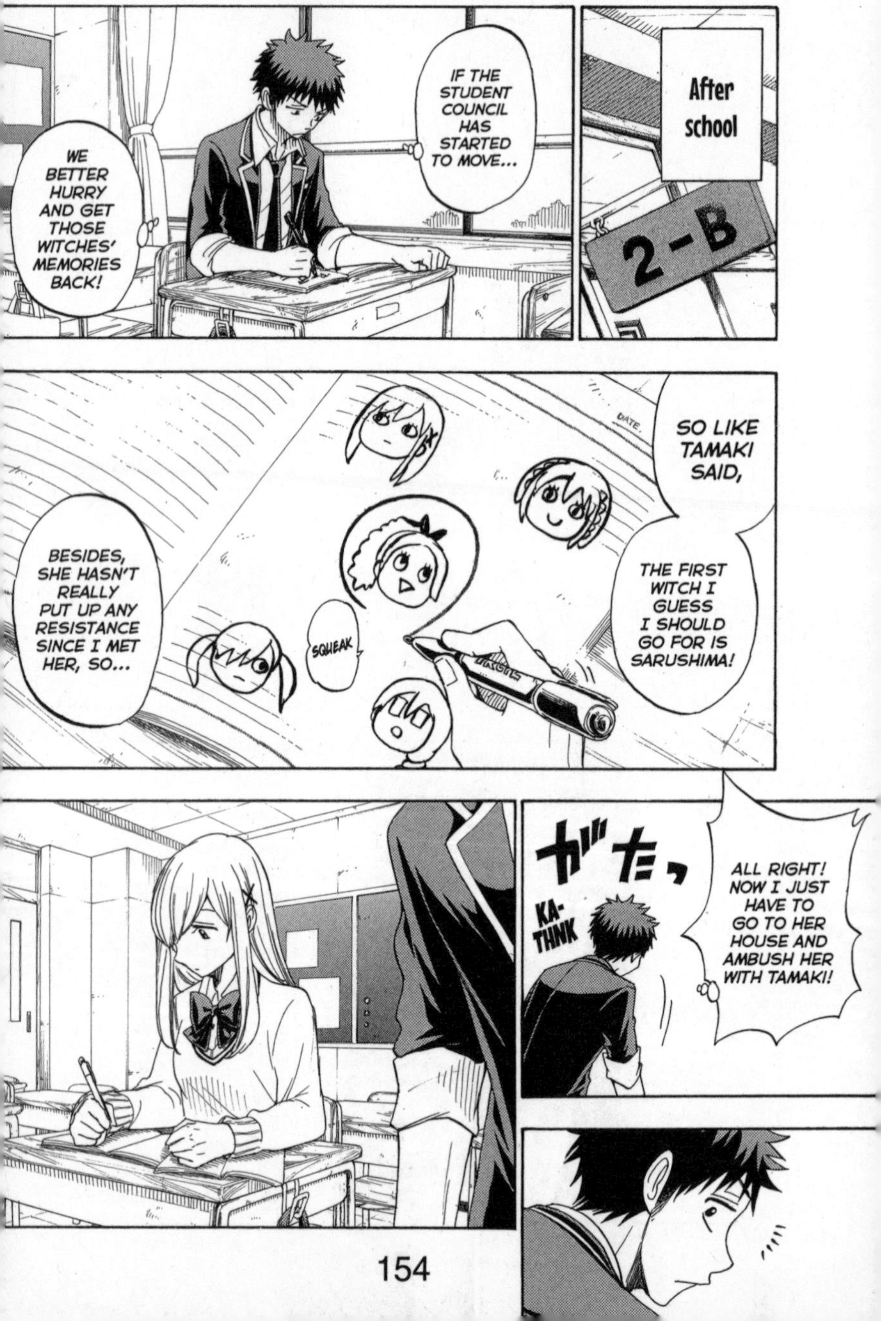
After school
2-B
IF THE STUDENT COUNCIL HAS STARTED TO MOVE...
WE BETTER HURRY AND GET THOSE WITCHES' MEMORIES BACK!
SO LIKE TAMAKI SAID,
THE FIRST WITCH I GUESS I SHOULD GO FOR IS SARUSHIMA!
SQUEAK
BESIDES, SHE HASN'T REALLY PUT UP ANY RESISTANCE SINCE I MET HER, SO...
ALL RIGHT! NOW I JUST HAVE TO GO TO HER HOUSE AND AMBUSH HER WITH TAMAKI!
ガタッ
KA-THNK

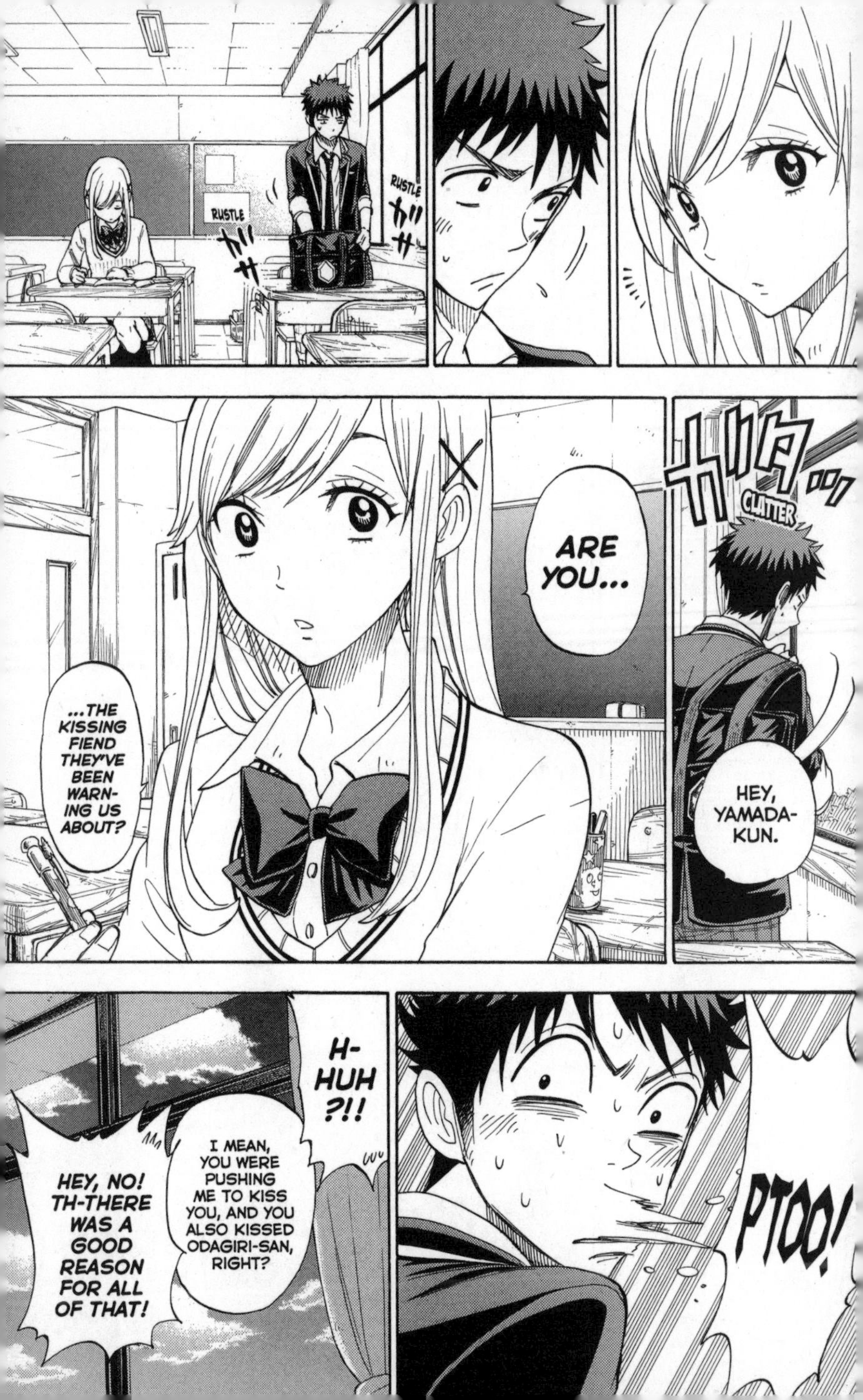
RUSTLE
ガサ
RUSTLE
ガサ
カタ
CLATTER
HEY, YAMADA-KUN.
ARE YOU...
...THE KISSING FIEND THEY'VE BEEN WARNING US ABOUT?
PTOO!
H-HUH?!!
I MEAN, YOU WERE PUSHING ME TO KISS YOU, AND YOU ALSO KISSED ODAGIRI-SAN, RIGHT?
HEY, NO! TH-THERE WAS A GOOD REASON FOR ALL OF THAT!

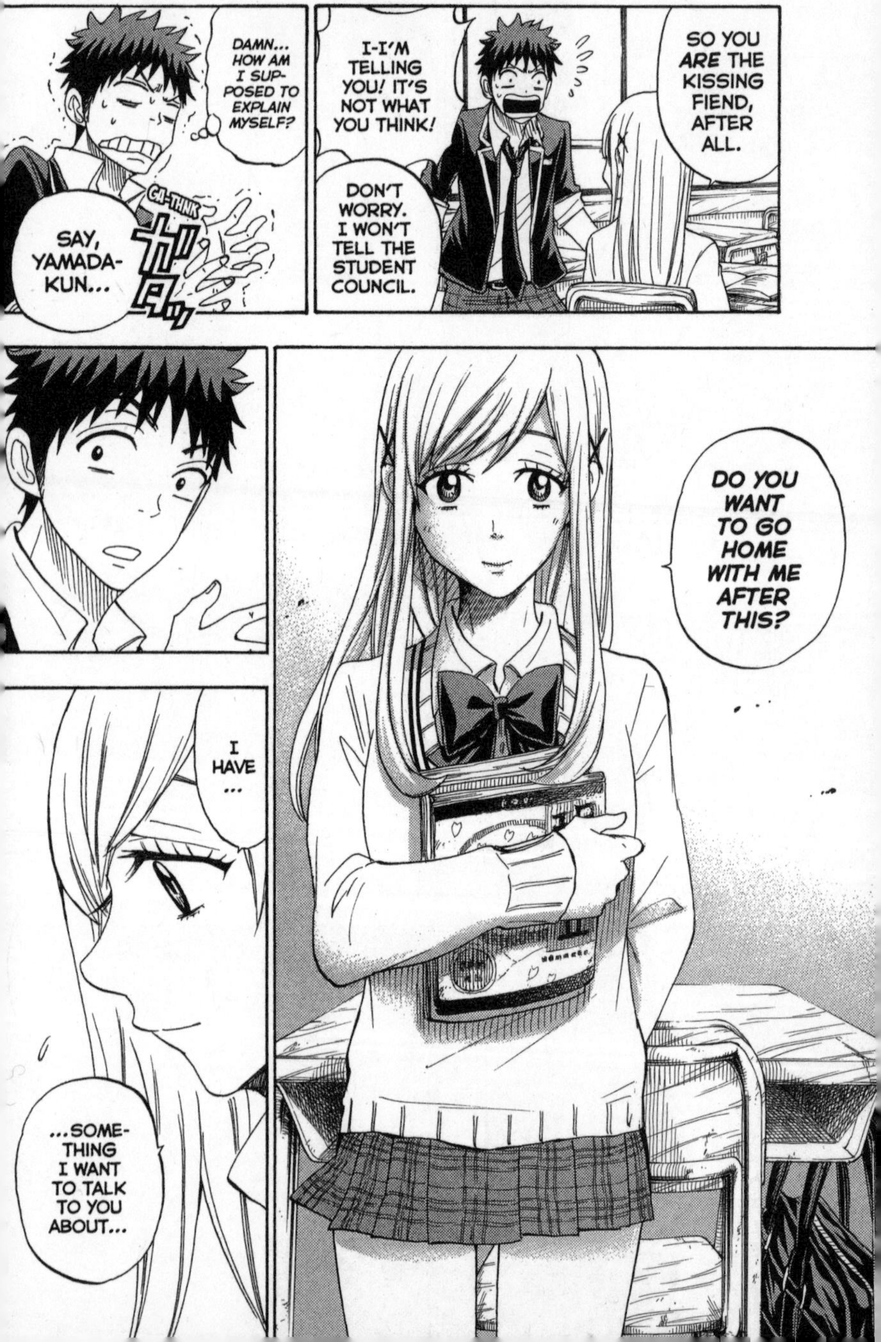
SO YOU ARE THE KISSING FIEND, AFTER ALL.
I-I'M TELLING YOU! IT'S NOT WHAT YOU THINK!
DON'T WORRY. I WON'T TELL THE STUDENT COUNCIL.
DAMN... HOW AM I SUP-POSED TO EXPLAIN MYSELF?
GA-THNK
SAY, YAMADA-KUN...
DO YOU WANT TO GO HOME WITH ME AFTER THIS?
...
I HAVE...
...SOME-THING I WANT TO TALK TO YOU ABOUT...

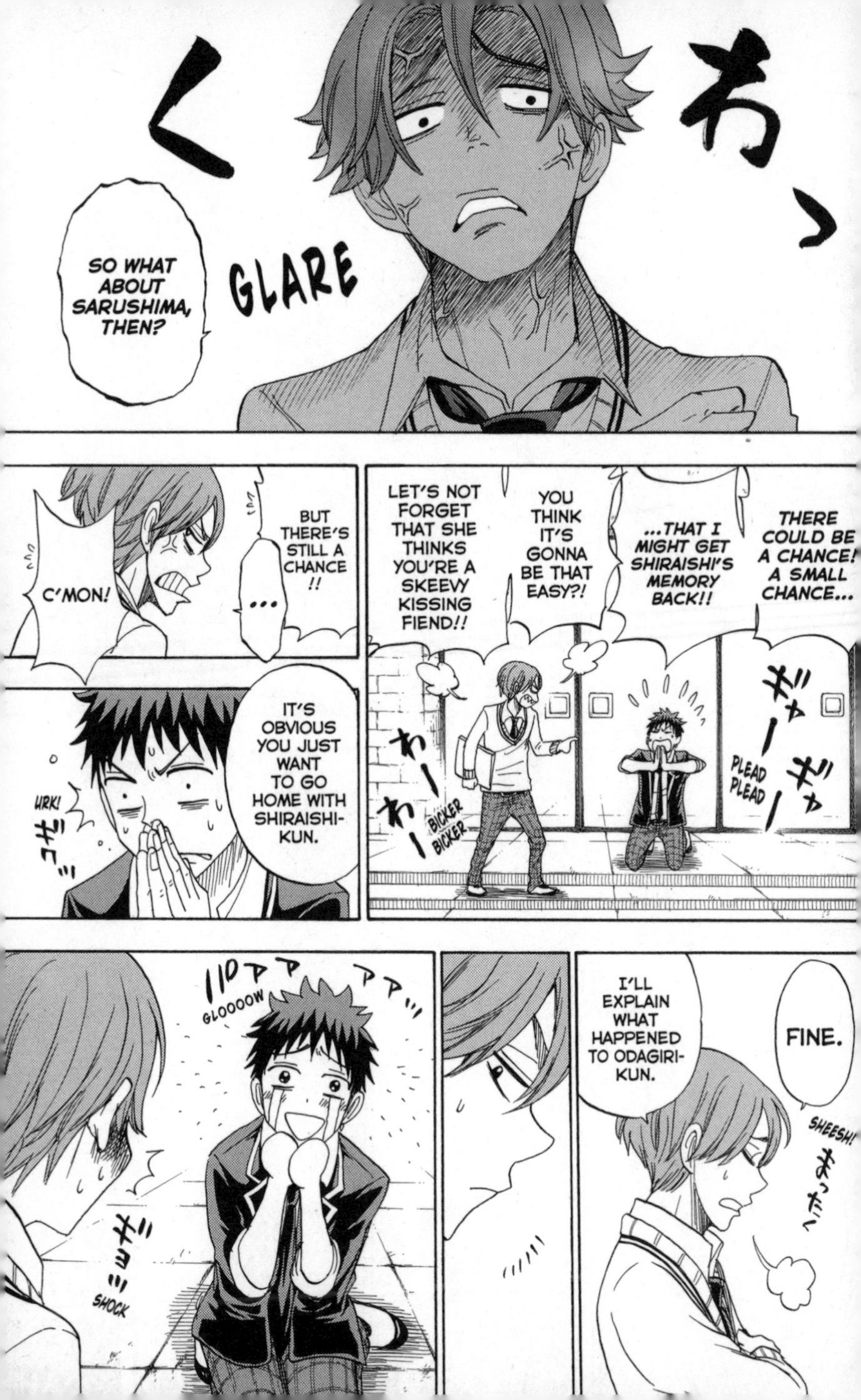
くわっ
GLARE
SO WHAT ABOUT SARUSHIMA, THEN?
THERE COULD BE A CHANCE! A SMALL CHANCE...
...THAT I MIGHT GET SHIRAISHI'S MEMORY BACK!!
YOU THINK IT'S GONNA BE THAT EASY?!
LET'S NOT FORGET THAT SHE THINKS YOU'RE A SKEEVY KISSING FIEND!!
ギャーギャー
PLEAD PLEAD
わーわー
BICKER BICKER
BUT THERE'S STILL A CHANCE!!
...
C'MON!
IT'S OBVIOUS YOU JUST WANT TO GO HOME WITH SHIRAISHI-KUN.
URK!
ギクッ
FINE.
I'LL EXPLAIN WHAT HAPPENED TO ODAGIRI-KUN.
SHEESH!
まったく
GLOOOOW
ギョッ
SHOCK

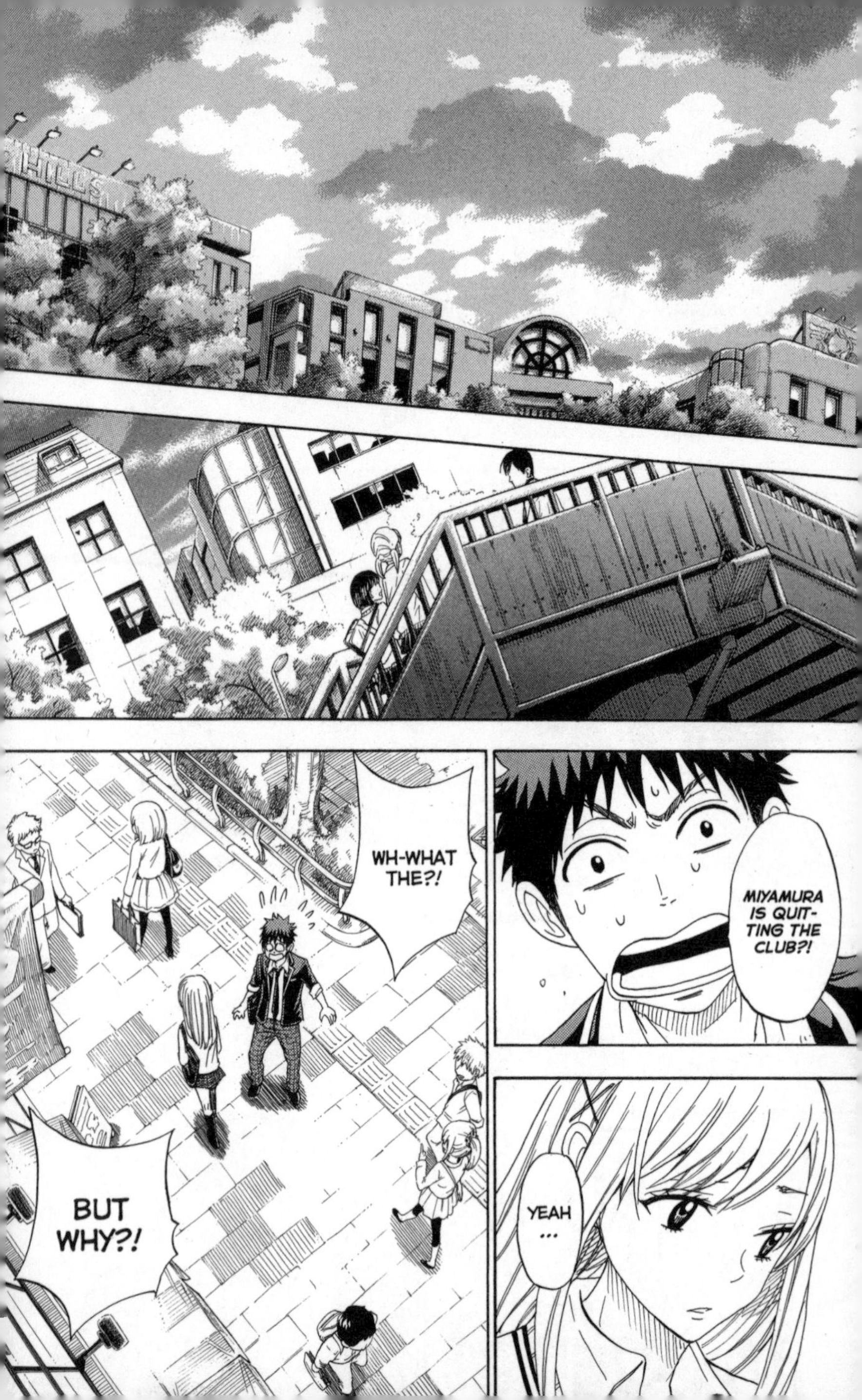
MIYAMURA IS QUIT-TING THE CLUB?!
YEAH ...
WH-WHAT THE?!
BUT WHY?!

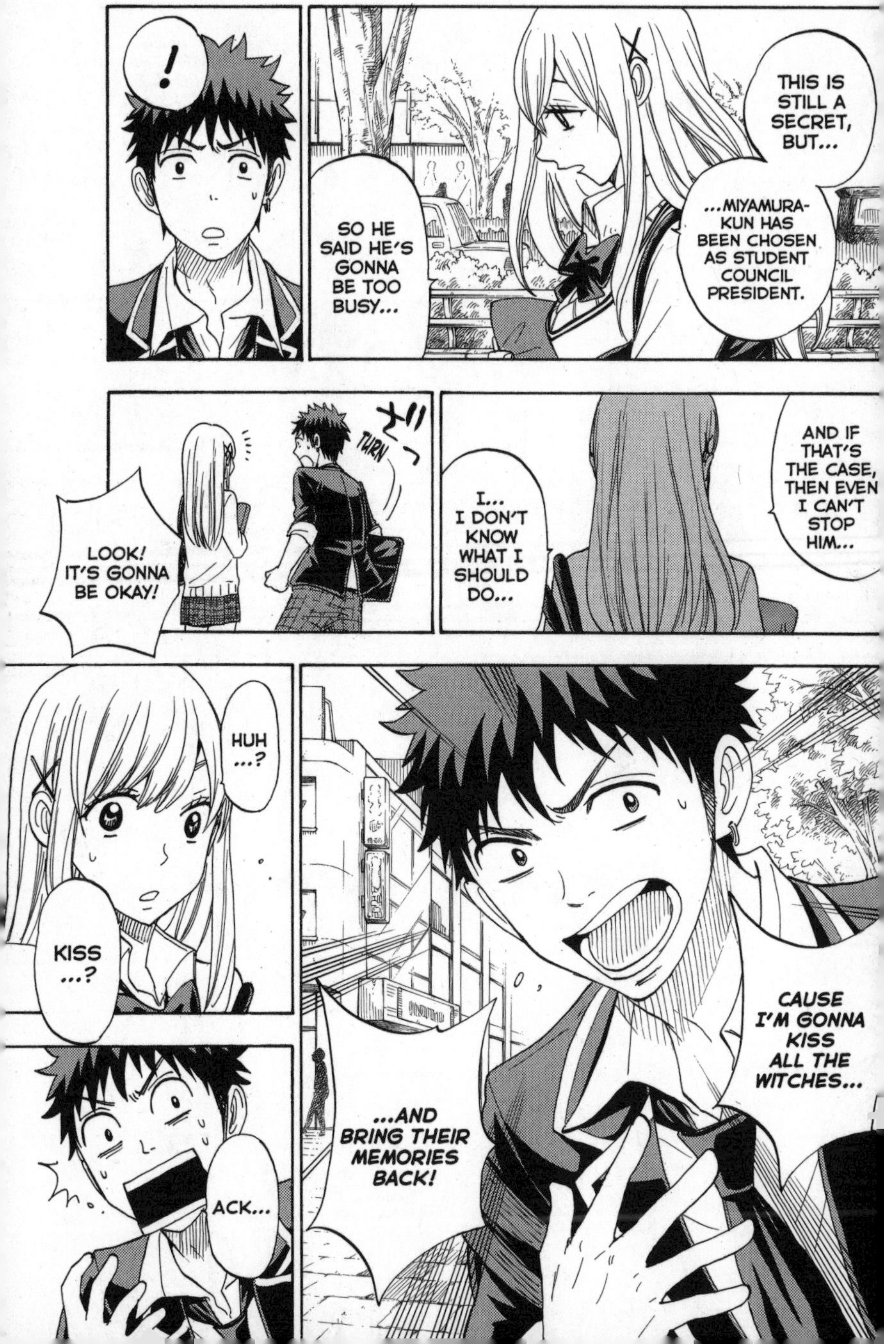
THIS IS STILL A SECRET, BUT...
...MIYAMURA-KUN HAS BEEN CHOSEN AS STUDENT COUNCIL PRESIDENT.
SO HE SAID HE'S GONNA BE TOO BUSY...
!
AND IF THAT'S THE CASE, THEN EVEN I CAN'T STOP HIM...
I... I DON'T KNOW WHAT I SHOULD DO...
TURN
LOOK! IT'S GONNA BE OKAY!
CAUSE I'M GONNA KISS ALL THE WITCHES...
...AND BRING THEIR MEMORIES BACK!
HUH ...?
KISS ...?
ACK...

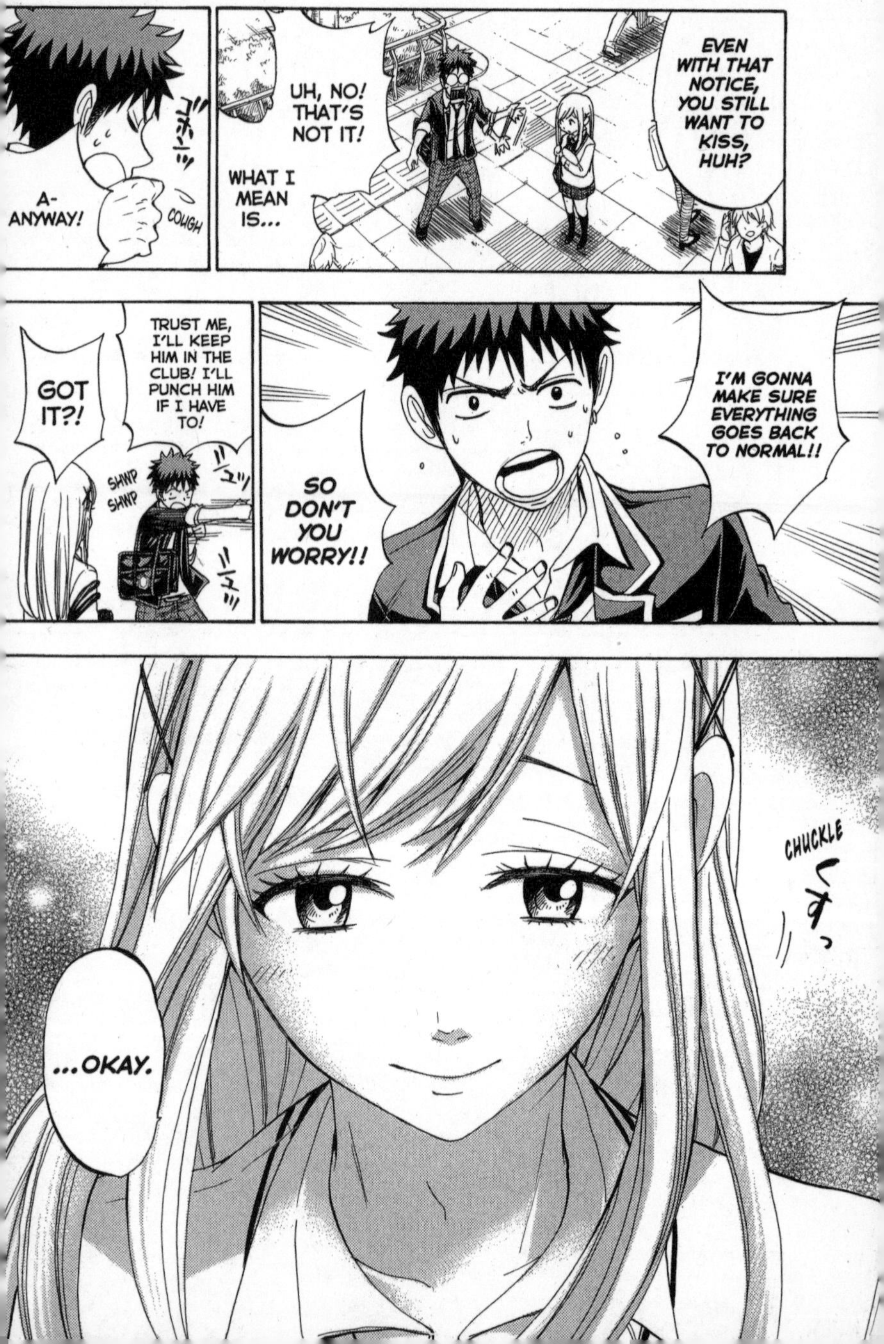
EVEN WITH THAT NOTICE, YOU STILL WANT TO KISS, HUH?
UH, NO! THAT'S NOT IT!
WHAT I MEAN IS...
COUGH
A-ANYWAY!
I'M GONNA MAKE SURE EVERYTHING GOES BACK TO NORMAL!!
SO DON'T YOU WORRY!!
TRUST ME, I'LL KEEP HIM IN THE CLUB! I'LL PUNCH HIM IF I HAVE TO!
SHWP SHWP
GOT IT?!
CHUCKLE
くすっ
...OKAY.

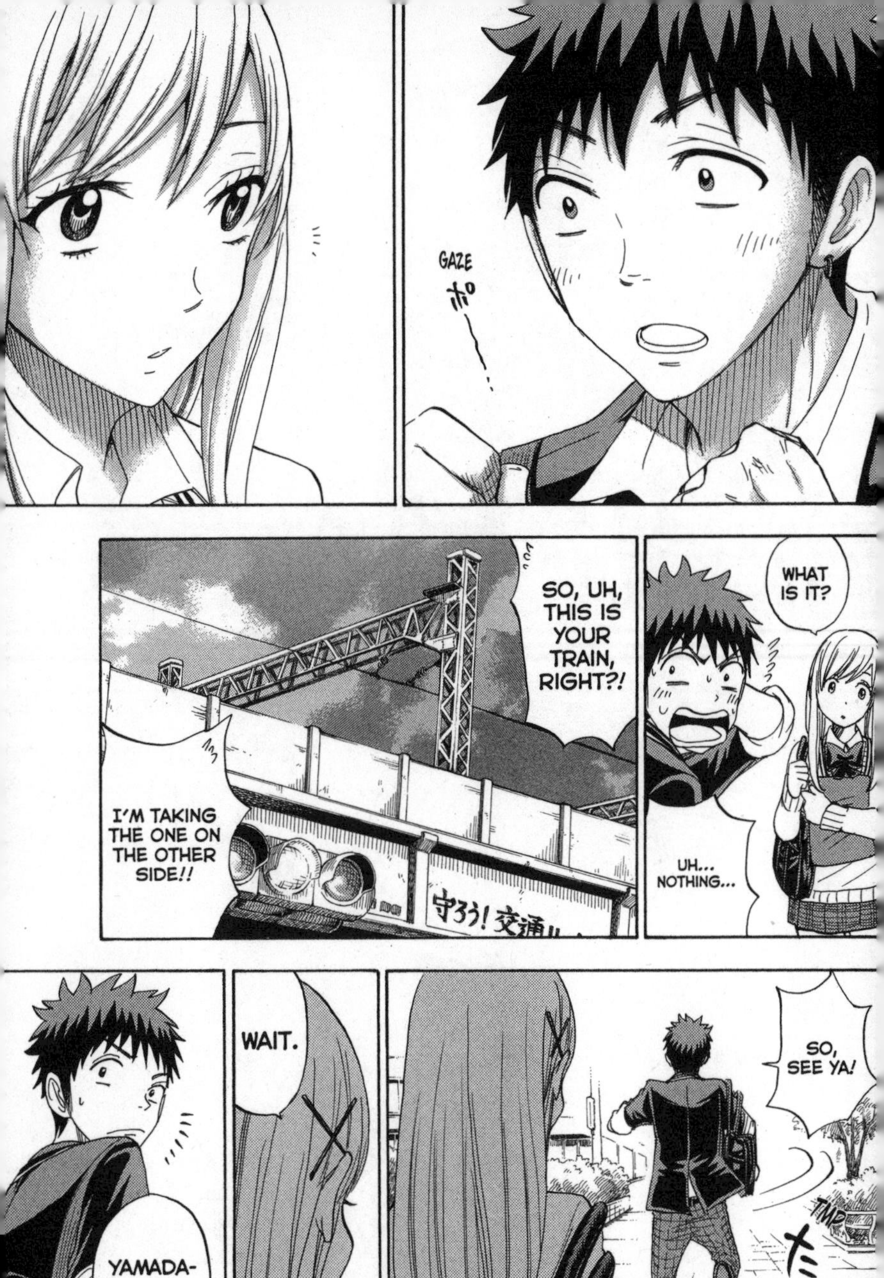
GAZE
ポ
WHAT IS IT?
UH... NOTHING...
SO, UH, THIS IS YOUR TRAIN, RIGHT?!
I'M TAKING THE ONE ON THE OTHER SIDE!!
守ろう! 交通
SO, SEE YA!
TMP
たっ
WAIT.
YAMADA-KUN...

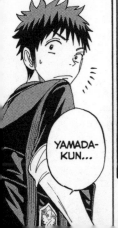

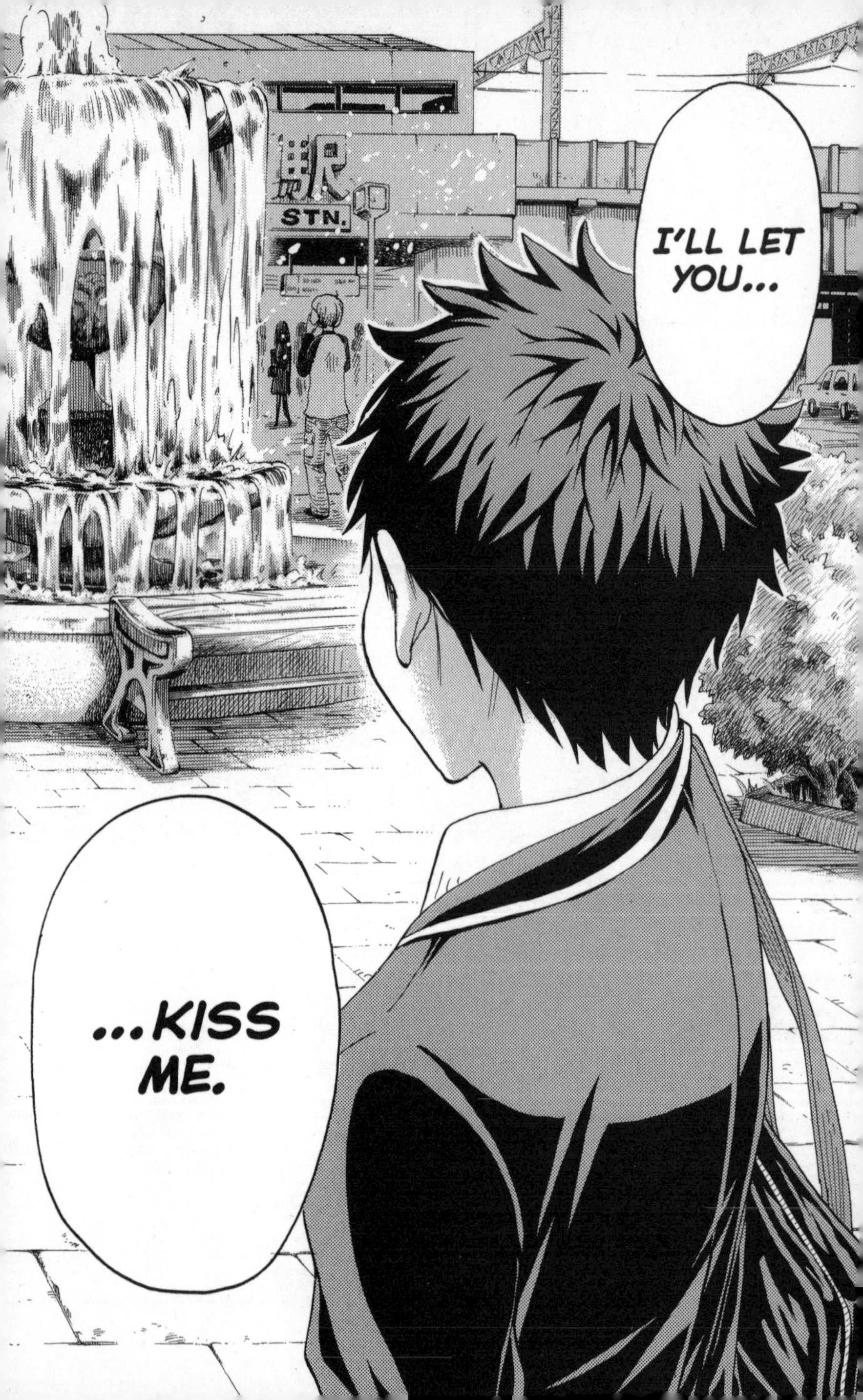
I'LL LET YOU...
駅
STN.
...KISS ME.

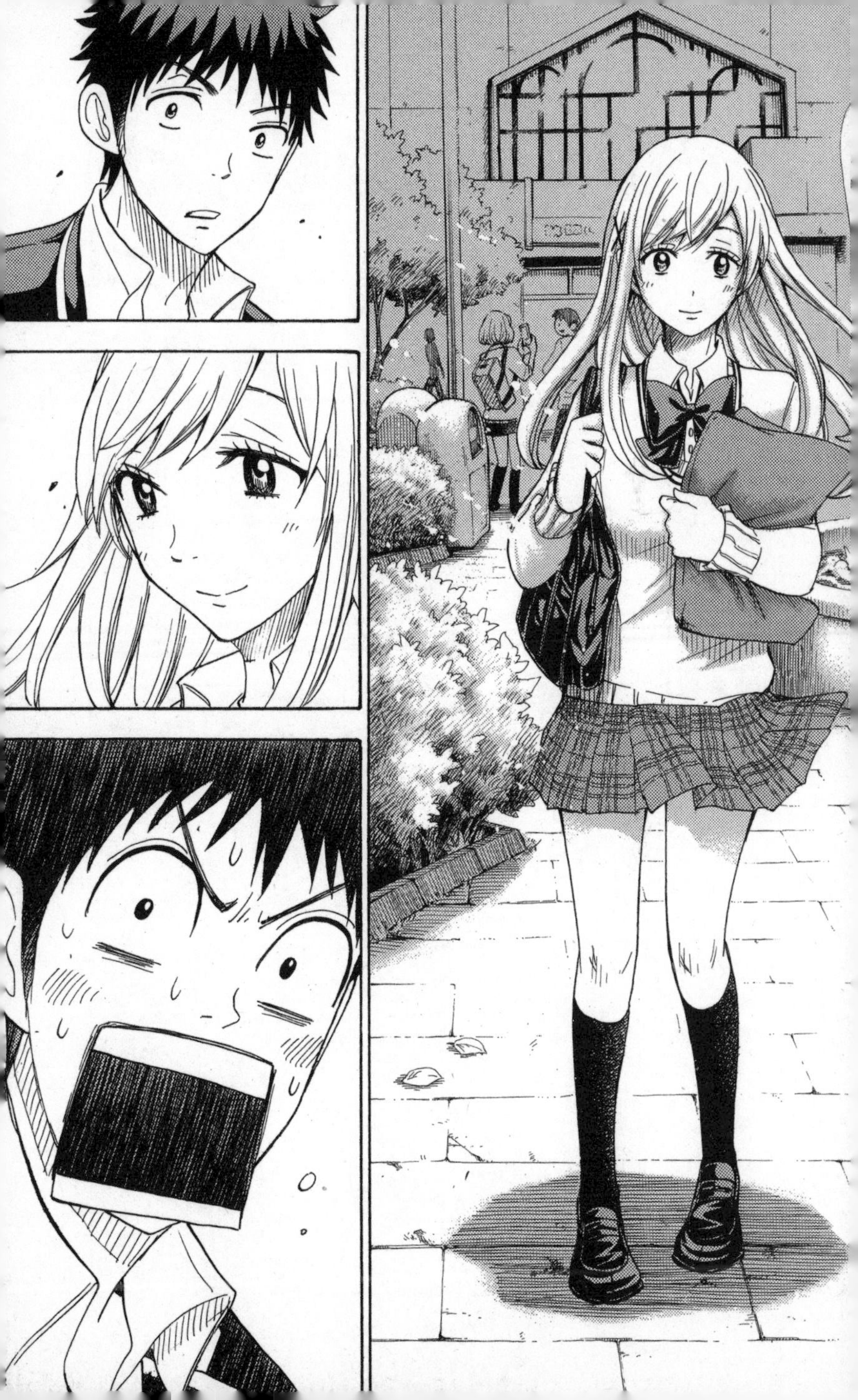

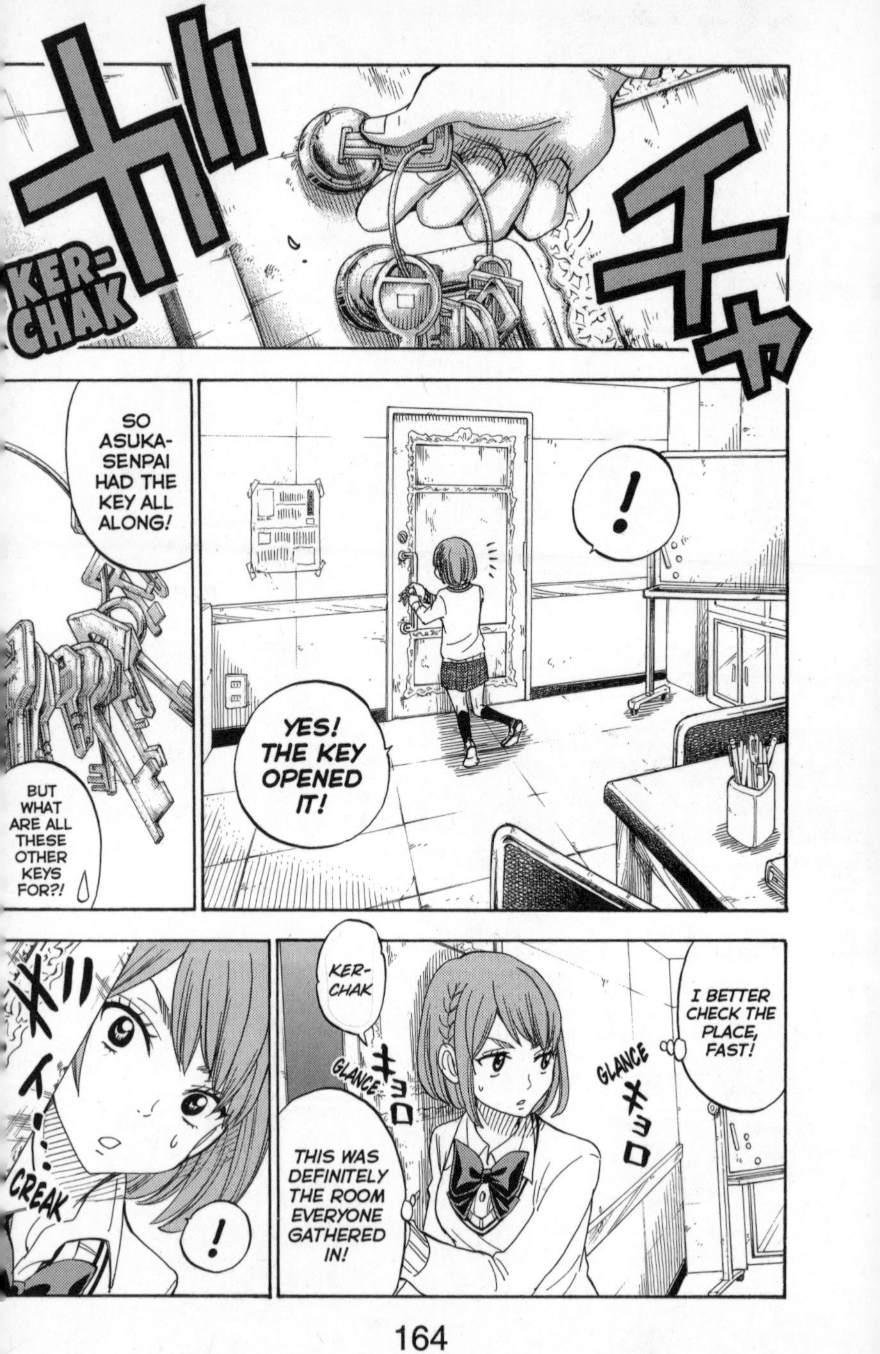
KER-CHAK
!
YES! THE KEY OPENED IT!
SO ASUKA-SENPAI HAD THE KEY ALL ALONG!
BUT WHAT ARE ALL THESE OTHER KEYS FOR?!
I BETTER CHECK THE PLACE, FAST!
GLANCE
KER-CHAK
GLANCE
THIS WAS DEFINITELY THE ROOM EVERYONE GATHERED IN!
CREAK
!

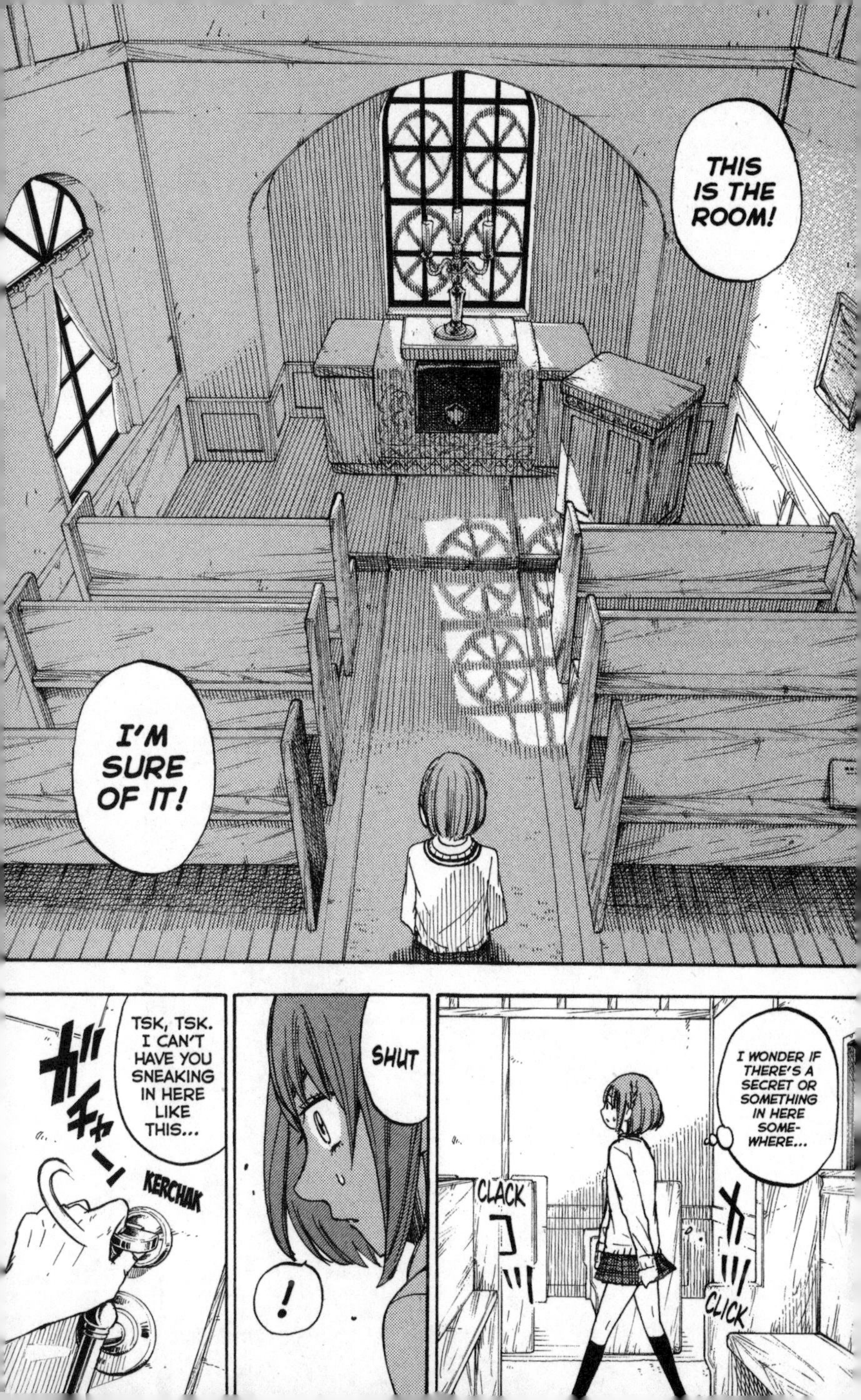
THIS IS THE ROOM!
I'M SURE OF IT!
I WONDER IF THERE'S A SECRET OR SOMETHING IN HERE SOME-WHERE...
CLICK
CLACK
SHUT
!
TSK, TSK. I CAN'T HAVE YOU SNEAKING IN HERE LIKE THIS...
KERCHAK

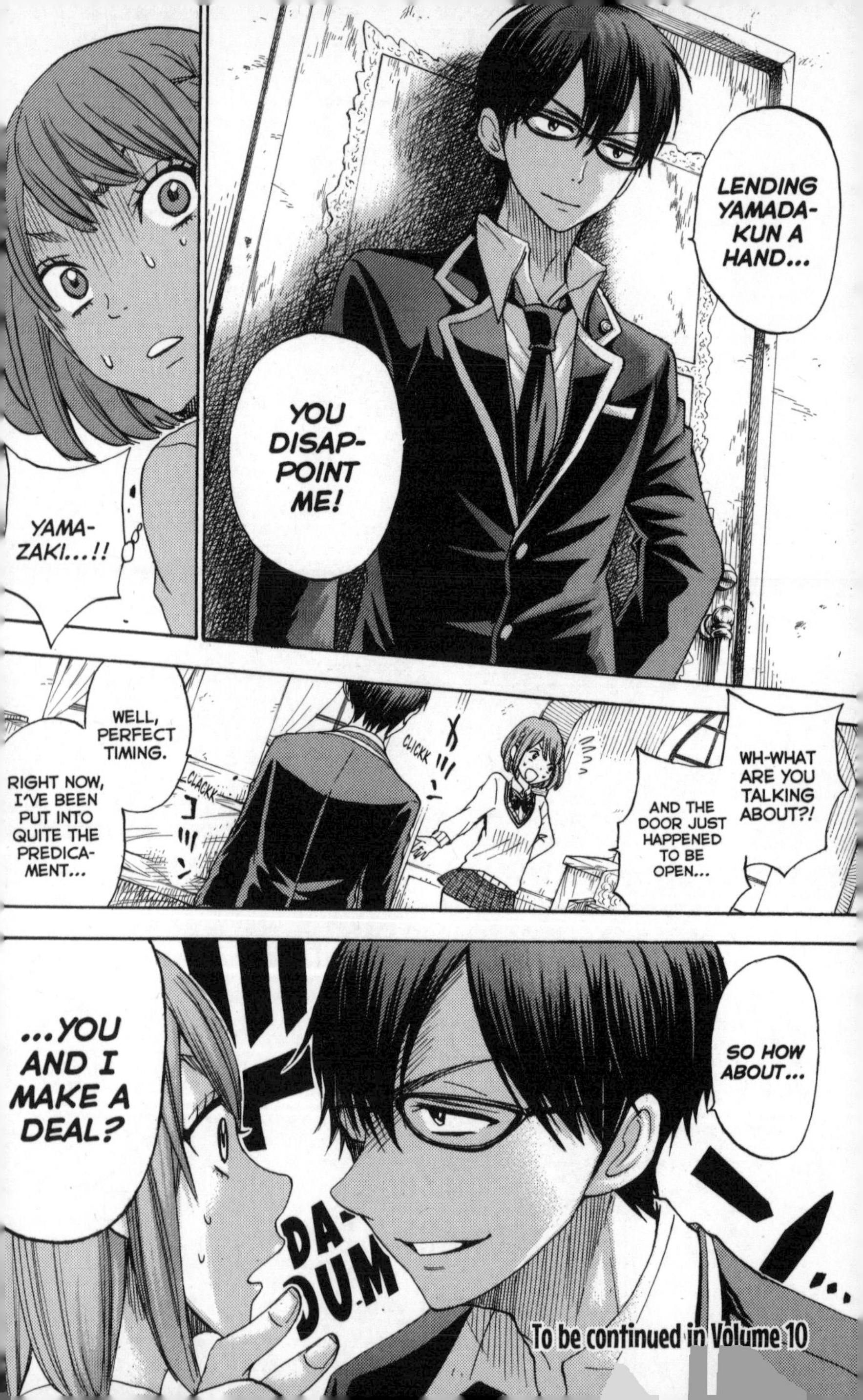
LENDING YAMADA-KUN A HAND...
YOU DISAP-POINT ME!
YAMA-ZAKI...!!
WH-WHAT ARE YOU TALKING ABOUT?!
AND THE DOOR JUST HAPPENED TO BE OPEN...
CLICKK
CLACKK
WELL, PERFECT TIMING.
RIGHT NOW, I'VE BEEN PUT INTO QUITE THE PREDICA-MENT...
SO HOW ABOUT...
...YOU AND I MAKE A DEAL?
DA-DUM
To be continued in Volume 10

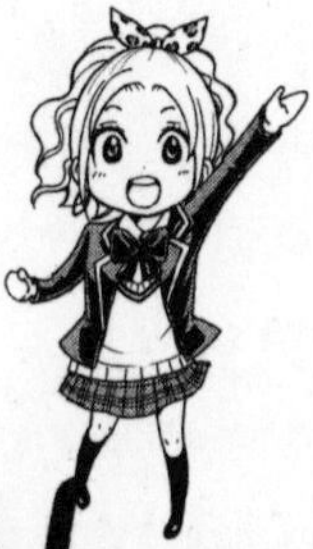

Yamada-kun and the Seven Witches

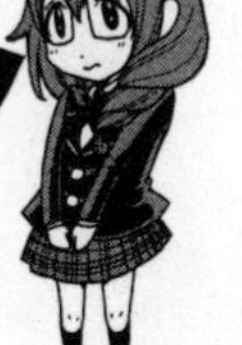

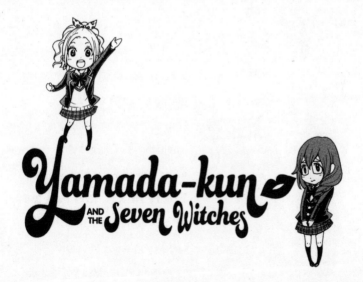

THE DEVIL'S CLASSROOM

魔王の教室

This work came about two years ago, right around the time I was coming up with the story for "Yamada-kun and the Seven Witches." I had suddenly thought to myself, "Oh! An elementary school story might be interesting!" and so I decided to draw one. Having said that, this work is very significant to me on a personal level, 'cause I mean, c'mon, **elementary school students are crazy** (in many ways)! Back when I was an elementary school student, I was very scared of my homeroom teacher. First, it started with me wondering, "Why do I have to listen to an adult who I don't even know?" followed by, "Why does the teacher always know when I'm lying?" and "How does the teacher know that I was out playing with so-and-so yesterday after school?" As an adult, it all makes sense now, but it was scary for me back then. This is the story I wrote as I recalled those memories.

HE'S UP TO NO GOOD AGAIN...

I WONDER WHAT TODAY'S SCHOOL LUNCH IS GONNA BE.

…Huh? You don't know what I'm talking about? I see…

I guess my commentary might be a little difficult to understand. But, well, to put it simply…

Pretty much, this is a story about a stupid teacher!!!

I hope you enjoy the story.

— August 2013. Miki Yoshikawa

Special One-Shot Comic — The Devil's Classroom

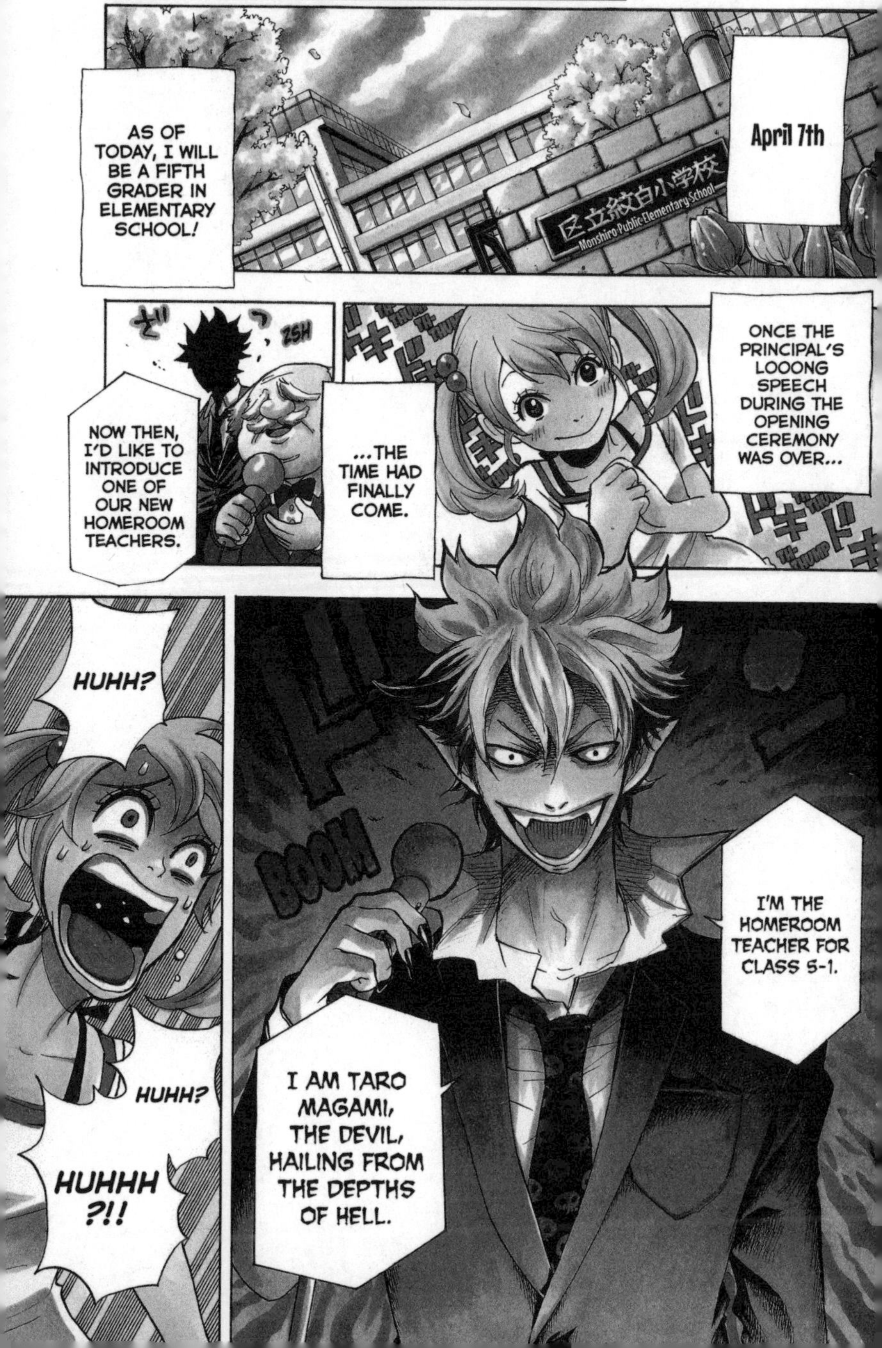
April 7th
区立紋白小学校
Monshiro Public Elementary School
AS OF TODAY, I WILL BE A FIFTH GRADER IN ELEMENTARY SCHOOL!
ONCE THE PRINCIPAL'S LOOONG SPEECH DURING THE OPENING CEREMONY WAS OVER...
TH-THUMP
...THE TIME HAD FINALLY COME.
ZSH
NOW THEN, I'D LIKE TO INTRODUCE ONE OF OUR NEW HOMEROOM TEACHERS.
BOOM
I'M THE HOMEROOM TEACHER FOR CLASS 5-1.
I AM TARO MAGAMI, THE DEVIL, HAILING FROM THE DEPTHS OF HELL.
HUHH?
HUHH?
HUHHH ?!!

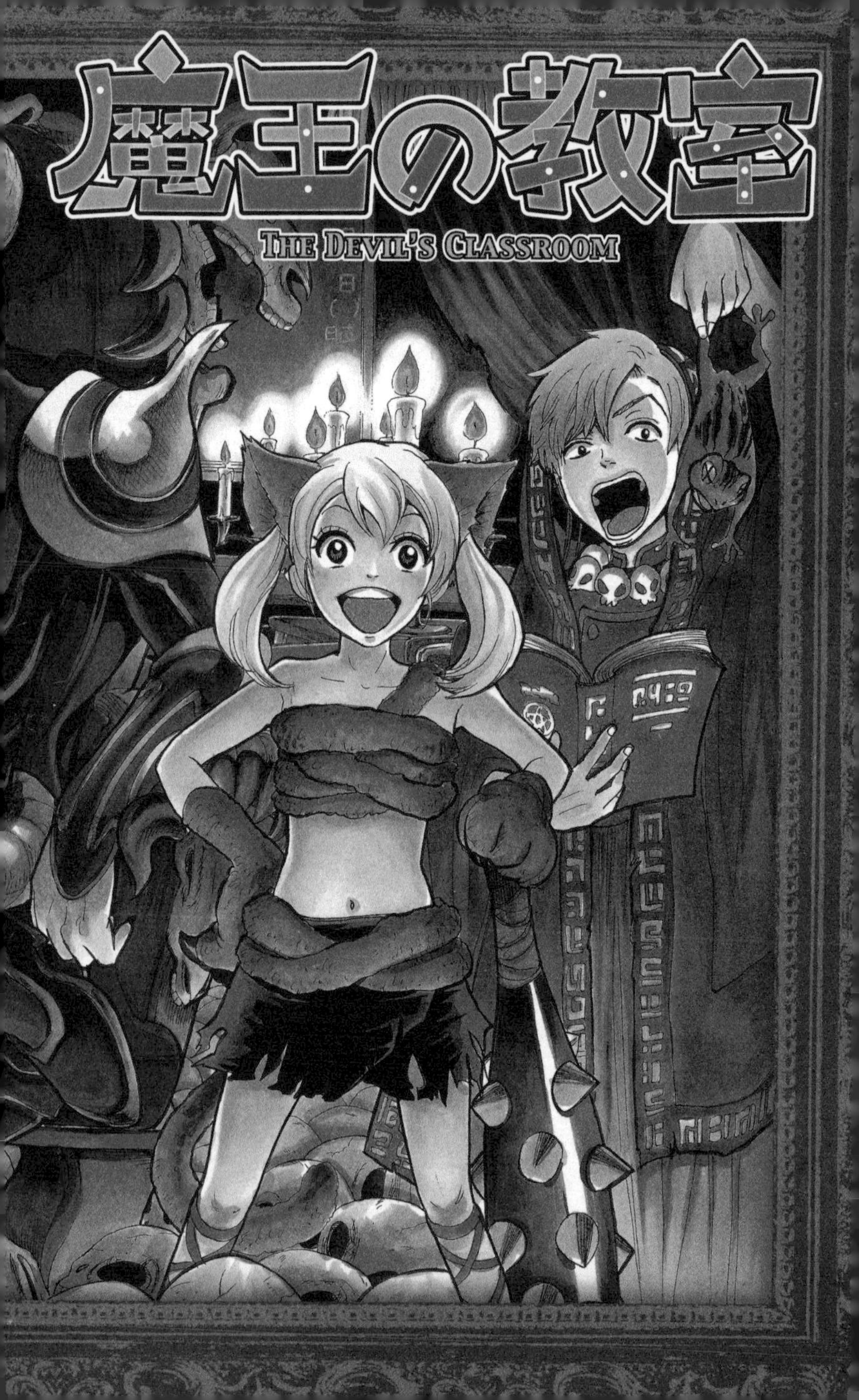

魔王の教室
THE DEVIL'S CLASSROOM

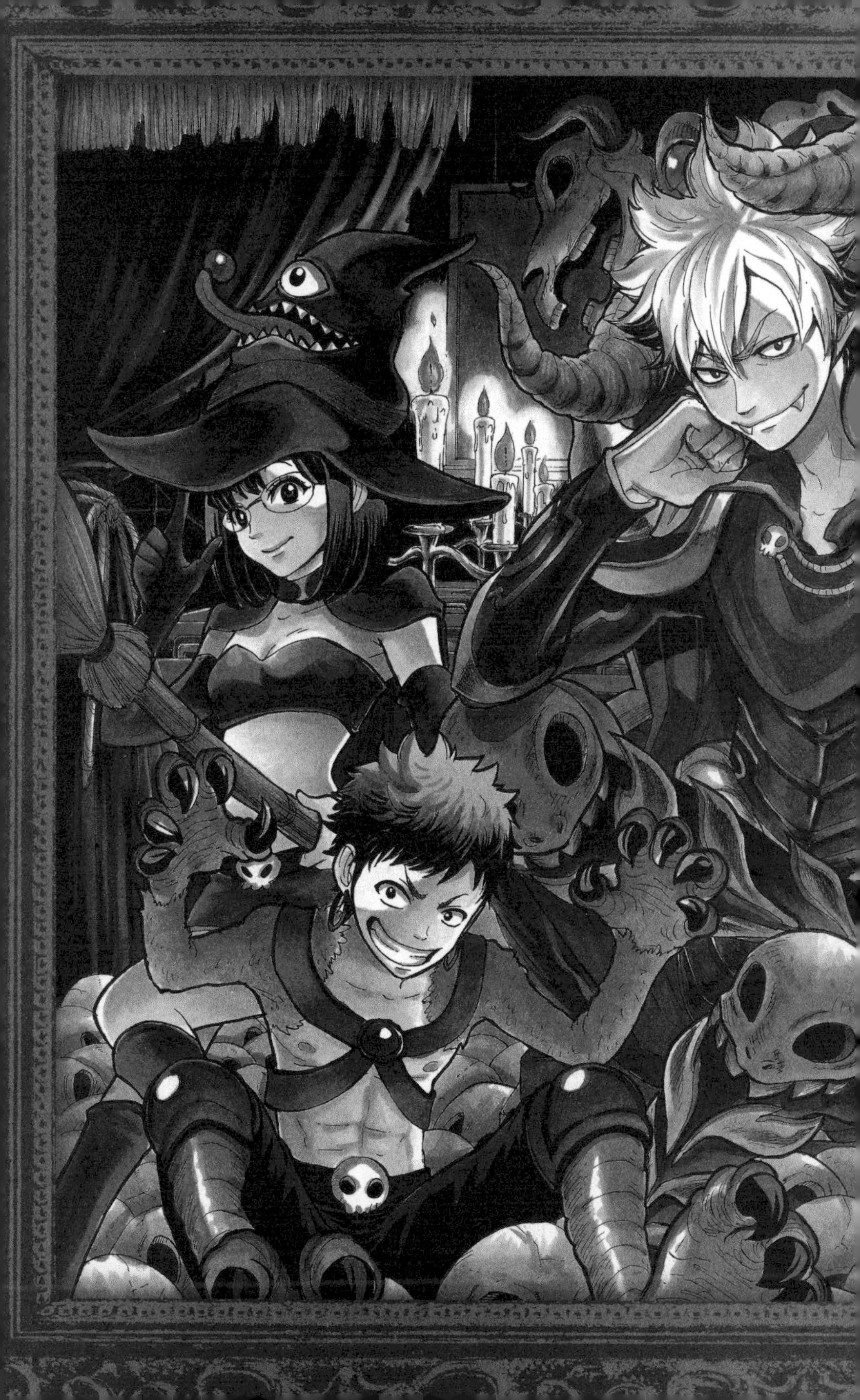

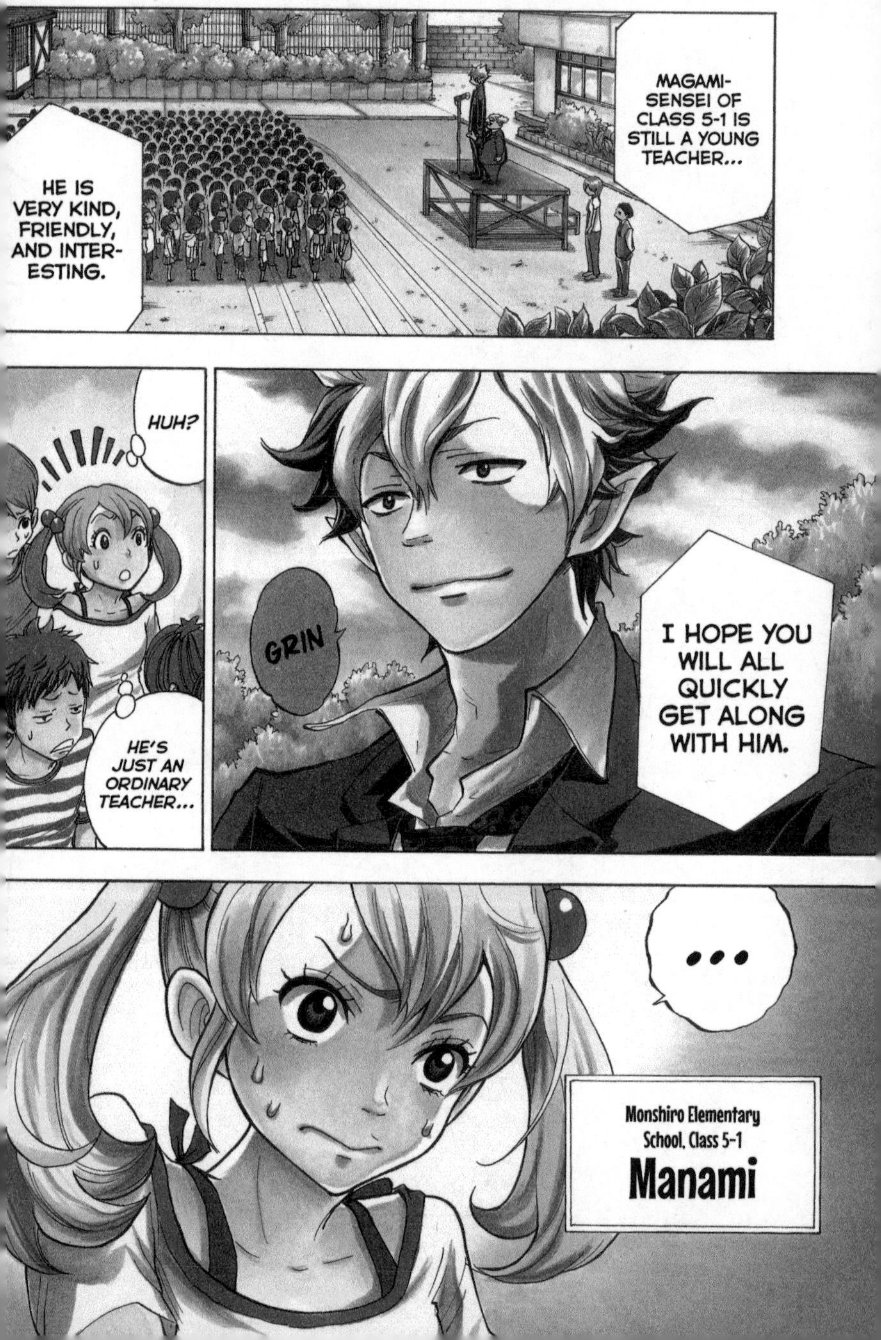
MAGAMI-SENSEI OF CLASS 5-1 IS STILL A YOUNG TEACHER...
HE IS VERY KIND, FRIENDLY, AND INTER-ESTING.
I HOPE YOU WILL ALL QUICKLY GET ALONG WITH HIM.
GRIN
HUH?
HE'S JUST AN ORDINARY TEACHER...
...
Monshiro Elementary School, Class 5-1
Manami

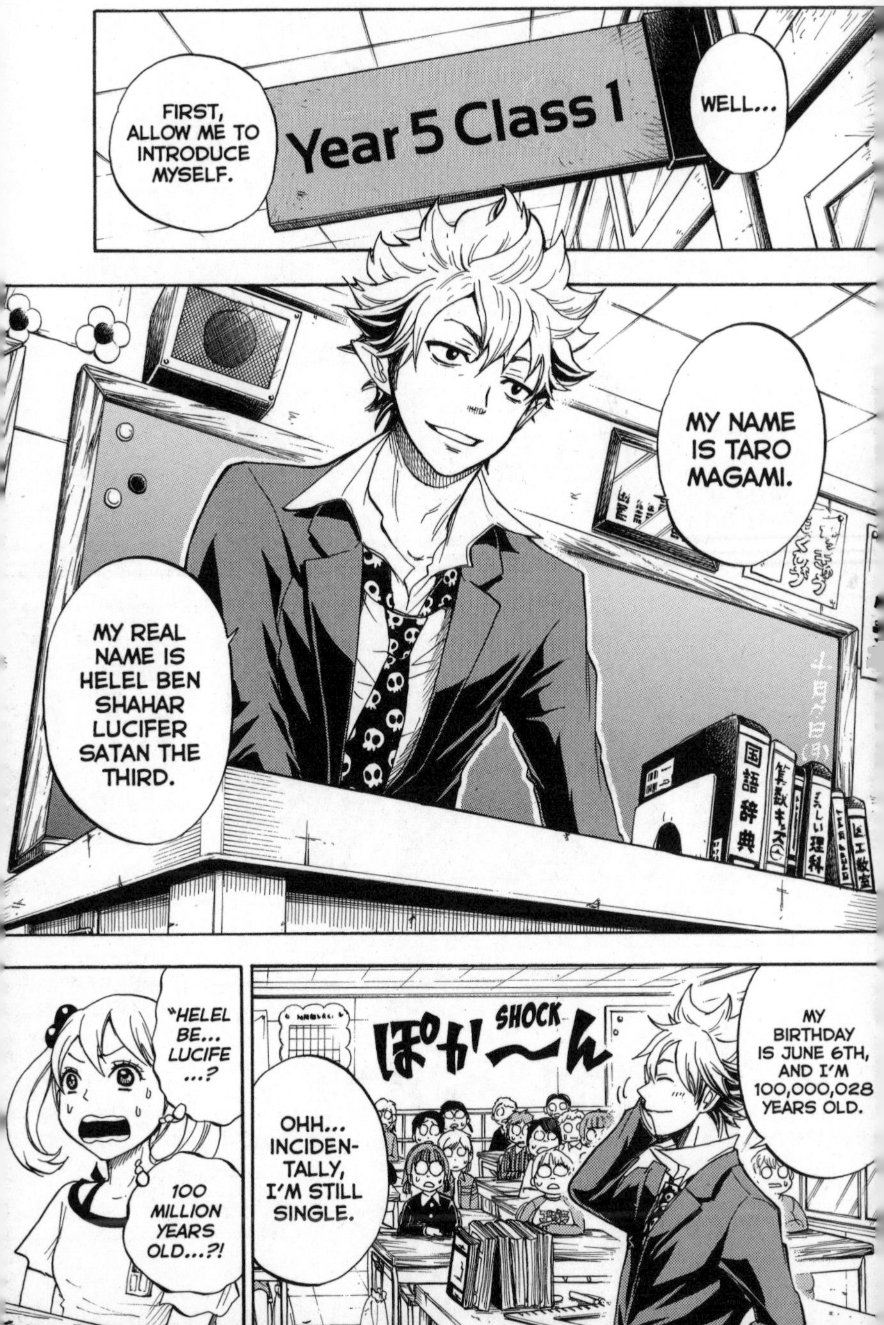
Year 5 Class 1
WELL...
FIRST, ALLOW ME TO INTRODUCE MYSELF.
MY NAME IS TARO MAGAMI.
MY REAL NAME IS HELEL BEN SHAHAR LUCIFER SATAN THE THIRD.
MY BIRTHDAY IS JUNE 6TH, AND I'M 100,000,028 YEARS OLD.
ぽか〜ん
SHOCK
OHH... INCIDENTALLY, I'M STILL SINGLE.
"HELEL BE... LUCIFE ...?
100 MILLION YEARS OLD...?!

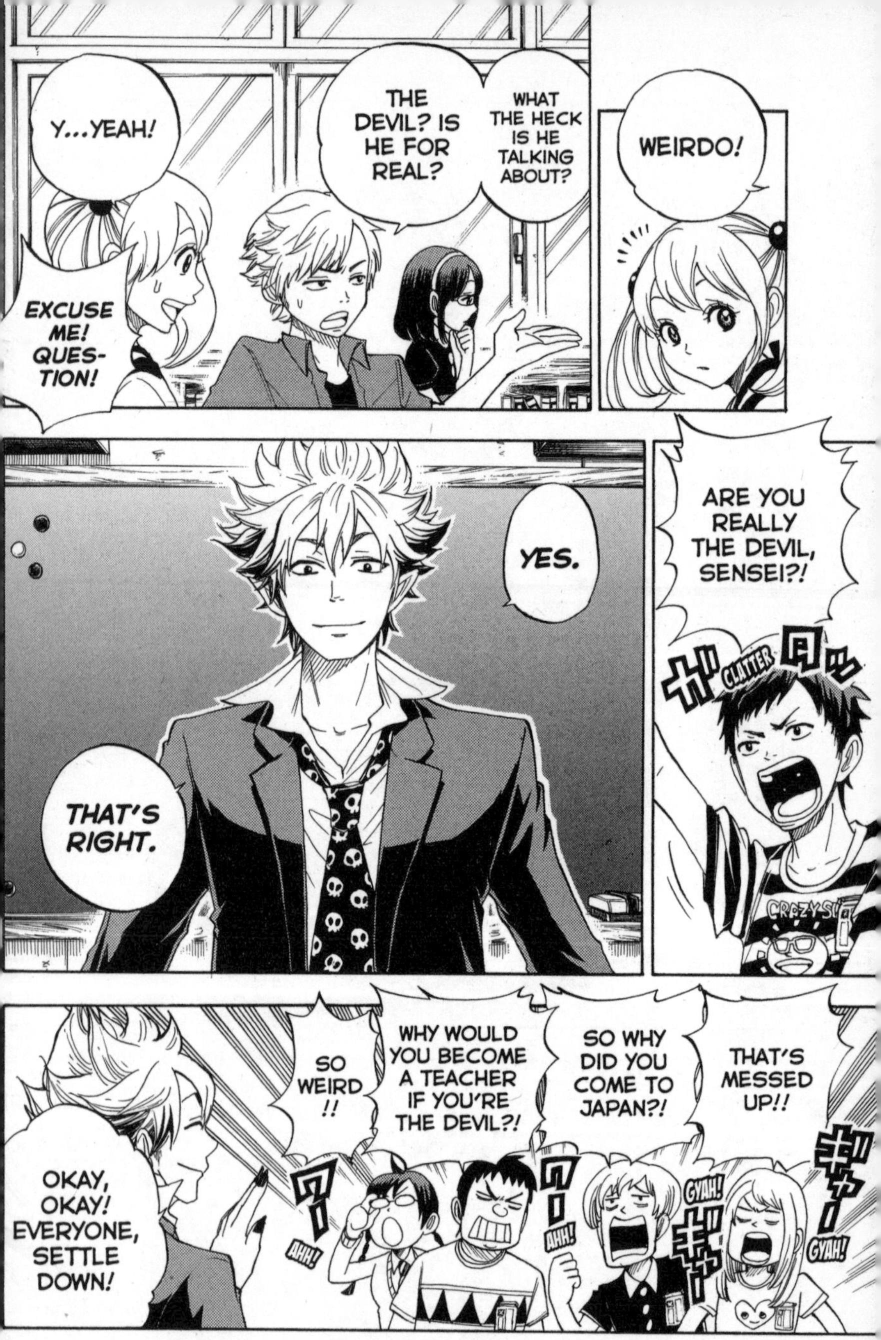
WEIRDO!
WHAT THE HECK IS HE TALKING ABOUT?
THE DEVIL? IS HE FOR REAL?
Y...YEAH!
EXCUSE ME! QUESTION!
ARE YOU REALLY THE DEVIL, SENSEI?!
CLATTER
YES.
THAT'S RIGHT.
THAT'S MESSED UP!!
GYAH!
SO WHY DID YOU COME TO JAPAN?!
GYAH!
WHY WOULD YOU BECOME A TEACHER IF YOU'RE THE DEVIL?!
AHH!
SO WEIRD!!
AHH!
OKAY, OKAY! EVERYONE, SETTLE DOWN!

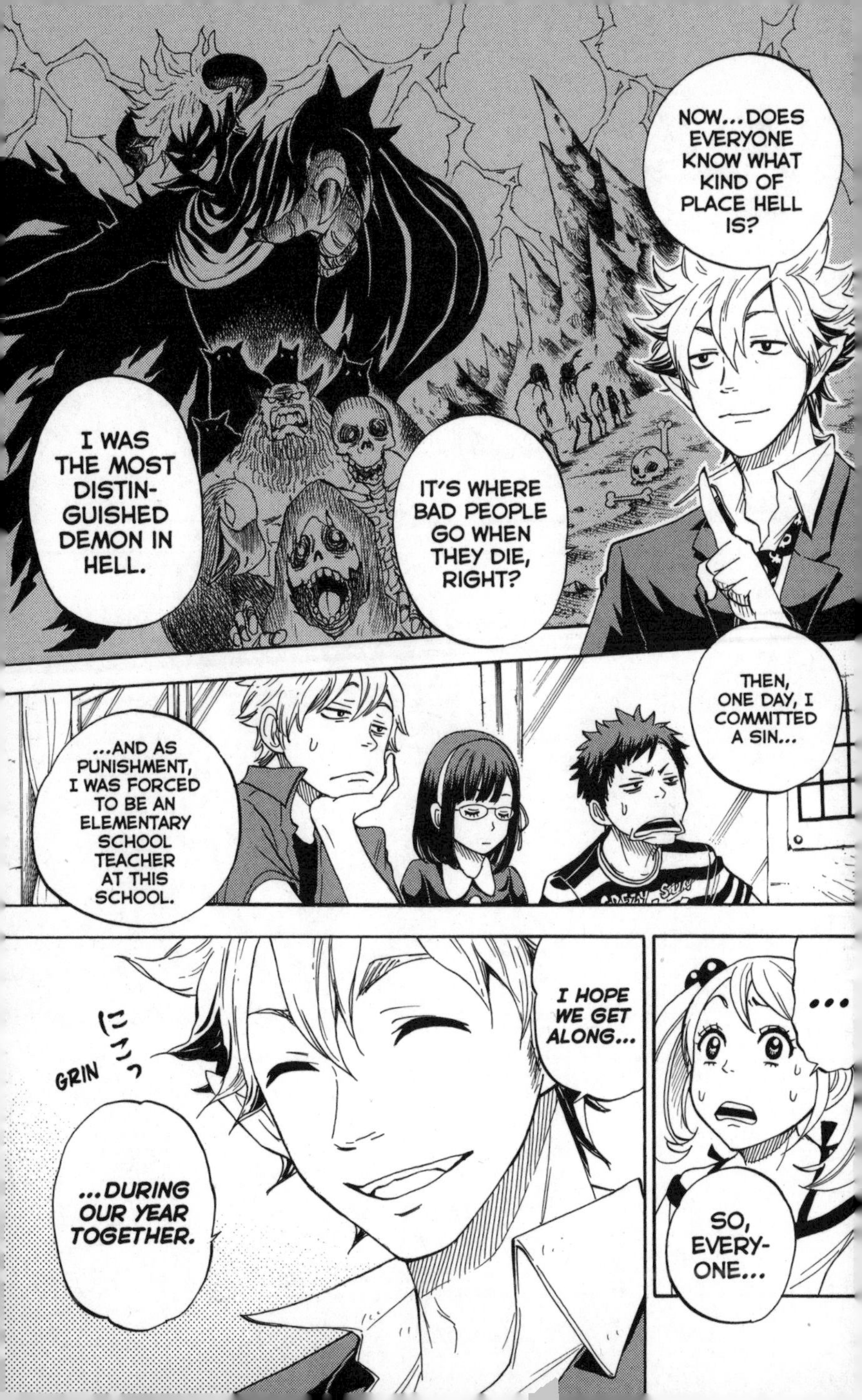
NOW...DOES EVERYONE KNOW WHAT KIND OF PLACE HELL IS?
IT'S WHERE BAD PEOPLE GO WHEN THEY DIE, RIGHT?
I WAS THE MOST DISTIN-GUISHED DEMON IN HELL.
THEN, ONE DAY, I COMMITTED A SIN...
...AND AS PUNISHMENT, I WAS FORCED TO BE AN ELEMENTARY SCHOOL TEACHER AT THIS SCHOOL.
...
SO, EVERY-ONE...
I HOPE WE GET ALONG...
にこっ
GRIN
...DURING OUR YEAR TOGETHER.

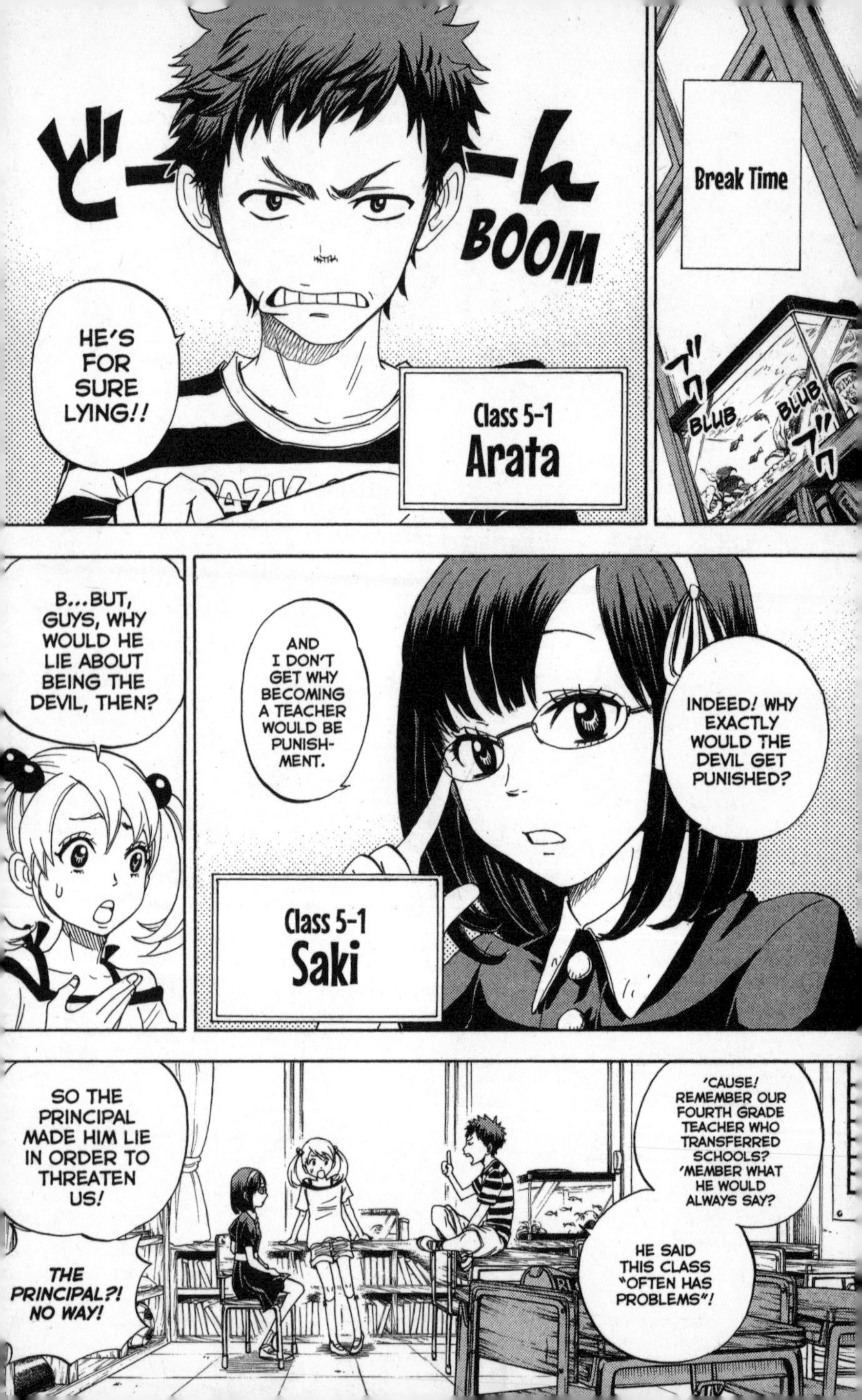
Break Time
BLUB BLUB
BOOM
HE'S FOR SURE LYING!!
Class 5-1 Arata
INDEED! WHY EXACTLY WOULD THE DEVIL GET PUNISHED?
AND I DON'T GET WHY BECOMING A TEACHER WOULD BE PUNISH-MENT.
Class 5-1 Saki
B...BUT, GUYS, WHY WOULD HE LIE ABOUT BEING THE DEVIL, THEN?
'CAUSE! REMEMBER OUR FOURTH GRADE TEACHER WHO TRANSFERRED SCHOOLS? 'MEMBER WHAT HE WOULD ALWAYS SAY?
HE SAID THIS CLASS "OFTEN HAS PROBLEMS"!
SO THE PRINCIPAL MADE HIM LIE IN ORDER TO THREATEN US!
THE PRINCIPAL?! NO WAY!

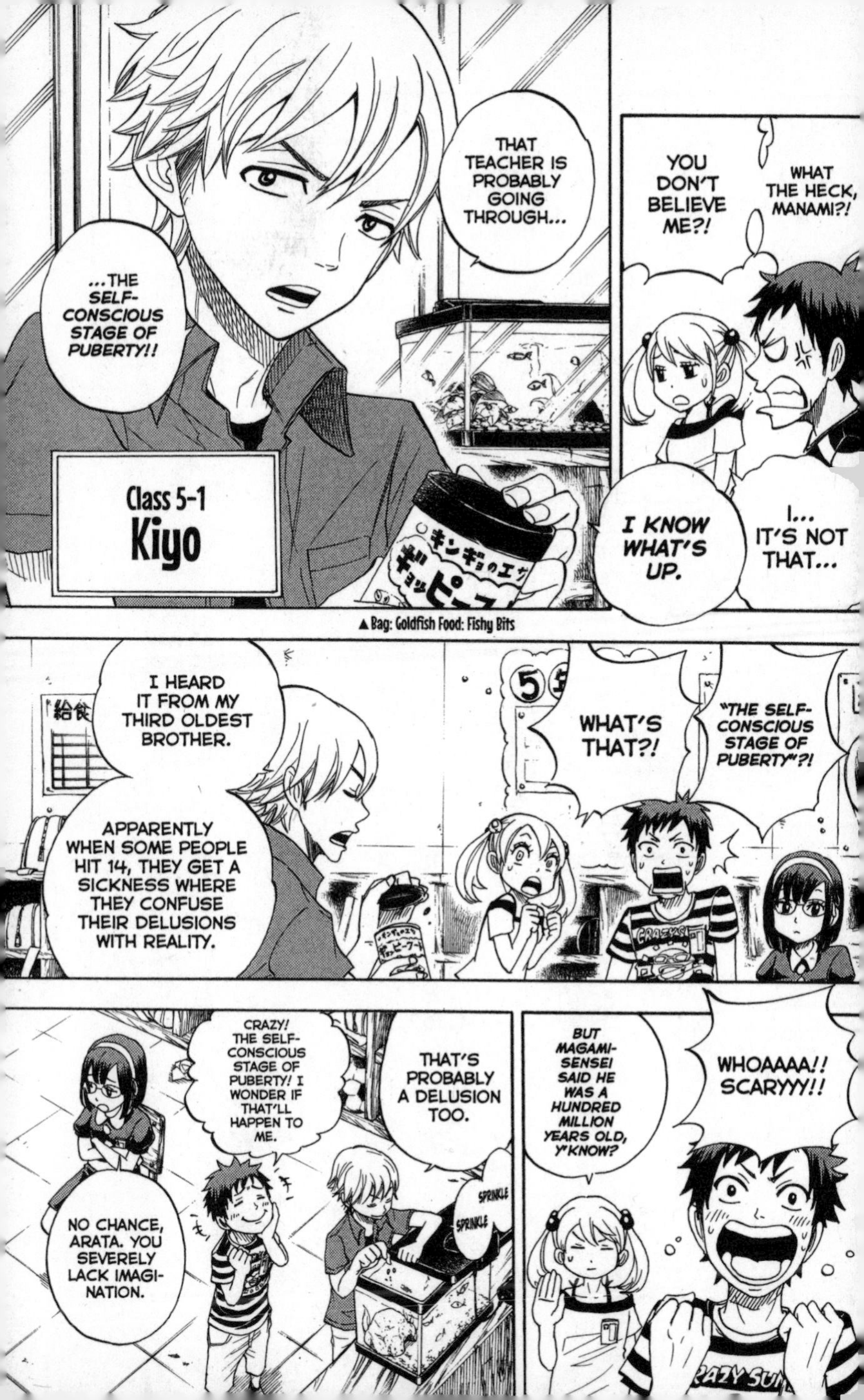
WHAT THE HECK, MANAMI?!
YOU DON'T BELIEVE ME?!
I... IT'S NOT THAT...
I KNOW WHAT'S UP.
THAT TEACHER IS PROBABLY GOING THROUGH...
...THE SELF-CONSCIOUS STAGE OF PUBERTY!!
Class 5-1
Kiyo
"THE SELF-CONSCIOUS STAGE OF PUBERTY"?!
WHAT'S THAT?!
I HEARD IT FROM MY THIRD OLDEST BROTHER.
APPARENTLY WHEN SOME PEOPLE HIT 14, THEY GET A SICKNESS WHERE THEY CONFUSE THEIR DELUSIONS WITH REALITY.
WHOAAAA!! SCARYYY!!
BUT MAGAMI-SENSEI SAID HE WAS A HUNDRED MILLION YEARS OLD, Y'KNOW?
THAT'S PROBABLY A DELUSION TOO.
SPRINKLE
SPRINKLE
CRAZY! THE SELF-CONSCIOUS STAGE OF PUBERTY! I WONDER IF THAT'LL HAPPEN TO ME.
NO CHANCE, ARATA. YOU SEVERELY LACK IMAGINATION.
▲Bag: Goldfish Food: Fishy Bits

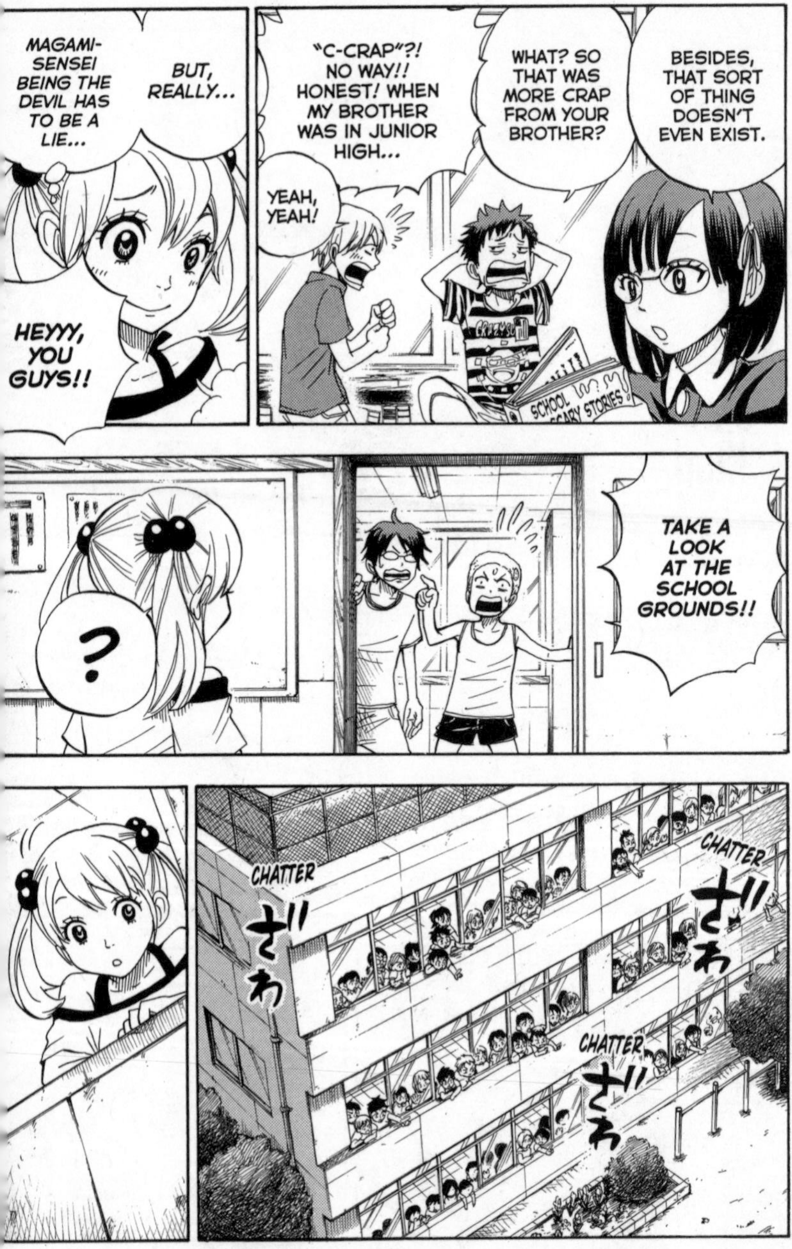
BESIDES, THAT SORT OF THING DOESN'T EVEN EXIST.
WHAT? SO THAT WAS MORE CRAP FROM YOUR BROTHER?
"C-CRAP"?! NO WAY!! HONEST! WHEN MY BROTHER WAS IN JUNIOR HIGH...
YEAH, YEAH!
SCHOOL SCARY STORIES
BUT, REALLY...
MAGAMI-SENSEI BEING THE DEVIL HAS TO BE A LIE...
HEYYY, YOU GUYS!!
TAKE A LOOK AT THE SCHOOL GROUNDS!!
?
CHATTER
ざわ
CHATTER
ざわ
CHATTER
ざわ

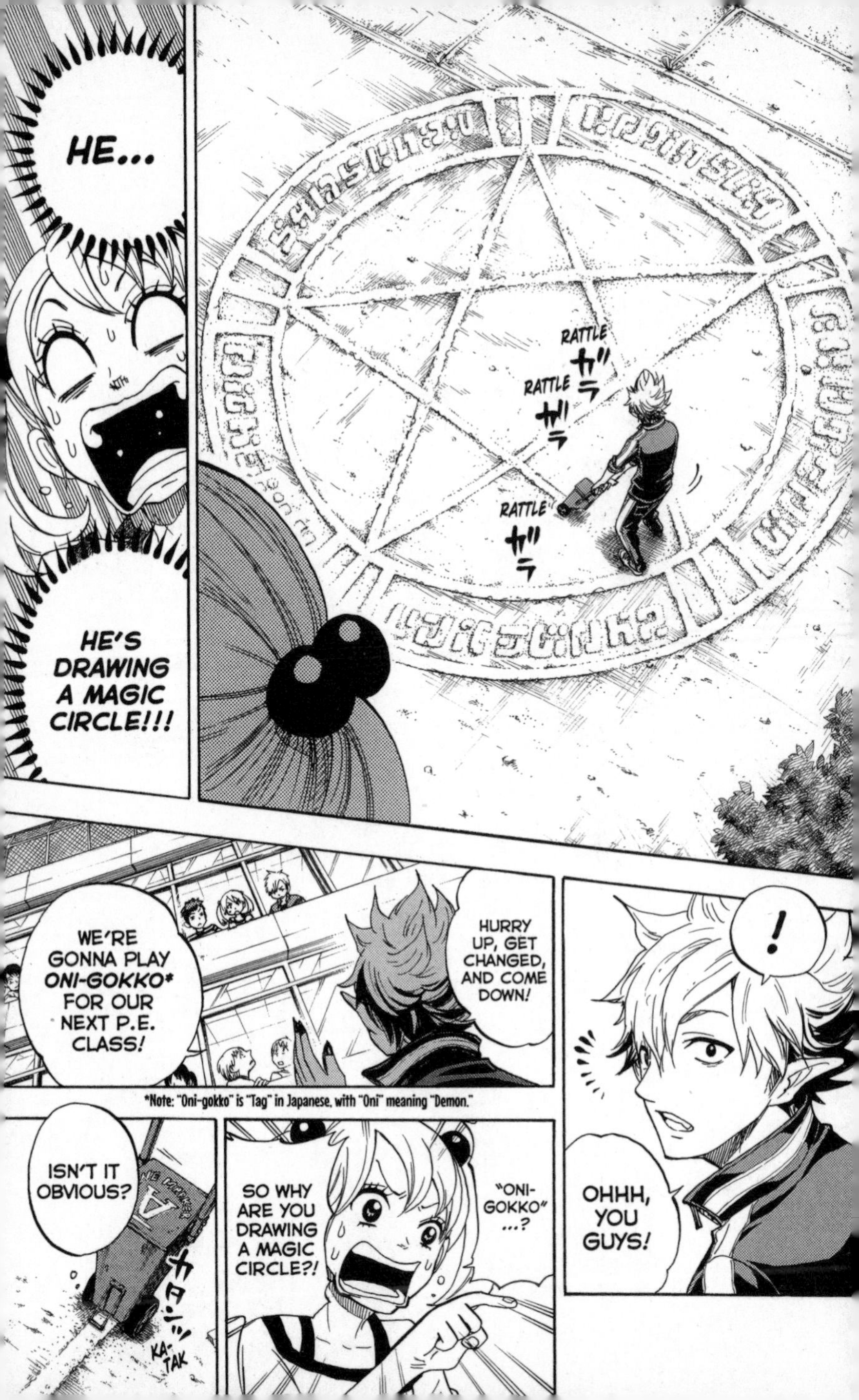
RATTLE
ガラ
RATTLE
ガラ
RATTLE
ガラ
HE...
HE'S DRAWING A MAGIC CIRCLE!!!
!
OHHH, YOU GUYS!
HURRY UP, GET CHANGED, AND COME DOWN!
WE'RE GONNA PLAY ONI-GOKKO* FOR OUR NEXT P.E. CLASS!
"ONI-GOKKO" ...?
SO WHY ARE YOU DRAWING A MAGIC CIRCLE?!
ISN'T IT OBVIOUS?
カタン
KA-TAK

*Note: "Oni-gokko" is "Tag" in Japanese, with "Oni" meaning "Demon."

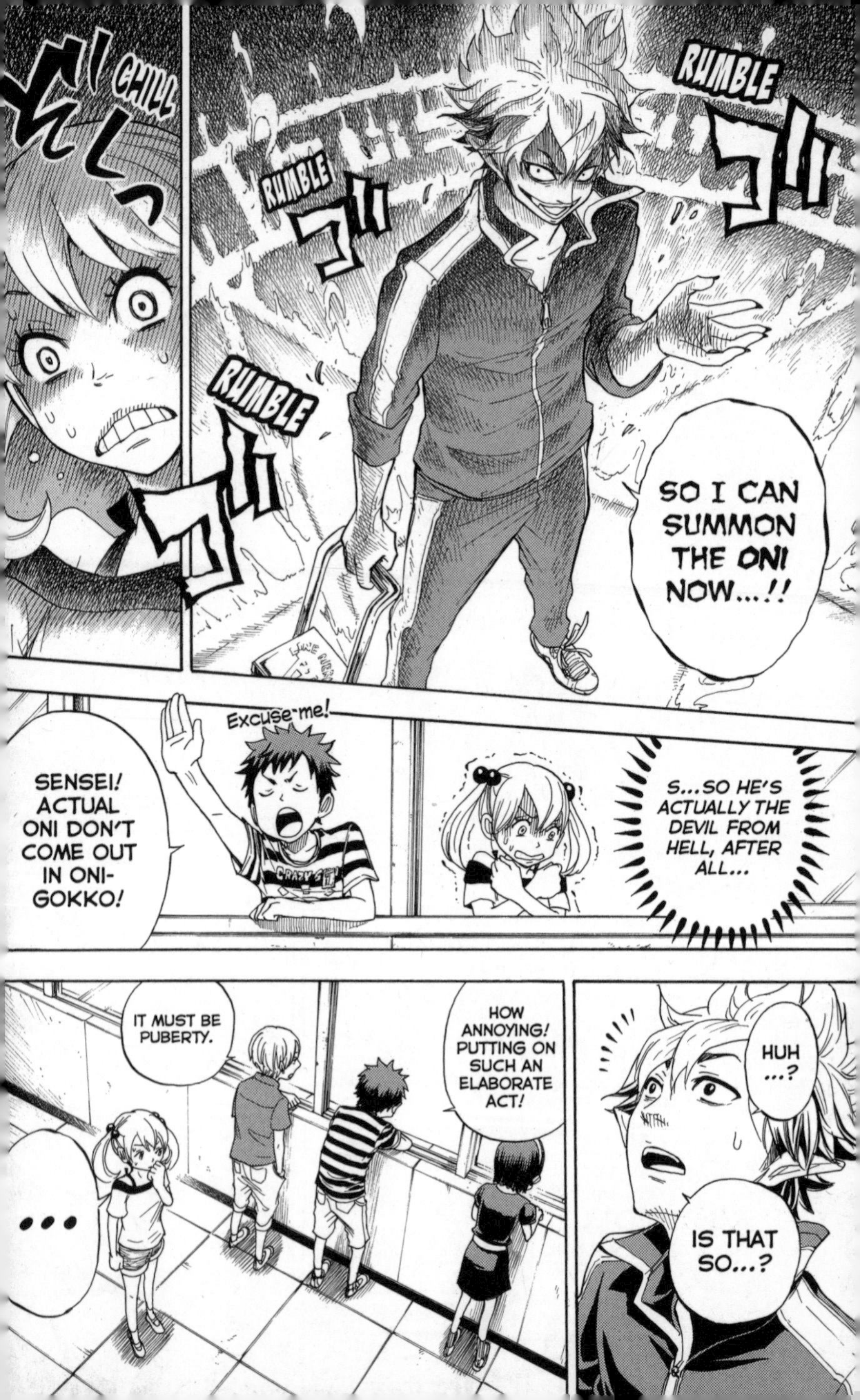
RUMBLE
RUMBLE
RUMBLE
SO I CAN SUMMON THE ONI NOW...!!
CHILL
S...SO HE'S ACTUALLY THE DEVIL FROM HELL, AFTER ALL...
Excuse me!
SENSEI! ACTUAL ONI DON'T COME OUT IN ONI-GOKKO!
HUH ...?
IS THAT SO...?
HOW ANNOYING! PUTTING ON SUCH AN ELABORATE ACT!
IT MUST BE PUBERTY.
...

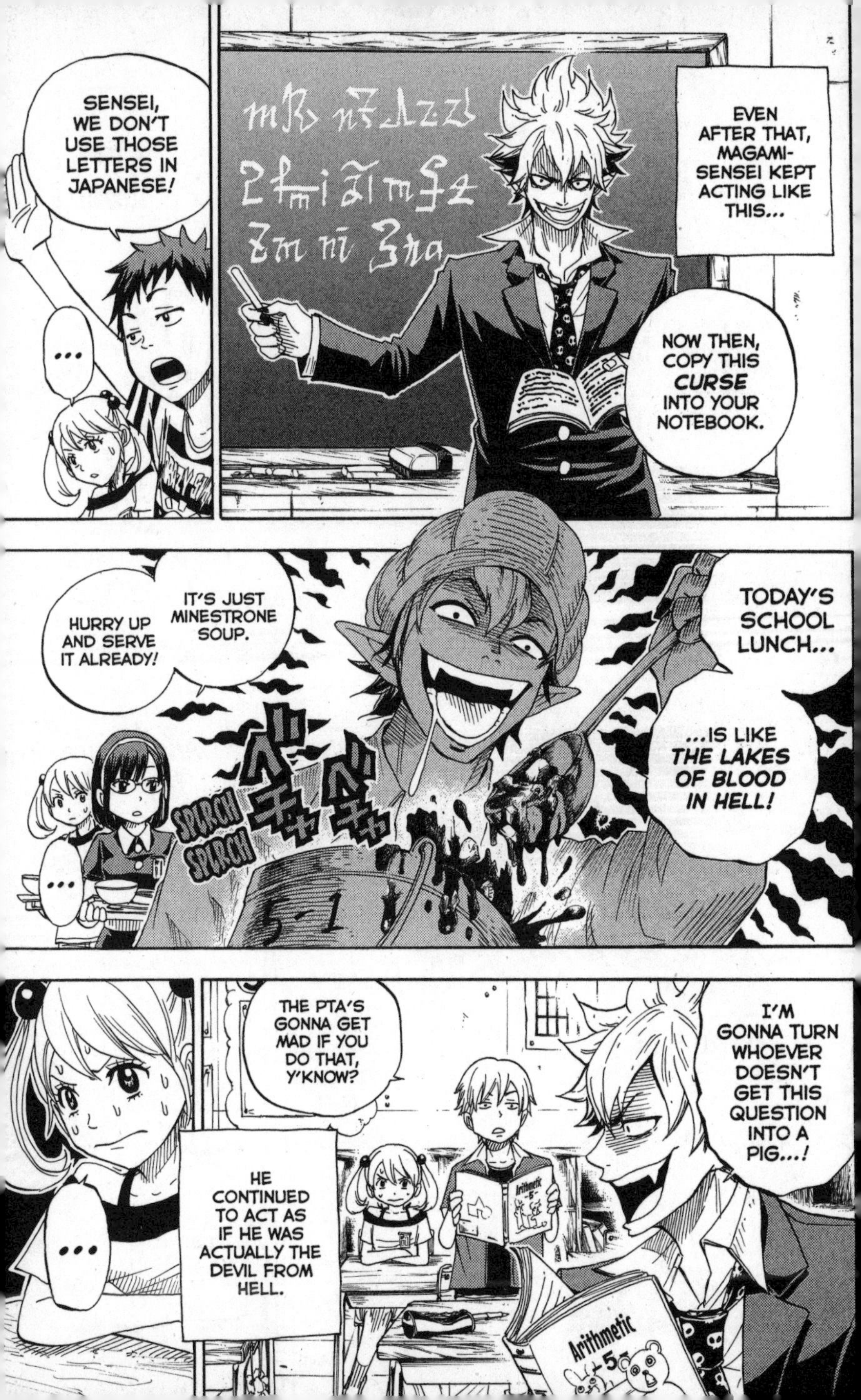
EVEN AFTER THAT, MAGAMI-SENSEI KEPT ACTING LIKE THIS...
NOW THEN, COPY THIS CURSE INTO YOUR NOTEBOOK.
SENSEI, WE DON'T USE THOSE LETTERS IN JAPANESE!
...
TODAY'S SCHOOL LUNCH...
...IS LIKE THE LAKES OF BLOOD IN HELL!
IT'S JUST MINESTRONE SOUP.
HURRY UP AND SERVE IT ALREADY!
SPLRCH SPLRCH
...
I'M GONNA TURN WHOEVER DOESN'T GET THIS QUESTION INTO A PIG...!
THE PTA'S GONNA GET MAD IF YOU DO THAT, Y'KNOW?
HE CONTINUED TO ACT AS IF HE WAS ACTUALLY THE DEVIL FROM HELL.
Arithmetic -5-
...

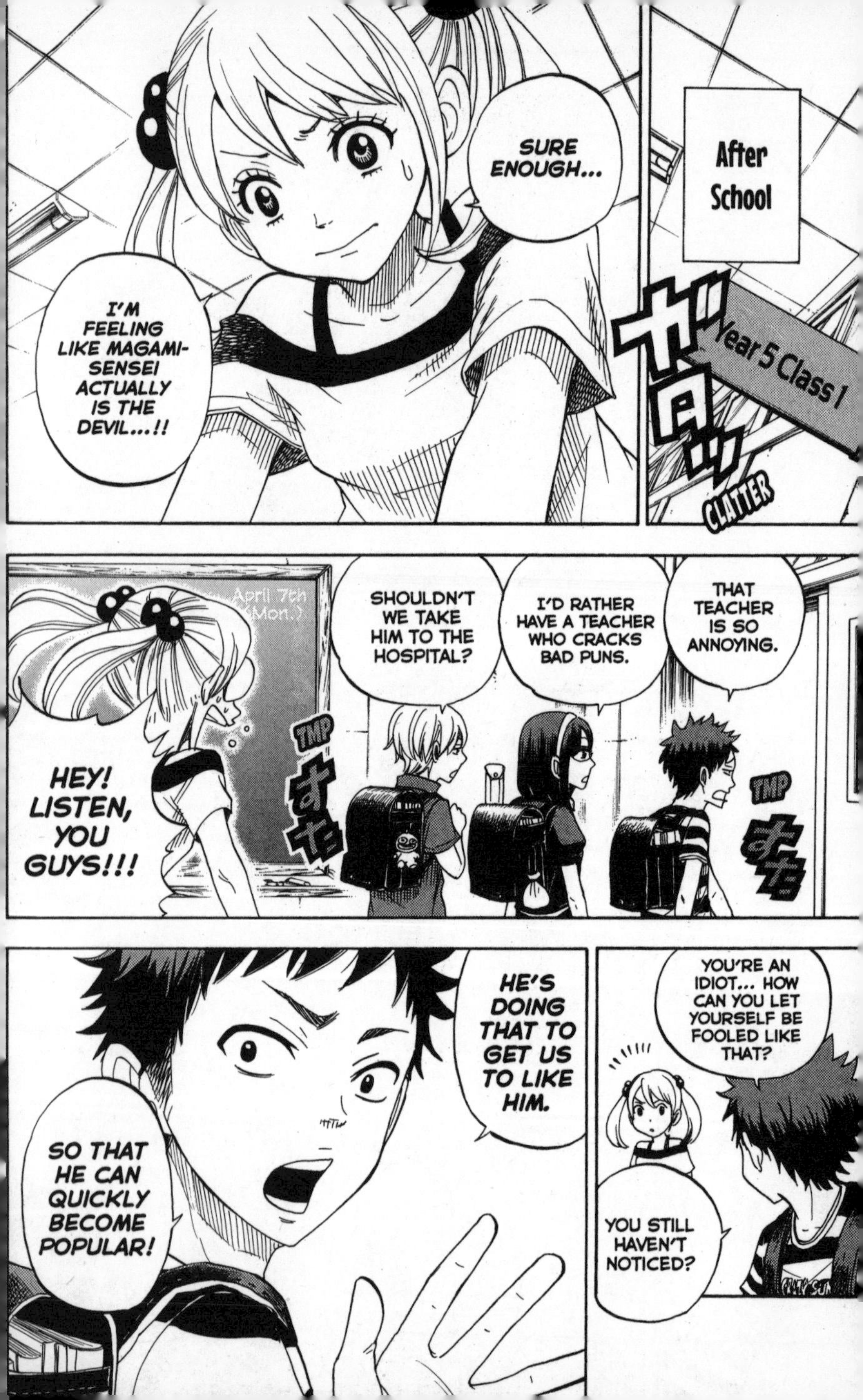
After School
Year 5 Class 1
ガラッ
CLATTER
SURE ENOUGH...
I'M FEELING LIKE MAGAMI-SENSEI ACTUALLY IS THE DEVIL...!!
THAT TEACHER IS SO ANNOYING.
TMP
I'D RATHER HAVE A TEACHER WHO CRACKS BAD PUNS.
SHOULDN'T WE TAKE HIM TO THE HOSPITAL?
TMP
April 7th (Mon.)
HEY! LISTEN, YOU GUYS!!!
YOU'RE AN IDIOT... HOW CAN YOU LET YOURSELF BE FOOLED LIKE THAT?
YOU STILL HAVEN'T NOTICED?
HE'S DOING THAT TO GET US TO LIKE HIM.
SO THAT HE CAN QUICKLY BECOME POPULAR!

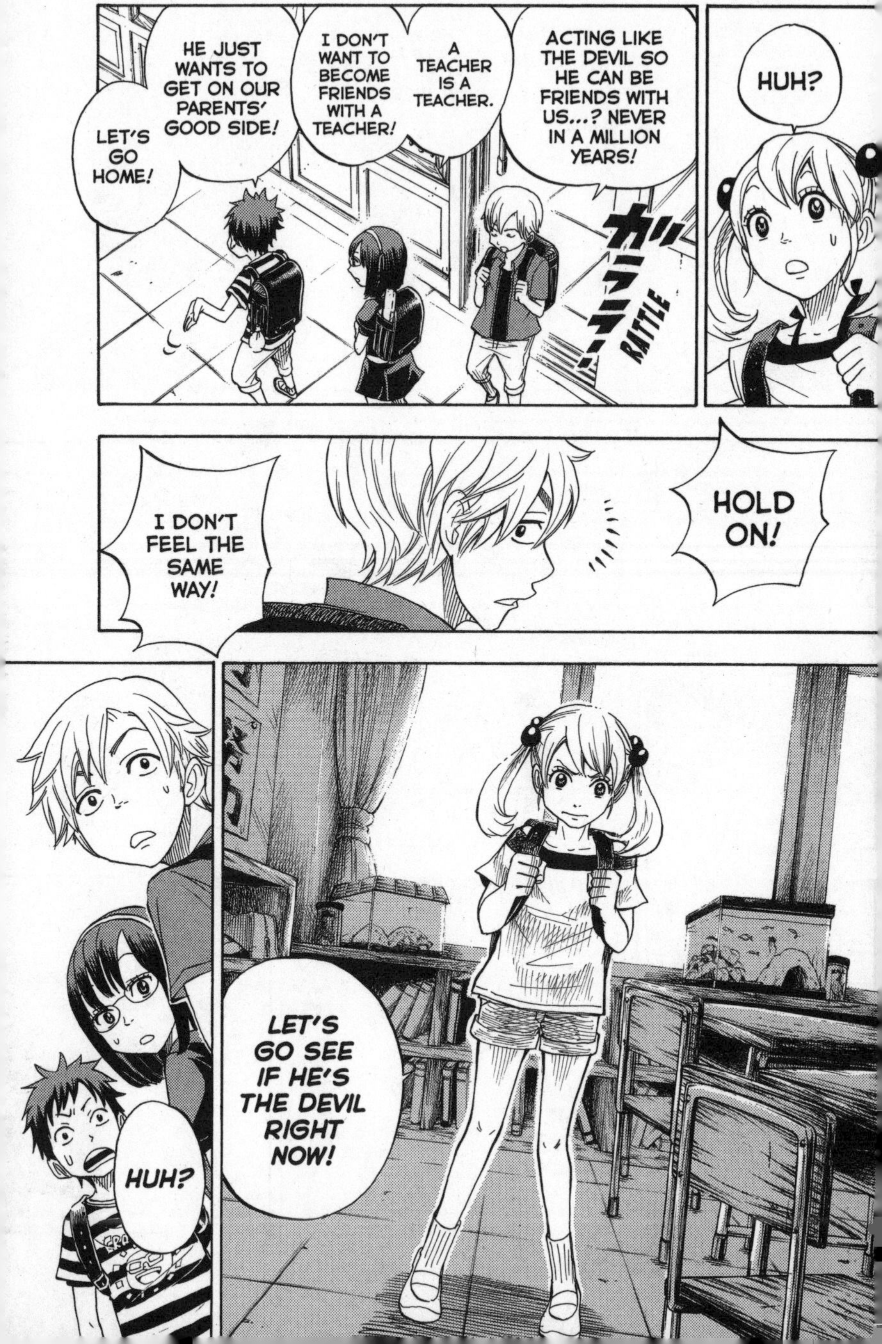
HUH?
ACTING LIKE THE DEVIL SO HE CAN BE FRIENDS WITH US...? NEVER IN A MILLION YEARS!
A TEACHER IS A TEACHER.
I DON'T WANT TO BECOME FRIENDS WITH A TEACHER!
HE JUST WANTS TO GET ON OUR PARENTS' GOOD SIDE!
LET'S GO HOME!
RATTLE
HOLD ON!
I DON'T FEEL THE SAME WAY!
LET'S GO SEE IF HE'S THE DEVIL RIGHT NOW!
HUH?

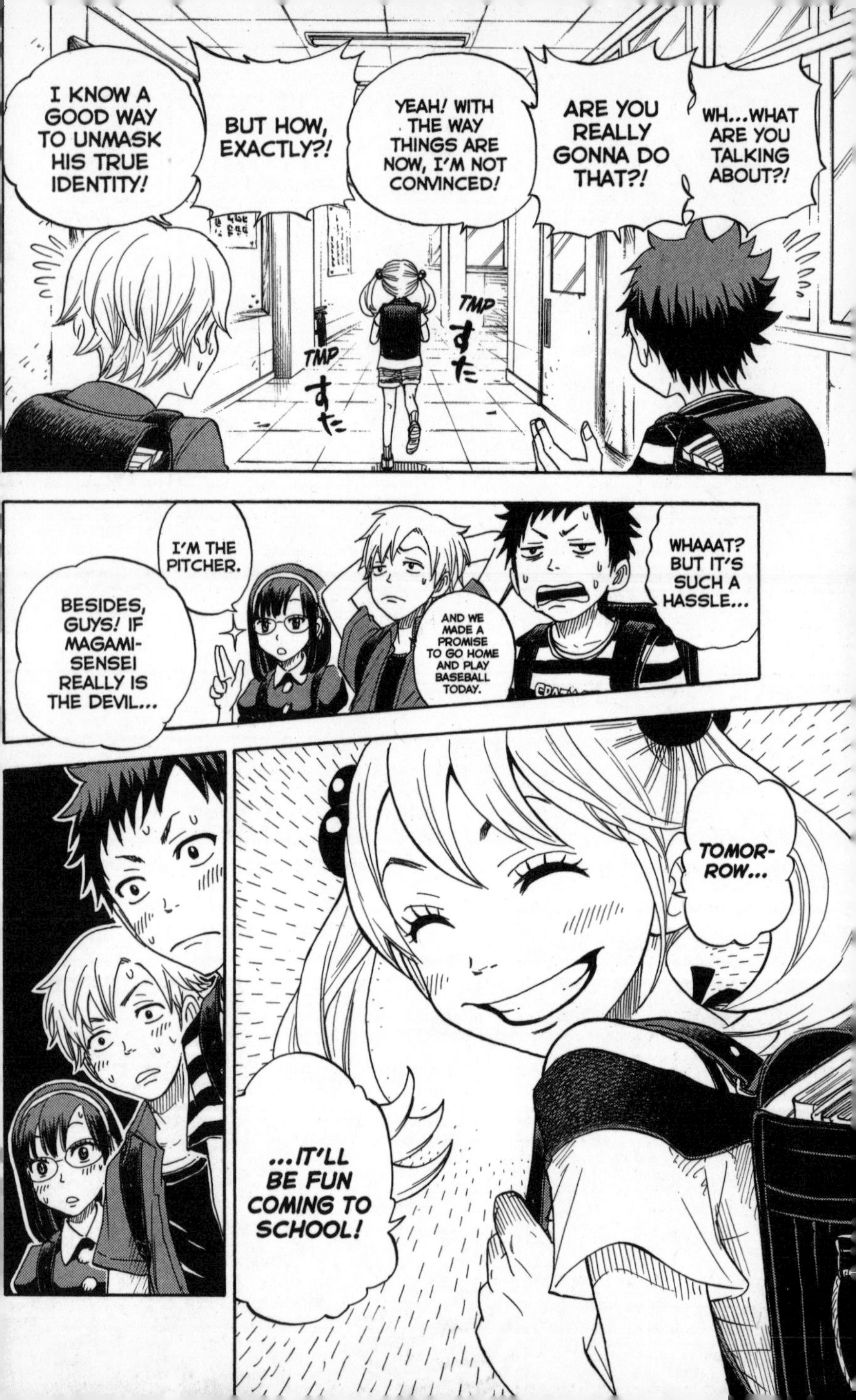
WH...WHAT ARE YOU TALKING ABOUT?!
ARE YOU REALLY GONNA DO THAT?!
YEAH! WITH THE WAY THINGS ARE NOW, I'M NOT CONVINCED!
BUT HOW, EXACTLY?!
I KNOW A GOOD WAY TO UNMASK HIS TRUE IDENTITY!
TMP すた
TMP すた
WHAAAT? BUT IT'S SUCH A HASSLE...
AND WE MADE A PROMISE TO GO HOME AND PLAY BASEBALL TODAY.
I'M THE PITCHER.
BESIDES, GUYS! IF MAGAMI-SENSEI REALLY IS THE DEVIL...
TOMOR-ROW...
...IT'LL BE FUN COMING TO SCHOOL!

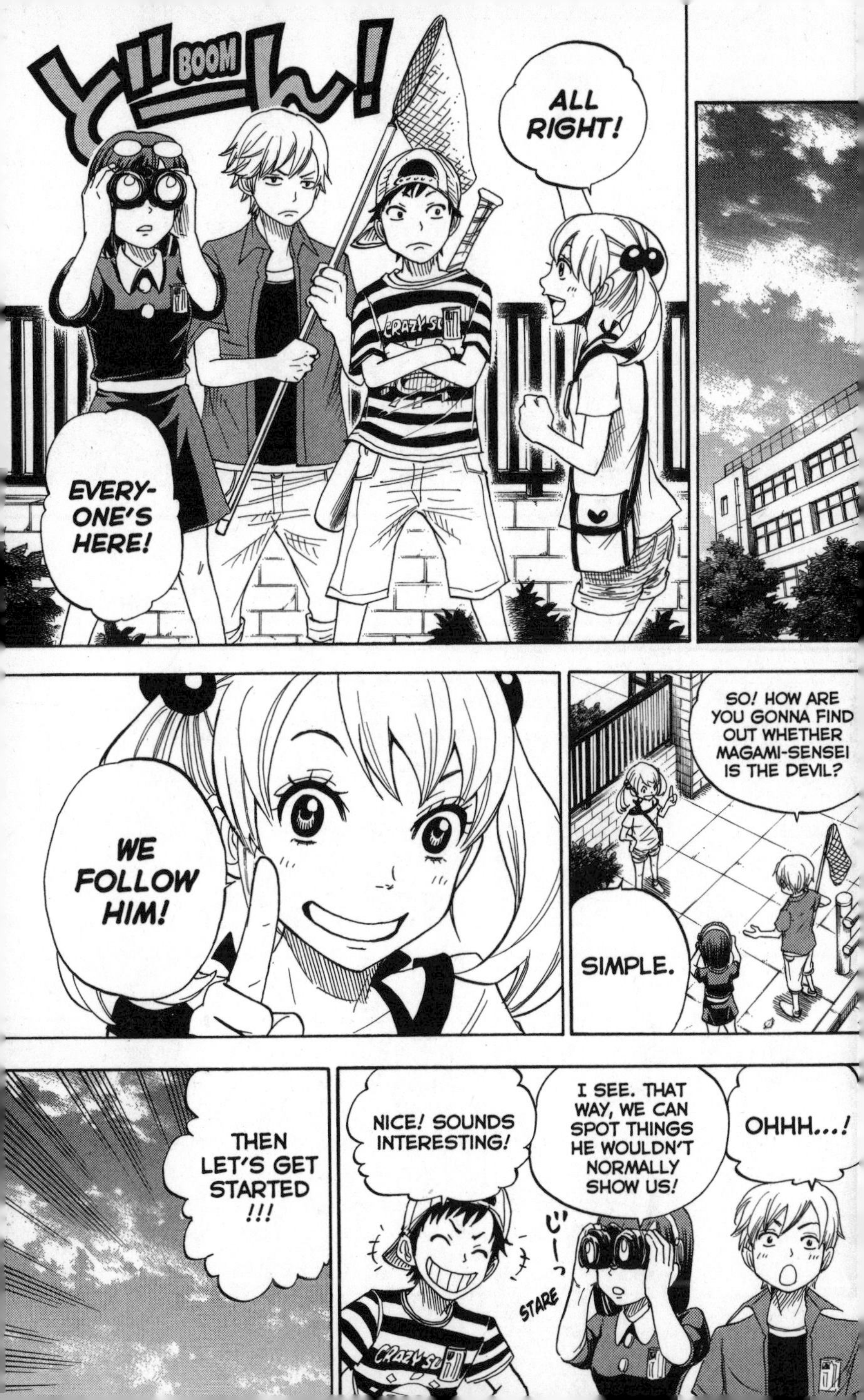
ALL RIGHT!
BOOM
EVERY-ONE'S HERE!
SO! HOW ARE YOU GONNA FIND OUT WHETHER MAGAMI-SENSEI IS THE DEVIL?
SIMPLE.
WE FOLLOW HIM!
OHHH...!
I SEE. THAT WAY, WE CAN SPOT THINGS HE WOULDN'T NORMALLY SHOW US!
STARE
NICE! SOUNDS INTERESTING!
THEN LET'S GET STARTED!!!

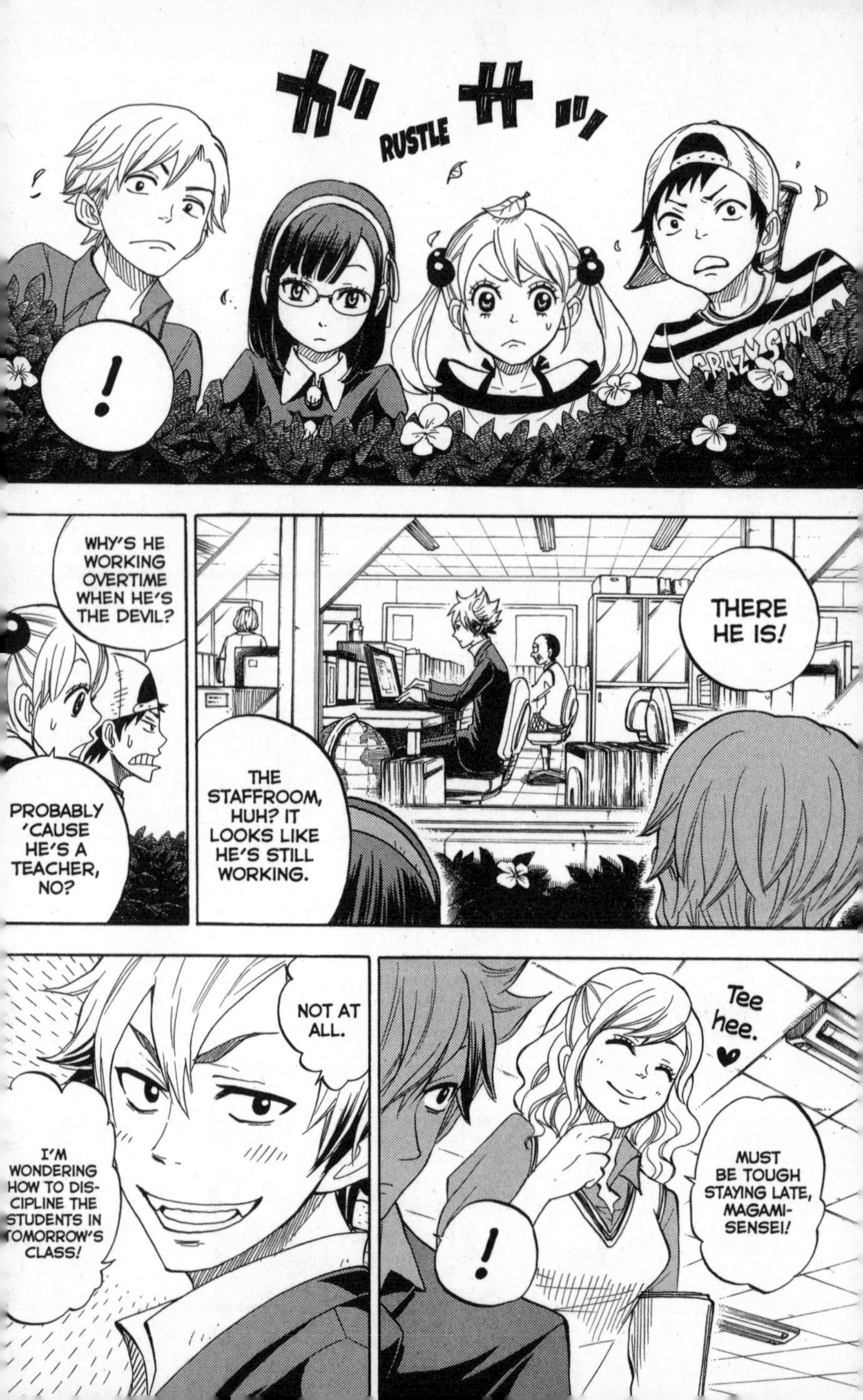
RUSTLE
!
THERE HE IS!
THE STAFFROOM, HUH? IT LOOKS LIKE HE'S STILL WORKING.
WHY'S HE WORKING OVERTIME WHEN HE'S THE DEVIL?
PROBABLY 'CAUSE HE'S A TEACHER, NO?
Tee hee.
MUST BE TOUGH STAYING LATE, MAGAMI-SENSEI!
!
NOT AT ALL.
I'M WONDERING HOW TO DISCIPLINE THE STUDENTS IN TOMORROW'S CLASS!

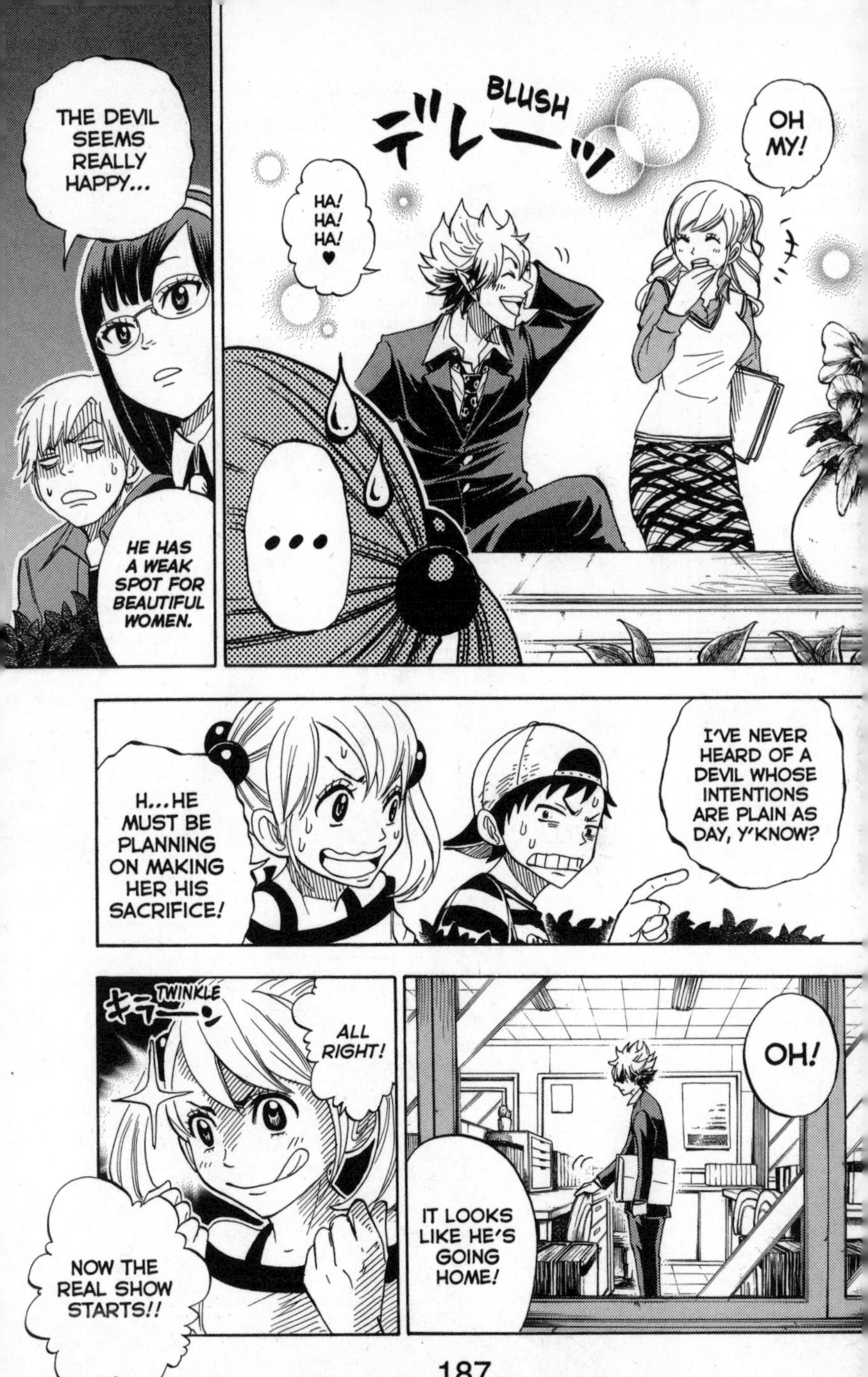
OH MY!
BLUSH
デレーッ
HA! HA! HA! ♥
...
THE DEVIL SEEMS REALLY HAPPY...
HE HAS A WEAK SPOT FOR BEAUTIFUL WOMEN.
I'VE NEVER HEARD OF A DEVIL WHOSE INTENTIONS ARE PLAIN AS DAY, Y'KNOW?
H...HE MUST BE PLANNING ON MAKING HER HIS SACRIFICE!
OH!
IT LOOKS LIKE HE'S GOING HOME!
TWINKLE
キラーン
ALL RIGHT!
NOW THE REAL SHOW STARTS!!

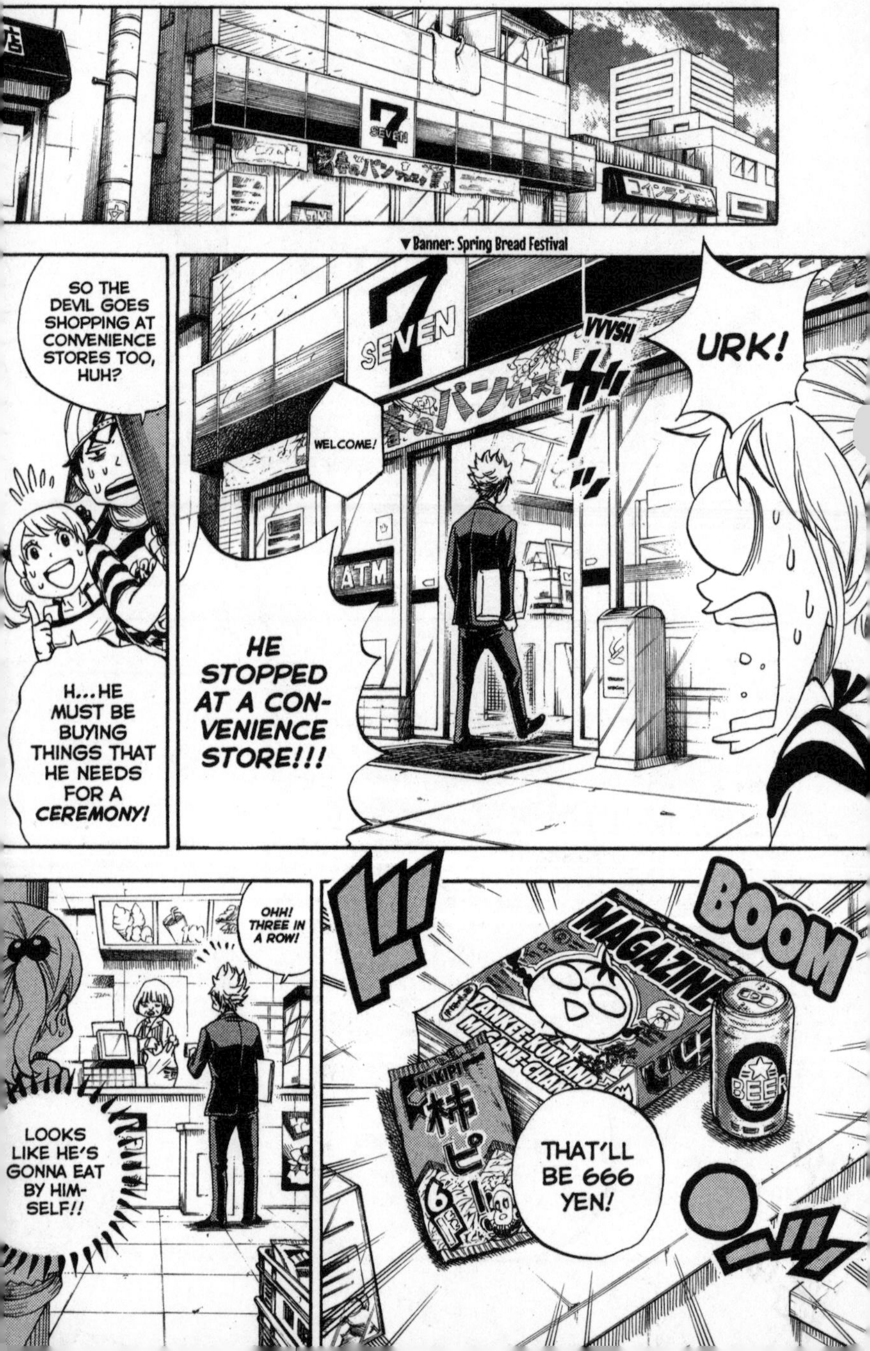
▼Banner: Spring Bread Festival
URK!
VVVSH
WELCOME!
HE STOPPED AT A CON-VENIENCE STORE!!!
SO THE DEVIL GOES SHOPPING AT CONVENIENCE STORES TOO, HUH?
H...HE MUST BE BUYING THINGS THAT HE NEEDS FOR A CEREMONY!
BOOM
MAGAZINE
YANKEE-KUN AND MEGANE-CHAN
KAKIPI
BEER
THAT'LL BE 666 YEN!
OHH! THREE IN A ROW!
LOOKS LIKE HE'S GONNA EAT BY HIM-SELF!!

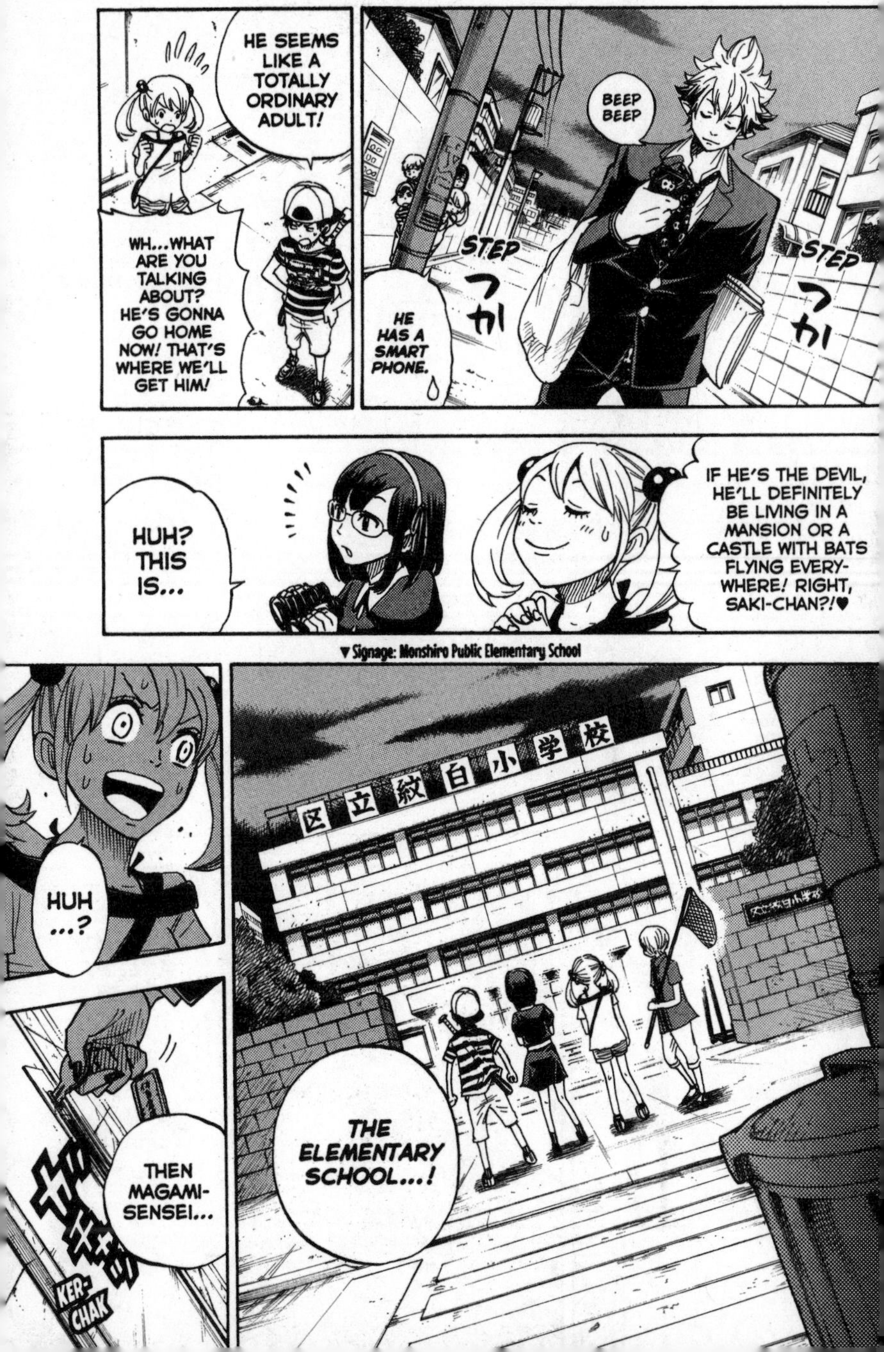
BEEP BEEP
STEP
つか
STEP
つか
HE HAS A SMART PHONE.
HE SEEMS LIKE A TOTALLY ORDINARY ADULT!
WH...WHAT ARE YOU TALKING ABOUT? HE'S GONNA GO HOME NOW! THAT'S WHERE WE'LL GET HIM!
IF HE'S THE DEVIL, HE'LL DEFINITELY BE LIVING IN A MANSION OR A CASTLE WITH BATS FLYING EVERY-WHERE! RIGHT, SAKI-CHAN?!♥
HUH? THIS IS...
▼Signage: Monshiro Public Elementary School
区立紋白小学校
THE ELEMENTARY SCHOOL...!
HUH ...?
THEN MAGAMI-SENSEI...
ガチャッ
KER-CHAK

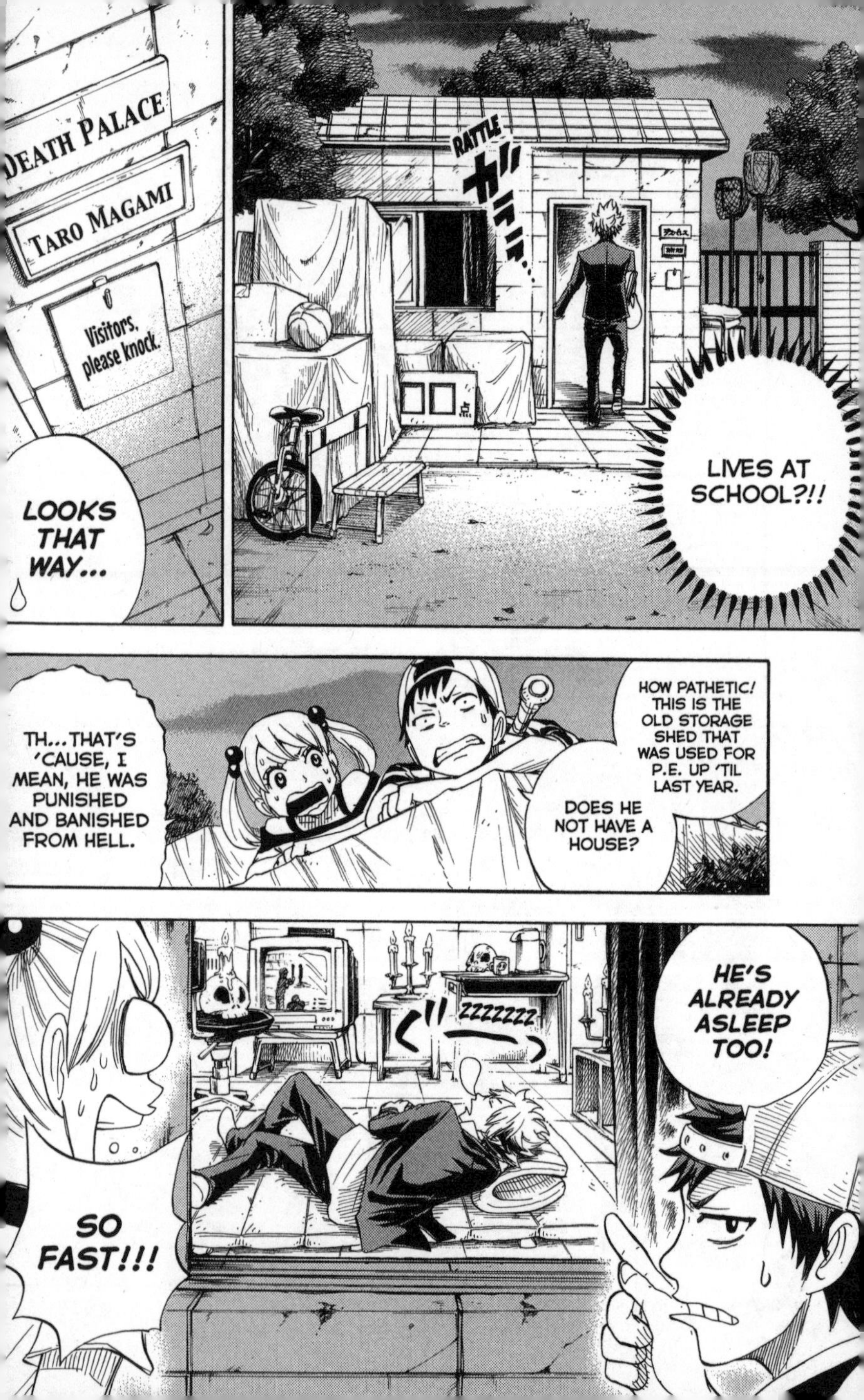
RATTLE
LIVES AT SCHOOL?!!
DEATH PALACE
TARO MAGAMI
Visitors, please knock.
LOOKS THAT WAY...
HOW PATHETIC! THIS IS THE OLD STORAGE SHED THAT WAS USED FOR P.E. UP 'TIL LAST YEAR.
DOES HE NOT HAVE A HOUSE?
TH...THAT'S 'CAUSE, I MEAN, HE WAS PUNISHED AND BANISHED FROM HELL.
HE'S ALREADY ASLEEP TOO!
ZZZZZZZ
SO FAST!!!

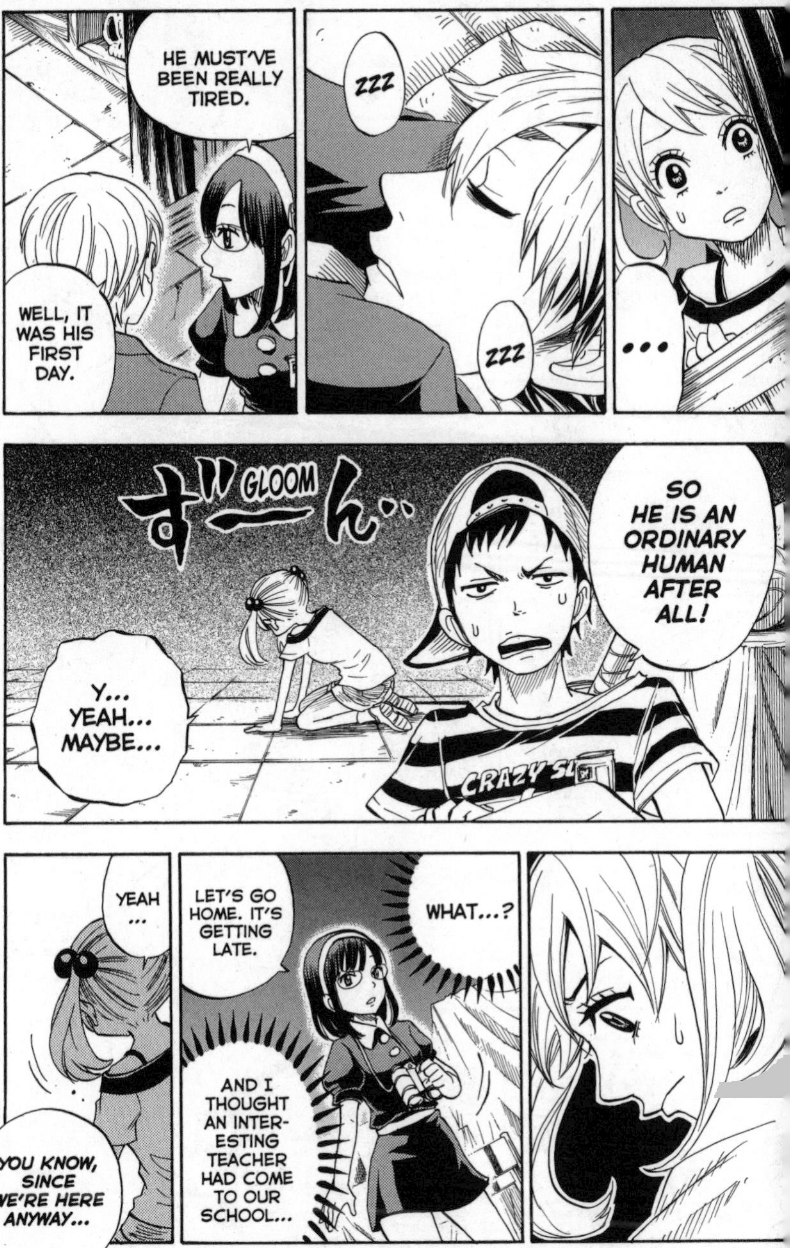
...
ZZZ
ZZZ
HE MUST'VE BEEN REALLY TIRED.
WELL, IT WAS HIS FIRST DAY.
SO HE IS AN ORDINARY HUMAN AFTER ALL!
ずーん GLOOM
Y... YEAH... MAYBE...
WHAT...?
LET'S GO HOME. IT'S GETTING LATE.
AND I THOUGHT AN INTERESTING TEACHER HAD COME TO OUR SCHOOL...
YEAH ...
YOU KNOW, SINCE WE'RE HERE ANYWAY...

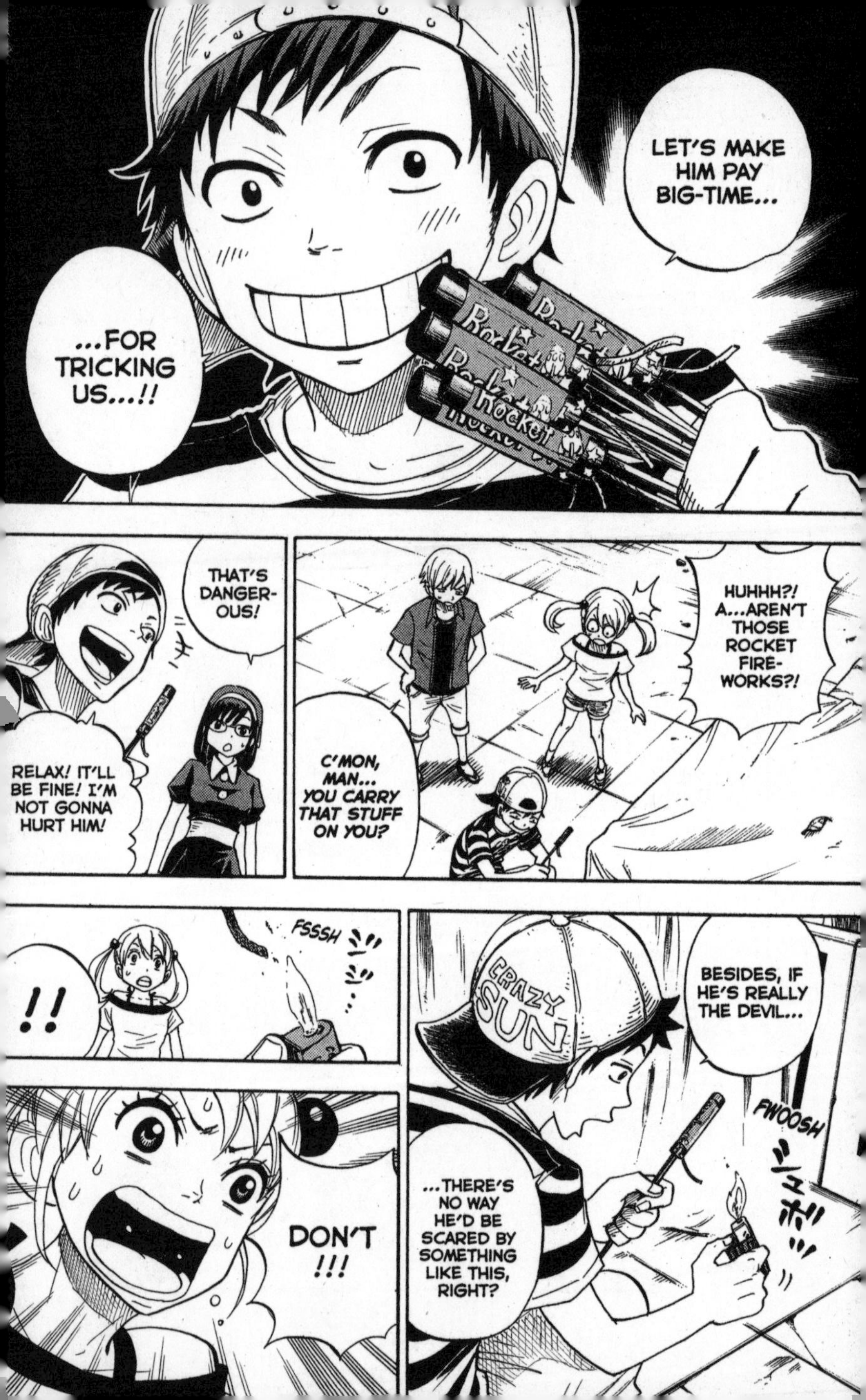
LET'S MAKE HIM PAY BIG-TIME...
...FOR TRICKING US...!!
HUHHH?! A...AREN'T THOSE ROCKET FIRE-WORKS?!
C'MON, MAN... YOU CARRY THAT STUFF ON YOU?
THAT'S DANGER-OUS!
RELAX! IT'LL BE FINE! I'M NOT GONNA HURT HIM!
BESIDES, IF HE'S REALLY THE DEVIL...
FWOOSH
...THERE'S NO WAY HE'D BE SCARED BY SOMETHING LIKE THIS, RIGHT?
FSSSH
!!
DON'T !!!

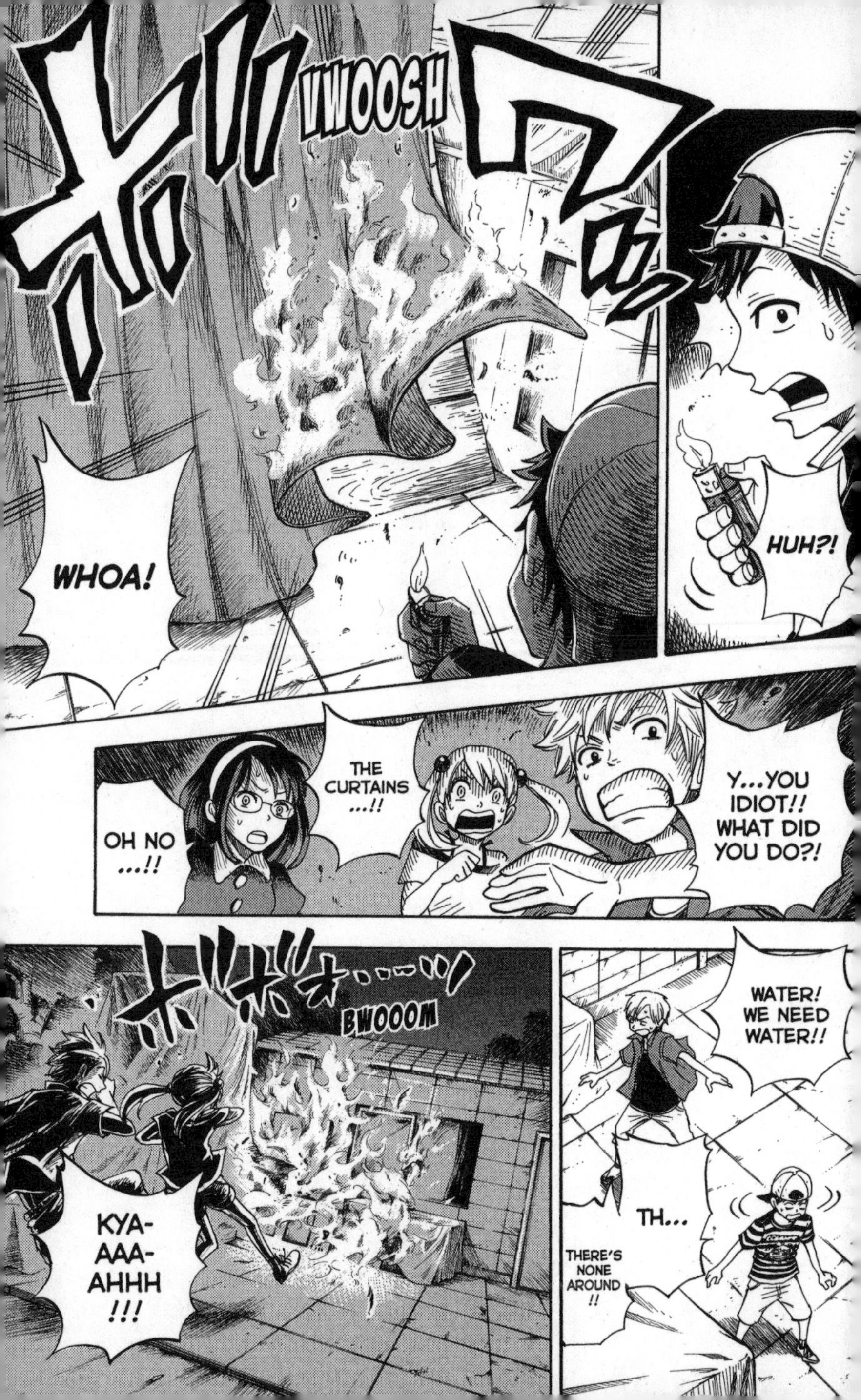
HUH?!
VWOOSH
WHOA!
Y...YOU IDIOT!! WHAT DID YOU DO?!
THE CURTAINS ...!!
OH NO ...!!
WATER! WE NEED WATER!!
TH...
THERE'S NONE AROUND !!
BWOOOM
KYA-AAA-AHHH !!!

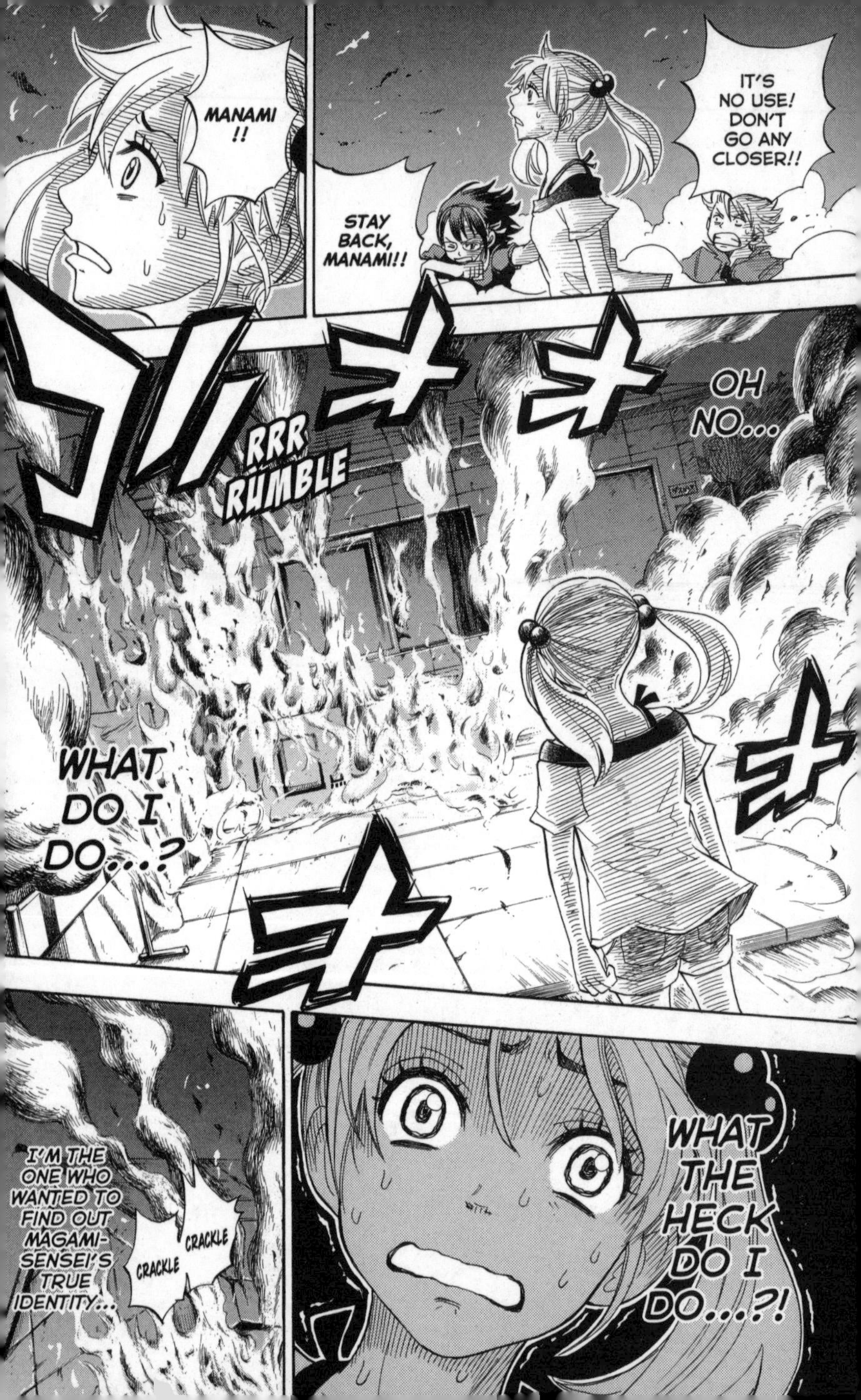
IT'S NO USE! DON'T GO ANY CLOSER!!
STAY BACK, MANAMI!!
MANAMI!!
OH NO...
RRR RUMBLE
WHAT DO I DO...?
WHAT THE HECK DO I DO...?!
I'M THE ONE WHO WANTED TO FIND OUT MAGAMI-SENSEI'S TRUE IDENTITY...
CRACKLE
CRACKLE

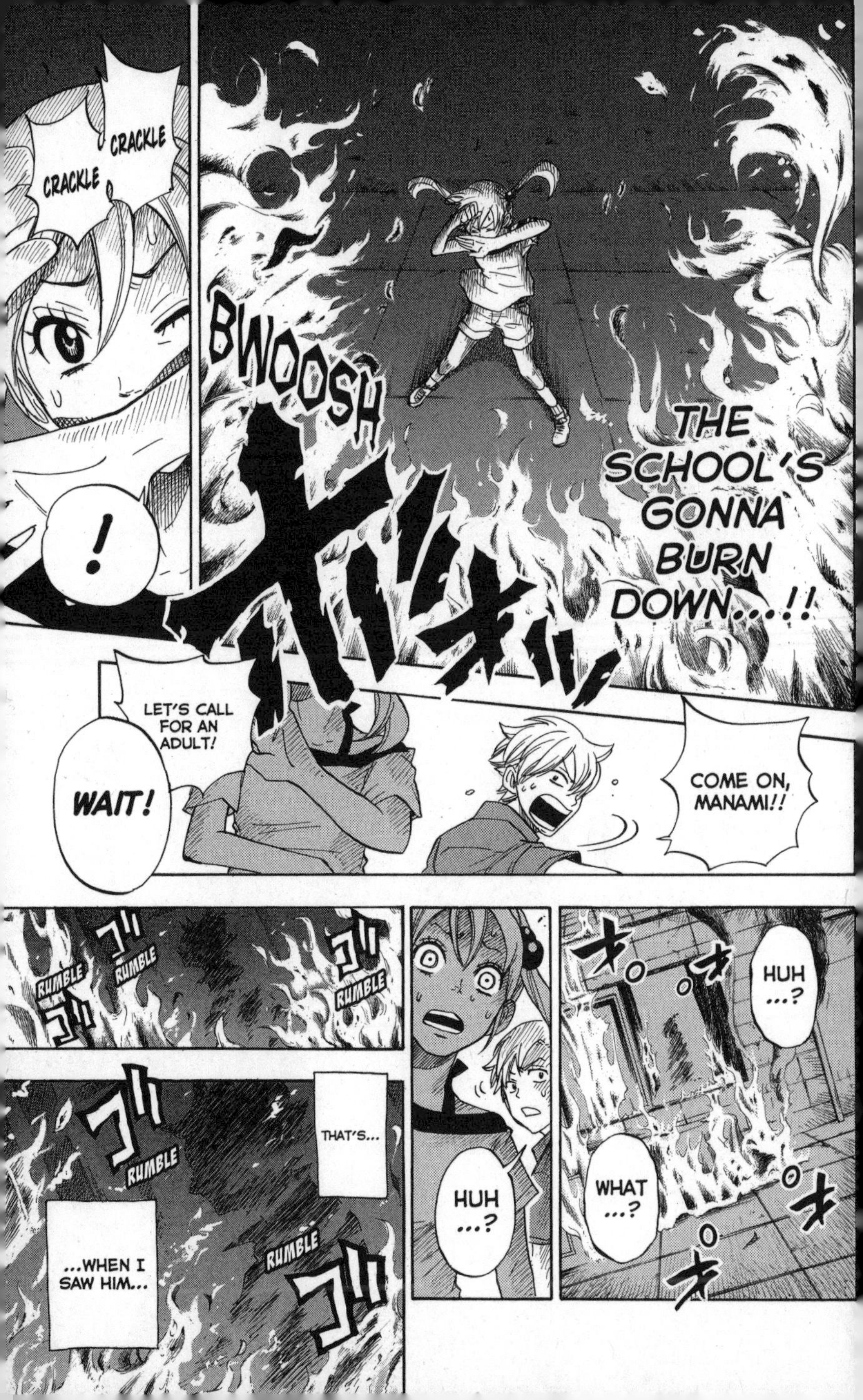
BWOOSH
THE SCHOOL'S GONNA BURN DOWN...!!
CRACKLE
CRACKLE
!
COME ON, MANAMI!!
LET'S CALL FOR AN ADULT!
WAIT!
HUH ...?
WHAT ...?
HUH ...?
RUMBLE
RUMBLE
RUMBLE
THAT'S...
RUMBLE
RUMBLE
...WHEN I SAW HIM...

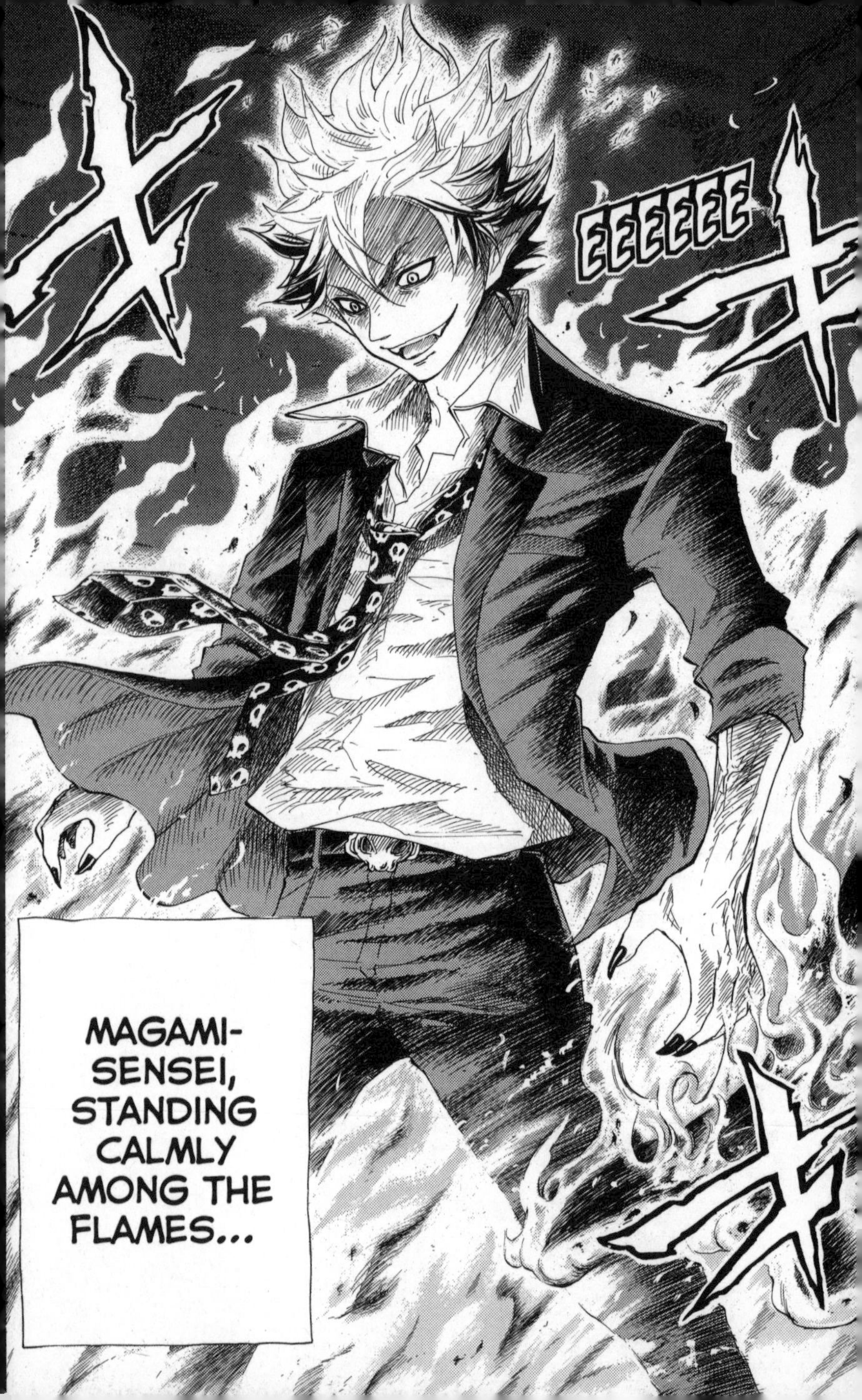
EEEEEE
MAGAMI-SENSEI, STANDING CALMLY AMONG THE FLAMES...

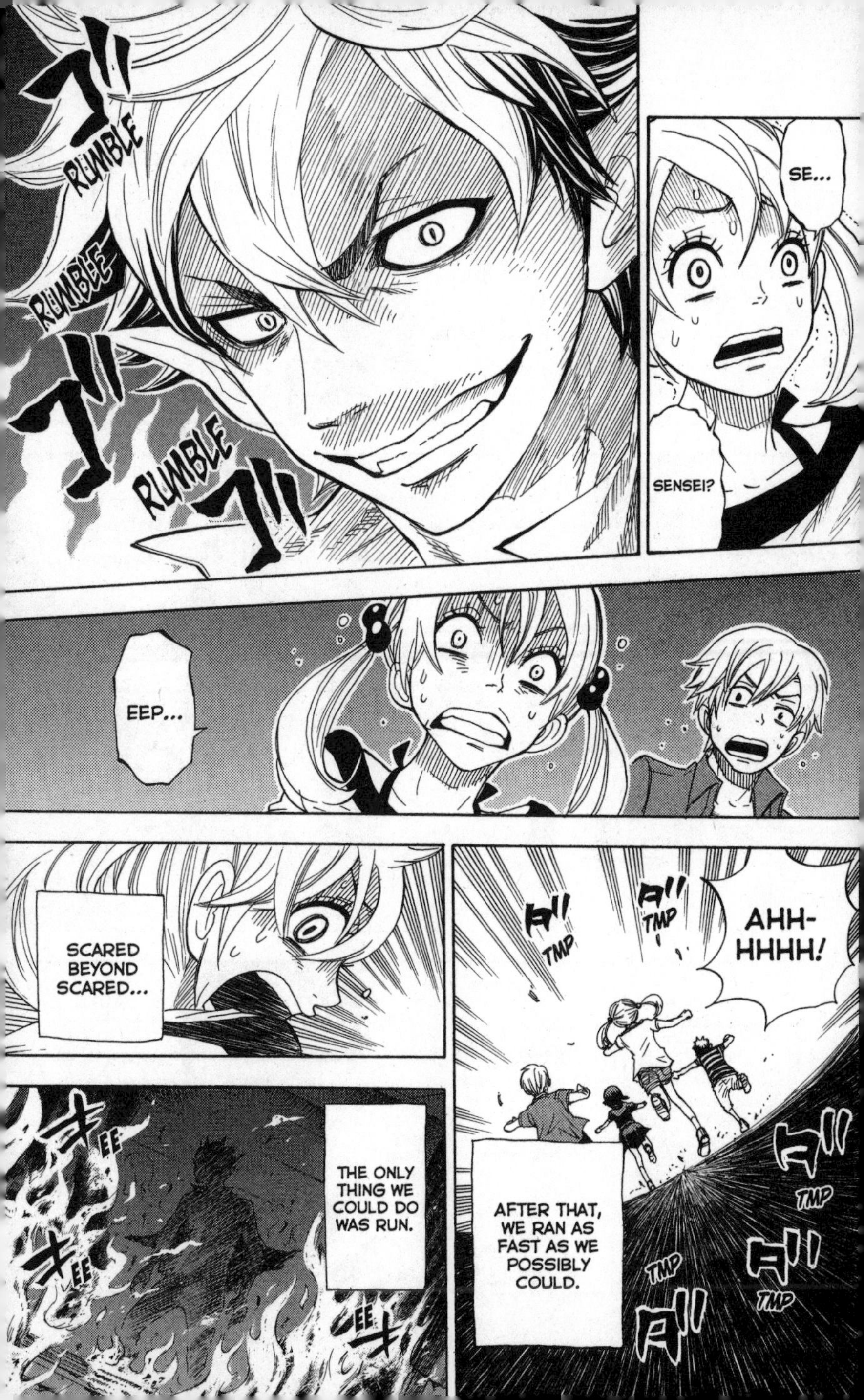
SE...
SENSEI?
RUMBLE
RUMBLE
RUMBLE
EEP...
TMP
TMP
AHH-HHHH!
AFTER THAT, WE RAN AS FAST AS WE POSSIBLY COULD.
TMP
TMP
TMP
TMP
SCARED BEYOND SCARED...
THE ONLY THING WE COULD DO WAS RUN.
EE
EE
EE

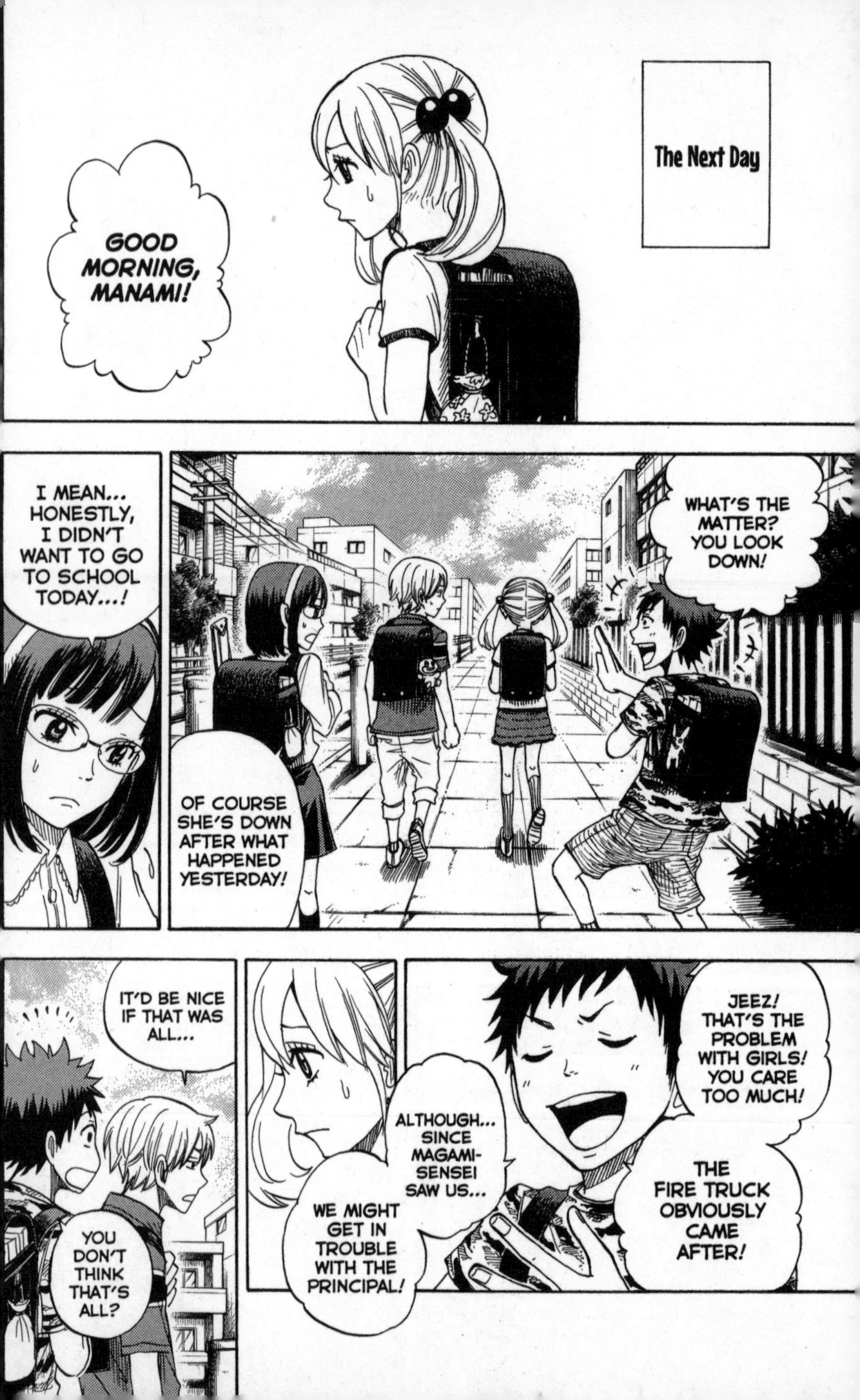
The Next Day
GOOD MORNING, MANAMI!
WHAT'S THE MATTER? YOU LOOK DOWN!
OF COURSE SHE'S DOWN AFTER WHAT HAPPENED YESTERDAY!
I MEAN... HONESTLY, I DIDN'T WANT TO GO TO SCHOOL TODAY...!
JEEZ! THAT'S THE PROBLEM WITH GIRLS! YOU CARE TOO MUCH!
THE FIRE TRUCK OBVIOUSLY CAME AFTER!
ALTHOUGH... SINCE MAGAMI-SENSEI SAW US...
WE MIGHT GET IN TROUBLE WITH THE PRINCIPAL!
IT'D BE NICE IF THAT WAS ALL...
YOU DON'T THINK THAT'S ALL?

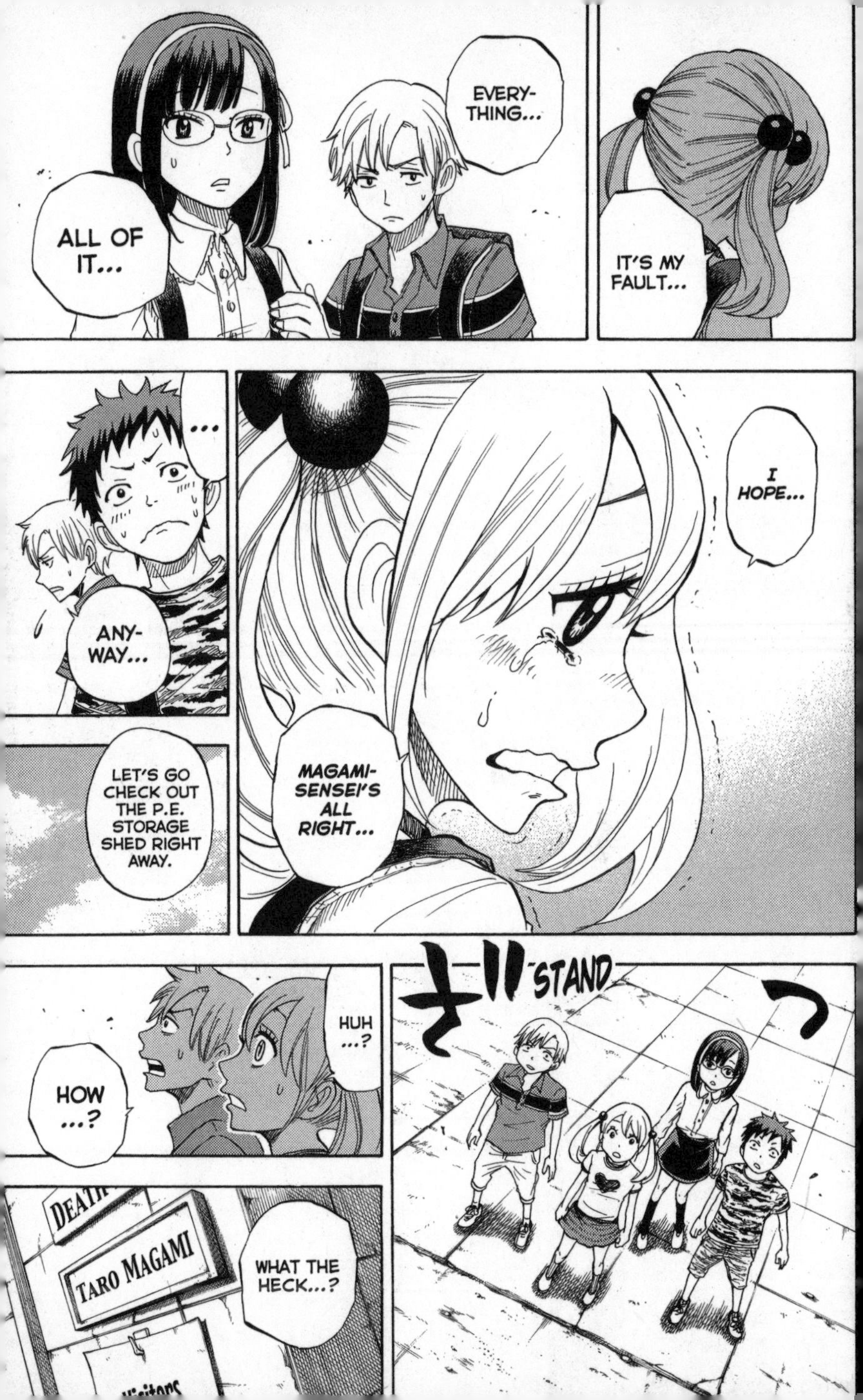
IT'S MY FAULT...
EVERY-THING...
...
ALL OF IT...
I HOPE...
MAGAMI-SENSEI'S ALL RIGHT...
...
ANY-WAY...
LET'S GO CHECK OUT THE P.E. STORAGE SHED RIGHT AWAY.
STAND
HUH ...?
HOW ...?
DEATH
TARO MAGAMI
WHAT THE HECK...?

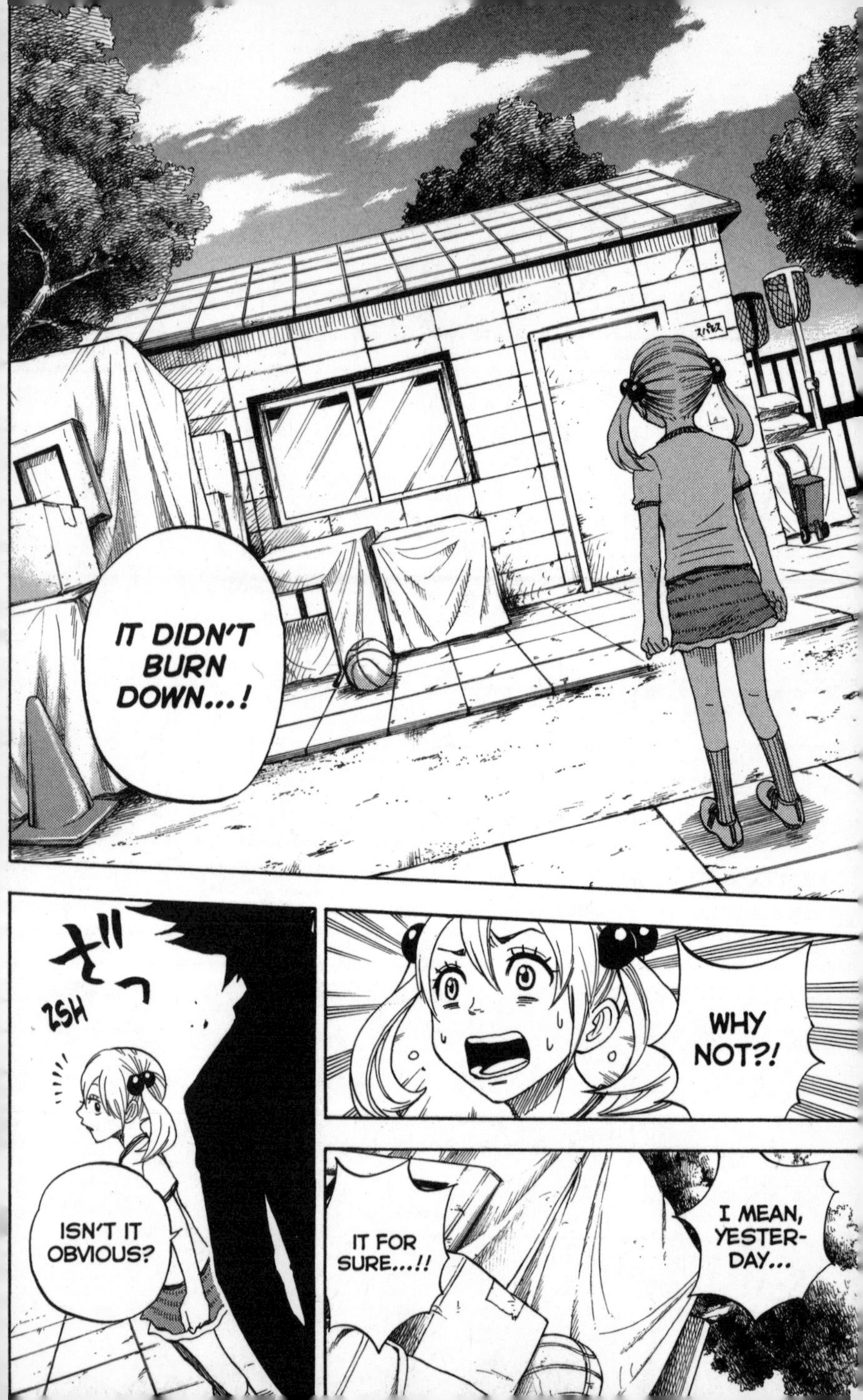
IT DIDN'T BURN DOWN...!
WHY NOT?!
I MEAN, YESTER-DAY...
IT FOR SURE...!!
ぞっ
ZSH
ISN'T IT OBVIOUS?

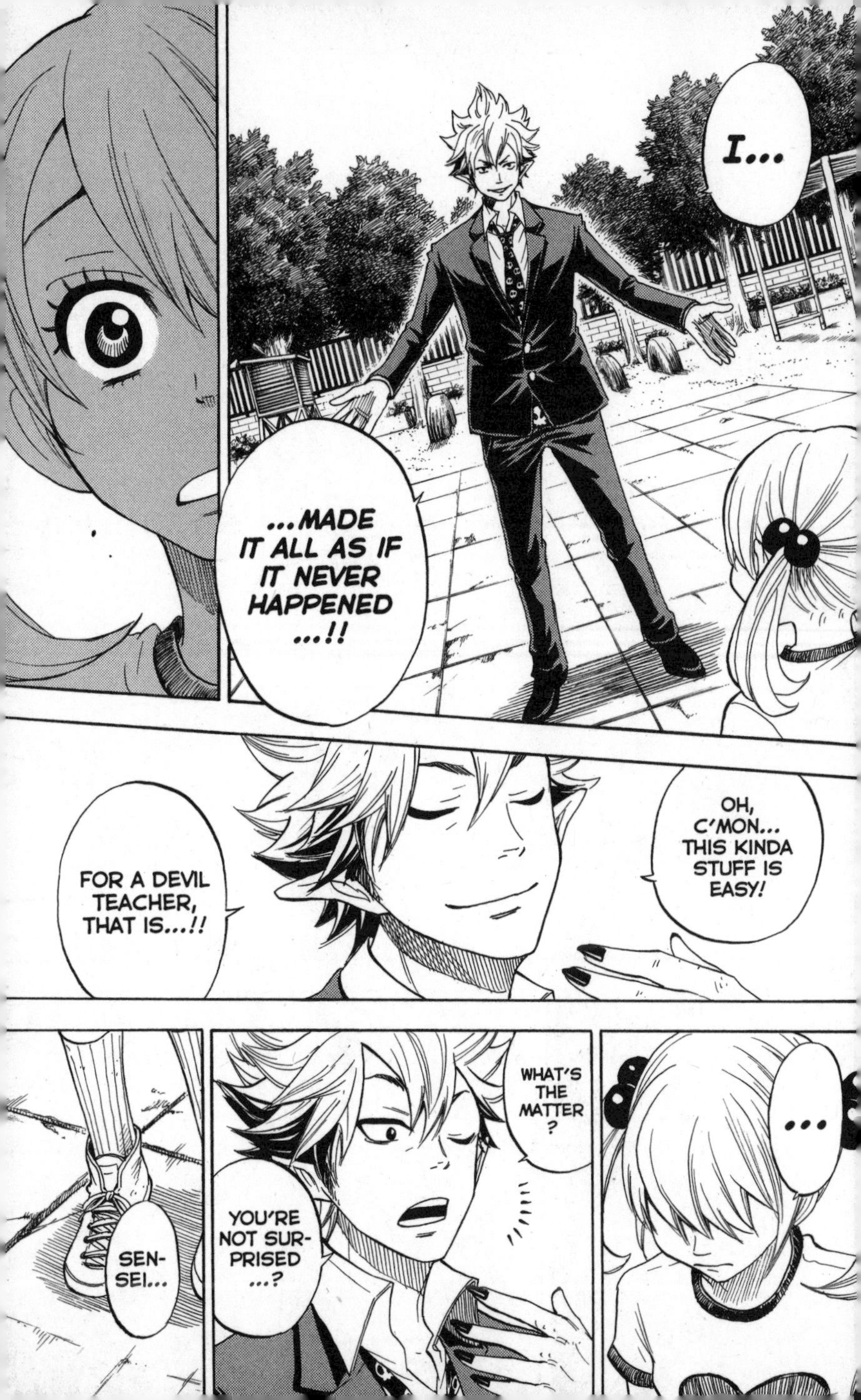
I...
...MADE IT ALL AS IF IT NEVER HAPPENED...!!
OH, C'MON... THIS KINDA STUFF IS EASY!
FOR A DEVIL TEACHER, THAT IS...!!
...
WHAT'S THE MATTER?
YOU'RE NOT SURPRISED...?
SENSEI...

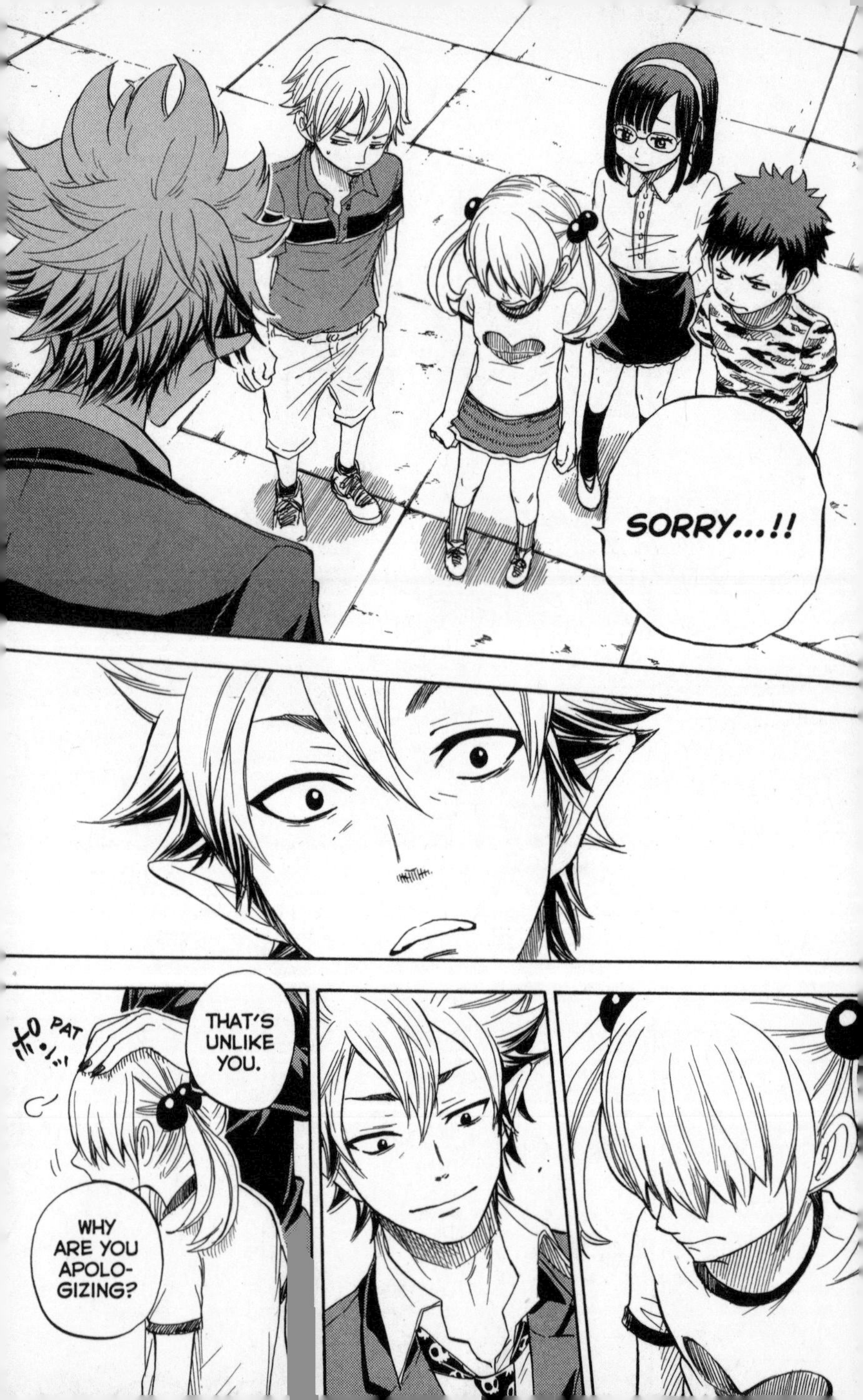
SORRY...!!
THAT'S UNLIKE YOU.
PAT
WHY ARE YOU APOLOGIZING?

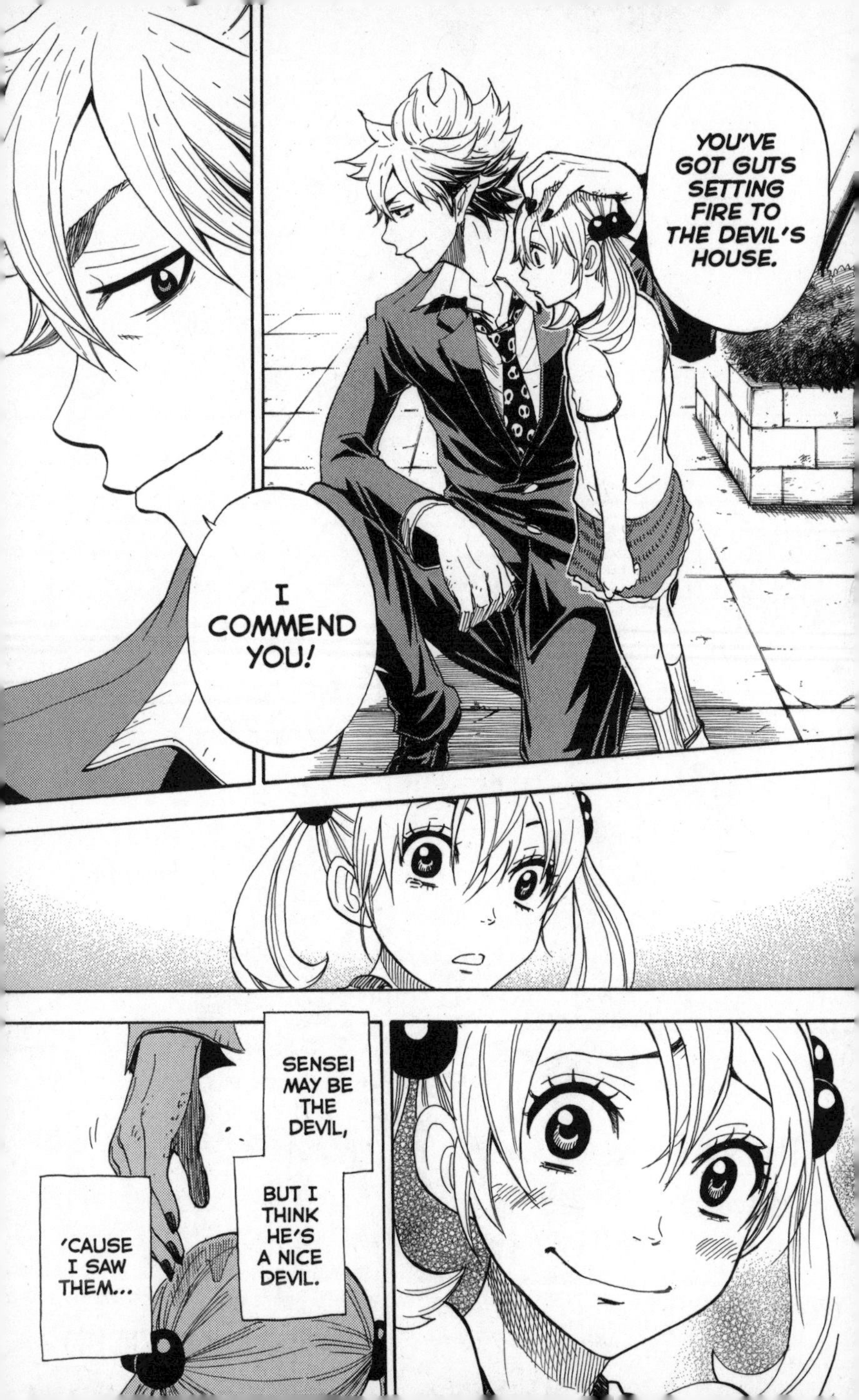
YOU'VE GOT GUTS SETTING FIRE TO THE DEVIL'S HOUSE.
I COMMEND YOU!
SENSEI MAY BE THE DEVIL,
BUT I THINK HE'S A NICE DEVIL.
'CAUSE I SAW THEM...

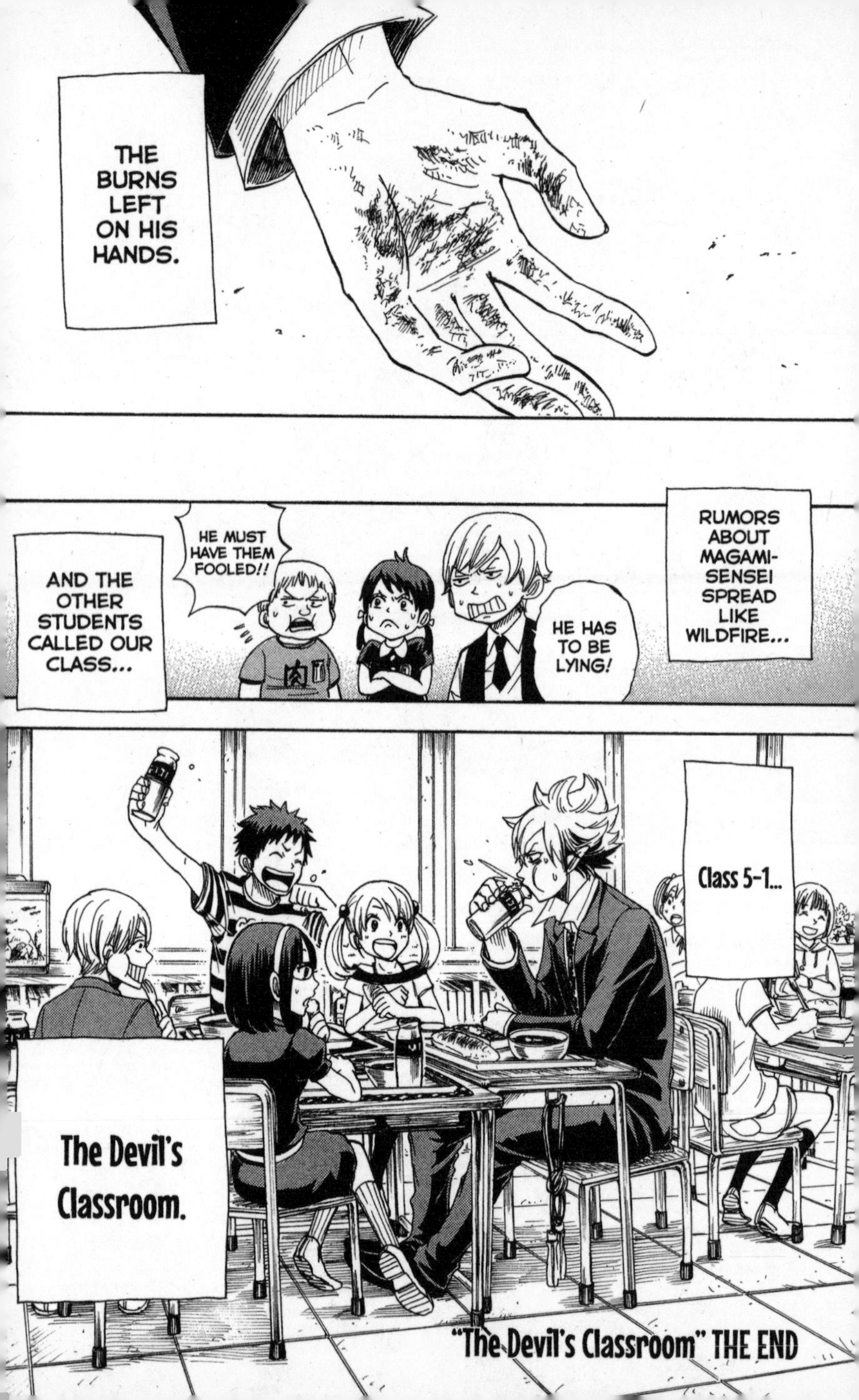
THE BURNS LEFT ON HIS HANDS.
RUMORS ABOUT MAGAMI-SENSEI SPREAD LIKE WILDFIRE...
HE HAS TO BE LYING!
HE MUST HAVE THEM FOOLED!!
AND THE OTHER STUDENTS CALLED OUR CLASS...
Class 5-1...
The Devil's Classroom.
"The Devil's Classroom" THE END

Yamazaki's ~~Miyabi Itou~~'s Witch Research Notes

File.5

By: Yamazaki

It's me! The Student Council President!

MONO

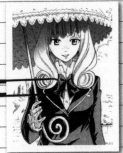

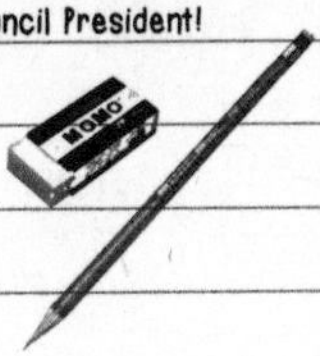

Rika Saionji

The Seventh Witch   Power: Rewrite

- Suzaku High third-year student.
- She and I are friends.

  She listens to my various requests.
- Her role is to erase all witch-related memories when someone learns the identity of all seven witches!

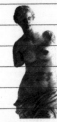

※ Yamada-kun is a special case, as witch powers don't work on him, so the memories of everyone around Yamada-kun were manipulated instead!

- It seems that the power doesn't work on someone who has been affected by the power before.

  This also surprised me!
- Between you and me, **she never wears underwear!**

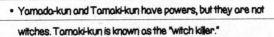

★ A review of the common rules regarding witches!

- One person, one power!
- When a person is under a spell, another power will have no effect on them even when kissed by a different witch!
- Powers have no effect on fellow witches.
- Yamada-kun and Tamaki-kun have powers, but they are not witches. Tamaki-kun is known as the "witch killer."
- There are always seven witches. When a witch disappears from the school or loses their power, another witch is born.

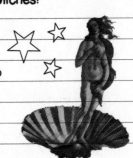

Translation Notes

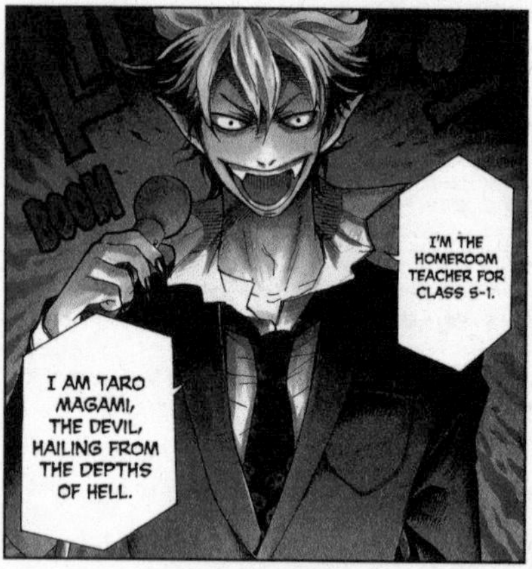
BOOM
I'M THE HOMEROOM TEACHER FOR CLASS 5-1.
I AM TARO MAGAMI, THE DEVIL, HAILING FROM THE DEPTHS OF HELL.

Magami, page 169

Magami may not have any particular meaning to an English-speaker, but in Japanese, it has a meaning that emphasizes the teacher's devilish persona. Taro Magami's last name is written using the Chinese characters for "demon" and "king," which is another way to say Satan, a.k.a. the Prince of Darkness.

The self-conscious stage of puberty, page 177

What the kids are talking about here is something called "*chūnibyō*," a slang term to describe certain behaviors that are said to occur in the second year of junior high school. *Chūnibyō* literally means second-year junior high illness and it's used to describe people who around that time become absorbed in delusional thoughts, like thinking that they have special powers or are otherwise better than other people. Since some of these behaviors could also be attributed to teenagers going through puberty, for the purposes of this manga it was translated as "the self-conscious stage of puberty."

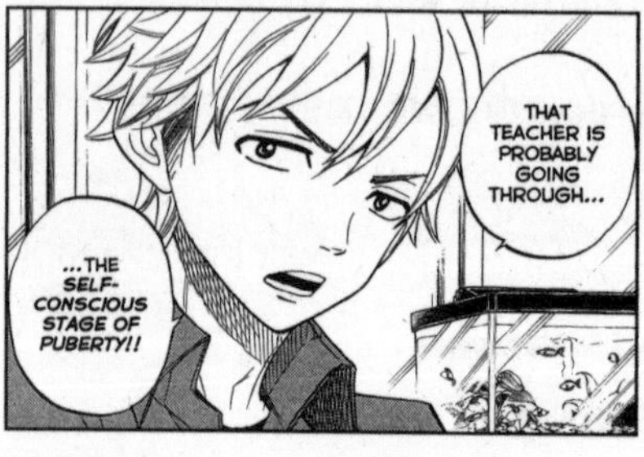
THAT TEACHER IS PROBABLY GOING THROUGH...
...THE SELF-CONSCIOUS STAGE OF PUBERTY!!

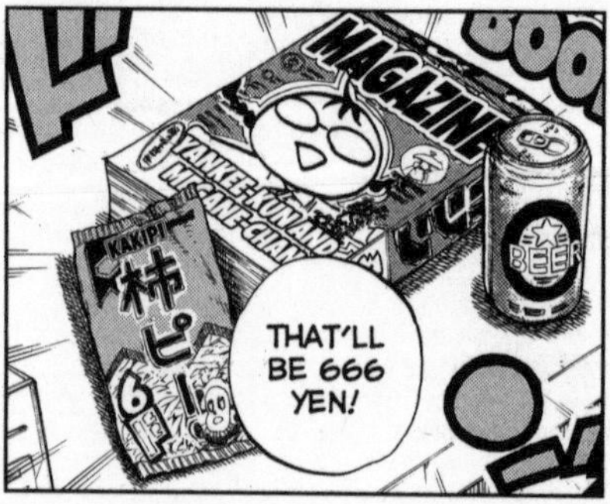
BOO
MAGAZINE
YANKEE-KUN AND MEGANE-CHAN
BEER
KAKIPI
柿ピー
THAT'LL BE 666 YEN!

Kakipi, page 188

Kakipi (short for *kaki* (EN: persimmon fruit) peanuts) or *kaki no tane* (EN: persimmon seeds) are the names of a Japanese snack that typically contains a mixture of oblong-shaped rice crackers and peanuts.

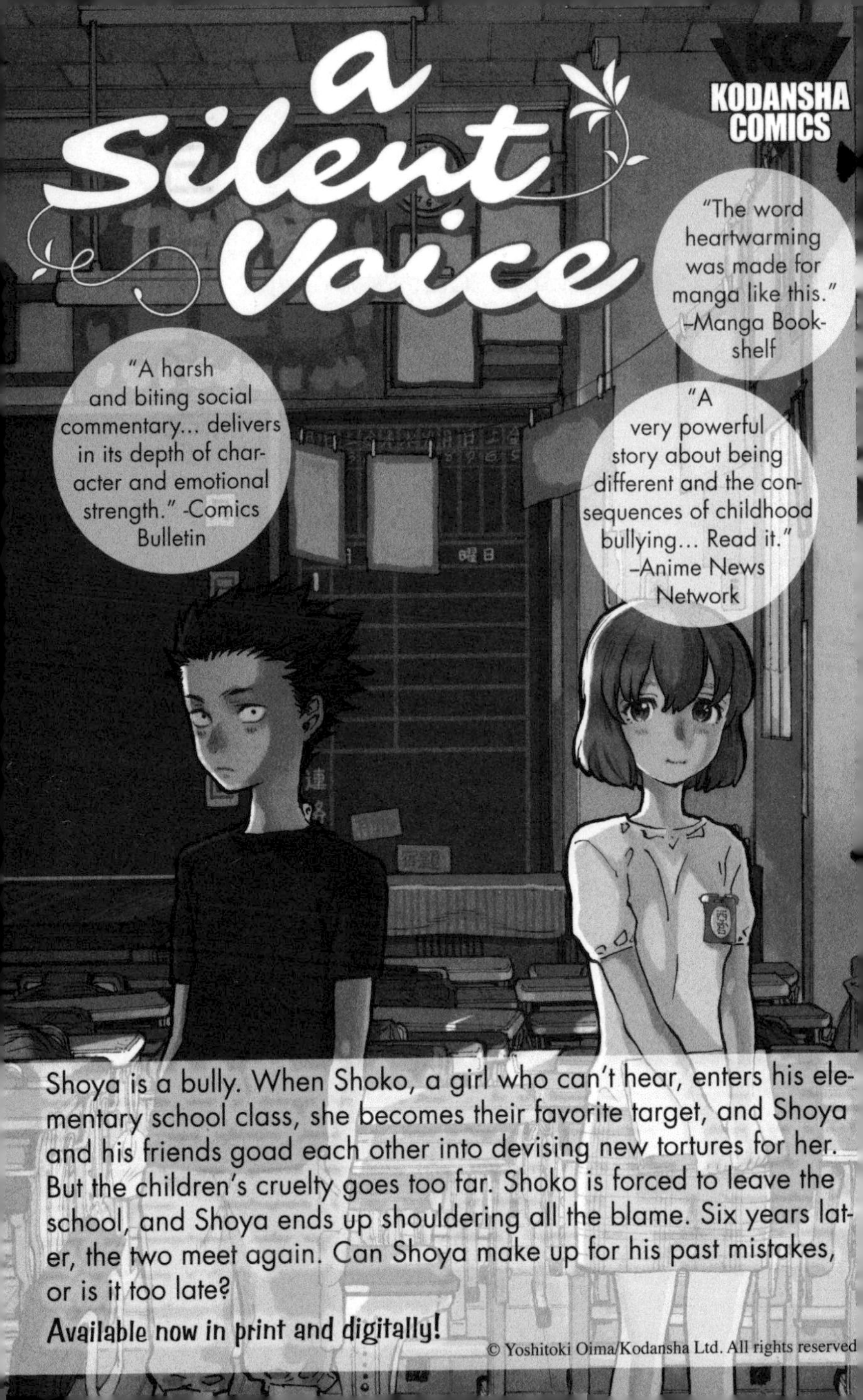
a Silent Voice
KODANSHA COMICS
"The word heartwarming was made for manga like this." –Manga Bookshelf
"A harsh and biting social commentary... delivers in its depth of character and emotional strength." -Comics Bulletin
"A very powerful story about being different and the consequences of childhood bullying... Read it." –Anime News Network
Shoya is a bully. When Shoko, a girl who can't hear, enters his elementary school class, she becomes their favorite target, and Shoya and his friends goad each other into devising new tortures for her. But the children's cruelty goes too far. Shoko is forced to leave the school, and Shoya ends up shouldering all the blame. Six years later, the two meet again. Can Shoya make up for his past mistakes, or is it too late?
Available now in print and digitally!
© Yoshitoki Oima/Kodansha Ltd. All rights reserved

Yamada-kun and the Seven Witches volume 9 is a work of fiction. Names, characters, places, and incidents are the products of the author's imagination or are used fictitiously. Any resemblance to actual events, locales, or persons, living or dead, is entirely coincidental.

A Kodansha Comics Trade Paperback Original.

Yamada-kun and the Seven Witches volume 9 copyright © 2013 Miki Yoshikawa
English translation copyright © 2016 Miki Yoshikawa

Published in the United States by Kodansha Comics, an imprint of Kodansha USA Publishing, LLC, New York.

Publication rights for this English edition arranged through Kodansha Ltd., Tokyo.

First published in Japan in 2013 by Kodansha Ltd., Tokyo, as *Yamada-kun to Nananin no Majo* volume 9.

ISBN 978-1-63236-138-7

Printed in the United States of America.

www.kodanshacomics.com

9 8 7 6 5 4 3 2 1

Translation: David Rhie
Lettering: Sara Linsley
Editing: Ajani Oloye
Kodansha Comics edition cover design: Phil Balsman